DATE DUE

ALMANAC *of* NAVAL FACTS

ALMANAC *of* NAVAL FACTS

United States Naval Institute
Annapolis, Maryland

11582

Copyright © 1964 by
United States Naval Institute
Annapolis, Maryland

Library of Congress Catalogue No. 64-12269

Printed in the United States of America by
George Banta Co., Inc., Menasha, Wisconsin

Foreword

The *Almanac of Naval Facts* was planned to provide naval personnel, public information officers, students and the general public a ready reference source of information about the Navy, especially those elusive bits of information which are usually only half remembered and always difficult to verify. The material contained herein was collected from a wide range of sources, official and unofficial, both published and unpublished.

The book is not offered as history, nor is it to be considered as official. Rather, it gives the reader, in condensed form, the most complete information available on several subjects of general naval interest. If it answers some questions, arouses more interest in the Navy, and induces some readers to delve deeper into naval history, it will have served its purpose.

U.S. NAVAL INSTITUTE

Acknowledgment

The idea for this book was suggested by Captain James C. Shaw, U.S. Navy; the first rough outline of the work was prepared by Commander Betty Winspear, U.S. Naval Reserve (W). It was researched and written by Arnold S. Lott, Lieutenant Commander, U.S. Navy; Joseph D. Harrington, Chief Journalist, U.S. Navy, and John L. Greene, Chief Journalist, U.S. Navy. They were assisted at various times by Lee Bair, Yeoman first class (W); Albert M. Cohen, Yeoman second class; Gene L. Henderson, Chief Journalist; James A. Hyde, Journalist third class; Lynn M. King, Chief Yeoman (WAVE); Caryl M. Mertz, Chief Yeoman (WAVE); and Richard R. Rohm, Journalist third class. The work could not have been completed without the interest of Rear Admiral William G. Beecher, Jr., U.S. Navy, Rear Admiral E. B. Taylor, U.S. Navy, and Rear Admiral Charles C. Kirkpatrick, U.S. Navy, each of whom, as Chief of Information, realized the merit of the work and provided "logistic support" to see it through; nor could it have been accomplished without the cooperation of the Director of Naval History, Rear Admiral John B. Heffernan, U.S. Navy (Retired), and later Rear Admiral Ernest M. Eller, U.S. Navy (Retired), who made available the extensive research facilities of the Naval Library.

Contents

CALENDAR

Calendar

1 January

1776 British Navy had 89 warships, with 2,576 guns, on North American station, as opposed to Continental Navy's 14 ships, with 332 guns.

1800 Schooner *Experiment* sank two West Indian pirate barges.

1819 Smith Thompson took office, seventh Secretary of the Navy.

1862 Gunboat *Ottawa* aided Army troops in attack on Fort Royal Ferry, S.C.

1863 U.S. blockading squadron at Galveston, Tex., attacked by Confederate "cotton-clad" steamers, *Bayou City* and *Neptune*.

1900 First Marine Regiment organized at Cavite, P.I.

1901 Second Marine Regiment organized at Cavite, P.I.

First Brigade formed in the Philippine Islands.

1940 Tenth Naval District established, with H.Q. at San Juan, Puerto Rico.

1942 Naval Supply Depot, Seattle, Wash., established.

1943 Naval Supply Depot, Spokane, Wash., established.

1944 First four-star Marine general, Thomas Holcomb, appointed.

1950 First woman doctor, Mary T. Sproul, commissioned commander in the Medical Corps.

2 January

1794 Congress passed resolution to provide a navy for protection of commerce.

1890 Gunboat *Omaha* visited by Nelly Bly, during her trip around the world.

1909 President Theodore Roosevelt offered use of battleship fleet to Italy to assist earthquake victims. (See 3 Jan. 1909)

1940 Charles Edison took office, forty-seventh Secretary of the Navy.

1942 Manila and Cavite, P.I., captured by Japanese.

1958 Seventh Fleet and Middle East Force units commenced flood relief operations in Ceylon. (See 9 Jan. 1958)

3 January

1861 Georgia state troops seized Fort Pulaski, Ga.
1909 Store ship *Culgoa* and armed yacht *Scorpion* carried relief to earthquake victims at Messina, Italy, through 15 Jan.
1912 RADM Robley D. Evans, who commanded battleship fleet on 1907-1909 world cruise, died, Washington, D.C.
1918 Eleventh Marine Regiment organized, Quantico, Va.
1933 U.S. Marines withdrew from Nicaragua.
1944 MAJ Gregory Boyington, USMC, taken prisoner by Japanese after shooting down 28 enemy planes.
1956 First landing on USS *Forrestal*.
1957 Navy's last operational CATALINA, a PBY-6A of NARTU Atlanta, ordered retired from service.

4 January

1847 First mayor of San Francisco, LT Washington A. Bartlett.
1962 Fred Korth assumed office as fifty-ninth Secretary of the Navy.

5 January

1776 First Continental Navy squadron ordered to sea.
1779 CAPT Stephen Decatur born at Sinnepuxent, Md.
1861 U.S. steamer *Star of the West* sailed from New York to relief of Fort Sumter, Charleston Harbor, S.C.
1875 Naval expedition sailed for Panama to determine best canal route.
1928 First landing made on USS *Lexington*.

6 January

1776 Continental Congress authorized appointment of surgeons and surgeon's mates.
1791 Senate Committee on Mediterranean trade reported that U.S. trade in that area could not be protected without a naval force.
1814 British ship *Bramwell* arrived at Annapolis, Md., bearing British peace offer.
1913 First naval aviation detachment used in Fleet maneuvers.
1928 First air evacuation of wounded in Nicaragua by LT Christian F. Schilt, USMC, who flew Marine wounded from Ocotal to Quilali.

7 January

1822 Schooner *Porpoise* captured six pirate vessels. Schooner *Spark* captured Dutch sloop.
1863 Joint Navy-Army expedition up Pamunkey River, Va.

1881   Nathan Goff, Jr., took office as twenty-ninth Secretary of the Navy.

1942   Navy's authorized aircraft strength increased from 15,000 to 27,500.

1952   Third Marine Division reactivated.

8 January

1815   Battle of New Orleans.

1847   Navy, Marines, and Army forces attacked Mexican troops along San Gabriel River, Calif.

1963   USS *Benjamin Stoddert* (DDG 22) launched at Seattle, Wash.

9 January

1847   Navy landing parties defeated Mexicans at Mesa, Calif.

1861   U.S. steamer *Star of the West* fired upon while attempting to relieve Fort Sumter.

1918   First American aviation unit to go overseas, First Marine Aeronautic Company, commanded by CAPT Francis T. Evans, USMC, sailed. (See 21 Jan.)

1945   Naval gunfire and carrier-based aircraft covered Army landing at Lingayen Gulf, P.I.

1958   Carrier *Princeton,* tender *Duxbury Bay,* and two destroyers ended seven days of flood relief operation in Ceylon.

1959   *Halibut* (SSGN 587), atomic submarine, launched.

10 January

1847   Joint Army-Navy expedition occupied Los Angeles, Calif.

1861   Louisiana state troops seized Forts Jackson and St. Philip, La.

1914   Josephus Daniels's announcement on future of Naval Aviation: "The science of aerial navigation has reached the point where aircraft must form a large part of our naval force for offensive and defensive operation."

1934   First U.S. to Hawaii squadron flight; six P2Ys, 2,460 miles, 24 hours.

1956   First Nuclear Power School established, New London.

1957   Naval Air Mine Defense Unit commissioned at Panama City, Fla.

11 January

1862   Armored steamers *Essex* and *St. Louis* engaged Confederate gunboats at Lucas Bend, Mo.

1863   Side-wheeler *Hatteras* captured by CSS *Alabama*.

1875   First nautical municipal school opened on board USS *St. Marys* in New York City.

1905   First Navy ship, gunboat *Petrel,* entered Pearl Harbor. (See 14 Dec. 1911)

1928   First landing aboard USS *Saratoga*.

1943   PT boats attacked Japanese destroyers off Cape Esperance.

1944   First aircraft rocket attack against an enemy submarine by TBF's from *Block Island.*

1959   Aircraft carrier *Independence,* 1,046 feet long, 252-foot beam, 56,000 tons, commissioned at New York Naval Shipyard.

12 January

1813   Frigate *Chesapeake* captured British *Volunteer.*

1848   Sloop *Lexington* attacked San Blas, Mexico.

1861   Florida state troops demanded surrender of Pensacola Navy Yard. Navy Yard surrendered to Florida State Commissioners.

1863   Naval expedition against White River, Ark.

1882   Screw gunboat *Marion* rescued shipwrecked crew of whaler *Trinity* on Heard Island in Indian Ocean.

1918   USS *P. K. Bauman,* scout patrol craft, struck rock and sank.

1963   USS *John Adams* (SSBN 620) launched, Portsmouth, N.H.
        USS *Nathan Hale* (SSBN 623) launched, Groton, Conn.

13 January

1813   British squadron began blockading Chesapeake and Delaware Bays.

1842   Landing party from USS *Wave* started battle with Seminole Indians in Florida.

14 January

1779   Continental ship *Alliance* sailed from Boston, carrying Lafayette to France.

1813   Frigate *Chesapeake* captured British *Liverpool* and frigate *Hero.*

1926   U.S. Naval party observed total solar eclipse in Sumatra.

1943   Casablanca Conference began, lasted until 23 Jan.

1959   Fleet Air Photographic Laboratory, NAS Jacksonville, established.

15 January

1776   Eighteen volunteers from Newburyport, Mass., boarded and captured a British supply ship.

1815   Frigate *President* captured by British squadron.

1865   Monitor *Patapsco* sunk by "torpedo," (mine).

1887   First hospital for military and naval forces opened. (Army and Navy Hospital, Hot Springs, Ark.)

1918   Tenth Marine Regiment organized, Quantico, Va.

1942   American-British-Dutch-Australian Supreme Command (ABDA) established.

1943 CAPT Joseph J. Foss, USMC, scored kill on twenty-sixth enemy plane. Japanese invaded Burma.

1954 U.S. Navy Supply Corps School, Athens, Ga., commissioned.

1957 100 KW Nuclear Research Center dedicated at NRL.

16 January

1758 William W. Burrows, second Commandant of the Marine Corps, born.

1863 CSS *Florida* escaped to sea through U.S. squadron blockading Mobile, Ala.

1917 Admiral of the Navy, George F. Dewey, died, Washington, D.C.

1941 President Franklin D. Roosevelt asked Congress to appropriate $350,000,000 for 200 new merchant ships.

1954 Wearing of swords on dress occasions made mandatory.

17 January

1898 Gunboat *Wilmington* ordered to await orders in West Indies. South Atlantic squadron ordered into Cuban waters.

1900 U.S. took formal possession of Wake Island.

1956 USS *Nautilus,* first atomic-powered ship in the world, completed her first year in operation.

18 January

1798 France declared all vessels conducting commerce with British to be lawful prize.

1814 Schooner *Enterprise* captured *Isabella,* Spanish prize of British.

1861 U.S. steamer, *Star of the West,* reached New York after unsuccessful attempt to relieve Fort Sumter.
Alabama state troops seized Fort Gaines and schooner *Alert.*

1862 CSS *Sumter,* commerce raider, arrived at Gibraltar.

1911 First airplane landing on board ship.

1943 Carrier aircraft hit targets at Wonsan, Songjin, Hungnam, and Changyon, Korea.
NEPTUNE patrol bomber downed by Red Chinese anti-aircraft fire, Swatow, China.

1957 Naval Air Facility, Lages, Azores, commissioned.

19 January

1813 William Jones took office, fifth Secretary of the Navy.

1815 Six boats under Purser T. Shields, USN, captured nine British vessels, Lake Borgne, La.

1840   Antarctic continent discovered by LT John Wilkes, commanding Wilkes Exploring Expedition.

1900   Gunboat *Marietta* supported Army troops battling insurgents, Taal, P.I.

20 January

1814   Schooner *Enterprise* captured *Sincerity*, Swedish prize of British.

1861   Confederates seized fort on Ship Island, Miss.

1865   Armed steamer *Monticello* captured Confederate blockade runners *Stag* and *Charlotte*.

1899   Cruiser *Philadelphia* departed San Francisco, en route Samoa to protect American interests.

1914   First school for naval air training started, Pensacola.

1958   Martin YP6M SEAMASTER made first flight.

21 January

1863   Armed ship *Morning Light* and armed schooner, *Velocity* captured by Confederate steamers *Josiah H. Bell* and *Uncle Ben*.

1869   American steamer *Aspinwall* seized by Spanish *Hernan Cortes*.

1892   U.S. sent Chile ultimatum demanding apology for assault on USS *Baltimore* sailors (See 27 Jan. 1892)

1918   First Marine Aeronautic Company reached Ponta Delgada, Azores.

1944   Fifth Marine Division activated.

1954   First atomic-powered submarine, USS *Nautilus,* launched.

1955   First flight of flying platform, one-man helicopter.

22 January

1800   First Superintendent of Washington Navy Yard, CAPT Thomas Tingey, ordered to duty.

1870   Screw gunboat *Nipsic* sailed for Central America to survey possible canal route.

1917   President Wilson made his address on "free seas."

1944   Allies landed at Anzio, Italy.

1953   Carrier aircraft attacked Hongwon-Hungnam area, Korea.

1957   Four U.S. destroyers rescued 126 passengers from New Zealand merchant ship, SS *Natua,* aground in Fiji Islands.

23 January

1777   Continental Congress authorized construction of two frigates.

1815   Sloop-of-war *Hornet* captured British *William*.

1890   First modern seagoing torpedo boat, USS *Cushing,* launched.

1946   First Congressional Medal of Honor awarded a Navy chaplain, LCDR Joseph Timothy O'Callahan.

1952   First Marine Air Wing's "Deathrattler" Squadron (VHF 323) completed ten thousandth combat air mission over Korea.

1957   Amundson-Scott South Pole Station dedicated.

1960   Bathyscaph *Trieste* reached the bottom of Marianas Trench off Guam, 35,800 feet below sea level, with LT Don Walsh and scientist Jacques Piccard aboard.

24 January

1800   Frigate *Adams* captured the first of three French privateers taken during the period from 24 Jan. to 1 March.

1861   Georgia state authorities seized U.S. Arsenal, Augusta, Ga.

1870   Screw sloop *Oneida* rammed and sunk by British steamer *Bombay*, off Yokohama, Japan, with 117 lives lost.

1898   Battleship *Maine* ordered to Havana, Cuba.

1942   Battle of Balikpapan (Battle of Makassar Strait).

25 January

1776   Marine Committee given full power to direct fleet under Esek Hopkins.

1859   U.S. squadron entered La Plata River, Paraguay, to call upon Paraguayan officials at Asunción.

1898   Battleship *Maine* entered Havana harbor.

1917   First governor of Virgin Islands, RADM James H. Oliver, took possession for U.S.

1918   USS *Guinevere*, scout patrol craft, struck rock and sank near Lorient, France. No casualties.

26 January

1856   Brig *Decatur* protected Seattle, Wash., from hostile natives.

1911   First naval seaplane flight in U.S., San Diego, Calif.

1942   First U.S. Expeditionary Force to Europe in World War II reached Northern Ireland.

1949   *Norton Sound*, first guided-missile experimental ship, launched first guided missile, a Loon.

1951   U.S. warships bombarded Inchon, Korea.

27 January

1837   Marine Corps Commandant, COL Archibald Henderson, led Second Army Brigade in Second Seminole Indian War in Florida at Battle of Hatchee-Lustee.

1892   Chile agreed to U.S. demands for apology and reparations in USS *Baltimore* case.

1928   First dirigible landing on ship. *Los Angeles* landed aboard *Saratoga* (See 8 Aug. 1924)
1942   First contingent of Seabees left U.S. (See 17 Feb. 1942) USS *Gudgeon* became first U.S. submarine to sink an enemy submarine.

28 January

1915   *W. P. Frye,* merchant vessel under U.S. colors, sunk by German raider *Prinz Eitel Friedrich.*

29 January

1814   Frigate *Adams* captured British *Prince Regent.*
1815   Three barges under LT Lawrence Kearney captured two British tenders.
1914   U.S. Marines landed in Haiti.
1919   American cargo ship *Plave* grounded and sank in Dover Straits. No casualties.
1943   Battle of Rennell Island.
1945   Naval attack group landed Army forces near San Antonio, P.I.

30 January

1848   Naval forces attacked Cochori, Mexico.
1862   First turreted warship, USS *Monitor,* launched.
1863   Armed steamer *Isaac Smith* captured forts at Stone River, S.C. Joint Navy-Army expedition against Hartford, N.C.
1933   Adolf Hitler became German Chancellor.
1942   Naval Supply Depot, Newport, R.I., established.
1951   U.S. warships bombarded Kansong, Korea.
1960   Guided-missile destroyer *John King* launched at Bath, Me.

31 January

1863   Armed steamer *Mercedita* captured by CSS *Palmetto State,* and USS *Keystone State* disabled by CSS *Chicora.*
1930   First operation of "parasite" aircraft from a dirigible. LT R. S. Darnaby made successful drop in a glider from *Los Angeles,* at altitude of 3,000 feet.
1944   Invasion of Marshall Islands: Marines and Army troops landed on Kwajalein and Majuro.
         First use of forward-firing rocket by plane from *Manila Bay.*
1945   Naval attack group landed Army troops, Masugbu, P.I.

1 February

1800   Frigate *Constellation* engaged French *Vengeance*.

1855   Paddle gunboat *Water Witch* fired upon by forts while making surveys in Paraguay River.

1913   Postgraduate School at Naval Academy opened.

1917   Germany's unrestricted submarine warfare policy placed in effect.

1941   Second Marine Division, formerly Second Marine Brigade, activated.
First Marine Division, formerly First Marine Brigade, activated.
Navy Department announced reorganization of United States Fleet.

1942   First air strike by U.S. forces in World War II launched by *Enterprise* and *Yorktown*.
Seventh Naval District reactivated.

1944   Invasion of Marshall Islands; Marines landed on Roi and Namur, Army troops landed on Kwajalein Island.

1951   Naval Supply Depot, San Pedro, Calif., established.

1952   Third Marine Air Wing recommissioned at Cherry Point, N.C.

1954   Task Force 43 established, to plan Antarctic operations (Operation Deep-Freeze).

1957   LCDR Frank H. Austin, Jr., (MC), became first Navy Flight Surgeon to qualify as a test pilot.

2 February

1848   U.S. concluded treaty of peace with Mexico.

1894   Screw sloop *Kearsarge* wrecked on Roncador Reef, West Indies. Crew saved by SS *City of Para*.

1944   Namur Island secured.
USS *Sam Houston* (SSBN 609), seventh Polaris submarine, launched at Newport News, Va.

3 February

1795   Birth date of Supply Corps.

1799   Frigate *United States* sank French privateer *Amour de la Patrie*.

1801   Congress ratified U.S. treaty with France.

1917   U.S. severed diplomatic relations with Germany.

1944   Cruisers and destroyers supported Army troops landing on Ebeye, Kwajalein Atoll, Marshall Islands.

1947   ADM Marc A. Mitscher died at Norfolk, Va.

1949   Lockheed R6O constitution carried 78 passengers and crew of 18 from Moffett Field, Calif., to Washington, D.C., in 9 hours 35 minutes.

11

4 February

1779 CAPT John Paul Jones took command of *Bon Homme Richard*.
1813 Brig *Hornet* captured British *Resolute*.
1873 VADM Joel R. P. Pringle born at Georgetown, S.C.
1952 Robert B. Anderson took office as fifty-third Secretary of the Navy.
1959 Keel of USS *Enterprise,* world's first nuclear-powered aircraft carrier, laid at Newport News, Va.

5 February

1854 First chapel built on Navy property dedicated at Annapolis, Md.
1864 Joint Navy-Army expedition into Florida began, lasted until 14 April.
1942 National Naval Medical Center, Bethesda, Md., established.
1946 Fifth Marine Division disbanded at Camp Pendleton, Calif.

6 February

1777 Great Britain authorized privateering against United Colonies.
1778 France signed treaties of alliance and commerce with United Colonies.
1802 Congress recognized a state of war with Tripoli.
1832 Frigate *Potomac* destroyed pirate villages at Qualla Battoo, Sumatra.
1862 U.S. gunboat squadron captured Fort Henry, Tenn. Naval expedition up Tennessee River ended 10 Feb.
1922 U.S., Great Britain, France, Italy and Japan signed treaty for limitation of naval armament.
1942 U.S. and Britain established combined chiefs of staff.
      Naval Coastal Frontiers redesignated Sea Frontiers.
1943 North African Theatre of Operations established.

7 February

1781 Continental Congress authorized appointment of Secretary of Marine.
1800 Frigate *Essex* became the first American warship to cross the Equator.
1815 Board of Naval Commissioners established.
1862 Joint Navy-Army expedition captured Roanoke Island, N.C.
1955 U.S. ships began evacuation of Chinese Nationalists from Communist-threatened Tachen Islands, near Formosa. (See 12 Feb., 1955)

8 February

1890 Landing party from screw gunboat *Omaha* assisted fire fighters at Hodogaya, Japan.

9 February

1799 Congress suspended all U.S. trade with France and her colonies. Frigate *Constellation* captured French *Insurgente*.

1943 Organized Japanese resistance on Guadalcanal ended.

1951 U.S., British, Australian, New Zealand, and Netherlands warships bombarded east and west coasts of Korea.

10 February

1862 U.S. squadron engaged Confederate squadron and shore batteries at Elizabeth City, N.C.

1900 First Naval Governor of Guam, Commodore Seaton Schroeder, appointed.

1960 *Sargo* (ssn 583) surfaced at North Pole.

11 February

1898 GEN Randolph M. Pate, twenty-first Commandant of the Marine Corps, born at Port Royal, S.C.

12 February

1935 Dirigible *Macon* crashed off Point Sur, Calif. Two lives lost.

1955 Evacuation of Tachen Islands completed; 24,000 civilian and military personnel moved by Seventh Fleet ships.

1957 Destroyer *William C. Lawe* rescued seven men and a dog from sinking Italian ship *Giocomo H. Altieri* in Mediterranean.

1962 USS *Barb* (SSN 596) launched at Pascagoula, Miss.

13 February

1844 Commodore Perry anchored off Yokosuka, Japan, to receive Emperor's answer to earlier proposals.

1864 Tinclad *Forrest Rose* drove off three Confederate attacks on Waterproof, La., during the period of 13-15 Feb.

1917 CAPT Francis J. Evans, USMC, made the first "loop-the-loop" in a "Jenny" N-9 floatplane at Pensacola.

1945 First U.S. naval units entered Manila Bay since May 1942.

14 February

1778 First official salute to U.S. flag, Quiberon, France. (See Nov. 16, 1776)

1813 First U.S. warship, frigate *Essex*, entered Pacific Ocean.

1840 First U.S. "landing" in Antarctic regions made on floating ice by several officers and a mascot dog from USS *Vincennes* (Wilkes Exploring Expedition).

1862   U.S. squadron attacked Fort Donelson, Tenn.
1919   Air Detachment, Atlantic Fleet, commenced active operations at Guantanamo Bay, Cuba.

15 February

1898   USS *Maine* blown up in harbor of Havana, Cuba; 250 lives lost. (See 16 March 1923)
1943   Women marines re-established as Marine Corps Women's Reserve.
1944   U.S. warships landed New Zealand troops in the Green Islands off New Ireland.
1944   Naval task group landed Army troops in Mariveles, P.I.
1960   Icebreakers *Burton Island* and *Glacier* reached Thurston Peninsula in Antarctic, first ships ever to do so.

16 February

1804   Frigate *Philadelphia* captured by Tripolitans, destroyed by party under LT Stephen Decatur, USN.
1862   U.S. squadron captured Fort Donelson, Tenn.
1933   Distinguished Flying Cross posthumously awarded Eugene Ely.
1945   U.S. carrier aircraft bombed Tokyo.
1943   Siege of Wonsan, Korea, entered third year.
1955   Bureau of Aeronautics issued instructions for painting operational aircraft in new gray and white combination.

17 February

1776   Continental Navy put to sea on first cruise.
1815   Congress ratified treaty of peace with Great Britain.
1864   First ship sunk by torpedo, screw sloop *Housatonic,* at Charleston, S.C. *Housatonic* torpedoed and sunk by Confederate submarine *Hunley,* first ship sunk by enemy submarine.
1865   U.S. squadron attacked and captured Fort Anderson, N.C.; siege lasted until 19 February.
1925   Naval scrapping program completed.
1942   First contingent of Seabees to leave U.S. arrived at Bora Bora, Society Islands.
1944   Carrier-battleship task force attacked Truk, Caroline Islands.
1953   Hospital ship *Repose* recorded one thousandth helicopter landing.
1956   First submarine, USS *Jallao,* to visit Port Elizabeth, Union of South Africa.

18 February

1846   Navy Department General Order made use of "port and starboard" mandatory, in place of "larboard and starboard."

1865 Confederates evacuated Charleston, S.C.

1944 Marines landed and secured Engebi Island, Eniwetok Atoll.

19 February

1844 Thomas W. Gilmer took office as sixteenth Secretary of the Navy.

1868 Naval forces landed at Montevideo, Uruguay, to protect foreign residents.

1900 Tutuila (Samoa) and nearby islands placed under Navy Department control.

1941 U.S. Coast Guard Reserve established.

1942 Battle of Badoeng Strait.

1944 Marines and Army troops landed on Eniwetok.

1945 Marines landed on Iwo Jima.

1954 Corner-stone of Marine Corps War Memorial, "Iwo Jima Monument," laid, Arlington, Va.

20 February

1815 Frigate *Constitution* captured British *Cyane* and *Levant*.

1942 Atlantic and Pacific Fleets directed to establish amphibious forces.

1962 LCOL John H. Glenn, USMC, became first U.S. man in orbit with three orbits of the earth in 5 hours, 17 minutes, was recovered by USS *Noa* (DD 841).

21 February

1944 Eniwetok Island secured.

22 February

1909 President Roosevelt reviewed battleship fleet on its return from around-the-world cruise (See 16 Dec. 1907)

1944 Marines landed, and secured Parry Island, in Marshall Islands.

1963 USS *Woodrow Wilson* (SSBN 624) launched, Mare Island, Calif.

23 February

1903 President Theodore Roosevelt signed lease agreement with Cuba for Guantanamo Bay.

1942 First naval chaplain's school convened, Norfolk, Va.

1944 First U.S. strike against the Marianas Islands.

1945 U.S. flag raised on Mt. Suribachi, Iwo Jima.

1955 Douglas F4D SKYRAY set record, first airplane to reach altitude of 10,000 feet in less than a minute. (See 23 April 1915)

24 February

1797 American merchant schooner *Zilpha* seized by French privateer.

1813   Brig *Hornet* captured British *Peacock.*
1815   Robert Fulton, inventor of the steamboat, died.
1885   FADM Chester H. Nimitz born at Fredericksburg, Tex.
1908   Cruiser *Des Moines* ordered to Cuba to protect American interests.
1927   Fourth Marine Regiment landed at Shanghai, China, to protect American lives and property.
1942   U.S. carrier task force bombarded Wake Island.
       USS *Swordfish* evacuated United States High Commissioner F. B. Sayre from Philippine Islands.
1945   Japanese resistance in Manila ended.
1956   USS *Jallao,* first submarine around the Cape of Good Hope.
1959   Navy announced plans to scrap 43 ships, including battleships *Tennessee, California, Colorado, Maryland* and *West Virginia.*

25 February

1799   Congress authorized 1 ship-of-the-line and 6 sloops-of-war.
1933   USS *Ranger,* first true aircraft carrier, commissioned.
1942   U.S. Coast Guard assumed responsibility for U.S. port security.
1944   U.S. carrier aircraft bombed aircraft factories and airfields near Tokyo.
1959   Guided missile cruiser *Galveston* successfully fired first TALOS supersonic surface-to-air missile.

26 February

1799   Frigate *United States* captured French privateer's British prize, and recaptured one American ship.
1811   Congress passed Act to provide Navy hospitals.
1918   USS *Mariner,* scout patrol craft foundered, no lives lost.
       USS *Cherokee,* scout patrol craft foundered, 22 lives lost.
1944   CAPT Sue Sophia Dauser became first woman commissioned as captain.
1960   Mid-air collision in Rio de Janeiro killed 19 members of Navy band.
1962   USS *Thomas Jefferson* (SSBN 618) launched at Newport News, Va.
1963   USS *Waddell* (DDG 24) launched at Seattle, Wash.

27 February

1797   Secretary of State reported on injuries inflicted upon U.S. merchants and mariners by France.
1840   CAPT Isaac Chauncey died at Washington, D.C.
1870   MAJ GEN Ben H. Fuller, fifteenth Commandant of the Marine Corps, born at Big Rapids, Mich.

1879   Congress authorized acceptance of yacht *Jeannette* for use in Arctic exploration.

1928   CDR T. G. Ellyson, Navy's first aviator, killed in air crash.

1942   First advance base depot established at Davisville, R.I.
        Battle of Java Sea.
        Aircraft tender *Langley* sunk off Tjilatjap, Java.

1952   USS *Shelton* hit by enemy shore batteries.

1960   Guided-missile destroyer *Lawrence* launched.

28 February

1803   Congress appropriated $96,000 for construction of four ships.

1844   Gun explosion aboard USS *Princeton,* in Potomac River, killed Secretary of State and Secretary of Navy.

1863   Monitor *Montauk* destroyed CSS *Nashville.*

1919   Destroyer *Ingram,* first Navy ship named for an enlisted man, launched.

1942   Battle of Sunda Strait.

29 February

1944   U.S. destroyer force landed Army troops on Los Negros Island, Admiralty Islands.
        U.S. destroyers bombarded Rabaul, New Britain.
        First Victory ship, SS *United Victory,* delivered.

1 March

1781 Articles of the Confederation (forerunner of Constitution) placed in effect.

1809 U.S. Embargo Act repealed by Non-Intercourse Act, which forbade U.S. commerce with Britain or France.

1862 Timber-clad river ships *Tyler* and *Lexington* attacked Confederate troops at Pittsburg Landing (Shiloh), Tenn.

1864 Armed steamers *Southfield* and *Whitehead* rescued Army gunboat *Bombshell* in Chowan River, N.C.

1909 CDR Peary left Cape Columbia base for final dash to North Pole. (See 6 April 1909)

1916 Marine Corps association published first issue, *Marine Corps Gazette*.

1941 Support Force, Atlantic Fleet established.
Bulgaria occupied by German troops and joined the Axis.

1942 First German submarine sunk by U.S. Navy aircraft in World War II.

1950 First flight of tailless carrier fighter plane, F7U-1 CUTLASS.

1960 *Sargo* (SSN 583) completed 6,000 mile trip, east to west across North Pole to Hawaii, having spent 14 days and 21 hours under the ice cap.

2 March

1794 Secretary of State reported to President Washington on plundering of neutral American ships.

1796 Congress ratified treaty of peace with Algiers. Construction of warships halted.

1797 France decreed Americans serving in enemy ships would be treated as pirates, and U.S. ships not having crew's list in proper form would be considered lawful prize.

1799 Congress passed act for government of the Navy, an act authorizing pensions, and an act increasing strength of Marine Corps.

1811 Non-Intercourse Act evoked against Great Britain.

1815 U.S. declared war on Algiers.

1859 First Navy ship built on west coast, paddle gunboat *Saginaw,* launched at Mare Island, Calif.

1867 Birthdate of Civil Engineering Corps.

1899 First Admiral of the Navy, George F. Dewey, appointed.

1942 Anti-submarine Warfare Unit, Atlantic Fleet, established.
First scheduled NATS flight. (See 15 May 1944, 20 Dec. 1955)

1943 Battle of Bismarck Sea.

18

3 March

1776 First amphibious landing operations by Continental Navy, U.S. Marines land at New Providence in the Bahamas.

1777 Continental brig *Cabot* captured by British *Milford.*

1801 Peace Establishment Act passed. Navy greatly reduced.

1805 Congress voted COMO Edward Preble a sword for conduct of operations against Tripoli.

1809 Act of Congress required for first time that pursers be bonded. (See 30 Mar. 1812)

1814 Congress passed act barring aliens from service in Navy ships.

1819 Congress authorized war on pirates in Gulf of Mexico.
First legislation passed governing naming of Navy ships.

1871 Congress directed that civil engineers be given relative rank at President's discretion.

1883 Congress appropriated funds for four steel warships.

1889 Congress appropriated $100,000 for construction of coaling station at Pago Pago, Samoa.

1891 Congress increased strength of Civil Engineering Corps to 40 officers.

1911 Congress appointed Robert E. Peary to rank of RADM.

1915 Office of Chief of Naval Operations (CNO) established.
National Advisory Committee for Aeronautics (NACA) established.

1916 CAPT Mark L. Bristol ordered to command of USS *North Carolina* and given broad aviation development responsibilities.

1956 F3H-2N DEMON all weather fighter became operational.

4 March

1801 Twenty Navy ships sold.

1848 CAPT Matthew C. Perry died at New York, N.Y.

1895 Navy landing party assisted in fighting fire at Port of Spain, Trinidad.

1911 First Naval Appropriations Act, provided $25,000 to develop aviation for naval purposes.

1913 Naval Appropriations Act limited naval aviation to 30 officers.

1918 Collier *Cyclops* sailed from Barbadoes, West Indies with 280 men on board, never seen again.

1925 Congress authorized restoration of USS *Constitution*

1933 Claude A. Swanson took office, forty-sixth Secretary of the Navy.

1942 Carrier task force bombed Marcus Island.

1949 Caroline Mars set word's record for passenger load, carried 269 men, including crew, from San Diego to Alameda, Calif. (See 19 May 1949)

1957 *ZP6-2*, airship commenced world record flight. (See 15 Mar. 1957)

5 March

1770   Boston Massacre.
1913   Josephus Daniels took office, forty-second Secretary of the Navy.
1921   Edwin Denby took office, forty-third Secretary of the Navy.
1929   Charles F. Adams took office, forty-fifth Secretary of the Navy.
1942   "Seabees" name and insignia authorized.
1943   First anti-submarine operations by escort carrier, USS *Bogue,* began.

6 March

1805   LT COL William Ward Burrows, second Marine Corps Commandant, died, Charleston, S.C.
1841   George E. Badger took office, thirteenth Secretary of the Navy.
1862   USS *Monitor* departed New York for Hampton Roads, Va.
1864   Armed steamer *Memphis* attacked by CSS *David.*
1889   Benjamin F. Tracy took office, thirty-third Secretary of the Navy.
1897   John D. Long took office, thirty-fifth Secretary of the Navy.
1899   Cruiser *Philadelphia* arrived at Apia, Samoa, to subdue native uprising.
1909   George Von L. Meyer took office, forty-first Secretary of the Navy.
1943   U.S. cruisers and destroyers bombarded Vila and Munda, Solomon Islands.

7 March

1778   Continental Frigate *Randolph* blew up while engaging British *Yarmouth.*
1797   American merchant ship *Cincinnatus* seized by French armed brig.
1861   Gideon Welles took office, twenty-fifth Secretary of the Navy.
1881   William H. Hunt took office, thirtieth Secretary of the Navy.
1885   William C. Whitney took office, thirty-second Secretary of the Navy.
1893   Hilary A. Herbert took office, thirty-fourth Secretary of the Navy.
1936   Germany annexed the Rhineland.
1956   First F3H-2N BANSHEES assigned to fleet delivered to Fighter Squadron 14 at NAS Cecil Field.
1957   First turbine powered catapult tested, launched 16,400 pound AD-4NA at 90 knots on 210 foot run.
1958   USS *Grayback,* first submarine built with guided-missile capability, commissioned at Mare Island.

8 March

1822   Schooner *Enterprise* captured four pirate vessels.
1849   William P. Preston took office, twentieth Secretary of the Navy.
1853   James C. Dobbin took office, twenty-third Secretary of the Navy.

1854 COMO Perry landed at Yokohama, Japan, to open treaty negotiations.

1862 CSS *Virginia* (formerly USS *Merrimac*) destroyed sloop-of-war *Cumberland* and frigate *Congress* at Hampton Roads, Va.

1889 John Ericsson, designer of USS *Monitor,* died at New York.

1915 USS *Baltimore,* first U.S. minelayer, placed in service.

1945 Phyllis Mae Daley, first Negro nurse, commissioned in Naval Reserve Nurse Corps.

1957 Navy announced USS *Nautilus* being refueled after sailing 60,000 miles on original atomic fuel supply (about size of a baseball).
F11F TIGER became operational.

1961 USS *Patrick Henry* (SSBN 599) reached Holy Loch, Scotland, setting new world record by cruising submerged for 66 days, 22 hours.

9 March

1773 COMO Isaac Hull born at Huntington, Conn.

1798 First surgeon in the new Navy, George Balfour, appointed.

1828 John Branch took office, ninth Secretary of the Navy.

1847 Siege of Vera Cruz, Mexico began.

1862 First engagement between iron-clad warships at Hampton Roads: USS *Monitor* vs. CSS *Virginia*.

1869 Adolph E. Borie took office, twenty-sixth Secretary of the Navy.

1911 Wilbur and Orville Wright offered to train an aviator if the Navy bought one plane for $5,000.

1920 USS subchaser *No. 282,* sank in Pacific, no casualties.

1942 First naval air transport service (NATS) squadron commissioned.

10 March

1797 American merchant brig *Calliope* seized by French privateer.

1911 Fourth Marine Regiment organized at Mare Island, Calif.

1933 Navy rendered assistance following earthquake at Long Beach, Calif.

1942 Aircraft from USS *Lexington* and USS *Yorktown* bombed Japanese shipping at Salamaua and Lae, New Guinea.

1948 First carrier operations of a jet squadron: Fighter Squadron 5-A commenced using FJ-1 FURY, aboard *Boxer*.

11 March

1845 George Bancroft took office, eighteenth Secretary of Navy.

1941 Lend-Lease Act became law.

1942 GEN Douglas MacArthur and RADM Francis W. Rockwell left Luzon, P.I., by motor torpedo boat for Mindanao, P.I.

1957   RADM Richard E. Byrd, first man to fly over both poles, died.

12 March

1799   Navy ordered to search suspicious French ships and retake any armed prizes.
1917   U.S. mechant ships authorized to arm against German submarines.
1956   First missile squadron deployed overseas: Attack Squadron 83, equipped with F7U-3M CUTLASS aircraft and SPARROW missiles, sailed aboard *Intrepid* for Mediterranean.

13 March

1862   U.S. squadron attacked and captured New Berne, N.C.
1877   Richard W. Thompson took office, twenty-eighth Secretary of the Navy.
1895   First submarine building contract awarded. (See 11 April 1900)
1900   Navy General Board established.
1947   First NEPTUNE P2V-1 delivered, at Miramar, Calif.
1959   Aerobee-Hi rocket made first ultraviolet photographs of sun, at 123 mile altitude.

14 March

1813   Frigate *Essex* arrived at Valparaiso, Chile.
1863   Paddle frigate *Mississippi* sunk by Confederate shore batteries as U.S. squadron ran past Port Hudson, La.
1864   Government drafted 200,000 men for Union Army.
1929   Navy planes from NAS Pensacola made 113 flights in flood rescue and relief.
1942   Amphibious Force, Atlantic Fleet established.

15 March

1796   President Washington urged Congress to authorize completion of warship construction.
1862   U.S. squadron began bombarding Confederate defenses at Island No. 10, Mississippi River. Bombardment lasted until 7 April.
1930   Frigate *Constitution* relaunched in Boston, Mass.
1943   Numbered fleet system established.
1947   First Negro officer, John Lee, commissioned in Regular Navy.
1951   UN forces re-entered Seoul, Korea.
        U.S. warships bombarded Wonsan, killing 8,000 Communist troops in seven minutes.

1957   *ZPG-2,* airship commanded by CDR J. R. Hunt, flew from South Weymouth, Mass. to near Portugal and returned to Key West, 9,448 miles in 264 hours, 12 minutes, without refueling.

1963   USS *James Madison* (SSBN 627) launched at Newport News, Va.

16 March

1889   Screw cruisers *Trenton* and *Vandalia* totally wrecked, gunboat *Nipsic* grounded by hurricane at Apia, Samoa.

1911   USS *Maine* raised, towed to sea, and sunk.

1918   Navy Department forbade sale of liquor within five miles of naval bases and stations.

1960   Hospital ship *Consolation* transferred to Project HOPE.
Nuclear attack submarine, *Shark* (SSN 591) launched at Newport News.
USS *Guadalcanal* (LPH 7) launched at Philadelphia, Pa.

17 March

1776   Boston evacuated by British.

1898   First practical submarine, USS *Holland,* made first dive.

1908   Screw sloop *Monongahela* burned at Guantanamo Bay, Cuba.

1921   First deployment of Marine Corps aviation west of San Francisco, at Guam.

1958   VANGUARD rocket successfully placed an earth satellite into orbit, with estimated life of 25 years.

1959   Atomic-powered *Skate* (SSN 578) surfaced at North Pole.

18 March

1942   U.S. Naval force ordered to join British Home Fleet.

19 March

1863   Screw sloop *Hartford* ran upriver past batteries at Grand Gulf, Miss.

1898   Operation of Naval Home transferred to Bureau of Navigation.

1918   First enemy plane shot down in World War I.

1924   Curtis D. Wilbur took office, forty-fourth Secretary of the Navy.

1942   Secretary of the Navy gave Civil Engineering Corps command of Seabees.

20 March

1833   First commercial treaty between U.S. and an Oriental power signed in Siam.

1918   U.S. requisitioned all Dutch vessels in U.S. ports.

1922   First aircraft carrier, USS *Langley*, commissioned.

1930   First Navy dive bomber designed to deliver 1,000 lb. bomb met strength and performance tests.

1942   USS *South Dakota* commissioned, New York, N.Y.

1951   USS *Missouri* bombarded Wonsan, Korea.

1943   U.S. warships bombarded Kosong, Korea.

1956   First HUK-1 helicopter delivered to fleet.

1959   First announcement of proposed merger of Bureau of Aeronautics and Bureau of Ordnance into new Bureau of Weapons.

21 March

1942   First Seabee training center, Camp Allen, commissioned at Norfolk, Va.

1957   An A3D-1 SKYWARRIER piloted by CDR Dale W. Cox, Jr., broke two transcontinental speed records; one for the round trip Los Angeles to New York and return in nine hours 31 minutes 35.4 seconds, and the other for the east to west flight in five hours 13 minutes 49 seconds.

22 March

1820   Duel between CDR Decatur and CDR Barron, near Washington, D.C. which resulted in Decatur's death.

1920   Navy free balloon took off from Pensacola, Fla., with five man crew and never seen again.

1929   U.S. warships protected American lives and property along western coast of Mexico during revolution, 22 Mar. to 3 May.

1944   First Provisional Marine Brigade activated at Guadalcanal.

23 March

1776   Continental Congress authorized privateering.

1810   Napolean signed Rambouillet Decree, allowing the sale of captured American vessels.

1815   Sloop *Hornet* captured British *Penguin*.

1912   Funeral services held at Arlington National Cemetery for bodies of 59 men removed from hulk of USS *Maine*.

24 March

1783   Continental Congress recalled all armed vessels sailing under American colors.

1917   First "Yale Unit" enlisted in Naval Reserve Flying Force.

1920 USS *H-1,* submarine, sank during salvage operations off Margurita Island, Mexico. Four lives lost.

1927 U.S. and British naval forces laid down protective artillery barrage around hill at Nanking, China, to protect American citizens there.

25 March

1804 First formal uniform order issued for Marine Corps by Secretary of the Navy.

1813 Frigate *Essex* captured Peruvian *Nereyda,* first prize taken by U.S. Navy in Pacific.

1814 Brig *Adams* captured British *Woodbridge.*

1822 First U.S. flag raised over Key West, Fla.

1898 Beginning of naval aviation. Assistant Secretary of the Navy, Theodore Roosevelt, proposed the Navy investigate Langley's "flying machine."

1915 Submarine *F-4* sank off Honolulu, Hawaii, with loss of 21 lives; first submarine disaster in Navy history.

1948 ADM Joseph M. Reeves died at Bethesda, Md.

1957 F8U-1 CRUSADER became operational.

26 March

1799 U.S. concluded treaty with Tunis.

1844 John Y. Mason took office, seventeenth Secretary of the Navy.

1863 River ram *Lancaster* sunk by Confederate shore batteries at Vicksburg, Miss.

1917 Joint Army-Navy Airship Board established.

1942 ADM King became Chief of Naval Operations.

1943 Battle of Komandorski Islands.

1945 Naval attack group landed Army troops on Kerama Retto, Ryukyu Islands.

1946 Fourth Marine Air Wing decommissioned.

27 March

1794 Congress passed Act founding present day Navy.

1798 Congress passed law to equip Frigates *Constitution, Constellation* and *United States.*

1880 Frigate *Constellation* departed New York with cargo of food for famine sufferers in Ireland.

1945 U.S. destroyers, PT-boats and carrier aircraft supported Army landing on Caballo Island, P.I.

1952 Navy aircraft cut enemy railway system in 256 places, Korea.

1957 First TV2-1 SEASTAR jet trainer delivered to NAATC Corpus Christi, Texas.

28 March

1800 First rounding of Cape of Good Hope by Navy ship, USS *Essex*.
1814 Frigate *Essex* captured British *Phoebe* and *Cherub*.
1864 Screw sloop *Niagara* fired upon by shore batteries at Lisbon, Portugal.

29 March

1844 First Jewish officer, Uriah Levy, appointed captain.
1865 *Osage*, monitor, "torpedoed" in Blakely River, Fla.
1890 First Naval Militia established.
1951 First Naval Air Reserves in action in Korea.

30 March

1812 Congress set pursers' bond at $10,000.
1863 U.S. squadron ran downriver past batteries at Grand Gulf, Miss.
1867 U.S. purchased Alaska from Russia. (See 18 Oct. 1867)
1898 Navy Yard, Mare Island, severely damaged by earthquake.
1912 First design for an automatic pilot submitted to Aeronautical Society.
1941 U.S. took possession of German, Italian and Danish ships in U.S.
1943 Naval Supply Depot, Scotia, N.Y., established.
1944 U.S. carrier aircraft bombed Caroline Islands.
      Carrier airplanes from Task Force 58 laid mines in Palau Harbor.
      Twenty-millimeter guns first used in Navy planes by SB2C HELL-DIVERS.

31 March

1854 COMO Perry signed U.S. treaty with Japan.
1917 RADM James H. Oliver took possession of Virgin Islands for U.S.
1931 Navy and Marines rendered assistance to victims of earthquake at Managua, Nicaragua.
1942 Superintendent Civil Engineers established as regional representatives of Chief, Bureau of Yards and Docks.
1946 Ninth Marine Air Wing decommissioned.
1955 First high speed target drone for guided-missile defense training placed in operation.
1956 First A3D-1 SKYWARRIORS delivered to fleet.
1960 *Sculpin* (SSN 590), launched.

1 April

1778 Continental ship *Virginia* captured by British squadron.

1847 Screw steamer *Scourge* captured Mexican *Relampago* and Alvarado, Mexico.

1862 Navy-Army forces attacked No. 1 Fort on Mississippi River.

1863 Screw sloop *Hartford* blockaded mouth of Red River, La.

1899 Landing party from protected cruiser *Philadelphia* ambushed in Samoa.

1905 U.S. and Santo Domingo agreed that U.S. would direct customs revenues at Santo Domingo.

1911 Officer in Charge, Naval Aviation, ordered to duty with General Board.

1917 U.S. Naval forces mobilized.

U.S. mechant ship *Aztec* torpedoed and sunk.

1925 First carrier night landing made, on *Langley*.

1934 First shipboard Divine service conducted by a Commander in Chief.

1942 First NATS squadron for operations in Pacific commissioned.

1944 Ninth Marine Air Wing commissioned at Cherry Point, N.C.

1945 Invasion of Okinawa.

Navy ships and aircraft supported Army troops landing near Legaspi, P.I.

1946 Sixth Marine Division redesignated Third Marine Brigade.

1948 First Navy Helicopter Utility Squadron commissioned.

1955 Career Incentive Act became law.

1957 Thomas S. Gates took office as fifty-fifth Secretary of the Navy.

2 April

1781 Frigate *Alliance* captured British *Mars* and *Minerva*.

1827 First Naval hospital construction begun, Portsmouth, Va.

1847 U.S. sailors and marines occupied Alvarado, Mexico.

1862 Navy-Army forces captured No. 1 Fort on Mississippi River.

1898 Naval Academy coat-of-arms adopted.

1916 LT R. C. Saufley set altitude record for Navy aircraft, 16,072 feet, in Curtiss pusher type hydroplane, Pensacola, Fla.

1945 U.S. destroyers supported Army troops landing on Sanga Sanga and Bangao, Islands, P.I.

1947 Former Japanese mandated islands placed under U.S. control.

1951 First jet aircraft with combat bomb loads launched from a carrier.

1953 Cruiser *Los Angeles* hit by enemy coastal batteries off Korea.

27

3 April

1800   Brig *Adams* captured French privateer *La Jason*.
1814   Sloop of war *Frolic* captured a British privateer.
1942   ADM Nimitz named Commander in Chief, Pacific Ocean Areas.

4 April

1776   First enemy warship captured by Continental Navy taken by brig *Lexington*.
1812   Embargo declared on all U.S. shipping for 90 days.
1818   Congress established present pattern of U.S. flag.
1854   U.S. and British naval forces battled Chinese terrorists at Shanghai.
1862   River ironclad *Carondelet* successfully ran past Confederate batteries on Island No. 10, Mississippi River.
1898   First Civil Engineering Corps officer, Mordecai T. Endicott, appointed Chief, Bureau of Yards and Docks.
1943   First Navy ship with a plural name, USS *The Sullivans,* launched.
1963   USS *Richmond K. Turner* (DLG 20) launched, Camden, N.J.

5 April

1914   U.S. demanded German reparations for sinking of SS *W. P. Frye*.

6 April

1776   Continental fleet attacked by British frigate *Glasgow*.
1779   Sloop-of-war *Ranger,* frigate *Queen of France,* and frigate *Warren* captured British *Hibernia* and seven other vessels.
1862   Timber-clad *Tyler* and timber-clad *Lexington* prevented defeat of Union troops at Pittsburg Landing (Shiloh), Tenn.
       River ironclad *Pittsburg* successfully ran past Island No. 10, Mississippi River.
1909   CDR Robert Peary reached North Pole, and raised first U.S. flag. (See 9 May 1926, 3 Nov. 1909)
1914   U.S. Naval personnel in Tampico, Mexico, arrested by local officials.
1917   U.S. declared war against Germany. Navy strength 4,376 officers and 69,680 men.
1945   First heavy attack of Japanese suicide planes on U.S. ships at Okinawa.

7 April

1776   Continental brig *Lexington* captured British *Edward*.
1814   Pettipaug, Conn., attacked by British barges.
1847   Sloop-of-war *Portsmouth* captured Chilean *Argo* and Mexican *Caroline*.

1863 U.S. squadron attacked forts at Charleston, S.C.
1905 Body of John Paul Jones located in Paris, France.
1913 Collier *Jupiter* commissioned, first electric-drive ship in Navy.
1917 Navy took control of all wireless stations in U.S.
1925 First radio broadcast of a ship launching, USS *Saratoga.*
1951 First United Nations Cemetery dedicated, Korea.
1958 F11F-1 set world altitude record of 76,932 feet.

8 April

1782 Pennsylvania ship *Hyder Ally* captured British *General Monk* (formerly Continental *George Washington*).
1823 USS *Musquito* and *Gallinipper* captured pirate schooner.
1848 U.S. flag first flown over Sea of Galilee.
1917 U.S. severed diplomatic relations with Austria-Hungary.
1942 Hydrographic Office and Naval Observatory transferred to Office of the Chief of Naval Operations.
1950 PRIVATEER patrol bomber disappeared during routine training flight over Baltic Sea, with 10 crew members.

9 April

1813 Schooner *Nonsuch* captured British privateer *Caledonia.*
1861 Second expedition to relieve Fort Sumter departed New York.
1865 Confederate Army surrended at Appomattox.
1940 Germany invaded Denmark and Norway.
1941 Battleship *North Carolina* commissioned.
      U.S. and Denmark signed "Agreement Relating to the Defense of Greenland."
1943 Rank of commodore (one star) re-established.
1960 *Patrick Henry* (SSBN 599) commissioned.

10 April

1778 CAPT John Paul Jones sailed from France in *Ranger* on raiding cruise in British waters.
1800 Frigate *President* launched.
1913 Secretary of the Navy Daniels approved issuance of Navy Air Pilot certificates.
1920 U.S. Marines reached Guatemala City, Guatemala, to protect American legation during revolution.
1940 President Roosevelt extended maritime danger zone for U.S. ships.
1943 Naval Supply Depot, Clearfield, Utah, established.
1945 Navy ships and aircraft supported Army troops landing on Tsuken Shima, off Okinawa.

1947   First underwater telecast made from submarine *Trumpetfish.*
1962   WAVE Chief Storekeeper Barbara Metras became first enlisted woman to transfer to Fleet Reserve.
1963   USS *Thresher* (SSN 593) sank while conducting diving tests, about 220 miles east of Cape Cod, with loss of crew of 112 and 17 civilians.

11 April

1783   Continental Congress proclaimed end of war with England.
1900   First submarine accepted by Navy, USS *Holland.*
1914   Mexico apologized for Tampico affair.
1918   USS *Mary B. Garner,* scout patrol craft, grounded and wrecked on Delaware coast, one life lost.

12 April

1780   British ships opened month-long bombardment of Charleston, S.C.
1811   American merchant ship *Tonquin* reached Point George on Columbia River, and established trading post and settlement at Astoria, Ore.
1861   First shot fired by Navy ship, USS *Harriet Lane,* in Civil War.
        Official date Civil War began.
        Second relief expedition arrived off Charleston.
        Seamen and marines from U.S. squadron reinforced Fort Pickens, Fla.
1864   Monitor *Osage* and timber-clad *Lexington* drove off Confederate troops attacking Blair's Landing, La.
1911   LT Glenn Ellyson qualified as the first naval aviator.
1914   U.S. demanded Mexico salute U.S. flag in Tampico affair.
1916   Bodies of 21 Spaniards, who had died while prisoners of war at Portsmouth, N.H., delivered to Spanish military attache.
1945   President Franklin D. Roosevelt died.

13 April

1847   U.S. naval forces began five-day battle for capture of Tlacotalpam, Talascosa and Tuxpan, Mexico.
1861   Fort Sumter surrendered to Confederates.
1914   Mexico offered to salute U.S. flag provided salute was returned.

14 April

1865   President Lincoln assassinated.
1898   USS *Solace* became first ambulance ship to enter Naval service.
1911   Office of Naval Aviation transferred to Bureau of Navigation.

1914 Fourteen warships of Atlantic Fleet ordered to Mexico.
1927 Navy set world's altitude record for Class C-2 airplanes—LT G. R. Henderson, USN, in Vought CORSAIR O2U, reached 22,178 feet, Washington, D.C.
1956 Carrier *Saratoga* (CVA 60), largest, most powerful warship in the world, commissioned, New York Naval Shipyard.

15 April

1781 Continental ship *Confederacy* captured by British *Roebuck* and *Orpheus*.
1783 Continental Congress ordered all naval prisoners of war released.
1861 President Lincoln called for 75,000 volunteers.
1885 Naval forces landed at Panama to protect American interests during revolution.
1912 Light cruiser *Chester* sailed from President Roads, Mass., to assist survivors of SS *Titanic* sunk by iceberg in North Atlantic.
1918 The First Marine Aviation Force was formed at Marine Flying Field, Miami, Fla.
1944 Alaskan Sea Frontier and Seventeenth Naval District established.
1961 USS *Bainbridge* (DLGN 25), first nuclear-powered frigate, launched at Quincy, Mass.

16 April

1823 Sloop-of-war *Peacock* captured two pirate vessels.
1862 U.S. squadron opened bombardment of Forts Jackson and St. Philip, La.
1863 U.S. squadron bombarded batteries at Vicksburg, Miss.
1924 Navy commenced relief operations in Mississippi Valley floods, until 16 June.
1945 Navy ships and aircraft supported Army troops landing on Ie Shima, Ryukyu Islands.
1947 Act of Congress gave Navy Nurse Corps members commissioned rank.
1951 First Presidential Unit Citation awarded to First Marine Division for action in Korean War.
1946 First F4D SKYRAY delivered to operating unit.

17 April

1778 Sloop-of-war *Ranger* captured British brig.
1798 Congress authorized purchase of 12 vessels for war.
1808 Napoleon issued Bayonne Decree, ordering American ships entering French-controlled ports in violation of the Embargo Act be seized.

1861   Paddle sloop *Powhatan* arrived with reinforcements for Fort Pickens, Fla.

1866   Congress appropriated $5,000 to test use of petroleum oil as fuel for ships' boilers.

1882   William E. Chandler took office, thirty-first Secretary of the Navy.

1923   Navy set world record for Class C airplanes, 11,609 feet.

1945   Naval attack group landed Army troops near Malabang, Parang, and Cotabato, P.I.

1952   Distribution of UN service ribbon began.

18 April

1906   Navy rendered assistance during San Francisco earthquake and fire.

1914   U.S. demanded that Mexico salute U.S. flag before 6 P.M., 19 April.

1916   U.S. ultimatum to Germany on unrestricted submarine warfare.

1942   First U.S. air raid on Japan, launched by USS *Hornet*.

1958   LCDR G. C. Watkins flying F11F-1F at Edwards AFB set world altitude record of 76,938 feet.

19 April

1775   Battle of Lexington and Concord.
        Revolutionary War began.

1778   Sloop-of-war *Ranger* captured British *Lord Chatham* and three smaller vessels.

1783   Commander-in-Chief, George Washington proclaimed cessation of hostilities. American Revolution ended. British naval strength: 469 warships with 174 mounting 60-150 guns. Peak of American naval strength during Revolution, 27 ships averaging 20 guns.

1861   President Lincoln proclaimed part of Confederate coast blockaded.

1864   Armed steamer *Southfield* sunk by *CSS Albemarle*.

1914   Mexico rendered apology and salute in Tampico affair.

1920   First German submarine brought to U.S. after WWI, *U-111,* arrived at New York.

1960   A2F-1 INTRUDER made first flight.

20 April

1796   Congress authorized completion of three frigates.

1814   Sloop-of-war *Frolic* captured by British *Orpheus.*

1861   Norfolk Navy Yard partially destroyed and abandoned.

1862   Gunboats *Itasca* and *Pinola* rammed and broke barrier across Mississippi River.

1914   First combat damage received by a Navy plane, Vera Cruz, Mexico.

1915 First Navy contract for lighter-than-air craft awarded.

1940 First true seaplane tender, USS *Curtiss*, launched.

1942 USS *Wasp* launched British aircraft for reinforcement of Malta.

1953 Battleship *New Jersey* shelled Wonsan, Korea from inside the harbor.

21 April

1861 Sloop-of-war *Saratoga* captured slaver *Nightingale*.

U.S. Army took over Naval Academy grounds and buildings for duration of war.

1864 Tinclad *Petrel* and Tinclad *Prairie Bird* attacked Confederates at Yazoo City, Miss.

1898 U.S. and Spain at war. (See 25 April)

1906 Commander Robert Peary reached "farthest north" point.

1920 First aircraft carrier, USS *Langley* (formerly USS *Jupiter*) named.

1950 First carrier take-off by long-range attack aircraft AJ-1 SAVAGE from *Coral Sea*.

1952 Explosion aboard cruiser *Saint Paul* off Korea.

1956 F5D SKYLANCER made first flight.

22 April

1778 John Paul Jones raided Whitehaven, attempted to capture Earl of Selkirk.

1793 President Washington proclaimed U.S. neutrality in the French-British-Dutch-Spanish war.

1898 U.S. warships began blockade of Cuba. (See 22 Oct., 1962)

First shot of Spanish-American war fired.

Gunboat *Nashville* captured *Buena Ventura,* first prize of Spanish-American war.

1921 World's longest unguarded overwater flight completed by two Navy DH-4Bs, 4,842 mile trip, Washington, D.C., to Santo Domingo and return.

1941 Authorized enlisted strength of regular Navy increased to 232,000.

1944 Navy ships and aircraft supported Army troops landing at Aitape, Tanahmerah Bay, and Humboldt Bay in New Guinea.

1953 Cruiser *Manchester* and destroyer *Nicholas* steamed into Wonsan harbor and shelled coastal positions.

1959 *Henry B. Wilson,* first all-new guided-missile destroyer, launched.

23 April

1800 Congress passed "Act for the better Government of the Navy."

1806 Congress passed law stopping importation of British goods.

1814   British extended blockade to include entire U.S. coast.

1914   Third Marine Regiment organized at Philadelphia, Pa.

1915   LT P. N. L. Bellinger set American seaplane altitude record, reaching 10,000 feet in 1 hour, 19 minutes. (See 23 Feb. 1955)

1917   First battleship driven by electrical power, USS *New Mexico*, launched.

1934   First fleet movement of Navy ships through Panama Canal.

1945   Only U.S. use of guided missiles in WW II: two BAT missiles released at Balikiapan, Borneo.

1959   *Towers*, second all-new guided-missile destroyer, launched.

24 April

1778   Sloop-of-war *Ranger* captured British *Drake*.

1805   Frigate *Constitution* captured a Tripolitan gunboat, together with two prizes taken earlier by the pirate ship.

1862   Paddle frigate *Mississippi* engaged CSS *Manassas*.
       U.S. squadron ran past Forts Jackson and St. Philip, La., and routed Confederate flotilla in Mississippi River.

1884   USS *Thetis, Bear* and *Alert* sailed from New York, to search for Greely expedition in Arctic.

1899   Rebuilding of Naval Academy commenced.

1917   First contingent of destroyers sailed from Boston for overseas service in WW I. (See 4 May 1917)

25 April

1862   U.S. naval forces occupied New Orleans, La.
       U.S. squadron engaged batteries at Fort Macon, N.C.

1898   Congress declared war had existed between U.S. and Spain from 21 April, 1898.

1940   Aircraft carrier *Wasp* commissioned.

1951   Volunteer battalion from Belgium and Luxemburg in Korea praised U.S. Marine Corps pilots for combat air support.

26 April

1907   International Naval Review at Hampton Roads.

1914   ADM Fletcher placed Vera Cruz, Mexico, under martial law.

1915   U.S. interned German raider *Kronprinz Wilhelm*.

1943   U.S. task group bombarded Japanese installations at Attu, Aleutian Islands.

1952   Destroyer *Hobson* sunk in collision with USS *Wasp*, 176 lives lost.

1956   Naval Aircraft Factory, Philadelphia, replaced by Naval Air Engineering Facility (Ships Installations).

27 April

1805   U.S. naval forces captured Derne, Tripoli, by combined land-sea assault, and raised first U.S. flag over foreign soil.

1813   U.S. Navy-Army expedition captured York, Canada.

1861   President Lincoln proclaimed blockade of all Confederate ports.

1893   President Cleveland reviewed naval vessels of ten nations at Columbian Exposition.

1898   U.S. warships bombarded Matanzas, Cuba.

1963   USS *Daniel Webster* (SSBN 626) launched at Groton, Conn., USS *Jack* (SSN 605) launched at Portsmouth, N.H.

28 April

1690   First Colonial naval expedition.

1862   Naval forces captured Forts Jackson and St. Philip, La.

1917   First officer casualty of WW I, LT C. C. Thomas.

1919   USS *W. T. James,* scout patrol craft, sank off Armen Light, France, no casualties.

USS *Gypsum Queen,* scout patrol craft, exploded and sank, same location, 18 lives lost.

1960   Atomic-powered, hunter-killer submarine *Tullibee* (SSN 597) launched at Groton, Conn.

29 April

1813   Boat parties from frigate *Essex* captured British *Montezuma, Policy,* and *Georgiana.*

1814   Sloop of war *Peacock* captured British *Epervier.*

1862   U.S. Marines raised U.S. flag over Custom House at New Orleans, La.

1863   U.S. squadron attacked Confederate batteries at Grand Gulf, Miss.

1898   U.S. warships engaged Spanish gunboats and shore batteries at Cienfuegos, Cuba.

1944   Navy aircraft from twelve carriers bombed Truk, Caroline Islands.

1958   HSS-1N made first flight by helicopter cleared for instrument flight.

1961   USS *Kitty Hawk* commissioned at Philadelphia.

30 April

1777   Continental ship *Hannah* captured by British squadron.

1798   Navy Department established.

1804   Brig *Argus* captured Tripolitan sloop.

1822   Schooner *Alligator* captured pirate schooner *Ciehqua.*

1847   Schooner *Boneta* captured Mexican *Yucateca.*

1873   Newfoundland steamer *Tigress* rescued 19 survivors of Navy Polar Expedition.

1888 First Catholic chaplain, Charles Henry Parks, commissioned.

1942 First submarine built on the Great Lakes, *USS Peto,* launched.

1951 Colombian frigate *Almirante Padilla* reported for duty with UN forces in Korea. HTMS *Bangpakong,* Thai warship, commended by Commander UN Blockading and Escort Force, for conduct under enemy fire at Wonsan.

1955 ADM John H. Towers, Naval Aviator No. 3, died at Jamaica, N.Y.

1 May

1780 French reinforcements sailed from Brest.

1798 George Cabot nominated, first Secretary of the Navy. (Declined—see 18 May, 1798.)

1810 Non-Intercourse Act of 1809 suspended by new act, with proviso for re-application should Great Britain or France again disrupt American commerce.

1811 American merchant brig *Spitfire* stopped by British *Guerriere*. American seaman impressed.

1882 Men from schooner *Alligator* and schooner *Grampus* aided in capture of four pirate schooners.

1891 The first Marine Officers' School established at Marine Barracks, Washington, D.C.

1898 Battle of Manila Bay.

1902 William H. Moody took office, thirty-sixth Secretary of the Navy.

1915 First U.S. merchant ship, *Gulflight,* sunk by German submarine in WW I.

1925 Navy set world's endurance record for Class C-2 seaplanes, May 1 and 2, 28 hours, 35 minutes without refueling.

1941 Office of Public Relations established, later renamed Office of Information.

1945 Naval attack force landed Australian troops on Tarakan Island, Borneo.

1947 LOON, first guided missile launched from a submarine, fired by *Cusk.*

1951 First and only use of aerial torpedoes in Korean war.

1954 Charles S. Thomas took office, fifty-fourth Secretary of the Navy.

1957 First test vehicle of Project Vanguard successfully launched.

2 May

1810 Frigate *Constitution* sent merchant ships *Coloonda* and *Rose* into New York for violation of Non-Intercourse Act.

1822 American merchant brig *Belvedere,* using hidden guns, drove off pirate schooner.

1863 Battle of Chancellorsville began.

1898 Naval forces destroyed enemy guns and magazines at Cavite, P.I.

1919 U.S. subchaser *No. 58* burned, Charleston, S.C., no casualties.

3 May

1861 USS *Surprise* captured Confederate privateer *Savannah.*

1863 Naval expedition in Red River, La., began.

1898 Marines land at Cavite and raise American flag.

1945 U.S. warships supported Army troops landing at Santa Cruz, P.I.

1949 First Navy firing of a high altitude rocket, VIKING, at White Sands.

4 May

1780 First official Navy seal adopted.

1798 Congress authorized President Adams to buy or build ten vessels for defense of U.S.

1865 Acting RADM Henry K. Thatcher, USN, received surrender of Confederate naval forces in Mobile Bay, Ala.

1917 First Navy ships to commence combat operations in European waters in World War I reached Queenstown, Ireland.

1942 Battle of Coral Sea, first carrier-vs-carrier sea battle, began.

1962 World record altitude flight by Stratolab balloon, 113,500 feet in 2 hours 36 minutes, launched by USS *Antietam*. CDR Malcolm Ross and CDR Victor A. Prather were pilots.

5 May

1861 Naval Academy transferred to Newport, R.I., for duration of war.

1864 U.S. squadron engaged CSS *Albemarle*.

1919 U.S. subchaser *No. 343* sunk by fire and explosion in Bermuda, 1 life lost.

1948 First jet squadron qualified for carrier-flight operations.

1945 First round-the-world flight by a Navy squadron ended at Whidby Island, Wash.

1961 First American in space, CDR. Alan B. Shepard, made 15 minute flight in "Freedom 7" from Cape Canaveral, reaching altitude of 116 miles.

6 May

1811 Frigate *President* ordered to protect American shipping off Sandy Hook.

1864 Armed steamer *Commodore Jones* blown up by "torpedo" in James River, Va.

1875 FADM William D. Leahy born at Hampton, Iowa.

1916 First ship-to-shore radio telephone conversation, battleship *New Hampshire* to Washington, D.C.

1929 Navy set world balloon record, 952 miles in 43 hours and 20 minutes.

1936 Congress authorized construction of David Taylor Model Basin, Carderock, Md.

7 May

1777 Continental cutter *Surprise* captured British *Prince of Orange*.

1779   Continental ship *Providence* captured British *Diligent*.
1915   *Lusitania* sank.
1934   Frigate *Constitution* completed tour of principal U.S. seaports.

8 May

1776   Continental schooner *Wasp* captured British *Betsey*.
1862   Naval expedition up James River, Va.
        U.S. squadron engaged Confederate batteries at Sewell's Point, Va.
1911   Birthdate of naval aviation. TRIAD, first airplane, ordered.
1919   First trans-Atlantic flight commenced by *NC-4* (See 31 May 1919)
1929   World altitude record set by LT Apollo Soucek in Wright APACHEE, 39,140 feet.
1952   U.S. Marine Corps and Air Force planes bombed and strafed Suan, Korea.
1962   USS *Lafayette* (SSBN 616) launched at Groton, Conn.

9 May

1926   First flight over North Pole. (See 28 Nov. 1929)
1929   First aerial observation of a solar eclipse.
1942   USS *Wasp* launched British aircraft to reinforce Malta for second time.
1945   First German submarine surrendered after VE Day—*U 249*.

10 May

1797   Frigate *United States* launched.
1801   Tripoli declared war on U.S.
1862   Union forces occupied Pensacola, Fla., after Confederate evacuation.
        U.S. squadron engaged Confederate River Defense Fleet near Fort Pillow, Tenn.
1912   RADM Bradley A. Fiske, first "flying admiral," flew over New York City in an airplane piloted by Joseph Collier and Walter Brookins.
1929   First submarine lung tested.
1949   First shipboard launching of the LARK, guided missile, by USS *Norton Sound*.
1960   Submarine *Triton* (SSRN 586) completed 84 days, 36,014 mile circumnavigation of the world, submerged. (See 9 Nov. 1880)
1962   First nuclear power plant in Antarctic began furnishing electric power at NAF McMurdo Sound.

11 May

1862   CSS *Virginia* destroyed by Confederates at Norfolk, Va., to prevent capture by Union forces.

1865   Captain Edward Simpson, USN, accepted surrender of remnants of Confederate Navy.

1898   Torpedo boat *Winslow* crippled by enemy fire at Cardenas, Cuba. First officer casualty of Spanish-American War, ENS Worth Bagley, killed at Cardenas.

      Sailors and Marines from U.S. squadron cut telegraphic cables at Cienfuegos, Cuba.

1950   VIKING rocket launched from a ship, USS *Norton Sound,* for the first time.

1957   Navy South Pole Station recorded world's coldest thermometer reading, minus 101° Fahrenheit.

12 May

1780   Frigate *Queen of France,* sloop *Providence,* frigate *Boston* and sloop-of-war *Ranger* captured by British.

1880   The new Marine Corps made their first landing at Puerto Plata, Santo Domingo. .

1846   U.S. declared war on Mexico.

1898   U.S. squadron bombarded San Juan, Puerto Rico.

1918   First U.S. subchasers reached Portsmouth, England, for duty in European waters.

1938   Aircraft carrier *Enterprise* commissioned.

1941   Japanese ambassador Nomura presented Secretary of State Hull with Japanese proposal for establishment of "just peace in the Pacific."

13 May

1861   Blockade set at Pensacola, Fla.

1908   Navy Nurse Corps established.

1942   Bureau of Navigation (BUNAV) renamed Bureau of Naval Personnel (BUPERS).

14 May

1801   Tripoli opened hostilities against U.S.

1846   President Polk declared Mexico's east coast blockaded.

1917   Marine Barracks, Quantico, Va., established.

15 May

1809   Paul Hamilton took office, fourth Secretary of the Navy.

1862   U.S. squadron attacked Fort Darling, Va.

1930   USS *Narwhal* commissioned, first "streamlined" submarine.

1941   Battleship *Washington* commissioned.

1942   First NATS flight across Pacific. (See 20 Dec. 1955)

1944 Navy began flying special emergency trans-Atlantic flights supporting Normandy invasion.

1953 Destroyer *Brush* hit by enemy shore batteries at Wonsan.

1960 *Abraham Lincoln* (SSBN 602) launched at Portsmouth, N.H.

1963 USS *Kearsarge* (CVA 33) recovered Astronaut Gordon Cooper, Major, USAF, after he orbited the earth 22 times in "Faith 7" capsule. Landing made about 80 miles southeast of Midway, less than 5 miles from *Kearsarge*.

16 May

1797 President John Adams urged Congress to strengthen the Navy.

1820 First U.S. warship, frigate *Congress,* visited China.

1847 USS *Independence* captured Mexican *Correo* and a launch.

1916 Forces under Admiral Caperton landed and occupied Santo Domingo.

1920 First large group of Navy and Marine Corps dead returned from France.

1940 President Roosevelt asked Congress for $1,182,000,000 national defense funds.

1947 Congress increased Civil Engineering Corps strength to 3% of the Line.

1957 USS *Skate* (SSN 578), atomic submarine, launched.

17 May

1862 U.S. squadron attacked Confederates along Pamunkey River, Va.

1888 First naval battalion of Massachusetts State Militia organized.

1940 President Roosevelt announced plans for recommissioning 35 destroyers.

1951 USS *New Jersey* joined Navy forces off Korea. Aircraft from carriers *Princeton, Boxer* and *Philippine Sea* supported ROK troops and blasted six bridges between Wonsan and Hamhung.

18 May

1775 General Benedict Arnold captured *Enterprise.*

1798 Benjamin Stoddert appointed first Secretary of the Navy.

1898 Navy boat parties cut telegraph cables at Santiago, Guantanamo, and Mole St. Nicholas, Cuba.

1942 Office of Naval Inspector General established.

19 May

1861 Armed steamer *Monticello* engaged Confederate battery at Sewall's Point, Va.

1863   U.S. squadron began bombardment of Vicksburg batteries.

1871   U.S. squadron on diplomatic mission arrived at mouth of Han River, Korea.

1882   COMO R. W. Shufeldt landed from USS *Swatara* to commence treaty negotiations with Korean commissioners.

1912   First North Atlantic ice patrol established.

1944   James Forrestal took office, forty-ninth Secretary of the Navy.

1949   Martin flying boat MARS lifted 301 passengers and 7 crew members from Alameda to San Diego.

1958   Worlds largest submarine, USS *Triton* (SSRN 586) launched. Atomic-powered, radar picket type is 447 feet long, displaces 5900 tons. (See 10 May 1960)

20 May

1801   Four warships dispatched to Mediterranean for protection of American commerce.

1815   U.S. squadron sailed for Mediterranean to suppress piracy.

1844   Frigate *Constitution* sailed from New York on round-the-world cruise.

1862   Naval forces occupied Stone River, S.C.

1863   Two naval expeditions captured Yazoo City, Miss.

1909   USS *Mississippi,* first battleship to visit an inland city, reached Natchez, Mississippi.

1918   Battleship *New Mexico* commissioned.

        USS *Annie E. Gallup,* scout patrol craft, wrecked, no casualties.

1930   First airplane catapulted from a dirigible. (See 31 Jan. 1930)

1943   Tenth Fleet established.

1950   Armed Forces Day first observed.

21 May

1777   Continental ships *Hancock* and *Boston* sailed from Boston in company with nine American privateers.

1917   First torpedo fired in WW I, by USS *Ericsson*.

1941   American freighter *Robin Moor* sunk by German submarine.

1960   Aircraft carrier *Kitty Hawk,* first armed with guided missiles, launched at Camden, N.J.

1961   USS *John Marshall* (SSBN 611) commissioned.

22 May

1864   USS *Columbine* and gunboat *Ottawa* attempted to rescue Army troops in St. John's River, Fla.; rescue attempt continued until 28 May.

1882 U.S. signed treaty opening Korea to foreign trade.

1912 Birthdate of Marine Corps aviation—1st LT Alfred A. Cunningham was first Marine officer ordered to flight training.

1917 President Wilson signed bill increasing strength of Navy to 150,000, Marine Corps to 30,000.

1918 USS *Wakiva II,* converted yacht, sunk in collision with *Wabash* in Bay of Biscay; 2 lives lost.

1958 Through May 22-23, F4D-1 SKY RAY set 5 world speed-to-climb records—3, 6, 9, 12 and 15 thousand meters in 44.392, 66.095, 90.025, 111.224 and 156.233 seconds respectively.

23 May

1831 Levi Woodbury took office, tenth Secretary of the Navy.

1834 Frigate *Potomac* arrived at Boston after circling the world.

1939 Submarine *Squalus* sank off Portsmouth, N.H., in 240 feet of water, 26 lives lost. Ship later refloated, renamed *Sailfish,* and served through WW II.

24 May

1850 USS *Rescue* and brigantine *Advance* sailed from New York in search of Franklin Expedition, lost in Arctic.

1917 First Atlantic convoy of WW I sailed from Hampton Roads, Va.

1918 First landing of U.S. naval forces in Russia during WW I.

1961 Three F4H PHANTOM II fighters set new Los Angeles to New York record of 2 hours, 47 minutes for 870 mph average.

1962 LCDR M. Scott Carpenter successfully completed second U.S. manned orbital space flight with three trips around the world. (See 20 Feb. 1962)

25 May

1862 U.S. Marines recaptured Norfolk Navy Yard from Confederates.

1885 Last U.S. Marines withdrawn from Panama.

1918 Three small schooners damaged by German submarine *U 151,* off Cape Charles, Va.

1949 Francis P. Matthews took office, fifty-first Secretary of the Navy.

1952 Battleship *Iowa* bombarded Chongjin, Korea.

1954 Airship *ZP6-2* completed 200.1 hours in the air.

26 May

1823 Schooner *Grampus* captured 2 pirate vessels.

1861   Blockade set at Mobile, Ala.
1958   USS *Galveston,* first Talos guided-missile cruiser, commissioned.

27 May

1813   Joint Navy-Army attack on Fort George, Canada.
1863   River ironclad *Cincinnati* attacked Confederate Army's left flank at Vicksburg.
1941   State of unlimited national emergency declared.
1944   U.S. warships supported Army troops landing on Biak, off New Guinea.

28 May

1798   President John Adams instructed public armed vessels to make reprisals on French commerce.
1813   Frigate *Essex* and prize, *Georgiana,* captured five British whalers.
1861   Blockade set at Savannah, Ga.
1882   Four members of DeLong Arctic expedition arrived at New York.

29 May

1781   Frigate *Alliance* captured British ships *Atlanta* and *Trepassy.*
1917   RADM Albert Gleaves appointed Commander, Convoy Operations.
1944   USS *Block Island* torpedoed and sunk by German submarine; only U.S. carrier lost in Atlantic during WW II.
1957   Seventh Fleet ships effected emergency repairs for Chinese Nationalist steamer *Ping Tung,* aground off Okinawa.

30 May

1814   Boats under Master-Commandant M. T. Woolsey captured three British gunboats at Sandy Creek, N.Y.
1868   First formal observance of Memorial Day.

31 May

1853   First U.S. expedition to the Arctic sailed from New York.
1861   Potomac flotilla engaged Confederate batteries at Aquia Creek, Va.
1863   U.S. squadron covered Army retreat at West Point, Va.
1900   Sailors and marines arrived in Peking, China, to form Legation Guard.
1916   Battle of Jutland.

1918 Second Division, AEF, composed of Army and Marine troops (Fourth Marine Brigade) participated in the Aisne offensive. USS *President Lincoln*, troop transport sunk by submarine *U-90* off French coast; 26 lives lost.

1919 First successful trans-Atlantic flight completed by *NC-4*.

1 June

1780   Continental ship *Trumbull* engaged British privateer *Watt.*
1792   John Paul Jones appointed special envoy and Consul to Algiers.
1813   Frigate *Chesapeake* captured by British ship *Shannon.*
1871   Navy surveying party fired upon by fort in Han River, Korea.
1940   Battleship *Washington* launched.
1944   First trans-Atlantic crossing by non-rigid lighter-than-air aircraft completed by airship *ZP-14,* 3,145 miles, 58 hours flight time.
1955   First Electronic Countermeasures squadron commissioned.
1959   William B. Franke succeeds Thomas S. Gates, Jr., as fifty-sixth Secretary of the Navy.

2 June

1941   USS *Long Island,* first escort carrier, commissioned.
1958   F8U-3, all weather fighter, made initial flight.
1962   USS *Worden* (DLG 18) launched at Bath, Maine.

3 June

1785   Last ship remaining in Continental Navy, frigate *Alliance,* ordered sold. Until 1794 there was no Navy.
1805   Preliminary articles of peace treaty with Tripoli signed.
1813   Sloop *Eagle* and sloop *Growler* captured by British on Lake Champlain.
1861   Armed cutter *Perry* captured Confederate privateer *Savannah.*
1865   Confederate naval forces in Red River, La., surrendered to U.S. squadron.
1898   Collier *Merrimac* sunk in Santiago harbor in effort to block entrance.
        First "campaign medal," for Battle of Manila Bay, authorized.
1949   First Negro, John Wesley Brown, graduated from Naval Academy.
1953   First podiatrist commissioned in the Naval Medical Service Corps.

4 June

1800   Navy Department purchased site of Portsmouth Navy Yard, N.H.
1829   Floating battery *Fulton* destroyed by explosion at Brooklyn Navy Yard.
1900   Boxer Rebellion (China) began.
1930   Lieutenant Apollo Soucek set world's aircraft altitude record, 43,166 feet.

1934 USS *Ranger* commissioned, first carrier designed as such.
1942 Battle of Midway began (turning point in Pacific war).
1944 German submarine *U 505* captured by U.S. Navy hunter-killer group.
1947 Landing field at NAS Ocean, Va., named Soucek Field in honor of VADM Apollo Soucek. (See 1930 above)

5 June

1794 First officers of new Navy announced.
1863 Naval shore battery began action against Vicksburg.
1901 Ammunition magazines destroyed by explosion at Mare Island Navy Yard. (See 17 July)
1917 First Selective Service registration in WW I. First naval Aeronautical Detachment reached France.
1918 U.S. subchaser *No. 132* sunk in collision with USS *Tacoma* off Barnegat Light, no casualties.
     Close of the Aisne offensive.
1945 Typhoon off Okinawa damaged many U.S. warships.

6 June

1776 James Nicholson appointed senior CAPT of Continental Navy.
1862 Battle of Memphis, Tenn.
1881 USS *Rogers* sailed from Mare Island in search of USS *Jeannette*.
1898 U.S. squadron bombarded Santiago.
1918 Battle of Belleau Wood.
1926 First use of aerial photography in Alaska as aid to mapping.
1944 Allies invaded Normandy, at UTAH and OMAHA Beaches. *Osprey* (minesweeper), *Curry* (destroyer) and *PC-1261* sunk by mines off Normandy.
1957 First carrier-to-carrier, ocean-to-ocean flight made by two F8U CRU-SADERS (3 hours, 28 minutes) and two A3D SKYWARRIORS (4 hours, 1 minute). Planes flew from *Bon Homme Richard* off California to *Saratoga* off Florida.
1958 USS *Independence,* fourth *Forrestal*-class carrier, launched.

7 June

1777 Frigate *Hancock* captured British frigate *Fox*.
1861 Blockade set at Key West, Fla.
1921 Secretary of the Navy authorized Brevet Medal, only decoration specifically for Marine Corps personnel.

1952   1st LT John Andre, USMC, became second Marine night fighter ace in history by shooting down YAK-9.

8 June

1830   Sloop-of-war *Vincennes,* first U.S. warship to circle the globe. (See 31 Aug. 1826)

1880   Congress authorized office of Judge Advocate General.

1925   First Naval Academy course in flight instruction commenced.

1926   ADM Charles F. Hughes appointed Commander in Chief, U.S. Fleet.

9 June

1772   First overt act of resistance to England by the Colonies.

1863   Naval shore battery began bombarding Port Hudson, La.

1869   Navy ordered construction of first torpedo manufacturing station on Goat Island, Newport Bay.

1871   Navy and Marine landing party attacked forts in Han River, Korea, in retaliation for Koreans' having fired on surveying party.

1880   CAPT William B. Remey, USMC, appointed first Judge Advocate General with rank of COL.

1882   Office of Naval Records of the War of Rebellion (now Naval History Division) established.

1917   Six converted yachts sailed from New York to form nucleus of U.S. patrol squadron in European waters.

1928   Carrier *Lexington* made record speed run from San Pedro to Honolulu, 9-12 June.

1945   Marines landed on Aguni Shima, Ryukyu Islands.

1948   First Navy Reserve Science Seminar convened.

1953   UN fleet launched heavy air and surface attacks against enemy battleline positions in the east-control sector of Korean front.

1959   USS *George Washington* (SSBN 598), first nuclear-powered Fleet Ballistic Missile Submarine, is launched at Groton, Conn.

10 June

1804   U.S. signed peace treaty with Tripoli.

1854   First formal graduation exercises held at Naval Academy.

1896   First experimental ship model tank authorized.

1898   U.S. Marines landed at Fisherman's Point, Guantanamo, Cuba; first U.S. troops ashore in enemy territory during Spanish-American War.

1915 U.S. asked Germany to take measures safeguarding American lives and ships.

11 June

1871 First American military man killed in action in Korea, LT Hugh W. McKee.

1927 Light cruiser *Memphis* arrived at Washington, D.C., after record speed run from France, with Charles A. Lindbergh and his plane, Spirit of St. Louis.

1940 President Roosevelt declared Mediterranean and mouth of Red Sea combat zones.

1944 U.S. battleships off Normandy gave gunfire support to Army troops ten miles inland.

12 June

1775 First sea fight of Revolution.

1941 Naval Reserves called to active duty.

1944 Aircraft from 15 U.S. carriers began bombing islands in the Marianas chain.

1951 Destroyer *Walke* damaged by mine off Korea.

1957 International Naval Review, Hampton Roads, Va.

13 June

1812 Two seamen impressed from USS *Chesapeake* freed by British.

1867 Navy landing party destroyed Formosan village in retaliation for massacre of American merchant seamen.

1881 USS *Jeanette* crushed in Arctic ice pack.

1899 Navy-Army forces drove off insurgent attack on arsenal at Manila Bay.

1913 Navy set American altitude record for seaplanes, 6,200 feet.

1917 USCG *McCulloch* sunk in collision with SS *Governor,* Point Conception, Calif., no casualties.

1942 Four German agents put ashore from submarine at Long Island, N.Y.

14 June

1777 Continental Congress adopted basic design of present National Ensign.

1847 Second naval expedition against Tabasco, Mexico began.

1898 Marines attacked Cuzco Well, Cuba. SGT John H. Quick, USMC, won Medal of Honor for gallant conduct.

1917 First contingent of American Expeditionary Force sailed from New York under Navy convoy.

1940   President Roosevelt signed "11% Naval Expansion Act."

1951   USS *Thompson* hit by Communist shore batteries near Songjin, Korea.

1952   Keel of world's first nuclear-powered ship, USS *Nautilus,* laid.

15 June

1775   First armed vessels commissioned by public authority in U.S.

1898   U.S. ships destroyed fort and took possession of outer bay at Guantanamo, Cuba.

1944   Marines landed on Saipan, Marianas Islands.

1956   World's second guided-missile cruiser, *Canberra,* commissioned at Philadelphia Naval Base.

1963   USS *Bronstein* (DE 1037), first of new escort class, commissioned.
        USS *Mars* (AFS 1), first of new class underway replenishment ship, commissioned.

16 June

1898   U.S. squadron bombarded Santiago.

1941   USS *0-9* sunk in test dive off Portsmouth, N.H., 33 lives lost.

1960   First woman to land aboard a carrier in a jet plane, Jacqueline Cochrane, landed aboard USS *Independence* as passenger in A3D SKYWARRIOR.

17 June

1800   Schooner *Enterprise* captured French privateer *Cygne.*

1802   American merchant brig *Franklin* captured by Tripolitan pirates.

1815   U.S. squadron captured Algerian *Mashouda.*

1862   U.S. squadron captured Confederate batteries at St. Charles, Ark.

1863   Monitor *Weehawken* captured CSS *Atlanta.*

1870   Screw sloop *Mohican* burned pirate ship *Forward* in Teacapan River, Mexico.

1898   Navy Hospital Corps established.

1909   Fort Severn demolished.

1915   Battleship *Colorado* sailed for Tabari Bay, Mexico, to assist distressed Americans.

1917   First enlisted man buried in France, WW I—Seaman Louis Reinhardy, drowned on 12 June.

1940   Chief of Naval Operations asked Congress for $4,000,000,000, to build a "two ocean" Navy.

1944   Allied task force landed French troops on Elba, Italy.

1952   *ZPN-1,* world's largest non-rigid airship, delivered to the Navy.

18 June

1798 Benjamin Stoddert took office, second Secretary of the Navy.
1812 U.S. declared war on Great Britain. U.S. had only 18 seaworthy ships, with but one, USS *Wasp,* actually at sea.
1942 First Negro officer, Bernard W. Robinson, commissioned in Naval Reserve.

19 June

1815 U.S. squadron captured Algerian *Estedio.*
1864 Screw sloop *Kearsarge* sank CSS *Alabama.*
1944 Battle of the Philippine Sea began.
1950 *Caroline Mars* flew from Honolulu to San Diego with 144 persons aboard.

20 June

1913 In first fatal accident of Naval Aviation, ENS W. D. Billingsley killed at Annapolis.
1940 Bureau of Ships and Office of Under Secretary of the Navy established.
1953 Destroyer *Gurke* stopped enemy trains at Tanchon and Pukchong with gunfire.

21 June

1812 U.S. squadron sailed from New York to intercept British convoys and draw enemy warships away from U.S. ports.
1866 Act of Congress separated Hydrographic Office from Naval Observatory.
1898 Cruiser *Charleston* captured Guam.
1918 USS *Schurz,* gunboat, sunk in collision with SS *Florida* off Cape Lookout, one life lost.
1919 German crews scuttled ships interned at Scapa Flow.

22 June

1803 Brig *Adams* sank Tripolitan *Mashouda.*
1807 USS *Chesapeake-Leopard* Incident.
1814 Schooner *Rattlesnake* captured by British *Leander.*
1865 Last shot of Civil War fired in Bering Sea by Confederate raider *Shenandoah.*
1884 USS *Thetis* and *Bear* rescued seven members of Greely expedition.
1898 Twin screw schooner *St. Paul* engaged Spanish *Terror* and *Isabel II.*
1963 USS *Tecumseh* (SSBN 628) and USS *Flasher* (SSBN 613) launched at Groton, Conn.; USS *Daniel Boone* (SSBN 629) launched at Mare

Island, Calif.; USS *John C. Calhoun* (SSBN 630) launched at Newport News, Va.

1937   12 PBY-1 planes flew non-stop, San Diego to Coco Solo, 3,292 miles in 27 hours, 58 minutes.

1945   CAPT Robert Baird, USMC, became first night-fighter ace.

1952   Naval ships and aircraft bombarded both coasts of Korea.

23 June

1812   Frigate *President* engaged British *Belvedere.*

1903   U.S. Fleet units visiting Germany entertained by Emperor at Kiel.

1933   USS *Macon,* last Navy dirigible, commissioned.

1942   Servicemen's Dependents Allowance Act became law.

1952   UN forces made most destructive air attack of Korean campaign.

24 June

1497   John and Sebastian Cabot first reached the American continent.

1810   Brig *Vixen* fired into by British *Moselle.*

1843   Secretary of the Navy Abel P. Upshur appointed *ad interim* Secretary of State.

1873   Screw sloop *Juniate* sailed from New York in search of USS *Polaris.*

1926   Congress authorized expanded Navy aircraft building program.

25 June

1798   President John Adams authorized U.S. merchant ships to repel French interference with force.

1859   Paddle sloop *Powhatan* aided British and French forces in attack at forts on Peiho River, China.

1940   Naval Construction Corps abolished.

1950   North Korea invaded South Korea.

1956   FADM Ernest J. King died at Portsmouth Naval Hospital in New Hampshire.

26 June

1861   First officer casualty of Civil War, CDR James Harmon Ward, killed by musket ball.

1869   George M. Robeson took office, twenty-seventh Secretary of the Navy.

1884   Congress passed act authorizing commission of Naval Academy graduates as ensigns.

1918   Marine brigade captured Belleau Wood.

1942   Germany announced unrestricted submarine warfare off U.S. Atlantic Coast.

1944   Marines landed on Kume Shima, Ryukyu Islands.

27 June

1863   U.S. Revenue Schooner *Cabel Cushing* captured by CSS *Archer.*

1889 Office of Inspector General, Pay Corps, established.

1891 Bodies of 19 men drowned in 1889 Samoan hurricane buried in Naval Cemetery, Mare Island, California.

1956 First annual Fleet Air Gunnery Meet held at NAAS, El Centro, Calif.

1958 WW II carrier *Enterprise,* the "Big E," sold as scrap.

28 June

1776 British fleet attacked Charleston, S.C.

1786 American representatives signed peace treaty with Morocco.

1794 First warship builder, Joshua Humphreys, appointed.

1798 Congress passed act authorizing prize money for crews of U.S. ships.

1814 Sloop-of-war *Wasp* captured British *Reindeer.*

1815 U.S. squadron arrived at Algiers to effect final treaty with Dey.

1862 Contingent of U.S. squadron successfully dashed past Confederate batteries at Vicksburg, Miss.

1863 Screw steamer *Princess Royal* engaged Confederates at Donalds-ville, La.

1869 First Surgeon General, William M. Wood, appointed.

1879 First shipboard electrical lighting system installed in USS *Jeanette.*

1898 President McKinley proclaimed southern coast of Cuba and port of San Juan, Puerto Rico, blockaded. U.S. gunboats engaged enemy gunboats and shore batteries at Manzanillo, Cuba.

1914 Archduke Ferdinand of Austria assassinated.

1919 Treaty of Versailles signed.

1952 Public Law 412 fixed personnel strength of Marine Corps and established relation of Commandant of Marine Corps to Joint Chiefs of Staff.

29 June

1860 Screw gunboat *Mystic* seized slaver *Thomas Achorn.*

1925 Earthquake at Santa Barbara, Calif.; Navy rendered assistance for one month after the quake.

1943 Navy forces began bombarding Vila-Stanmore on Kolombangara, and Buin-Shortland Harbor, Bougainville.

1950 First bombardment of Korean War, by USS *Juneau,* USS *Dehaven.*

30 June

1798 Congress authorized President John Adams to procure 12 ships for the Navy.

1815 Last action of War of 1812, USS *Peacock-Nautilus.*
    Captain Stephen Decatur concluded treaty for U.S. with Dey of Algiers.

1834   Congress clarified status of Marine Corps.
       Congress authorized $5,000 for steam engine experiments.

1847   Naval forces captured Tamultay, Mexico.

1861   CSS *Sumter,* commerce raider, escaped to sea through U.S. blockading squadron at mouth of Mississippi.

1940   Navy strength 1,099 ships and 203,127 men.

1941   Navy strength 1,899 ships and 358,021 men.
       France severed relations with Russia.

1942   Navy strength 5,612 ships and 843,096 men.

1943   U.S. warships landed Marines and Army troops in New Georgia area, Solomon Islands.
       Navy strength 18,493 ships and 2,207,720 men.

1944   Navy strength 46,032 ships and 3,623,205 men.

1945   Navy strength 67,952 ships and 4,031,097 men.

1950   Naval Aviation at lowest strength since WW II.

1956   Navy Coffee Roasting Plants in New York and Oakland were inactivated and Navy began using coffee from commercial sources.

1957   NRL launched, in Japan, first of radio carrying free balloons to provide regular weather coverage of trans-Pacific sea and air lanes.

1 July

1797 New "Navy Regulations" passed by Congress.

1800 First convoy duty, by USS *Essex*.

1801 U.S. squadron reached Gibraltar.

1824 American merchant brig *Castor* seized by Caribbean pirates.

1834 Mahlon Dickerson took office, eleventh Secretary of the Navy.

1838 James K. Paulding took office, twelfth Secretary of the Navy.

1847 Marine Regiment landed in Vera Cruz for service with Army in Mexican War.

1850 Naval School renamed Naval Academy.

1851 Four year course of study adopted at Naval Academy.

1863 Battle of Gettysburg began.

1897 International Rules of the Road first went into effect. (See 7 Oct. 1897)

1898 Gunboat *Helena* hauled off the grounded transport *Florida* while under enemy fire near Port Tunas, Cuba. Armed yacht *Scorpion* and armed tug *Osceola* engaged Spanish ships and shore batteries at Manzanillo, Cuba.

1904 Paul Morton took office, thirty-seventh Secretary of the Navy.

1905 Charles J. Bonaparte took office, thirty-eighth Secretary of the Navy.

1914 Prohibition proclaimed for the Navy.
Office of Naval Aeronautics established.

1918 USS *Covington*, troop transport, sunk by submarine off Brest, France, six lives lost.

1933 Navy Clothing Depot, Brooklyn, N.Y., established.

1941 Naval Coastal Frontiers established.

1942 Naval Supply Depot, Bayonne, N.J., established.

1947 Naval Supply Depot, Great Lakes, Ill., established.

1951 First enemy aircraft destroyed at night in Korea by VMFCN 513.

1952 Naval Supply Depot, Yokosuka, Japan, established.

1955 Keel of USS *Independence* (CVA 62), fourth *Forrestal*-class carrier, laid.
First Assault Helicopter Aircraft Carrier, USS *Thetis*, designated.
First Dental Corps admiral, George C. Paffenberger, USNR, appointed.

1958 First joint Civil-Navy Radar Air Traffic Control Center (RATCC) went into operation at NAS, Miramar, Calif.

1961 USS *Leahy* (DLG 16) launched at Bath, Maine.
USS *Permit* (SSN 549) launched at Mare Island, Calif.

2 July

1807   President Jefferson ordered all armed British ships out of U.S. ports.
1812   Frigate *Essex* sailed against British, flying flag with legend "Free Trade and Sailors' Rights."
1813   Frigate *President* captured British *Traveller*.
1861   Blockade set at Galveston, Texas.
1898   Gunboat *Helena* and armed yacht *Peoria* engaged shore batteries at Port Tunas, Cuba.
1923   Naval Research Laboratory (NRL) commissioned.
1937   Aviatrix Amelia Earhart disappeared in Pacific. Navy conducted extensive unsuccessful search.
1940   Export Control Act passed.
1944   Allied naval force landed Army troops on Noemfoor Island off Netherlands New Guinea.
1946   First jet aircraft operated from a carrier.

3 July

1775   Washington took command of Continental Army.
1871   Naval exploring expedition sailed from New York for Arctic in USS *Polaris*.
1898   Battle of Santiago.
1918   Thirteenth Marine Regiment organized at Quantico, Va.
1942   First airborne test firing of a retro-rocket by PBY-5A at Goldstone Lake, Calif.
1950   First combat action for carrier aircraft in Korea—Air Group 5 from USS *Valley Forge*.
       First Navy "kills" in aerial combat over Korea; 2 YAK-9s shot down at Pyongyang by F9Fs.

4 July

1776   United Colonies declared their independence. Continental Navy strength, 18 ships.
1777   First "Stars and Stripes" flag unfurled in a Continental warship.
1800   Schooner *Enterprise* captured French privateer *L'Aigle*.
1801   First Presidential Review of U.S. Marine Band and Marines at the White House.
1813   Frigate *President* captured British *Duchess*.
1814   Sloop-of-war *Wasp* captured British *Regulator*.
1831   U.S. concluded indemnity treaty with France.
1842   First electrically-operated underwater "torpedo" tested.
1863   Timber-clad *Tyler* beat off Confederates attacking Union troops at Helena, Ark.

1898   U.S. squadron prevented Spaniards sinking *Reina Mercedes* in order to block Santiago channel.

1927   World altitude record for seaplanes set by LT C. C. Champion in 425 HP Wright APACHE, 37,995 feet. (See 25 July)

1960   First 50-star U.S. flag flown at Fort McHenry, Baltimore, Md.

5 July

1801   David Glasgow Farragut born near Knoxville, Tennessee.

1814   Sloop-of-war *Peacock* captured British *Stranger, Venus, Adiona,* and *Fortitude.*

1815   Decatur's squadron arrived at Tripoli to present U.S. demands.

1859   Midway Island discovered.

1862   Navy Department reorganized into eight Bureaus.

1898   Armed yacht *Eagle* captured Spanish *Galleto.*

1920   President Roosevelt invoked Export Control Act against Japan.

1943   U.S. warships bombarded Vila, Kolombangara, and Bairoko Harbor, New Georgia, Solomon Islands.

6 July

1747   John Paul Jones born at Arbigland, Scotland.

1776   Continental sloop *Sachem* captured British privateer *Three Brothers.*

1814   Sloop-of-war *Wasp* captured British *Jenny.*

1898   Armed auxiliary *Dixie* captured Spanish *Three Bells, Pilgrim,* and *Greeman Castle.*

1908   Commander Robert Peary sailed from New York in steamer *Roosevelt* to explore Arctic..

1943   Battle of Kula Gulf.

1960   Blimp *ZPG-3W* crashed off New Jersey coast, 18 men dead or missing.

7 July

1777   Frigate *Hancock* and her prize, the frigate *Fox,* captured by British squadron.

1798   Frigate *Delaware* captured French privateer *Croyable.*

1846   Sailors and marines from U.S. squadron occupied Monterey, Calif.

1917   USS *Saxis,* patrol craft, grounded and lost, West Point, Va., no casualties.

1920   First radio compass used in Naval aircraft.

1941   U.S.-Iceland agreement announced.

        First Marine Air Wing organized at Quantico, Va.

        Marines landed at Reykjavik, Iceland.

1948   First WAVE enlisted women sworn into Regular Navy.

8 July

1778 French fleet under D'Estaing arrived off Delaware coast to join American forces.

1879 USS *Jeannette* departed San Francisco to explore Arctic.

1944 Naval bombardment of Guam began.

9 July

1798 Congress authorized privateering against French shipping. In the succeeding 9 months, 364 American privateers were commissioned.

1846 First U.S. flag raised over San Francisco, Calif.

1960 Nuclear-powered submarine *Thresher* (ssn 593) launched (bow first) at Portsmouth, N.H. (See 10 April 1963)

10 July

1863 U.S. squadron attacked Fort Wagner, Morris Island, Charleston, S.C., and landed troops on Morris Island.

1934 First visit of a U.S. President to South America, Franklin D. Roosevelt in heavy cruiser *Houston*.

1941 Second Marine Air Wing organized at San Diego, Calif.

1943 Allies invaded Sicily.

1945 Aircraft from 14 U.S. carriers began striking Japanese homeland.

11 July

1798 Act approved "for the establishing and organizing of a Marine Corps."

1846 Richmond Aulick, first Naval Academy graduate, commissioned passed midshipman.

1898 U.S. ships engaged shore batteries at Santiago. Armed yachts *Hist* and *Hornet* cut telegraph cable between Santa Cruz and Manzanillo, Cuba.

1917 Sixth Marine Regiment organized at Quantico, Va.

1918 *Westover,* cargo vessel, sunk by German submarine *U-92* off French coast, 11 lives lost.

1919 Pay Corps renamed Supply Corps.

1934 First U.S. President, Franklin D. Roosevelt, sailed through Panama Canal.

1940 Frank Knox took office, forty-eighth Secretary of the Navy.

1943 U.S. warships bombarded beaches near Gela, Sicily, and stopped German tank attack.

12 July

1775 American ships under Jeremiah O'Brien captured two British ships in Bay of Fundy.

1780 French fleet under Admiral Ternay arrived at Newport, R.I.

1798 Major William Ward Burrows appointed second Commandant of the Marine Corps.

1813 Frigate *President* captured British *Jean-and-Ann*.

1814 Brig *Siren* captured British *Adventure*.

1836 First Engineer officer, Charles Haswell, commissioned.

1919 American trawler *Richard Buckley* sunk by mine in North Sea, seven lives lost.

1943 First women completed submarine escape tests.

1951 Ninth Naval District forces took part in flood relief work in Kansas City area, through 20 July.

1953 UN fleet launched heavy air and sea attack on Wonsan. MAJ John F. Bolt, USMC, first jet ace in Marine Corps history.

13 July

1776 Continental brig *Reprisal* captured British *Peter*.

1813 Frigate *Essex* captured British *Charlton, Seringapatam,* and *New Zealander*.

1854 Sloop-of-war *Cyane* bombarded San Juan de Nicaragua in retaliation for ill-treatment of American citizens.

1863 U.S. squadron captured one Confederate steamer and forced enemy to destroy four others at Yazoo City, Miss.

1914 Fifth Marine Regiment organized at Vera Cruz, Mexico.

1943 Battle of Kolombangara (Solomon Islands).

14 July

1800 Frigate *Insurgent* with crew of 340, sailed from Norfolk for West Indies, and was never seen again.

1813 LT John M. Gamble, USMC, became first Marine officer to command a ship in battle.

1814 Gunboat *No. 88* captured British *Chebaoque*.

1853 COMO Matthew C. Perry held first meeting with Japanese officials. Landing force of Marines commanded by MAJ Jacob Zeilen, USMC.

1862 U.S. naval and marine forces landed at Alexandria, Egypt, to help extinguish fires started by bombardment from British ships.

1882 Sailors and marines help restore order at Alexandria, Egypt.

1901 Perry Monument at Kurihama, Japan, unveiled.

1950   U.S. Marines sailed from San Diego for Korean War.

1952   Keel of USS *Forrestal,* first 59,900 ton aircraft carrier, laid.

1955   First flight of jet-propelled Martin P6M seaplane.

1956   Navy's first Radio Station, Arlington, Virginia, deactivated after 41 years of operation. (See 21 Oct. 1918)

       First SIDEWINDER missile unit deployed overseas sailed for Sixth Fleet duty aboard *Randolph.*

1959   Nuclear-powered cruiser *Long Beach* (CGN 9) launched at Quincy, Mass.

15 July

1819   CAPT Oliver H. Perry, in USS *Adams,* arrived at Orinoco River on mission to discourage piracy.

1862   CSS *Arkansas* passed safely into Vicksburg, Miss., through U.S. blockading squadron.

1870   Act of Congress established Pay Corps.

1942   First NATS squadron for operations within the U.S. established.

       USS *Terror,* first minelayer built as such, commissioned.

1945   U.S. warships bombarded steel and iron works at Muroran, Japan.

1952   Nearly 10,000 Communist water craft sunk, damaged or captured by UN naval forces to this date off Korea.

1957   RADM Robert E. Dixon relieved RADM J. S. Russell as Chief of the Bureau of Aeronautics.

1958   Sixth Fleet landed 1,800 Marines at Beirut, Lebanon, to help support Lebanese government against rebel forces. (See 25 Oct. 1958)

       Several thousand more Marines and Army troops followed in next few days.

1961   USS *John Marshall* (SSBN 611) launched at Newport News, Va.

16 July

1798   Congress authorized construction of three frigates on which work had been halted.

1860   Screw gunboat *Mystic* seized slaver *Triton.*

1862   Congress created rank of rear admiral; Farragut appointed as first rear admiral. (See 25 July 1866)

1863   Screw sloop *Wyoming* fired upon by shore batteries at Shimonoseki, Japan.

1912   First patent for airborne torpedo granted to RADM Bradley A. Fiske, USN.

1915   First Navy ships, battleships *Ohio, Missouri,* and *Wisconsin,* transited Panama Canal (Atlantic-to-Pacific). (See 12 Oct. 1914)

1927 First use of aircraft in direct support of ground units by Marines in Nicaragua.

1945 First atomic bomb test held at Alamogordo, N.M.

1957 F8U-1P CRUSADER, piloted by MAJ John H. Glenn, set transcontinental record, from Los Alamitos, Calif., to Floyd Bennett Field, N.Y., in 3 hours, 23 minutes.

Two A3D SKYWARRIORS on routine flight flew from Moffett Field, Calif. to Honolulu in 4 hours, 43 minutes.

17 July

1812 Frigate *Constitution* escaped from British squadron.

1861 Congress passed act requiring promotions to "Corps of Paymasters" be made from list of assistant paymasters.

1898 Santiago, Cuba, surrendered to U.S. naval forces.

1919 First units of newly reorganized Pacific Fleet sailed from Hampton Roads for Panama Canal.

1944 Ammunition explosion at Port Chicago, Calif. (near Mare Island Navy Yard) destroyed two merchant ships, killed about 250 men.

1945 Aircraft from U.S. and British carriers attacked airfields around Tokyo, Japan.

1953 USS *T-1* launched.

18 July

1741 British landed troops at Guantanamo for assault on Santiago, Cuba.

1779 Sloop-of-war *Ranger,* frigate *Queen of France* and sloop-of-war *Providence* sailed on raid against British shipping.

1792 John Paul Jones died in Paris, France.

1813 Frigate *President* captured British *Daphne, Eliza Swan, Alert,* and *Lion.*

1863 U.S. squadron bombarded Fort Wagner, S.C.

1918 In attack on Soissons, France, Sergeants Louis Cukela and Matej Kocak, USMC, won both Army and Navy Medals of Honor.

1920 Naval aircraft sank ex-German cruiser *Frankfurt* in target practice.

1936 Second Division Memorial dedicated.
Spanish Civil War began.

1943 *K-47* shot down by enemy sub, first and only Navy airship lost to enemy action.

19 July

1892 Bureau of Provisions and Clothing renamed Bureau of Supplies and Accounts (BUSANDA).

1898 LT Robert E. Peary sailed from Boston on an expedition to the Arctic.

1918 USS *San Diego,* cruiser, sunk by mine off Fire Island, New York, six lives lost.

1940 President Roosevelt signed Naval Expansion Act.

20 July

1814 Joint Navy-Army expedition against British forts on Lakes Huron and Superior.

1846 First ship to visit Japan, USS *Columbus,* reached Tokyo Bay.

1942 ADM William D. Leahy reported as Chief of Staff to the President.

1953 Planes from four U.S. carriers attacked enemy targets from front lines to Chongjin, Korea.

1956 USS *Thetis Bay* (CVHA 1), first helicopter assault carrier, commissioned.

1960 Destroyers *Ammen* and *Collett* collide in fog off California killing 12 men.

1960 Polaris missile launched for first time from underwater position by USS *George Washington,* running submerged off Cape Canaveral, for 1000 mile flight.

21 July

1822 Navy landing party under LT David Farragut, destroyed pirate stronghold in Cuba.

1823 USS *Greyhound* and *Beagle* captured Cuban town and eight boats.

1905 Gunboat *Bennington* wrecked by boiler explosion at San Diego, Calif., 65 lives lost.

1944 Marines and Army troops invaded Guam.
    Last SBD DAUNTLESS dive bomber, No. 5936, completed by Douglas Aircraft Co.

22 July

1802 Frigate *Constellation* sank two Tripolitan gunboats.

1951 ADM Forrest P. Sherman, Chief of Naval Operations, died at Naples, Italy.

1953 U.S. warships laid down heavy barrage in support of UN troops on eastern front in Korea.

1955 Cesar S. Kycoco became the first foreign citizen to graduate with top honors from Navy submarine school, New London, Conn.

23 July

1800 Schooner *Enterprise* captured French privateer *Flambeau.*

1947   First Navy all jet air squadron received its first jet aircraft.

1948   First UN flag flown by Navy ship when *Putnam* entered Haifa, Israel.

24 July

1840   Landing party under LT Cadwallader Ringgold attacked Fiji Islands natives for having massacred a U.S. shore party.

1843   David Henshaw took office, fifteenth Secretary of the Navy.

1861   Navy-Army expedition in Black River, Va., destroyed two Confederate ships and captured a third.

1863   U.S. squadron drove back a sortie from Fort Wagner against Union batteries landed for offensive against the Fort earlier.

1905   Body of John Paul Jones brought to U.S.

1944   Marines landed on Tinian, Marianas Islands.

25 July

1777   Continental Congress authorized subsistence of Naval officers while in foreign ports.

1779   Amphibious expedition against British in Penobscot Bay, Me.

1785   American merchant schooner *Maria* seized by Algerian pirates.

1863   U.S. squadron bombarded Fort Wagner, N.C.

1866   First admiral in U.S. Navy, David G. Farragut, appointed. (See 16 July 1862, 21 Dec. 1864)

1898   Landing party from armed yacht *Gloucester* occupied Guanica, P.R.

1912   First general specifications for naval aircraft published.

1927   Seaplane altitude record pushed to 38,418 feet by former holder. (See 4 July 1927)

1934   First President to visit Hawaii, Franklin D. Roosevelt, reached Hilo on board USS *Houston*.

1941   First Navy "E" certificates for industry issued by Bureau of Ordnance.

1943   First ship named in honor of a Negro, destroyer escort *Harmon*, launched.

1946   Naval Air Station, Cubi Point, P.I., commissioned.

26 July

1812   Frigate *Essex* captured British brig *Leander*.

1814   Decatur's squadron arrived at Tunis to present U.S. demands.

1852   John P. Kennedy took office, twenty-second Secretary of the Navy.

1912   First test of airborne radio conducted at Annapolis; plane sending letter "D" was received by destroyer *Stringham* a mile away.

1940 President Roosevelt extended list of items forbidden for shipment to Japan.
1945 Potsdam Declaration.

27 July

1776 Continental brig *Reprisal* attacked by British *Shark*.
1801 Robert Smith took office, third Secretary of the Navy.
1917 Construction of Naval Aircraft Factory, Philadelphia, ordered.
1953 159th Plenary Session Convened at Panmunjom. Korean War ended.

28 July

1814 Frigate *Adams* captured British schooner *Favorite*.
1833 CAPT William Bainbridge died at Philadelphia, Pa.
1861 USS *St. Lawrence* captured the privateer schooner *Petrel*.
1914 World War I began.
1915 Sailors and marines landed in Haiti to restore order.
1918 BRIG GEN John A. Lejeune, USMC (promoted to major general 7 Aug., 1918) assumed command of Second Marine Division.
1943 Japanese evacuated Kiska, Aleutian Islands.
1945 Destroyer *Callaghan* sunk off Okinawa, last ship lost in WW II due to suicide plane.

29 July

1846 Sailors and marines from sloop-of-war *Cyane* captured San Diego, Calif.
1861 Screw gunboat *Yankee* fired upon by a hidden battery at Marlborough, Va.
1858 Second attempt made to lay trans-Atlantic cable. (See 4 Aug. 1858)
1945 U.S. warships bombarded Hamamatsu, Japan.

30 July

1785 American merchant ship *Dauphin* captured by Algerian pirates.
1813 Joint Navy-Army attack on York, Canada.
1877 Marines called out to quell labor riots.
1918 Units of First Marine Aviation Force arrived at Brest, France.
1919 USS *G-2,* submarine, accidentally sunk near New London, Conn., 3 lives lost.
1941 First Navy ship, gunboat *Tutuila,* damaged by Axis in World War II.
1942 WAVES established. (See 3 Aug. 1942)

1944 Naval task force landed Army troops near Cape Opmarai, New Guinea.

1945 Heavy cruiser *Indianapolis* sunk by Japanese submarine in Philippine Sea; 880 lives lost.

31 July

1813 British fleet took control of Lake Champlain.

1861 Office of Assistant Secretary of the Navy established.

1874 First U.S. warship equipped with torpedoes, USS *Intrepid,* commissioned.

1933 Frigate *Constitution* commenced tour of principal U.S. seaports.

1941 Dan A. Kimball took office, fifty-second Secretary of the Navy.

1956 A3D SKYWARRIOR, carrier jet attack plane, flew 3,200 miles from Honolulu to Albuquerque, New Mexico, non-stop, non-refueling, in 5 hours, 40 minutes.

1 August

1801   Schooner *Enterprise* captured Tripolitan ship *Tripoli*.

1814   British fleet entered the Patuxent River for advance against Washington.

1914   Germany declared war on Russia.

1925   Marine guard at American Legation, Managua, withdrew from Nicaragua.

1940   Alaskan Sector established as a military command.

1946   Office of Naval Research (ONR) established.

1947   Naval Supply Center, Oakland, Calif., established.

1950   Control of Guam transferred to Department of the Interior.

1953   Navy Fuel Depot, Casco Bay, Portland, Me., established.

1961   VADM George W. Anderson, Jr., relieved ADM Arleigh Burke as Chief of Naval Operations.

2 August

1850   William A. Graham took office, twenty-first Secretary of the Navy.

1927   Keel of submarine *Narwhal* laid.

1943   Naval task groups bombarded Kiska, Aleutian Islands.

1950   Marines landed in Korea.

3 August

1492   Columbus sailed from Spain.

1800   Corvette *Trumbull* captured French *Vengeance*.

1804   U.S. squadron made 5 attacks on defenses of Tripoli harbor, ending 3 Sept.

1812   Frigate *Essex* captured British brig *Brothers*.

1814   Sloop-of-war *Peacock* sank British *Peggy-and-Jane*.

1861   First Navy "balloon carrier," *Fanny*, in operation.
         Construction of USS *Monitor* authorized.

1914   Germany declared war on France.

1942   First woman naval officer, Mildred McAfee, commissioned.

1944   Office of the General Counsel, Navy Department, established.

1950   First Marine Corps aviation mission against North Koreans by carrier-based aircraft.

1958   First ship to reach the North Pole, submarine *Nautilus*, reached 90° North enroute from Hawaii to Atlantic Ocean.

4 August

1790   The Revenue Cutter Service (now the U.S. Coast Guard) organized.

1858   First trans-Atlantic cable completed by USS *Niagara* and British ship *Agamemnon.*

1898   USS *Monterey,* first monitor to cross the Pacific, reached Manila from San Francisco.

1914   Great Britain declared war on Germany.

1918   US subchaser *No. 187* sunk in collision with SS *Sapto* off Virginia coast, no casualties.

1943   First Navy Expert Pistol Shot Medal awarded a woman, ENS Rosalie Thorne.

1947   Birthdate of the Medical Service Corps.

1950   First helicopter evacuations in Korea by VMO-6.

5 August

1815   CAPT Decatur collected $25,000 indemnity from Bashaw of Tripoli.

1832   First ship to entertain royalty, frigate *Potomac,* visited by King and Queen of Sandwich Islands, in Honolulu.

1843   First trans-Atlantic crossing by steam-driven ship of Navy commenced by paddle sloop *Missouri.* (See 25 Aug. 1843)

1846   First U.S. flag raised over Santa Barbara, California.

1864   Battle of Mobile Bay.

1882   Beginning of "modern Navy." First steel warships authorized.

1915   First air spotting for shore batteries.

1921   Yangtze River Patrol Force established.

1951   Second Presidential Unit citation awarded to First Marine Division for action in Korean War.

6 August

1862   Screw gunboat *Essex* engaged CSS *Arkansas. Arkansas* destroyed.

1864   Monitor *Chickasaw* bombarded Fort Gaines, Mobile Bay, Ala.

1912   Armored cruiser *Tennessee* sailed with $6,000,000 for relief of U.S. citizens in Europe.

1943   Battle of Vella Gulf began.

1945   First atomic bomb dropped on Hiroshima, Japan.

1958   Department of Defense Reorganization Act approved by President.

7 August

1789   Congress established War Department.

1813   U.S. naval forces engaged the British on Lake Ontario.

1846   First U.S. flag raised over San Pedro, Calif.
       First shot in Mexican War fired.

1861   Contract signed for construction of seven iron-clad gunboats.
1864   U.S. squadron captured Fort Gaines, Ala.
1942   First American land offensive of WW II commenced in Solomon Islands.
1940   Marine ground forces in first Korean action at Pusan perimeter.
1951   Navy Douglas SKYROCKET, flown by test pilot Bill Bridgeman, reached speed of 1,238 MPH.
1958   Nuclear-powered *Nautilus* (SSN 571) completed a history-making cruise under the Arctic ice pack and across the North Pole: In 4 days, traveled 1,830 miles under the polar ice.

8 August

1924   First dirigible mooring, USS *Shenandoah,* to a ship underway, oiler *Patoka.* (See 27 Jan. 1928)
1942   Marines won control of Tulagi, Gavutu, and Tanambogo, Solomon Islands.

9 August

1781   Frigate *Trumbull* captured by the British *Iris.*
1790   Merchant ship *Columbia* arrived at Boston, first U.S. ship to circumnavigate the globe. (See 30 Sept. 1787)
1812   Stonington, Conn., bombarded by British squadron.
1815   CAPT Decatur concluded treaty for U.S. with Tripoli.
1865   Naval Academy returned to Annapolis after 4 years at Newport, R.I.
1942   Battle of Savo Island.
1945   Second atomic bomb dropped on Nagaski, Japan.
1949   First pilot-ejection seat used in emergency escape.

10 August

1831   U.S. flag nicknamed "Old Glory."
1921   Bureau of Aeronautics (BUAER) established.
1944   First American territory, Guam, recaptured in WW II.
1957   USS *Ranger,* CVA 61, commissioned at Norfolk, Va.

11 August

1807   Robert Fulton's steamboat, *Clermont,* made first trip up Hudson River.
1846   Joint Navy-Army expedition seized Los Angeles, California.
1923   Recruit Depot, San Diego, California, established.

12 August

1957   In first test of Automatic Carrier Landing System, F3D SKYNIGHT with LCDR Don Walker aboard landed on *Antietam.*

1959 MAJ GEN David M. Shoup named Commandant of the Marine Corps.

13 August

1812 First naval action of War of 1812—frigate *Essex* vs. *Alert*.

1868 USS *Fredonia* and double-ender *Wateree* wrecked by tidal wave at Arica, Peru.

1870 Armed tug *Palos* became first U.S. Navy ship to transit Suez Canal. (See 12 Oct. 1914)

1898 Spanish forces in Manila surrendered to U.S.

1918 First woman Marine, Opha M. Johnson, enlisted in Marine Corps Reserve.

14 August

1765 Stamp Act issued.

1819 Brig *Argus* captured by British *Pelican*.

1870 ADM David G. Farragut died at Portsmouth, N.H.

1917 Seventh Marine Regiment organized at Philadelphia, Pa.

1945 Japan agreed to surrender.
      Last Japanese ships sunk by U.S. Navy in World War II.

15 August

1799 Frigate *Congress* launched.

1845 Fort Severn, Annapolis, Maryland, transferred from War Department to Navy Department.

1864 Screw sloop *Niagara* captured CSS *Georgia*.

1908 First naval post offices established in *Illinois, Prairie,* and *Rhode Island.*

1914 Panama Canal officially opened. (See 16 July 1915, 12 Oct. 1914)

1930 First submarine escape training tank placed in operation.

1943 Naval task force landed U.S. Army and Canadian troops at Kiska, Aleutian Islands.

1944 Naval attack force landed Allied troops in Southern France.

1945 Cessation of hostilities with Japan.
      Last U.S. air strike against Japan.

1951 Navy Douglas SKYROCKET, flown by test pilot Bill Bridgeman, reached world altitude record of 79,494 feet.

1958 SPARROW III missile became operational.

16 August

1822 Schooner *Grampus* captured pirate schooner *Palmyra.*

1909 Acting Secretary of the Navy disapproved request for 2 aircraft:

"The Department does not consider that the development of an aeroplane has progressed sufficiently at this time for use in the Navy."

1943   Fourth Marine Division activated.

1958   USS *Seadragon* (SSN 584), launched.

17 August

1863   Combined attack on Fort Sumter by U.S. squadron and naval battery on Morris Island, S.C.

1942   First amphibious attack launched from submarines *Nautilus* and *Argonaut*.

1959   ADM Arleigh Burke, fifty-seven, reappointed Chief of Naval Operations for an unprecedented third two-year term.

1962   Navy's first hydrofoil patrol craft, USS *High Point* (PCH 1) launched at Seattle, Wash.

18 August

1911   First Navy Nurse Corps superintendent, Esther Voorhees Hasson, appointed.

1962   USS *Haddo* (SSN 604) launched at Camden, N.J.
         USS *Alexander Hamilton* (SSBN 617) launched at Groton, Conn.

19 August

1812   Frigate *Constitution* captured British *Guerriere*.

1818   CAPT James Biddle took possession of Oregon Territory for U.S.

1916   Naval Reserve Force established.

1929   First all-metal dirigible, *ZMC-3*, flown.

1939   First observation of National Aviation Day.

20 August

1958   First production model F8U-2 CRUSADER flown.

21 August

1858   Schooner *Dolphin* captured slaver *Echo*.

1918   USS *Montauk*, scout patrol craft, sank in gale off Cumberland, Ga., nine lives lost.

1945   Asiatic Wing, NATS, established.

1951   First contract for a nuclear-powered submarine awarded.

1956   Speed record of 1015.428 set by Commander R. W. Windsor in F8U-1 CRUSADER.
         MPSA—Military Petroleum Supply Agency—established to procure all military POL supplies.

1958 USS *Enterprise,* famous as "Big E" in WW II, towed to Kearney, N.J., to be scrapped.

22 August

1814 Gunboat flotilla in Patuxent River destroyed to avoid capture by British.

1912 Birthdate of Dental Corps.

1932 Monument to RADM Robert E. Peary, USN, completed at Cape York, Greenland.

1940 James Forrestal became first Under Secretary of the Navy.

1942 Fouth Marine Air Wing commissioned at Ewa, T.H.

1945 Destroyer escort *Levy* received surrender of first Japanese garrison to capitulate in WW II.

1956 Last scheduled passenger run for MARS aircraft completed, Honolulu to Alameda, by *Marianas Mars.*

23 August

1864 U.S. squadron captured Fort Morgan, thus winning control of Mobile harbor.

1890 Cruiser *Baltimore* sailed from Boston, carrying body of John Ericsson, inventor of *Monitor,* to his homeland.

1914 Japan declared war on Germany.

1951 USS *Essex,* first of the postwar carrier conversions, entered Korean combat.

24 August

1814 Battle of Bladensburg, near Washington, D.C.
Washington Navy Yard, and ships burned to avoid capture by British, who burned Capitol, Treasury, White House and other buildings.

1912 First electrically-propelled Navy ship, collier *Jupiter,* launched.

1942 Battle of Eastern Solomons.
First woman naval inspector, Mrs. Jean Hales, appointed.

1955 First carrier night landing with mirror system made, USS *Bennington.*

1956 First landings on the *Saratoga* made by Carrier Air Group.

1958 Units of Seventh Fleet moved to Taiwan area as Chinese Communists increased activity here.

1958 *Nautilus* (SSN 571) completed a record-setting trans-Atlantic crossing for underwater craft—six and one-half days, surfaced only twice during the voyage.

25 August

1812 American merchant brig *Edwin* taken by Algerian pirates.

1843   First trans-Atlantic crossing by a steam powered Navy ship, completed at Gibraltar by USS *Missouri*.

1917   USS *Elfreda*, converted yacht, damaged by explosion.

1948   MAJ Marion Cord, USMC, in Douglas SKYSTREAK D-588-1 set world record of 650.6 MPH, Muroc, Calif.

26 August

1803   Frigate *Philadelphia* captured Morrocan *Meshboha*.

1831   Frigate *Potomac* became first U.S. warship to make an easterly circumnavigation of the earth.

1839   Line of battleship *Washington* captured Spanish slaver *Amistad*.

1865   Civil War ended. Navy strength 58,500 men and over 600 ships.

1949   Submarine *Cochino* sank in Arctic Sea.

27 August

1918   US subchaser *No. 209* mistaken for enemy and sunk by gunfire from SS *Felix* Taussig, off Long Island, 18 lives lost.

1926   CDR John Rodgers, USN, killed in air crash.

1945   Victorious U.S. fleet stood into Sagami Bay, Japan.

1948   *Caroline Mars* set non-stop seaplane flight record, 4,478 miles from Honolulu to Chicago, with 42 passengers and seven ton cargo.

1957   *Swordfish* (SSN 579) fourth nuclear-powered submarine, launched.

28 August

1861   U.S. squadron captured Forts Hatteras and Clark, N.C.

1867   First U.S. flag raised over Midway Island.

1945   Destroyer *Callaghan* sunk off Okinawa, last victim of suicide plane.

29 August

1781   Office of Agent of Marine created.

1916   Congress passed act for expansion of Navy.
Congress set Civil Engineering Corps strength at two per cent of the Line.
Cruiser *Memphis* wrecked at Santo Domingo, 33 lives lost.

1929   First dirigible-to-airplane transfer of a human made.

30 August

1776   Continental Army under GEN Washington, trapped on Long Island, escaped by boats.

1942   U.S. Naval and Army forces occupied, Adak, Aleutian Islands.

31 August

1826　First U.S. warship to circle the globe, sloop-of-war *Vincennes,* sailed from New York. (See 8 June 1830)

1842　Congress passed act establishing five Navy bureaus.

1861　Daily rum issue for enlisted men abolished.

1863　USS *Roanoke,* first turreted frigate, altered to an ironclad.

1931　Yangtze Patrol Force and other Navy ships rendered relief after disastrous flood in central China.

1934　First Marine Brigade withdrew from Haiti.

1944　Naval ships and aircraft attacked Iwo Jima and the Bonin Islands.

1951　Marine Helicopter Transport Squadron 161 landed in Korea.

1952　Drone aircraft first used in combat, Korea, when F6F-5K's from *Boxer* launched against a bridge at Hungnam.

1958　First flight of A3J-1 VIGILANTE carrier-based attack aircraft.

1962　Last flight of a Navy lighter-than-air ship made at NAS Lakehurst, N.J.

1 September

1781   French fleet prevented British fleet entering Chesapeake Bay to relieve British Army at Yorktown.

1800   Schooner *Experiment* captured French privateer *Deux Amis.*

1814   Sloop-of-war *Wasp* sank British *Avon.*

1916   Gendarmerie d'Haiti established.

1920   USS *S-5* submarine, accidentally sunk, no casualties.

1925   First San Francisco-Hawaii flight commenced by CDR John Rodgers in *PN-9* and crew of four. (See 10 Sept. 1925)

1939   World War II began, as German troops marched into Poland.

1941   Navy assumed responsibility for trans-Atlantic convoys.

1942   Air Force, Pacific Fleet, established.
Naval Supply Depot, Mechanicsburg, Pa., established.

2 September

1918   Navy ships and men rendered assistance to earthquake victims at Yokohama and Tokyo, Japan.

1945   Japanese surrender signed on board USS *Missouri,* Tokyo Bay.

3 September

1782   Navy's first 74-gun ship, *America,* given to France.

1783   American and British emissaries signed Treaty of Paris.

1814   Schooner *Tigress* and schooner *Scorpion* captured on Lake Huron by British.
Brig *Adams* burned to prevent capture by British at Hampden, Me.

1885   First classes commenced at Naval War College.

1919   Naval Supply Depot, San Diego, Calif., established.

1925   USS *Shenandoah,* dirigible, wrecked over Ohio.

1939   Great Britain, France, Australia and New Zealand declared war on Germany.

1940   "Destroyers-for-bases" agreement signed between U.S. and Great Britain.

1944   Naval task group attacked Wake Island.

4 September

1777   Continental frigate *Raleigh* disabled British *Druid.*

1804   Ketch *Intrepid* blown up in Tripoli harbor, 13 lives lost.

1941   Destroyer *Greer* attacked by German submarine.
Cunningham Field, Cherry Point, N.C., dedicated.

1954   First transit of McClure Strait (Northwest Passage) made by Navy icebreaker *Burton Island* and Coast Guard icebreaker *Northwind*.

5 September

1774   First Continental Congress met in Philadelphia.
1775   First ship commissioned by Continental military establishment.
1776   First uniforms for Navy adopted.
1795   U.S. concluded treaty of peace with Algiers.
1813   Schooner *Enterprise* captured British *Boxer*.
1918   Fifth Marine Brigade organized at Quantico, Va.
1939   President Roosevelt issued two neutrality proclamations.
1956   William F. Durand, oldest living Naval Academy graduate (Class of 1880), received his diploma after delay of 76 years.

6 September

1918   First use of major caliber naval guns in land-based offensive.
1930   Mine sweeper *Grebe* arrived at Santo Domingo with supplies and medicines for victims of hurricane three days before.
1939   Neutrality Patrol formed.
1940   First destroyers transferred to Great Britain under "Destroyers-for Bases" agreement.
1947   First V-2 rocket successfully launched from a ship, fired by *Midway*.
1950   Yongchon, Korea, recaptured by UN Forces.

7 September

1775   First prize taken by Continental Navy, captured by *Hannah*.
1776   First submarine attack by "American Turtle."
1781   Robert Morris appointed Secretary of Marine Agent of Marine.
1797   Frigate *Constellation* launched.
1825   Frigate *Brandywine* received Lafayette on board for return to France after his tour of U.S.
1941   First U.S. merchant ship lost due to enemy air attack, *Steel Seafarer*.
1942   First air evacuation of casualties in WW II, Guadalcanal. (See also 6 Jan. 1913)
1944   First provisional Marine Brigade disbanded.
       Sixth Marine Division activated.
1956   USS *Barry*, *Sherman*-class destroyer, commissioned.

8 September

1863   Joint Navy-Army attack on Sabine Pass, Tex.
1923   Point Honda (California) disaster. Seven destroyers—*Delphy, S. P. Lee, Fuller, Chauncey, Woodbury, Nicholas, Young*—ran aground through faulty navigation, 22 lives lost.

1933   Six Consolidated P2Y-1 flying boats made record formation distance flight, 2,059 miles from Norfolk to Coco Solo, 25 hours, 19 minutes.

1939   President Roosevelt proclaimed limited national emergency.

1951   Japanese peace treaty signed at San Francisco, Calif.

9 September

1833   First federal drydock completed at Boston.

1841   First iron ship authorized by Congress.

1941   Naval Coastal Frontier Forces formed.

1943   Allies invaded Italy.

1950   First jet mission against enemy by Marine pilot, CAPT Leslie E. Brown, USMC, in Korea.

10 September

1813   Battle of Lake Erie. Forces under Oliver Hazard Perry achieved first defeat in history of a British naval squadron.

1846   John Y. Mason took office, nineteenth Secretary of the Navy.

1851   Paddle frigate *Mississippi* carried refugees of "Hungarian Republic" from Dardanelles to Gibraltar.

1861   Timber-clad *Lexington* and timber-clad *Conestoga* supported Army advance at Lucas Bend, in Mississippi River.

1919   USS *Mary Pope*, scout patrol craft, wrecked, no casualties.
        USS *Katherine K,* scout patrol craft, wrecked, no casualties.

1925   Crew of *PN-9* rescued by submarine *R-4,* 10 miles from Kaui, Hawaii, after plane had been lost 10 days. Plane set world record for seaplanes, flying 1,841 miles before running out of fuel.

11 September

1814   Battle of Lake Champlain.
        Naval expedition against pirates at Barataria, Gulf of Mexico.

1941   Navy ordered to attack any vessel threatening U.S. shipping or ships under U.S. escort.

1943   Italian Fleet surrendered.

12 September

1804   Frigate *Constellation* and frigate *President* captured two ships attempting to enter Tripoli Harbor, while brigs *Argus* and *Constellation* captured a third.

1814   British attacked Baltimore.

1906   U.S. squadron ordered to Cuba to protect American interests during rebellion.

1916 First automatic pilot for aircraft demonstrated.

1941 USCG *Northland* seized Norwegian trawler *Buskoe*.

13 September

1847 U.S. Forces stormed Chapultepec, gateway to Mexico City.

1906 Sailors and marines from cruiser *Denver* landed at Havana, Cuba, to restore order.

1954 President Eisenhower ordered Navy to give "full logistic support" to Chinese Nationalists in defense of Quemoy Island.

14 September

1847 American flag raised over Mexico City.

1899 Gunboat *Concord* and monitor *Monterey* captured two insurgent schooners at Aparri, P.I.

1957 Keel of carrier *Constellation* laid at New York Naval Shipyard.

15 September

1846 LT Washington A. Bartlett, USN, elected first Alcalde (mayor) of San Francisco under U.S. rule.

1941 Marine Barracks, New River, N.C., established.

1942 Carrier *Wasp* torpedoed.

1944 Marines landed at Peleliu, Palau Islands.

1950 Navy and Marine forces made amphibious assault on Inchon, Korea. USS *Missouri* began bombarding east coast of Korea.

1953 Keel of second nuclear-powered submarine, USS *Seawolf,* laid.

1962 USS *Andrew Jackson* (SSBN 619) launched at Mare Island, Calif.

16 September

1823 Samuel Southard took office, eighth Secretary of the Navy.

1854 CDR David G. Farragut took possession of Mare Island, Calif., first West Coast Navy Yard.

1917 Navy Department authorized establishment of 16 Naval air stations abroad.

1918 American cargo ship *Buena Ventura* sunk by submarine off Spain, 19 lives lost.

1940 President Roosevelt signed Selective Training and Service Act.

1942 Third Marine Division activated.

1950 First Marine Division and ROK Marines secured Inchon Peninsula.

1951 Destroyer *Perkins* hit by enemy fire, Korea.

1956 Statue of COMD John Barry unveiled in Wexford, Ireland.

1958 In first launch at sea, REGULUS II fired from submarine *Grayback*.

17 September

1787   Constitution of U.S. ratified by States convention.
1950   First Marine Division captured Kimpo airfield.

18 September

1924   U.S. Marines withdrew from Santo Domingo.
1926   Navy rendered relief to Miami, Fla., after severe hurricane.
1936   U.S. squadron dispatched to Spanish waters for protection of American evacuees.
1947   National Security Act, unifying Armed Forces, became effective. John L. Sullivan took office, fiftieth Secretary of the Navy.
1952   Destroyer *Barton* damaged by floating mine, Korea.

19 September

1777   Brig *Lexington* captured by British *Alert*.
1950   U.S. Marines, Army troops and ROK Marines surrounded Seoul.
1957   Bathyscaph *Trieste,* making series of ONR sponsored drive in Mediterranean, reached record depth of 3,200 meters—two miles down.

20 September

1951   First helicopter-borne landing of a combat unit in history, Korea.

21 September

1814   Sloop-of-war *Wasp* captured British *Atlanta*.
1858   Screw sloop *Niagara* departed Charleston, S.C., for Liberia with Negro slaves rescued from slave ship *Echo*.
1872   First Negro Midshipman, James Henry Conyers, entered Naval Academy. (See 3 June 1949)
1939   President Roosevelt asked Congress to repeal arms embargo provision of Neutrality Act.
1944   Aircraft from 12 U.S. carriers attacked Japanese shipping and airfields on Luzon, P.I.
1956   F11F-1 TIGER shot itself down over Long Island by catching up with and flying into 20mm shells it had test fired.

22 September

1959   USS *Patrick Henry* (SSBN 599), sister ship of the FBM submarine *George Washington,* launched at Groton, Conn.

23 September

1779   CAPT John Paul Jones, in frigate *Bon Homme Richard,* captured British *Serapis*.

1931   First autogyro landing on aircraft carrier, LT A. M. Pride landed XOP-1 on *Langley*.

1944   Naval task group landed Army troops on Ulithi Atoll, Caroline Islands.

1947   James Forrestal took office, first Secretary of Defense.

24 September

1960   Nuclear-powered carrier, USS *Enterprise*, launched at Newport News, Va.

25 September

1513   Pacific Ocean first sighted by Balboa, from Panama.

1924   USS *S-51*, submarine, sunk in collision by SS *City of Rome*, 37 lives lost.

1942   First Marine Corps Reserve Officer promoted to general rank. Camp Pendleton, Calif., dedicated.

1957   Project STRATOSCOPE, conducted by ONR, obtained sharp photographs of sun's corona at 80,000 feet with first balloon-borne telescope.

26 September

1777   British Army occupied Philadelphia.

1814   American privateer *General Armstrong* engaged three British ships at Fayal, Azores.

1899   New York City staged a Navy parade to welcome ADM George Dewey.

1918   USCG *Tampa*, with crew of 118, disappeared in British Channel. Meuse-Argonne offensive.

1941   "Shoot on sight" order issued to Navy.

27 September

1778   Frigate *Raleigh* captured by British *Experiment*, *Wallace*, and *Unicorn*.

1922   First radar observations made.

1932   Navy won international Gordon-Bennett Balloon race.

1941   First Liberty ship, SS *Patrick Henry*, launched.

1950   First Marine Division captured Seoul.

1956   First A4D SKYHAWKS assigned to operating units.

28 September

1822   Sloop-of-war *Peacock* captured five pirate vessels.

1923   Navy planes took first and second places in Schneider Cup Race, top speed 177.38 MPH.

1957   LST *Alameda County* redesignated Advance Aviation Base Ship AVB 1.

29 September

1904   Battleship *Connecticut,* largest warship to this time, launched.

1918   USS *Minnesota,* battleship, damaged by mine.

1946   Lockheed P2V NEPTUNE, "Truculent Turtle," commenced longest flight, non-stop, non-refueling, 55 hours, 17 minutes, over 11,235 miles.

1956   USS *Ranger,* third Forrestal-class aircraft carrier, launched at Newport News, Va.

30 September

1787   First American merchant ship to circumnavigate the world, *Columbia,* sailed from Boston, Mass., for Pacific. (See 9 Aug. 1790)

1800   U.S. concluded treaty of peace with France.

1918   American cargo ship *Ticonderoga* sunk by German submarine, 213 lives lost.

1937   Carrier *Yorktown* commissioned.

1954   First atomic-powered ship, USS *Nautilus,* commissioned.

1957   USS *Saipan,* CVL 48, last light carrier in operation, was decommissioned.

1958   Last U.S. Marines left Lebanon.

1 October

1814 LT Thomas ap Catesby Jones arrived at New Orleans with pirate ships captured at Barataria.

1847 Landing party under LT Thomas A. M. Craven captured Mulege, Mexico.

1862 Command of Western Gunboat Fleet transferred from War Department to Navy Department.

1880 John Philip Sousa appointed leader of U.S. Marine Corps Band.

1884 International Meridian Conference convened at Washington, D.C., to select prime meridian.

1910 General storekeeper system established.

1917 USCG *Mohawk* sunk off Ambrose Lightship, no casualties.

1918 US subchaser *No. 60* sunk in collision off Ambrose Lightship, two lives lost.

1937 First "Type Command" status for Naval Aviation, VP 1-5.

1944 Office of Deputy Commander in Chief, U.S. Fleet, and Deputy Chief of Naval Operations established.

1948 First guided-missile experimental and test ship, USS *Norton Sound*, placed in operation.

1949 Military Sea Transportation Service (MSTS) activated.
Career Compensation Act became law.
Naval Supply Depot, Guam, Marianas Islands, established.

1955 Carrier *Forrestal* commissioned.

1957 NAS, Rota, Spain, established.

2 October

1799 Washington Navy Yard founded.

1918 Battle of Blanc Mont Ridge.

1956 Carrier *Enterprise,* famous "Big E" of WW II, ordered stricken from the Navy. (See 25 Nov. 1961)

3 October

1775 Rhode Island delegates to Continental Congress proposed construction of a Navy.

1779 CAPT John Paul Jones arrived at The Texel, France, in the captured British *Serapis*.

1921 Protected cruiser *Olympia* sailed from Newport, R.I., to bring home body of Unknown Soldier.

1951 First Helicopter Antisubmarine Squadron commissioned.

1959 *Theodore Roosevelt* (SSBN 500), launched at Mare Island Shipyard, Vallejo, Calif.

1962 CDR Walter M. Schirra Jr. made third U.S. orbital flight, circled earth six times in 10 hours and 46 minutes.

4 October

1910 U.S. sailors and marines assisted local governmental forces in battle at Masaga, Nicaragua.

1917 USS *Rehoboth,* patrol craft, sunk, no casualties.

1918 American cargo ship *Herman Frasch* sunk in collision off Nova Scotia, 23 lives lost.

1927 Twelfth Marine Regiment organized at Tientsin, China.

5 October

1861 Armed steamer *Monticello* fired on and routed Confederate troops at Hatteras, N.C.

1918 USS *Mary Alice,* scout patrol craft, sunk in collision, no casualties.

1925 First naval air Utility Squadron formed.

1940 Organized Naval Reserve placed on short notice for call to active duty.

6 October

1884 U.S. Naval War College established.

1912 U.S. Marines captured Leon, Nicaragua, last stronghold of revolutionists.
Curtiss A-2, at Annapolis, set world endurance record for hydro-aeroplanes: six hours, 10 minutes.

1915 First meeting Naval Advisory Board of Inventions.

1923 Navy set world's aircraft speed record for 100 to 200 kilometers, 243.60 MPH.

1943 Battle of Vella Lavella.

1958 Submarine *Seawolf* completed record submerged run of 60 days.

1962 USS *Bainbridge* (DLGN 25), first nuclear-powered destroyer, commissioned.

7 October

1765 First Colonial Congress met in New York.

1864 Screw sloop *Wachusett* captured CSS *Florida*

1897 Inland Rules of the Road effective in U.S. waters.

1913 Secretary of the Navy appointed Aeronautic Board.

1915 Cape Cod Canal opened for navigation.

1916 First German submarine, *U 53,* appeared in U.S. waters.

1918 American cargo ship *West Gate* sunk in collisoon off Nova Scotia, seven lives lost.

1924 First transcontinental dirigible flight commenced. (See 11 Oct. 1924)

1950 First Marine Division relieved in Seoul area.

1955 First submarine, midget, USS *X-1*, commissioned.

8 October

1780 Continental ship *Saratoga* captured British *Charming Molly*.

1793 American merchant ships *Thomas, Hope* and *Dispatch* taken by Algerian pirates.

1864 CSS *Shenandoah*, commerce raider, departed London, England, to prey on Union shipping.

1912 BUMED issued criteria for physical examination of naval aviation candidates.

1915 Light cruiser *Chester* transported British, French, and Russian refugees to Alexandria from Jaffa.

1955 USS *Saratoga*, second *Forrestal* class carrier, launched.

1960 USS *Constellation*, sixth *Forrestal* class carrier, launched at New York Naval Shipyard.

9 October

1779 First joint naval operations with France.

1780 Continental ship *Saratoga* disappeared off Delaware Cape.

1812 American night boat attack on British warships at Fort Erie.

1814 Sloop-of-war *Wasp*, with crew of 140, last seen.

1862 Naval forces received surrender of Galveston, Tex.

1917 Eighth Marine Regiment organized at Quantico, Va.

1918 USS *Shaw*, destroyer, rammed by HMS *Aquitania*.

1929 U.S. Britain, France, Italy, and Japan agreed to naval disarmament conference at London.

1945 ADM of the Fleet Chester W. Nimitz, with 13 other Navy and Marine heroes, greeted in New York.

10 October

1776 Continental Congress created Navy grade of captain.

1845 Naval School (now Naval Academy) opened at Annapolis, Md.

1861 Screw steamer *Daylight* engaged Confederate battery at Lynn Haven Bay, Va.

1902 Colombia government protested ADM Casey's refusal to permit transportation of troops across the Isthmus of Panama.

1913 President Wilson removed the last obstruction in the Panama Canal.

1923 First American-built dirigible, USS *Shenandoah,* christened.
1944 Aircraft from 17 U.S. carriers bombed Okinawa and other islands in the Ryukyus.
1945 Headquarters, Commander in Chief, U.S. Fleet, disestablished.
1955 Carrier *Saipan* with Helicopter Training Unit One abroad, left Tampico, Mexico, after a week of flood relief operations during which 5,439 people were rescued by helicopter.
1957 USS *Sargo* (SSN 583), launched.

11 October

1776 First Battle of Lake Champlain.
1793 American merchant ships *George, Olive Branch* and *Jane* taken by Algerian pirates.
1841 Abel P. Upshur took office, fourteenth Secretary of the Navy.
1916 Acting Secretary of War recommended joint Army-Navy study and development of lighter-than-air service.
1924 First coast-to-coast dirigible flight, by USS *Shanandoah,* ended at San Diego.
1942 Battle of Cape Esperance.
1944 Aircraft from two U.S. carrier task groups attacked enemy facilities on northern Luzon, P.I.
1945 Typhoon hit Okinawa.
1952 UN ships bombarded supply areas near Wonsan.

12 October

1492 Columbus landed in West Indies, on San ʾSalvador, probably now Watling Island.
1800 Frigate *Boston* captured French *Le Berceau.*
1803 Congress ratified and confirmed U.S. treaty with Morocco.
1861 First "ironclad" *St. Louis* launched. (See 5 Dec. 1843)
      U.S. squadron engaged Confederate ships on Mississippi River.
      Timber-clad *Tyler* and *Lexington* covered GEN Grant's retreat at Belmont, Mo.
1914 First Navy ship, collier *Jupiter,* completed transit of Panama Canal.
1944 U.S. carrier aircraft bombed Formosa and northern Luzon, P.I.
1950 USS *Missouri* bombarded Chongjin, Korea.

13 October

1775 Congress enacted first legislation regarding an American Navy.
1842 COMO Lawrence Kearney, commanding East India Squadron, established friendly relations with China.
1901 Chapel at Mare Island dedicated—now oldest in Navy.

1952   Minesweeper *Osprey* and destroyer *Perkins* damaged by enemy shore batteries, Korea.

14 October

1774   Great Britain first referred to Colonies as "foreign power."
1915   Keel of battleship *Mexico* laid.
1935   *XP3Y* set world distance record for seaplanes, 3,281 miles from Canal Zone to San Francisco; flight ended 15 Oct.

15 October

1805   Robert Fulton, inventor, successfully demonstrated a "torpedo."
1912   President Taft reviewed Atlantic Fleet at New York.
1918   USS *America,* transport, sank at dock in Hoboken, N.J., two men missing.
1940   Marine Corps Reserve Units ordered to mobilize.
1943   Naval Supply Depot, Guantanamo Bay, Cuba, established.
1944   First Marine Division relieved by 81st Infantry Division on Peleliu.
1948   First WAVE officers sworn into Regular Navy.
1955   Navy set world speed record for the 500 kilometer closed circuit course, Muroc, Calif. LT Gordon Gray flew A4D SKYHAWK at 695.163 MPH.

16 October

1827   Schooner *Porpoise* captured six Mediterranean boats and a schooner.
1842   Monterey, Calif., mistakenly seized by Navy squadron.
1846   Unsuccessful attemept to capture Tuspan, Mexico.
1891   Crewmen of protected cruiser *Baltimore* attacked by mob at Valparaiso, Chile.
1917   First enlisted casualty of WW I, Osmond K. Ingram, died.
First ship, USS *Ingram,* named for an enlisted man honors this man.
1940   First Selective Training and Service Act registration.
1942   First SeaBees killed in action, Guadalcanal.
1945   First aircraft landing in Peking, China, by U.S. plane.
1957   Cruiser *Lake Champlain* reached Valencia, Spain, to assist in flood rescue work.

17 October

1777   British Army under Burgoyne surrendered at Saratoga.
1886   Keel of battleship *Maine* laid.
1918   Last U.S. ship lost to enemy action in WW I, USS *Lucia,* torpedoed.
1922   First carrier take-off made from USS *Langley.*

1941   Destroyer *Kearny* torpedoed.
      All U.S. mechant ships in Asiatic waters ordered into friendly ports.
1951   Destroyer escort *Ulvert M. Moore* hit by Communist shore batteries off Hungnam.
1956   Navy R3Y TRADEWIND, turbo-prop seaplane, made first West Coast-Hawaii hop, covering 2,117 miles in eight hours 24 minutes.

18 October

1812   Sloop-of-war *Wasp* captured British *Frolic*. Both ships taken same day by British *Poictiers*
1859   U.S. Marines reached Harper's Ferry.
      U.S. Squadron departed for Ascuncion, Paraguay.
1867   Screw sloop *Ossipee* and screw gunboat *Resaca* participated in formal transfer of Alaska to U.S. at Sitka.
1901   Hereafter only U.S. citizens allowed to enlist in Navy.
1944   Aircraft from 13 U.S. carriers attacked Japanese installations and shipping in northern Luzon and Manila area, P.I.
1957   Strato-Lab balloon reached new record hieght of 84,300 feet feet.

19 October

1781   British Army surrendered to GEN Washington at Yorktown.
1915   Submarine base, New London, Conn., opened.
1941   U.S. merchant ship *Lehigh* sunk by German submarine.

20 October

1824   Schooner *Porpoise* captured four pirate vessels.
1926   U.S. Marines ordered to guard U.S. mails.
1941   Carrier *Hornet* commissioned.
1944   U.S. forces invaded Leyte, P.I.

21 October

1797   Frigate *Constitution* launched.
1881   Centennial of Battle of Yorktown celebrated by naval review.
1916   Destroyer *McDougal* rescued victims of German submarine.
      Navy department ordered 49 seaplanes.
1918   Navy Radio Station, Arlington, Va., began transmitting to Paris and Honolulu. (See 14 July 1956)

22 October

1846   Sloop-of-war *Germantown* christened by "Miss Watson of Philadelphia," first ship of U.S. Navy sponsored by a woman.

1962   U.S. announced naval blockade of Cuba, to prevent introduction of Soviet offensive weapons.

23 October

1793   American merchant ship *President* taken by Algerian pirates.
1846   U.S. naval forces captured Frontera and Tobasco, Mexico.
1855   Frigate *John Adams* bombarded towns in Fiji Islands.
1917   Fourth Marine Brigade organized in France.
1944   Battle for Leyte Gulf.
1958   Three-stage VANGUARD launching vehicle successfully flight tested.

24 October

1914   Battleship *Kansas* ordered to Port Au Prince, Haiti, to protect American interests.
1915   Five day patrol led by MAJ Smedley D. Butler, USMC, into caco country in Haiti.
1916   Battle between U.S. Marines and Santo Domingo rebels at Grosse Roche.
1944   Battle for Leyte Gulf continues.
1948   UN Day first observed.
1952   Cruiser *Helena* and destroyer *O'Brien* bombarded enemy battleline positions near Kosong, Korea.

25 October

1793   American merchant brig *Polly* taken by Algerian pirates.
1812   Frigate *United States* captured British *Macedonian*.
1861   Keel of USS *Monitor* laid.
1915   First school for divers ordered established.
1916   Keel of battleship *California* laid.
1944   Battle for Leyte Gulf continues.
1952   Battleship *Missouri* bombarded entrenched Communists near Tanchon.
1958   Last U.S. forces withdrew from Lebanon.

26 October

1807   American merchant ships *Mary Ann* and *Violet* taken by Algerians.
1863   U.S. squadron and naval shore batteries bombarded Fort Sumter, S.C.
1893   Battleship *Oregon* launched.
1912   LT (jg) P. N. L. Bellinger reported for flight training.
1921   First turntable catapult tested at Philadelphia Navy Yard.

1922   First carrier landing with ship, USS *Langley,* underway.
1942   Battle of Santa Cruz Islands.
1944   Battle of Leyte Gulf continues.
1950   U.S. Marines landed at Wonsan, Korea.

27 October

1775   Special committee presented Continental Congress a bill for acquisition of 13 ships.
1812   Frigate *Essex* departed Delaware Capes on first U.S. Navy cruise into Pacific Ocean.
1864   Naval expedition sank CSS *Albemarle.*
1922   First annual celebration of Navy Day.

28 October

1779   Board of Admiralty established.
1918   USS *Tarantula,* scout patrol craft, sunk in collision, no casualties.

29 October

1814   First steam warship, USS *Fulton,* launched.
1861   Naval expedition against Port Royal, S.C.
1870   Paddle gunboat *Saginaw* wrecked on Ocean Island, mid-Pacific, no casualties. (See 18 Nov., 19 Dec. 1870)

30 October

1775   Continental Congress authorized two additional vessels for defense of Colonies.
1799   First chaplain in new Navy, William Balch, commissioned.
1917   First Jewish chaplain, LT (jg) David Goldberg, appointed.
1918   Second Marine Division relieved 42nd Marine Division at Meuse-Argonne area.
1919   King Albert of Belgium reviewed Midshipmen at Naval Academy.
1955   Landing field at NAS Miramar (California) renamed Mitscher Field.

31 October

1803   Frigate *Philadelphia* captured by Tripolitans.
1919   Queen of Belgium activated drydock at Norfolk Navy Yard.
       Marine SGT Herman H. Hanneken, and CPL William R. Button killed Haitian bandit chief Charlemagne Peralte.
1941   Recruiting of Headquarters Construction Companies, forerunners of the SeaBees, authorized.
       First U.S. naval vessel, USS *Reuben James,* lost to enemy action in WW II.

1954 Ensign D. L. Varner flew F2H-2 BANSHEE from Los Alamitos, Calif., to Cecil Field, Fla., 1,900 miles, in three hours 58 minutes.

1956 R4D SKYTRAIN, *Que Sera Sera,* landed seven men at South Pole— first men to stand on that spot since CAPT Robert F. Scott, Royal Navy, reached it in 1912.

1958 End of the battleship era. Uncompleted hull of USS *Kentucky,* last battleship authorized for construction, sold as scrap.

1961 End of the lighter-than-air era. Navy's last blimps were placed out of service at Lakehurst, N.J.

1 November

1765   Stamp Act went into effect.

1784   Robert Morris retired as Secretary of Marine.

1862   U.S. squadron engaged CSS *Cotton* and Confederate shore batteries in Atchafalava River and Bayou Teche, La.

1905   British squadron visited Annapolis, Md.

1915   Marine Recruit Depot, Marine Barracks, Port Royal, S.C., established.

1919   US subchaser *No. 256,* scout patrol craft, sunk in mid-Atlantic.

1941   President Roosevelt placed Coast Guard under Navy control.

1943   U.S. Marines landed at Cape Torokina, Bougainville, Solomon Islands.

1945   Naval Air Reserve Training Command established.

1954   First observance of Veterans' Day, replacing Armistice Day.

1955   First guided-missile cruiser, USS *Boston,* commissioned.

1963   Fred Korth, fifty-fifth Secretary of the Navy, resigned.

2 November

1775   Continental Congress appropriated $100,000 for Marine Committee work.

1899   USS *Charleston,* cruiser, wrecked in Philippine Islands.

1903   Party from gunboat *Nashville* landed at Colon, Panama, to protect American interests.

1923   Navy set world's aircraft speed record for three kilometer course, 259.47 MPH.

1930   U.S. Navy, Army, and Marine forces supervised Nicaraguan congressional elections.

1943   Battle of Empress Augusta Bay.

1944   Navy Standard Stock Catalog put into use.

1950   U.S. Marines in first action with Chinese Communists.

1955   RADM Richard E. Byrd placed in charge of all U.S. Antarctic activities.

3 November

1841   "Mosquito Fleet," composed of sailors and Marines, sent into Florida Everglades against Seminole Indians.

1909   National Geographic Society confirmed Peary's claim to have discovered the North Pole. (See 4 Nov. 1909)

1931   Dirigible *Akron* set record for largest number of passengers (207) carried aloft.

1946   Airship XM-1 completed world record, non-refueling, duration flight, 170.3 hours.

4 November

1796   U.S. concluded treaty of peace with Tripoli.

1909   National Geographic Society voted CDR Robert E. Peary a gold medal for reaching North Pole.

1917   USS *Empress,* scout patrol craft, lost.

1923   Navy set world's aircraft speed record, 266.59 MPH.

1939   Neutrality Act of 1939 became law.

1942   Marine Corps Air Station, El Toro, Calif., established.

1951   CAPT William F. Guss, USMC, became the first Marine pilot to shoot down a Russian MIG.

1955   First woman appointed captain, Medical Corps, Gioconda R. Saraneiro.

5 November

1775   First commander in chief of the Fleet, Esek Hopkins, appointed.

1821   Schooner *Alligator* captured Portuguese *Marianno Flora.*

1865   First Confederate warship to circumnavigate the world, USS *Shenandoah,* arrived in London.

1915   First catapult launching from a ship underway by USS *North Carolina.*

1917   USS *Alcedo,* converted yacht, sunk by submarine, first loss due to enemy action in WW I.

1944   U.S. carrier aircraft bombed Manila, P.I.

6 November

1776   Continental Naval Board appointed.

1865   CSS *Shenandoah* surrendered to British authorities.

1918   American cargo ship *Lake Damita* grounded and sank, Brest, France, no casualties.

1941   Light cruiser *Omaha* and destroyer *Somers* captured German blockade runner *Odenwald.*

1945   Ryan FR-1 FIREBALL landed on USS *Wake Island,* first carrier landing by a jet aircraft.

7 November

1861   U.S. squadron captured Confederate batteries at Port Royal, S.C.
Boat party from frigate *Santee* captured Confederate privateer *Royal Yacht*.
Timber-clads *Tyler* and *Lexington* supported Army at Battle of Belmont, Mo.

1899   Navy ships covered Army landings at Lingayen, P.I.

8 November

1912   Armed cruisers *Tennessee* and *Montana* ordered to protect Americans in Turkey.

1921   U.S. Marines commenced guarding U.S. mails.

1940   First U.S. merchant ship, *City of Bayville*, sunk in WW II, by mine, off Australia. (See 7 Sept. 1941)

1941   First ship-type launching of a patrol bomber.
President Roosevelt approved withdrawal of Marines from Cuba.

1942   Allies invaded North Africa.

1956   Navy Strato-Lab balloon manned by LCDR M. D. Ross and LCDR M. L. Lewis, broke 1935 altitude record for manned balloons by reaching 76,000 feet.

9 November

1822   Schooner *Alligator* recaptured five American ships from pirates.

1863   Joint Navy-Army attack on Fort Sumter, S.C.

1880   *Ticonderoga,* Navy's first steam-powered ship to circle the globe, ended two year cruise commenced 7 Dec. 1878. (See 10 May 1960)

1906   First President to leave U.S. while in office, Theodore Roosevelt, sailed for Panama in *Louisiana*. (See 14 Nov.)

1921   Protected cruiser *Olympia* reached Washington, D.C. bearing body of the Unknown Soldier.

1950   First enemy jet aircraft, *MIG-15,* shot down by a Navy plane over Korea.

10 November

1775   Birthdate of the Marine Corps.

1918   Fifth Marines crossed the east bank of the Meuse River, France.

1921   First annual Marine Corps birthday celebration.

1941   First U.S. escorted troop convoy of WW II sailed from Halifax, Nova Scotia.

1942   U.S. warships and carrier aircraft engaged French naval forces at Casablanca, Morocco.
Third Marine Air Wing commissioned at Cherry Point, N.C.

1954 Marine Corps War Memorial, "Iwo Jima Monument," dedicated at Arlington, Va.

1959 The atom-powered radar-picket submarine *Triton* (SSRN 586) commissioned. The 447-foot boat, displacing 5,900 tons, was the largest submarine built by the U.S. to that date.

11 November

1807 Great Britain decreed neutral nations could not trade with France and her allies except under tribute to Great Britain.

1847 Naval forces occupied Mazatlan, Mexico.

1909 Navy commenced plans for a base at Pearl Harbor.

1918 World War I armistice signed.

1921 Unknown Soldier entombed at Arlington, Va.

1931 Tomb of the Unknown Soldier dedicated at Arlington, Va.

1942 Casablanca surrendered to U.S. forces.
Allied-French armistice signed.
Six U.S. Marines captured town of Mers-El-Kebir, North Africa.

1943 First combat use of Curtiss SB2C HELLDIVER.

1944 Naval assault on Iwo Jima opened.
Carrier aircraft attack Ormoc Bay, P.I.

1954 First Veterans Day (formerly known as Armistice Day) observed.

12 November

1776 Continental ship *Alfred* and brig *Providence* captured British transport *Mellish*.

1803 U.S. squadron began blockading Tripoli harbor.

1857 First artillery instruction in the Marine Corps.

1912 First successful catapult launching of an aircraft, at Washington Navy Yard. (See 5 Nov. 1915, 18 Nov. 1922)

1926 U.S. Marines landed at Chinwangtao, China.

1942 Naval battle of Guadalcanal.

13 November

1909 President Taft, in USS *Mayflower,* attended Hudson-Fulton celebration at New York.

1942 Navy Patrol Squadron 73 began air operations from French Morocco.

1943 First Japanese plane knocked out of the air by Marine Corps night fighter.

1944 First Negro women sworn into the WAVES.

14 November

1778 Continental Congress authorized Pursers for ships of 14 guns upwards.

1906 First President to visit a foreign country, Theodore Roosevelt, reached Panama.

1910 First airplane flight from a ship, light cruiser *Birmingham,* at Hampton Roads, Va.

1942 Battle of Guadalcanal continues.

1950 U.S. Marines swept across snow covered mountains toward Chosin Reservoir.

15 November

1776 Continental Congress adopted new pay scale for Navy.

1882 First naval attache, LCDR French E. Chadwick, received orders to London, England.

1918 USS *Elizabeth,* scout patrol craft, wrecked in Brazos River, Tex., 2 lives lost.

1940 Navy began air operations from Bermuda.

1942 Battle of Guadalcanal ended.

1950 U.S. Marines occupied Hagaru, Korea.

16 November

1776 First salute of U.S. flag by a foreign power, at St. Eustatia.

1798 Corvette *Baltimore* halted by British squadron; five American seamen impressed.

1856 Sloop-of-war *Portsmouth* fired upon by forts at Canton, China.

1899 Gunboat *Castine* combined with Army units to capture Zamboanga, P.I.

1927 Carrier *Saratoga* commissioned.

1940 Marine Corps Reserve aviation squadrons ordered to mobilize.

1942 Field Branch, Bureau of Supplies and Accounts, Cleveland, Ohio, established.

1958 First proficiency pay became effective.
First enlisted men promoted to new chief petty officer grades of E-8 and E-9.

17 November

1847 Landing parties from frigate *Congress* and sloop-of-war *Portsmouth* occupied Guaymas, Mexico.

1863 Screw sloop *Monongahela* and Army troops captured Arkansas Pass, Tex.

1915 Battle of Fort Riviere in Haiti.

1917 Destroyers *Fanning* and *Nicholson* sank *U-58*, first enemy submarine destroyed by U.S. Navy.

1941 Congress amended Neutrality Act to allow arming of U.S. merchant ships.

1958 USNS *Chain*, first of Navy's new oceanographic research ships, placed in service.

18 November

1867 Screw sloop *Monongahela* carried ashore by tidal wave at St. Croix, Danish West Indies, 5 lives lost.

1870 Five crew members of paddle gunboat *Saginaw*, wrecked on Ocean Island, sailed for Hawaii to get help.

1890 First battleship, USS *Maine*, launched, Brooklyn, N.Y.

1901 U.S. and Great Britain signed Isthmian Canal Treaty.

1909 U.S. warships ordered to Nicaragua.

1922 First catapult launching from an aircraft carrier made on USS *Langley*. (See 5 Nov. 1915)

1943 Aircraft from 11 U.S. carriers opened assault on Gilbert Islands.

1953 Jim Creek Navy radio station dedicated.

1954 Experimental "Pogo" plane, ultra-sonic seaplane, blew up in mid-air during first public demonstration.

19 November

1796 U.S. concluded treaty with England. No "impressment" provision included.

1835 First U.S. warship to visit Guam, sloop-of-war *Vincennes*, anchored off Apra.

1861 Screw sloop *San Jacinto* arrived at Boston with Confederate commissioners taken from British *Trent*.

1868 Marine Corps emblem authorized.

1917 USS *Chauncey*, destroyer, sunk in collision with SS *Rose*, off England, 64 lives lost.

20 November

1776 First 74 gun warship, *America*, authorized by Continental Congress.

1798 Schooner *Retaliation* captured by French *Insurgente* and *Volontaire*.

1846 Boat party from brig *Somers* destroyed Mexican *Creole*.

1846 U.S. squadron attacked forts at Canton, China. Landing force occupied one fort and raised American flag.

1917 Ninth Marine Regiment organized at Quantico, Va.

1918 First contingent of German fleet surrendered.

1932 Wright Brothers Memorial unveiled at Kitty Hawk, N.C.

1933 LCDR T. G. W. Settle and MAJ C. L. Fordney set world's altitude record for balloons, 61,236 feet.

1943 Marines landed on Tarawa, Gilbert Islands.

1952 Mine sweeper *Kite* hit by enemy battery near Wonsan, Korea.

1962 U.S. ordered cessation of Cuban blockade in which Navy used 184 ships, 85,000 men.

21 November

1806 Napoleon issued Berlin Decree, prohibiting neutral nations from commerce with Great Britain.

1918 German fleet surrendered to combined U.S. and British fleets.

1919 Battleship *California* launched.

1946 Harry S. Truman became first President to travel underwater in a submarine.

1952 Destroyer *Thompson* hit by enemy shore battery off Wonsan, Korea.

22 November

1961 F4H PHANTOM II set new world speed record of 1606.324 mph.

1963 John Fitzgerald Kennedy, thirty-fifth President of the United States, was assassinated in Dallas, Texas. Mr. Kennedy served as a Lieutenant in the Navy during WW II, commanded USS PT 109.

23 November

1793 American merchant brig *Minerva* taken by Algerian pirates.

1862 Armed steamer *Ellis* captured by Confederates after two day battle at Onslow, N.C.

1943 U.S. Marines captured Tarawa.

24 November

1852 Naval expedition to Japan sailed from Norfolk, Va.

1877 Gunboat *Huron* wrecked, Nags Head, N.C., 100 lives lost.

1950 UN forces launched offensive supposed to end the Korean War.

25 November

1924 USS *Los Angeles,* dirigible, christened.

1943 Battle of Cape St. George.

1944 Last carrier air strike launched in support of Leyte invasion.

1961 World's largest ship, USS *Enterprise* (CVAN 65) commissioned. Ship is 1102 feet long, displaces 85,350 tons, has 200,000 horsepower nuclear power plant.

26 November

1918 Scout patrol craft *Bonita* hit and sunk by American schooner *Russell* while moored in Boston harbor, no casualties.

1950 U.S. Marines seized Yudam-ni, Korea.

27 November

1941 "War warning" message sent to commanders of Pacific and Asiatic Fleets.

First contingent of Marines left Shanghai, China, for the Philippines.

1942 French fleet scuttled at Toulon, France.

28 November

1775 First NAVY REGULATIONS adopted.

Birthdate of the Navy Chaplaincy: Navy Regulations ordered that "The commanders of the ships of the thirteen United Colonies, are to take care that divine service be performed twice a day on board and a sermon preached on Sundays, unless bad weather or other extraordinary accidents prevent."

First Marine commission received by CAPT Samuel Nicholas. CAPT Nicholas served as first Commandant of the Marine Corps.

1861 CSS *Sumter* escaped capture by screw gunboat *Iroquois*.

1929 First flight over South Pole. (See 9 May 1926)

1941 Last U.S. Marines left China.

1945 Fourth Marine Division disbanded at Camp Pendleton, Calif.

29 November

1775 Continental schooner *Lee* captured British brig *Nancy*.

1776 First ship of Continental Navy to visit Europe, brig *Reprisal*, arrived in France.

1890 First Army-Navy football game. Navy—24, Army—0.

1910 Glenn Curtiss offered to "instruct 1 Naval officer in operation and construction of the Curtiss aeroplane.

1916 Captain Harry S. Knapp appointed military governor of Santo Domingo.

1941 Japan closed its Army office in the U.S.

30 November

1782 British and American emissaries signed preliminary peace treaty.

1941 Japanese Foreign Minister Tojo rejected U.S. proposals for settling Far Eastern crisis.

1942 Battle of Tassafaronga.

1961 End of lighter-than-air operations in the Navy, all blimps ordered deflated and stored.

1962 USS *Henry Clay* (SSBN 625) launched at Newport News, Va.

Catherine Murray, Master Sergeant, USMC, became first enlisted woman Marine to retire.

1 December

1842 USS *Somers* mutiny, only case in U.S. Navy.
1908 Truman H. Newberry took office, fortieth Secretary of the Navy.
1912 RADM Alfred T. Mahan died, Washington, D.C.
1914 First Navy flying school opened.
1918 Helium first used for lighter-than-air craft.
1931 Carrier *Langley* conducted cold weather aircraft tests off New England.
1938 Hepburn Board reported on naval aviation shore establishment.
1941 Marine Corps Air Station, Cherry Point, N.C., established.
1943 Naval Air Ferry Command established.
1940 U.S. Marines rescued 1,200 American soldiers at Chosin, Korea. U.S. Marines break out from Yudam-ni to Hagaru.
1959 Navy Bureau of Ordnance and Bureau of Aeronautics merged to become the Bureau of Naval Weapons, headed by RADM Paul D. Stroop.

2 December

1799 Frigate *Chesapeake* launched.
1812 Brig *Argus* captured British brig *Recovery*.
1823 First statement of Monroe Doctrine.
1891 Screw cruiser *New York* launched.
1903 Panama Canal treaty ratified.
1908 RADM Cowles sent memorandum to Secretary of the Navy recommending government assistance in development of flying machines.
1909 U.S. Marines and other naval forces ordered to Nicaragua.
1941 First Armed Guard Crew of WW II reported on board SS *Duboyne*. SS *Duboyne*.
1955 First "Texas tower" turned over to Air Force.

3 December

1864 U.S. gunboat flotilla defeated left wing of Confederate Army at Bell's Mill, Tenn.
1915 U.S. requested the recall of German diplomats.
1954 USS *Gyatt*, first TERRIER missile destroyer, commissioned. USS *Compass Island*, first ship converted to support Fleet Ballistic Missile Program, commissioned.

4 December

1861   Armed steamer *Montgomery* engaged CSS *Florida*.
1918   President Wilson sailed from New York in USS *George Washington* for Paris peace conference.

5 December

1813   Frigate *Congress* captured British *Atlantic*.
1843   First prefabricated ship (also first iron ship), paddle sloop *Michigan*, launched. (See 12 Oct. 1861)
1953   Submarine *Albacore* commissioned.

6 December

1796   President Washington urged Congress to increase naval strength.
1812   Brig *Argus* captured British schooner *Dorothy*.
1830   First national observatory (Naval Observatory) established at Washington, D.C.
1846   First gold from California delivered to Washington, D.C., by LT G. F. Beale.
1863   USS *Weehawken,* monitor, foundered off Morris Island, S.C. Crew of 30 lost.
1917   Destroyer *Jacob Jones* sunk by submarine off English coast, 64 lives lost.
1944   Commissioning of Evacuation Squadrons directed.
1946   First squadron equipped with AD-1 SKYRAIDER attack planes.
1950   U.S. Marines broke out from Hagaru to Koto-ri, Korea.
1959   A Navy McDonnell F4H flown by CDR Lawrence E. Flint, reached an altitude of 98,560 feet. Previous high was 94,658 feet, reached in USSR by a TU-431 jet.

7 December

1862   U.S. ships engaged Confederates at Corpus Christi, Tex.
1912   Civilian personnel in Navy Department placed under Civil Service.
1917   U.S. battleships joined British fleet at Scapa Flow.
1941   At about 0755, Sunday morning, Japanese carrier-based planes heavily attacked ships of the U.S. Pacific Fleet and military installations at Pearl Harbor and other places on Oahu, T.H. About 360 enemy planes were involved. Navy Yard and Naval Base, Pearl Harbor; NAS, Ford Island, Naval Patrol Plane Station, Kaneohe; Marine Corps airfield, Ewa; Army airfields at Hickam, Wheeler and Bellows damaged. A total of 188 Army and Navy aircraft were destroyed. Killed or missing: Navy, 2,004; Marine Corps, 75; Army,

360. The Japanese lost 5 midget submarines, 28 aircraft, and fewer than 100 men. U.S. ships sunk were battleships *Oklahoma, Arizona, California, West Virginia;* minelayer *Ogala;* target ship *Utah.* U.S. ships damaged were battleships *Nevada, Pennsylvania, Tennessee, Maryland;* cruisers *Raleigh, Honolulu, Helena;* destroyers *Cassin, Shaw, Downes;* seaplane tender *Curtiss;* repair ship *Vestal.*
Same day, Midway Island was bombarded by two Japanese destroyers.
President Roosevelt ordered mobilization.

1944 Naval task group landed Army troops at Ormac Bay, P.I.

8 December

1846 Brig *Somers* capsized in squall, Vera Cruz, Mexico, no casualties.
1868 First Japanese Midshipman enrolled at Naval Academy.
1933 Fleet Marine Force organized and made part of U.S. Fleet.
1941 U.S. declared war on Japan.
First and only U.S. warship of WW II to surrender, gunboat *Wake.*
Potomac River Naval Command and Severn River Naval Command established.
Japanese landed on Bataan and east coast of Malay.
Japan interned U.S. Marines and American nationals at Shanghai, Peiping, and Tientsin, China.

9 December

1917 USS *Washington,* scout patrol craft, sunk in Ambrose Channel, no casualties.
1929 Armored cruiser *Pittsburgh* and eleven destroyers sent to Shanghai.
1941 First plane shot down by a Marine pilot in WW II, at Wake Island.
1950 U.S. Marines break out from Koto-ri to Hamhung.
Navy laid down protective curtain of shells for five days during evacuation of UN forces from Wonsan.

10 December

1814 British ships entered Lake Borgne, La.
1815 First training school for naval officers established.
1843 First steam ship with screw propeller, USS *Princeton,* launched.
1846 Naval expedition against Tampico, Mexico.
1898 U.S. concluded treaty of peace with Spain.
1899 Protected cruisers *Olympia* and *Baltimore* took possession of navy yard at Olangapo, P.I.

1941   U.S. Navy Yard, Cavite, P.I., heavily damaged by Japanese air attack.

First submarine lost, due to enemy action, USS *Sealion,* bombed.

1950   Allied naval forces evacuated 7,000 soldiers and civilians from Pyongyang area.

11 December

1918   American cargo ship *Lake Bloomington,* grounded and sank, Gironde River, France, no casualties.

1941   Germany and Italy declared war on the U.S.

U.S. declared war on Germany and Italy.

1947   Naval Supply Center, Norfolk, Va., established.

1950   Evacuation of Hungnam completed.

1954   Carrier *Forrestal* launched

12 December

1812   Frigate *Essex* captured British packet *Norton.*

1941   Naval Air Transport Service (NATS) established.

French ships in U.S. ports seized.

1942   PT-boats attacked Japanese destroyers off Guadalcanal.

1950   U.S. Marines fought through six Chinese divisions near Chosin reservoir.

13 December

1775   Continental Congress passed bill for acquisition of 13 ships.

1855   First U.S. frigate equipped with turrets, USS *Roanoke,* launched.

1900   Transport *Yosemite* wrecked.

1937   Gunboat *Panay* bombed and sunk by Japanese aircraft, Yangtze River, China. Two men killed, 43 injured.

14 December

1775   Marine Committee increased to 13 members.

1799   George Washington died, Mount Vernon, Va.

1814   U.S. squadron of gunboats captured by British on Lake Borgne, La.

1911   First ship, USS *California,* entered Pearl Harbor after it was made a naval base.

1927   Carrier *Lexington* commissioned.

1944   Rank of fleet admiral established. (See 15 Dec. 1944)

1945   First Distinguished Service Medal awarded a Navy nurse received by CAPT Sue S. Dauser.

1950   Successful withdrawal of UN forces from Chinnampo announced.

15 December

1814 Congress asked Army to furnish Navy with horses wherever necessary.

1897 First submarine to utilize internal combustion engine demonstrated.

1941 USS *Swordfish* became first U.S. submarine to sink a Japanese ship in WW II.

1944 First three fleet admirals appointed: Ernest J. King, William D. Leahy, and Chester W. Nimitz.

1950 First Marine Division evacuated to Masan area, Korea.

16 December

1773 Boston Tea Party.

1835 Sailors and Marines assisted in fighting greatest fire in history of New York City.

1907 First fleet of warships to circumnavigate the world left Hampton Roads, Va. (See 22 Feb. 1909)

1921 First ship constructed as a lighter-than-aircraft tender, USS *Wright*, commissioned.

1923 Destroyer *Bainbridge* rescued 482 persons from burning French transport *Vinh-Long*.

17 December

1810 David G. Farragut appointed midshipman. (See 21 Dec. 1864)

1812 Brig *Argus* captured British schooner *Vancise*.

1907 Victor H. Metcalf took office, thirty-ninth Secretary of the Navy.

1917 USS *F-1*, submarine, rammed and sunk by USS *F-3* off San Pedro, Calif., 19 lives lost.

1927 USS *S-4*, submarine, sunk in collision with Coast Guard destroyer, *Paulding*, Provincetown, Mass., 39 lives lost.

1929 U.S. ships ordered from Manila to Shanghai.

1951 First successful jet-assisted take-off by a helicopter.

1952 First aircraft equipped with hydro-skis tested.

18 December

1807 Congress authorized 188 new gunboats.

1929 First use of a ship to furnish electrical power for a major city, USS *Lexington*, at Tacoma, Wash.

1959 *Robert E. Lee* (SSBN 601) launched.

19 December

1782 Continental ship *South Carolina* captured by British squadron.

1870 USS *Saginaw's* gig reached Kauai, Hawaii. Only coxswain, William Halford, survived the landing.

1893 Protected cruiser *San Francisco* and armored cruiser *New York* ordered to Rio de Janeiro.

1913 Law passed limiting tenure of office for Commandant of the Marine Corps.

1941 Naval Academy Class of 1942 graduated.

1949 *Scorpion* (SSN 589) launched.

20 December

1822 Congress authorized Navy squadron for suppressing Caribbean pirates.

1838 Brig *Adams* bombarded pirates at Qualla Battoo, Sumatra.

1860 South Carolina seceded from the Union.

1941 ADM King designated Commander in Chief, U.S. Fleet.

1942 Marine Barracks, New River, N.C., redesignated Camp Lejeune.

1944 Organized enemy resistance ended on Leyte, P.I.

1955 First air link to Antarctic continent, two P2V NEPTUNES and two R5D SKYMASTERS flew from Christ Church, N.Z., to McMurdo Sound.

1961 John B. Connally, fifty-eighth Secretary of the Navy, resigned. (See 4 Jan. 1962)

21 December

1783 Colonel Archibald Henderson, fifth Commandant of the Marine Corps, born at Colchester, Fairfax County, Va.

1821 Schooner *Enterprise* captured a West Indian pirate schooner.

1861 Medal of Honor authorized.

1864 David G. Farragut appointed vice admiral.

1941 Naval defense forces in Philippine Islands moved headquarters to Corregidor.

1951 First helicopter landing aboard a hospital ship—USS *Consolation*.

22 December

1775 First regular naval officers' commissions approved.
First "Flag of America" unfurled on board an American warship.
First commander in chief, Esek Hopkins, designated.

1807 U.S. declared an embargo, prohibiting all foreign commerce.

1917 US subchaser *No. 117* burned.

1950 World's passenger-carrying record set by SS *Meredith Victory* which evacuated 14,000 refugees from Hungnam, Korea.

23 December

1803 Brig *Enterprise* captured Tripolitan *Mastico*.
1814 Schooner *Carolina* supported Army attack on New Orleans.
1816 Final treaty of peace signed between U.S. and Algiers.
1862 Naval forces cleared Yazoo River, Miss., of "torpedoes."
1898 Guam placed under Navy Department control.
1910 First naval aviator, LT T. G. Ellyson, ordered to flight training.
1941 Wake Island surrendered to Japanese.

24 December

1800 Brig *Enterprise* captured French privateer *Amour de la Patrie*.
1814 U.S. concluded treaty of peace with Great Britain.
1864 U.S. squadron opened bombardment of Fort Fisher, N.C.
1947 Operation HIGHJUMP commenced.
1940 Hungnam withdrawal completed.
1955 First baptism performed south of Antarctic Circle.

25 December

1796 American merchant ship *Commerce* fired upon by French privateer.
1864 U.S. squadron bombarded Fort Fisher. Army troops attempted landing.
1915 First of the traditional Navy shipboard Christmas parties held on board USS *New York*, Edinburgh, Scotland.
1958 Navy aircraft from Port Lyautey rescued 134 persons from flooded areas in Morocco.

26 December

1837 Admiral of the Navy George F. Dewey born at Montpelier, Vt.
1839 Wilkes Expedition sailed from Sydney, Australia, for the South Seas.
1862 First hospital ship, *Red Rover*, placed in use.
1918 Secretary of the Navy Daniels reviewed fleet units at New York.
1941 Manila declared an open city.
1943 U.S. Marines landed at Cape Gloucester, New Britain.

27 December

1860 U.S. revenue cutter *William Aiden* surrendered to South Carolina authorities.
1862 U.S. squadron engaged Confederate batteries in Yazoo River, Miss.
1956 The keel of USS *Kitty Hawk*, fifth in *Forrestal* series, was laid.

28 December

1867 Midway Island claimed by the U.S., first territory annexed outside Continental limits.

1918 USS *Tenadores,* troop transport, grounded and lost, Brest, France, no casualties.

1941 Chief of the Bureau of Yards and Docks requested construction battalions be recruited.

1945 Third Marine Division disbanded.

29 December

1798 First annual report by Secretary of the Navy. (See 31 Dec. 1948)

1812 Frigate *Constitution* captured British *Java.*

1863 Joint Navy-Army attack on Matagorda Bay, Tex.

1941 Corregidor bombed for first time by Japanese.

30 December

1812 New York Flotilla captured British ships *Abrantes* and *Mina.*

1918 USS *Katherine W. Cullen,* scout patrol craft, sunk off Boston, no casualties.

1941 ADM King assumed duties as Commander in Chief, U.S. Fleet.

31 December

1776 From 10 March, 1776, to this date 140 American vessels were captured by the British.
American ships made 342 captures of British ships.

1777 During the year 464 vessels were taken from the British.

1779 During the year the British lost 516 ships.

1780 During the year the British lost 596 ships.

1781 During the year the British lost 625 ships, and captured 317.

1861 Naval forces occupied Biloxi, Miss.

1862 USS *Monitor* foundered off Cape Hatteras, 16 lives lost.

1941 ADM Chester W. Nimitz assumed command of Pacific Fleet.

1942 Carrier *Essex* commissioned.

1945 Third Marine Air Wing decommissioned.
Naval Supply Center, Pearl Harbor, T.H., established.

1947 Seabee Organized Reserve authorized.

1948 Last annual report of Secretary of the Navy made to Congress and the President.

CAMPAIGNS, BATTLES,
AND ACTIONS

Campaigns, Battles, and Actions

First Sea Battle of the Revolution (12 June 1775)

Though there was no American Navy at the time, this was the first clash occurring on water. The British cutter *Margaretta,* entering the harbor of Machias, Me., with two sloops to commandeer a load of lumber for GEN Gage's army at Boston, was challenged by Jeremiah O'Brien, leading a group of lumberjacks and fellow townsmen brandishing pitchforks. *Margaretta* stood out into the stream, whereupon O'Brien seized *Unity,* one of the sloops, and went after her. The Maine men pitted rifles against cannon, used stacks of lumber as bulwarks, and picked off British gunners through *Margaretta's* ports. In thirty minutes O'Brien's men killed the midshipman skipper of the enemy ship, boarded her and ran up a home-made white flag bearing a green pine tree and the legend "AN APPEAL TO HEAVEN."

Lee vs. Nancy (29 November 1775)

CAPT John Manly, Marblehead fisherman and former boatswain's mate in the Royal Navy, was sailing in *Lee,* a 4-gun schooner, under orders from GEN George Washington. While cruising off Massachusetts for the purpose of intercepting supplies destined for the British army, he took the British *Nancy.* Her cargo included 2,000 muskets with bayonets, 8,000 fuses, 31 tons of musket shot, 3,000 24-pound round shot, several barrels of powder, two cannon, and a 13-inch mortar described as "the noblest piece of ordnance ever landed in America." These supplies proved most valuable to the Continental Army. GEN Washington used the cannon when forcing the British to evacuate Boston four months later.

Attack on New Providence, Bahamas (3-4 March 1776)

First amphibious assault launched by the U.S. Navy. Almost every ship the Navy had was involved, under COMO Esek Hopkins. U.S. Marines first saw combat. CAPT Samuel Nicholas led 250

Marines ashore from the fleet, combined them with 50 sailors under *Cabot's* LT Weaver, and captured Nassau, New Providence, Bahamas, with only slight resistance and no bloodshed. Though marines and sailors captured 88 cannons, 15 mortars, and 24 casks of gunpowder, the island's British governor was able to spirit away most of his munitions on the night of 3 March in a merchant schooner. After holding the island two weeks, the fleet sailed for Rhode Island, taking the governor and other officials with them as hostages.

American Turtle vs. Eagle (7 September 1776)

SGT Ezra Lee of the Continental Army, piloting a one-man submarine devised by David Bushnell, approached the enemy warship in New York Harbor, with the intention of fastening a "time bomb," or mine to her hull. Due to *Eagle's* bottom being copper-plated, however, Lee's attempt was unsuccessful. The mine was set adrift and exploded without damage. This was the first American submarine attack on an enemy warship.

First Battle of Lake Champlain (11-13 October 1776)

BRIG-GEN Benedict Arnold led a force of one sloop, three schooners, eight gondolas, and four galleys, mounting 94 cannon and manned by about 700 men against a British force of 29 vessels. Arnold's "navy" was defeated, but the time they had caused the British army to consume in building a fleet to win control of the lake proved valuable. British forces shortly thereafter became so scattered in various campaigns that they could not combine to cut off New England from the rest of the Colonies, as they had hoped to do earlier by taking Lake Champlain and controlling the Hudson River.

Alfred vs. Mellish (12 November 1776)

While crusing in company with *Providence* (CAPT Hoysted Hacker), the 24-gun ship *Alfred* under CAPT John Paul Jones captured the British transport *Mellish* and 150 prisoners. The British cargo included 10,000 suits of winter uniform, destined for GEN Burgoyne's army at Montreal, Canada. While convoying *Mellish* and seven other prizes into port *Alfred,* having parted company with *Providence,* encountered the British frigate *Milford.* Jones drew the enemy warship off while his prizes ran for shore, then, having made sure the Englishman was too far away to chase them, loosed all sail and slipped away. He joined his prizes later off Nantasket, Mass., and brought them safe into port, where the uniforms were transferred to the Continental Army.

Ranger vs. Drake (24 April 1778)

After having raided Whitehaven, England, in the *Ranger,* John Paul Jones put into the harbor of Carrickfergus, where the British warship *Drake* lay moored, taking on supplies. After waiting for the enemy to come to quarters, Jones opened fire. Within 30 minutes *Drake's* captain lay dying, and 40 of her crew were dead. *Ranger* lost six men in the battle, during which Jones fought the enemy while putting down a mutiny on his own ship. This was the first defeat of a British warship by an American naval vessel.

Bon Homme Richard vs. Serapis (23 September 1779)

The *Bon Homme Richard,* 42-guns, under John Paul Jones, acting with three ships under French captains, sighted the British ships *Serapis* and *Countess of Scarborough,* escorting a merchant convoy off Flamborough Head, England. Jones engaged the *Serapis,* a frigate of 50-guns, and the French *Pallas* captured the *Countess of Scarborough* after a two-hour battle. The two remaining French ships gave no assistance, and the convoy fled. When *Bon Homme Richard* fired her first broadside, two of her lower deck cannons exploded, killing the gun crews. The men refused to fire any more of these guns and Jones was left with only small cannon on the upper deck. When *Bon Homme Richard* was being rapidly destroyed, Jones lashed her alongside the *Serapis* and sent men into the rigging to fire on the enemy. *Bon Homme Richard* was on fire and leaking badly, when one of the gunners cried for quarter and attempted to haul down the colors. Jones killed him by throwing a pistol at his head. CAPT Pearson of the *Serapis* asked Jones if he surrendered. Jones replied, "Surrender? I have not yet begun to fight!" Jones's master-at-arms, seeing the fires and leaks, thought his ship was sinking, and so released all prisoners. The English would have turned on the U.S. crew, but were told both ships were sinking

and that they must man *Bon Homme Richard's* pumps to save their
own lives. Meanwhile Jones's men in the rigging had climbed over
into the masts of *Serapis*. One of them dropped a grenade, which
fell down an open hatch of *Serapis* and started a powder fire. At
this point *Alliance,* under the French CAPT Landais, entered the
engagement by firing broadsides into both *Bon Homme Richard*
and *Serapis*. As Pearson could not see that *Alliance* was damaging
Bon Homme Richard as much as the *Serapis,* he thought that
further fighting was useless, and surrendered. The battle lasted
three and one-half hours. As *Bon Homme Richard* was sinking,
Jones transferred his prisoners and crew to the *Serapis*. This is the
only instance in which the victor lost his own ship and returned to
port in the ship he captured.

Alliance vs. Atalanta and Trepassy (29 May 1781)

While enroute home after landing Lafayette in France, CAPT
John Barry's 32-gun ship *Alliance* met *Atalanta* and *Trepassy* on a
calm day with little wind. *Atalanta* had 20 guns and 130 men, while
her consort mounted 14 guns and had an 80-man crew. Though
wounded early in the battle, Barry rallied his men and, taking advantage of a slight wind, ran between the enemy ships and gave each
a broadside. This lessened his enemies' zeal considerably, for they
surrendered shortly afterward.

Hyder Ally vs. General Monk (8 April 1782)

General Monk had formerly been the Continental ship *George
Washington,* captured by the British in the occupation of Phila-
delphia, and had over 60 captures of American ships to her credit.
With four other British ships, she sighted the Pennsylvania-owned
Hyder Ally, 16 guns, under Joshua Barney, escorting a fleet of
merchantmen through the mouth of the Delaware River. *General
Monk* stood in alone to take what looked like an easy prey, but
Barney (by having his helmsman follow the "rule of contrary") lured
the Englishman alongside. Barney ordered his steersman to turn
left, whereupon the Britisher followed suit in order to stay parallel
for a broadside. *Hyder Ally* turned right, instead, and fouled her
jib in *General Monk's* rigging. The enemy's guns were pointed into
empty space, while *Hyder Ally* could rake her opponent's decks.

General Monk surrendered in 30 minutes, and Barney dashed upstream with his prize before other British ships realized what had happened.

Delaware vs. Croyable (9 July 1798)

While cruising along the Atlantic coast in USS *Delaware*, 20 guns, CAPT Stephen Decatur, Sr., sighted four schooners. Decatur stood off, pretending he was a merchantman anxious to avoid them and one schooner gave chase. Decatur let the Frenchman approach, then suddenly turned to give battle. The Frenchman, discovering he was facing a warship, attempted to escape, but a few rounds from *Delaware's* guns forced his surrender. The French ship was the privateer *Croyable*, 14 guns. Taken into Philadelphia, she was renamed USS *Retaliation*. For this capture Decatur and his men received the first prize money awarded men of the "new" Navy.

Constellation vs. Insurgente (January-December, 1800)

In the space of 11 months this little 12-gun schooner, whose crew never exceeded 83 men, struck blows at the French all out of proportion to what had been expected of her when she was purchased to deal with small privateers. Under LT John Shaw she took eight French privateers and recaptured four American merchantmen. Her prize victory was the privateer *Flambeau*, carrying 12 ninepounders and 110 men. During the cruise, LT Shaw's health broke down, and he was relieved by LT Andrew Sterrett, but he could boast upon returning home that he had "taken 13 sail . . . really more than I could have contemplated." Sterrett continued where Shaw left off, taking three privateers in December alone.

Constellation vs. Vengeance (1-2 February 1800)

CAPT Truxtun won another victory in a running battle, almost yardarm to yardarm on parallel courses, during which *Vengeance* struck her colors, then escaped in the darkness because the Americans could not see she had surrendered. *Vengeance* received 160 battle casualties, *Constellation* 39.

Destruction of USS Philadelphia (16 February 1804)

While pursuing a pirate vessel into the harbor of Tripoli on 31 Oct. 1803, CAPT William Bainbridge's 36-gun frigate went aground and all hands were captured by the pirates. Since *Philadelphia* posed a threat to the blockading American squadron by augmenting pirate shore batteries, CAPT Bainbridge managed to smuggle out a letter written in lemon juice to CAPT Edward Preble, suggesting that a small ship slip in at night, board the frigate and burn her. LT Stephen Decatur, who had just captured the Tripolitan ketch *Mastico* and renamed her USS *Intrepid*, volunteered for the venture. With 74 officers and men from USS *Enterprise* and *Constitution*, Decatur ran alongside *Philadelphia* in the darkness, boarded and set her afire, then withdrew under fire from shore batteries with only one man wounded. *Philadelphia* burned, exploded, and sank. Horatio, Lord Nelson, called Decatur's exploit "the most bold and daring act of the age."

Bombardment of Tripoli Harbor (3 August-3 September 1804)

During this period a U.S. squadron under COMO Edward Preble made five attacks on the pirate stronghold. Ships involved at first were *Constitution*, flagship; three 16-gun brigs, *Argus, Scourge,* and *Siren;* three 12-gun schooners, *Vixen, Nautilus,* and *Enterprise;* two mortar-carrying bomb vessels; and six gunboats. These mounted 156 guns and were manned by 1,060 men. Opposing them were 115 shore guns, plus one brig, two schooners, two galleys, and 19 gunboats. Total enemy guns were 227, and Tripolitan forces numbered 25,000 men. On 7 Aug. USS *John Adams* joined the U.S. squadron. While maneuvering carefully to avoid boarding, American ships sank three enemy gunboats and captured four, while suffering only 54 casualties. This was the first effective action taken against the Tripolitan pirates, and had great effect on the execution of a treaty some months later.

Chesapeake vs. Leopard (22 June 1807)

Having been ordered to duty in the Mediterranean, CAPT James Barron put to sea on 21 June, planning to train his hurriedly-gathered crew and mount his guns while crossing the Atlantic. Next day, just outside U.S. waters, he was hailed by the 50-gun British frigate *Leopard*. Though not prepared for battle, Barron refused to let the British search his ship for English-born seamen, whereupon *Leopard* fired a broadside that killed three U.S. sailors and wounded 18 others, including CAPT Barron. During the next 15 minutes Barron was able to fire only one token shot before hauling down the American colors. A boarding party from *Leopard* then boarded *Chesapeake* and seized four men claimed to be British deserters. The aftermath of this incident was the court-martial and five-year suspension of CAPT Barron for not having his ship battle-ready, and an embargo against Great Britain.

USS *President* vs. *Little Belt* (16 May 1811)

While cruising from Annapolis to New York, CAPT John Rodgers received word from a coasting vessel that an American seaman had been impressed into a British warship near Sandy Hook. Next day he sighted a sail, and closed in to hail the ship, which he recognized as British, but whose strength he could not measure in the poor weather. At his second hail, the British ship opened fire. Broadsides were exchanged, but when Rodgers' saw the enemy ship was smaller than his he stood off to await her next move. Two 32-pound shot crashed into his mainmast, and *President* returned to action, and silenced the English guns. After lying alongside all night, Rodgers sent a boat to the other ship in the morning, and learned she was the 18-gun sloop-of-war *Little Belt,* with nine British crewmen dead, 22 wounded. *Little Belt* limped into Halifax, and *President* continued cruising. This is the American version of the incident. The British version differed completely, and resentment on both sides of the Atlantic was so great that many U.S. cities began making preparations for war. When President Madison stated that U.S. warships had the right to challenge foreign vessels near her shores, and simultaneously presented proof the British were operating an espionage ring in this country, the matter was closed.

USS *President* vs. *Belvedere* (23 June 1812)

While cruising off the Atlantic coast as flagship of a squadron that included *United States, Congress,* and *Argus,* CAPT Rodgers' frigate sighted an English warship. The entire squadron gave chase but only *President,* being fastest, caught up. Her first three shots smashed in *Belvedere's* stern, and as the American gunners prepared to fire a few more shots from their long guns, they were confident that the battle would be a short, and victorious one. On the fourth shot, a bow chaser exploded, killing or wounding 18 men, and breaking CAPT Rodgers' leg. Rodgers hoped to disable the Englishman before it could damage his ship extensively, but the enemy kept cutting away rigging, jettisoning material, and repairing damage at a great rate. By nightfall CAPT Byron of *Belvedere* had thrown over his spare anchor, barge, yawl and jolly boat, while pumping 14 tons of water from *Belvedere's* hold. This had the desired effect, and she gained way on *President*. By 11:30 P.M., seeing further pursuit was useless, Rodgers broke off the chase. *Belvedere* escaped into Halifax.

USS *Essex* vs. *Alert* (13 August 1812)

While cruising in USS *Essex*, 32 guns, CAPT David Porter sighted a British warship, and used the popular device of pretending to be a merchant ship to draw the enemy within range. The 18-gun ship *Alert*, under CAPT Thomas Laugharne sped in on *Essex's* quarter and opened fire as her crew gave three cheers. Then the gunports on *Essex* flew open, and a broadside slammed into *Alert*. This was followed in rapid succession by others, and in eight minutes *Alert* surrendered, ending the first conclusive naval action of the War of 1812.

Constitution vs. Guerriere (19 August 1812)

Because enemy shot caromed off her thick bulkheads, *Constitution*, under CAPT Isaac Hull, won her nickname "Old Ironsides" in this battle. She met the British warship, *Guerriere*, about 700 miles off Boston, and in 30 minutes reduced her to a helpless wreck. CAPT Dacres, of *Guerriere*, had previously been an arrogant man, and had offered to bet a new hat that he could defeat within 15 minutes any ship the Americans could produce. Upon surrendering, he offered his sword to the victor. Hull declined it, adding, "But if you don't mind, Captain, I'll trouble you for that hat."

PSS *Wasp* vs. *Frolic* (18 October 1812)

Two days out of port CAPT Jacob Jones in USS *Wasp* sighted and chased a sloop-of-war guarding a convoy. As the vessel came about to challenge, Jones saw her break a Spanish flag, but believed her to be running under false colors, a common practice in those days. As he closed to about 60 yards range the sloop-of-war hauled down the Spanish flag, ran up a British flag, and fired a broadside. She had fired on an uproll, however, and her fire tore into *Wasp's* rigging. Jones' gunners were ready, and their broadside did tremendous damage. *Wasp* hauled off and raked her enemy effectively, then stood by to observe damage, since the heavy seas made any attempt at boarding dangerous both to ship and crew. Then the ships collided and Seaman Jack Lange, an American who had once been impressed by the British, leaped on board the other ship, cutlass in hand, followed by a few of his shipmates. All that confronted them was one wounded steersman and three British officers. *Wasp's* fire had killed or wounded more than 90 of her enemy's 110-man crew, while she had only 10 casualties herself.

United States vs. Macedonian (25 October 1812)

Off the Canary Islands *United States,* under CAPT Stephen Decatur, encountered *Macedonian,* under CAPT John S. Carden, whose crew included seven impressed American seamen. *Macedonian* opened fire first, scoring hits on the American sails, but *United States'* return volley showed her guns had a longer range. *Macedonian* then tried to utilize her superior speed to close, but had her rigging smashed and decks swept by American gunners before she could do any damage. Thirty minutes of fighting saw the battle ended. *Macedonian* had 105 casualties, while only seven of Decatur's men were killed or wounded.

Constitution vs. Java (29 December 1812)

Some 30 miles off Salvador, Brazil, the speedier *Java* was able to rake *Constitution* several times as the American ship bore down to close with her enemy. Though twice wounded, CAPT William Bainbridge directed his fire until the British ship was helpless. *Constitution* stood off to repair her battered sails, then closed again, and had maneuvered into position for raking *Java* when the British ship surrendered. *Java* had 60 killed and 170 wounded: *Constitution* had only 34 casualties.

Hornet vs. Peacock (24 February 1813)

Off the coast of South America, CAPT Stephen Lawrence's 18-gun ship encountered the 22-gun British brig, and, after maneuvering for position more than an hour, they exchanged broadsides. *Pea-*

cock's shots were high, while *Hornet's* caught her enemy in the lower rigging. Lawrence then took advantage of his own better condition, and moved to the enemy's starboard quarter. In 15 minutes *Peacock*, sinking, surrendered. The British vessel had 38 killed and wounded, including her captain, William Peake. *Hornet* lost four men, three of whom were drowned with nine *Peacock* men when the enemy ship suddenly sank during rescue operations. Three other Americans were wounded.

USS Chesapeake vs. *Shannon* (1 June 1813)

Despite the story that the American ship sailed out of Boston to answer a British challenge, CAPT Stephen Lawrence left port without ever having received the letter sent him by British CAPT Philip Broke. He did, however, sail with the knowledge he would likely have to go into battle with inexperienced officers and men. The 38-gun British frigate was far more prepared for battle. Broke had commanded *Shannon* for six years, and his crew had been with him for five. Unlike most naval officers of his day, he held daily gunnery practice, and gave a prize of tobacco to the best musket marksman.

Against such well-trained men, *Chesapeake* never had a chance.

Battle commenced about 6 P.M., and the double-shotted guns of the British did terrible damage. Marksmen in her tops shot down three *Chesapeake* helmsmen, one after another. In 15 minutes the battle was over, with CAPT Lawrence wounded fatally, and the British boarding party in control. As he was being carried below Lawrence called out, "Don't give up the ship!" Casualties in *Chesapeake* were 24 killed and 50 wounded. *Shannon* lost 47 killed and 99 wounded.

USS Argus vs. *Pelican* (14 August 1813)

In less than 10 months the 16-gun American brig *Argus* captured or destroyed 22 British ships. Under Master Commandant Arthur Sinclair she took five. The other 17 were taken by *Argus* under Master Commandant William Henry Allen.

Argus sighted *Pelican* early in the morning. The battle began at 6 A.M., Sinclair and his first lieutenant were soon wounded, and LT William Howard Allen took command. English shot quickly wrecked *Argus'* rigging and her wheel ropes; then they stood off and poured broadside after broadside into the motionless ship. LT Allen led one last attempt to board the enemy ship, but it was easily driven back and *Argus* had to surrender. *Argus* casualties totalled a fifth of her crew, while *Pelican* lost two killed and five wounded.

Enterprise vs. Boxer (5 September 1813)

Enterprise, 14 guns, engaged the 14-gun British brig off Portland, Me. In a 20-minute action the American ship received one hit to the enemy's 18. *Boxer* counted 42 casualties to 14 in *Enterprise.* The engagement was won in the first eight minutes, though the American ship did not know it. All her crew saw was that the British ship still had colors flying. After pouring shot into *Boxer* for another 12 minutes, *Enterprise* closed to hail, then found the colors were nailed in place. *Boxer* was taken into Portland, Me., by LT E. R. McCall, her second-in-command. Both commanding officers were killed in the battle.

Battle of Lake Erie (10 September 1813)

In order to stop British military operations in the upper Mississippi Valley, it was planned to cut off their communication with eastern Canada by obtaining control of the Great Lakes, Master Commandant Oliver H. Perry hurriedly built nine ships on Lake Erie—five of green timber. His opponent, CAPT Barclay, built a similar fleet of six ships. On 10 Sept. 1813, the two home-made flotillas met at the western end of the lake. On his flagship, *Lawrence,* Perry hoisted a blue flag bearing the dying words of CAPT James Lawrence, "Don't give up the ship." *Lawrence* was soon wrecked and Perry rowed in an open boat to the *Niagara* with a few survivors. He brought the rest of his ships into action then, and soon won the engagement. Perry reported the victory on the back of an old letter, saying, "We have met the enemy and they are ours— two ships, two brigs, one schooner, and one sloop." This victory regained the Michigan-Detroit territory for the United States and had a marked effect on peace negotiations.

USS Essex vs. Phoebe and Cherub (28 March 1814)

Essex, under CAPT David Porter, captured a mail packet, two schooners, and 13 whalers on a cruise that brought her into the

Pacific Ocean, first U.S. warship to enter those waters. The havoc she wrecked on the British whaling industry soon brought retaliation, and the 36-gun frigate *Phoebe,* accompanied by *Cherub,* 18-gun sloop, trapped *Essex* in the harbor of Valparaiso, Chile.

When the British ships blockaded him Porter led a surprise night boat attack on *Phoebe,* but called off the venture when he discovered that all the British seamen were waiting at their guns. After six weeks of being bottled up, Porter tried to make a dash out of the harbor but a sudden squall caried his main topmast away. Porter ran for shore and anchored, whereupon the two enemy ships took up raking positions and opened fire. After two hours and 20 minutes Captain Porter surrendered. Of 225 *Essex* men, 58 had been killed, 66 wounded, and 31 lost by drowning. *Phoebe* had four killed and seven wounded out of 300 men, while *Cherub* lost one man killed and three wounded of 121-man crew.

USS Peacock vs. Epervier (29 April 1814)

CAPT Lewis Warrington slipped his 18-gun sloop through the British blockade off New York, and cruised down the East coast before sighting an enemy sail off Florida. Both ships were prepared to fight, and sailed straight for each other without the usual formality of a preliminary hail. *Peacock* took two 32-pound shots in her fore-yard with the first exchange, but her return broadside smashed most *Epervier's* rigging and guns. *Epervier* closed for an attempt at boarding, but another broadside, plus several volleys from U.S. Marines in *Peacock,* turned her back. American casualties were two killed and two wounded; British 15 killed and 23 wounded.

This battle was hailed as a tribute to American gunnery. *Epervier* had 45 shot holes in her port side, and five feet of water in her hold when the 45-minute battle ended. *Peacock* received not one hit in her hull, and less than an hour after the engagement ended had repaired her rigging and was ready in all respects to fight again.

Cruise of USS Peacock (June 1814-June 1815)

After capturing *Epervier,* CAPT Warrington took his ship into Savannah, Ga. He was voted a gold medal by Congress, each of his officers received a silver one and each sailing-master and midshipman was awarded a sword, for the capture of *Epervier* and $125,000 in gold she had been carrying. A month later he sailed on a cruise lasting 147 days, during which *Peacock* captured or destroyed 14 British ships, valued at $493,000, and took 150 prisoners. These actions occurred in areas as far apart as Newfoundland, Portugal, North Ireland, and the West Indies.

Last Cruise and Disappearance of USS *Wasp* (May-October 1814)

This sloop, named for the ship which had captured the British *Frolic,* only to be taken with her prize that same evening by *Poictiers,* sailed from Portsmouth, N.H., on 1 May and ranged the ocean for six months against the enemy, before her mysterious disappearance. During this time she captured or sank 15 enemy ships, two of them warships, all in English waters. Eleven of her actions, in fact, were fought in the English Channel itself.

Her most notable captures were *Reindeer* (June 28) and *Avon* (1 Sept.) *Reindeer,* 21-gun sloop, was taken 19 minutes after *Wasp* opened fire. When the British captain, R. William Manners, was killed leading an attempt to board *Wasp,* his men surrendered.

MC Blakeley's crew then took a prize, *Mary,* right under the nose of the British ship-of-the-line, *Armada,* burned it, and was driven off in attempting to seize another ship *Armada* was convoying. That night *Wasp* ran down on *Avon,* a sloop of *Wasp's* size, and after exchanging broadsides with her was about to board the enemy by boat when she sighted another enemy ship closing. *Wasp* drew away, leaving *Avon* in fire and sinking.

On 9 Oct., the Spanish brig *Adonis* was hailed and boarded by men who said they were from the *Wasp.* After obtaining information as to the whereabouts of a British convoy, they returned to their ship. She set sail in the direction of the convoy, and was never seen again.

Battle of Bladensburg (near Washington, D.C., 24 August 1814)

During the War of 1812, the British sent a strong expeditionary force into Chesapeake Bay, under MAJ GEN Robert Rose, to operate with a British Squadron under VADM Sir Alexander Cochrane. The only American force in the bay was CAPT Joshua Barney's flotilla of 26 small craft manned by some 900 sailors and Marines. Barney was soon trapped in the Patuxent River and although he once repulsed the British he destroyed his boats to prevent their capture. On 23 Aug., the British began to march towards Washington. A force of about 7,000 troops under BRIG GEN Winder made a small show of resistance against this force at Bladensburg, then retreated in panic. Barney, with a couple of hundred sailors, had been joined by CAPT Samuel Miller from the Marine Barracks in Washington with a hundred Marines; this small force reached the battlefield at Bladensburg just as Winder's army began to withdraw. Three times they repulsed the superior British forces before they were flanked on both sides. Both Barney and Miller were wounded; they ordered their men to withdraw and remained behind, where they were captured by the British. With no one to stop their movements, the British marched on into Washington and set fire to several buildings, then returned to their ships.

Attack on Baratharia, Gulf of Mexico (11 September–1 October 1814)

With the U.S. Navy arrayed against the British fleet during the War of 1812, pirates in the Gulf of Mexico had grown increasingly bolder. Finally a squadron of two schooners (USS *Carolina* and *Seahorse*), six gunboats, and one launch moved out from New Orleans to attack the island of Barataria, where the pirates maintained headquarters. Though the pirate force numbered about 1,000 men of assorted nationalities, they burned several of their armed ships and fled as soon as the naval squadron appeared. COMO Patterson bombarded the pirate ships, captured 11 of them, and landed a force of soldiers and Marines to destroy the fort and village. The captured craft were taken back to New Orleans.

Second Battle of Lake Champlain (11 September 1814)

In the latter part of the War of 1812, a British army of 11,000 men advanced into northern New York from Canada, relying on supplies transported from Canada by water over Lake Champlain. The British attempted a combined land-sea attack on Plattsburg, and MC Thomas Macdonough, USN, defended the town from waterborne attack with four sailing ships, and 10 galleys, having a total of 86 guns. Opposing him, CDR Downie had four ships and 12 galleys, with a total of 92 guns. Macdonough's force was inferior, so he anchored his ships in such a position that the ends of his battle line were protected by harbor headlands, forcing British ships to attack head on, thus being able to use only a few guns at a time. The British ships suffered heavily in approaching, and finally anchored about 500 yards from the U.S. fleet. The battle was fought at this range in smooth water.

It lasted two and one-half hours and ended in capture of the entire British squadron. The loss of Lake Champlain deprived the British army of means for obtaining supplies from Canada, and it was forced to make a hasty retreat. (This is one of the few instances in history where ships at anchor won a battle.)

Capture of USS *President* (15 January 1815)

Hoping to escape southward through the British blockade and raid enemy shipping in the East Indies. CAPT Stephen Decatur headed his 44-gun frigate *President* out of New York. The pilot, lacking beacon lights, ran her aground, and Decatur wanted to return to harbor, but adverse wind conditions prevented this. He forced her over a sand bar and put to sea, next day meeting up with the three-ship blockading squadron.

His damaged ship had no hope of escaping, so Decatur pointed a cannon into *President's* hold, set a watch on it, then swiftly turned, planning to capture the leading British ship by boarding, scuttle *President*, and run for New York harbor. As he wore around, however, *Endymion*, 40 guns, retreated. *President* finally ran down on her at dusk and fired four broadsides that crippled the Englishman.

Decatur then decided to run for New York harbor, but British reinforcements arrived. *Majestic, Pomone,* and *Tenedos* outran *President* and positioned themselves so as to keep her continually under fire. After 24 of his men had been killed, and 56 wounded, CAPT Decatur surrendered. Upon surrendering his sword to CAPT John Hayes, senior British officer present, it was returned to him with an expression of praise for "an officer who defended his ship so proudly."

USS *Hornet* vs. *Penguin* (23 March 1815)

MC James Biddle sailed his 20-gun sloop *Hornet* from New York on 23 Jan. 1815, not knowing peace had been earlier attained in London by American emissaries. The British 19-gun brig *Penguin* knew nothing of this either. Upon sighting the British ship Biddle slowed down, waiting for her to come up, while *Penguin,* afraid her adversary would recognize her as a warship and run away, kept to a bow-on approach. At about 1:40 P.M. *Penguin* was near enough to join battle. She hauled up her colors and fired a broadside, which *Hornet* answered immediately. In the ensuing action *Hornet* shot up *Penguin's* rigging badly, *Penguin* closed, and fouled her bowsprit in *Hornet's* rigging, but for some reason made no attempt to board. Biddle, realizing he had the sailing advantage, refused to let his men leap to the enemy ship. A swell carried the ships apart, and *Penguin's* foremast tore loose, falling over her port guns so that they could not be used. Biddle asked if she had struck, whereupon two English seamen fired, wounding him through the neck. They were immediately shot down by U.S. marines, and Biddle's officers had difficulty restraining *Hornet's* men from slaughtering the entire enemy crew.

The action was over in 22 minutes. *Hornet* lost one man killed, and 11 wounded, while *Penguin's* casualties were 10 dead and 28 wounded.

Capture of Algerian *Mashouda* and *Estedio* (17 June and 19 June 1815)

During the War of 1812 the U.S. continued paying tribute to the Mediterranean pirates. When the Dey of Algiers sent a ransom note for the captain and crew of the American merchantman *Edwin* in 1815, however, President Madison decided this matter had to be cleared up once and for all. On 20 May, COMO Stephen Decatur sailed for the Mediterranean in his flagship *Guerriere,* in command of a squadron composed of *Constellation, Macedonian, Epervier, Ontario, Firefly, Spark, Flambeau, Torch,* and *Spitfire.*

After stopping at Gibraltar, where he learned the Algerians had ships out in force, Decatur entered the Mediterranean. *Mashouda* was spotted first. Cut off from Algeria, she tried to run for a neutral Spanish port. *Constellation* first led the chase, then *Ontario. Guerriere,* and *Epervier* forced *Mashouda's* surrender. Only one American had been killed and three wounded by enemy fire, while *Mashouda* lost 30 killed and 406 taken prisoner, including many wounded.

Two days later the pirate brig *Estedio* was sighted and ran immediately into shallow water where the frigates could not follow, but *Epervier, Spark, Torch,* and *Spitfire* forced her aground whereupon some of the corsairs escaped by boat. A few broadsides brought surrender, with 80 prisoners taken and 30 wounded found on the brig's decks.

Nine days later Decatur was off Algiers, demanding an indemnity from the Dey. News of these two ship captures, as related by *Mashouda's* first officer, convinced the Dey that peace with America, at any price, was worthwhile.

USS *Peacock* vs. *Nautilus* (30 June 1815)

Having received no word of the peace treaty, *Peacock* was cruising in the Indian Ocean against British commerce when she encountered the 14-gun brig *Nautilus*. On coming within hail, British LT Charles Boyce, commanding *Nautilus,* asked *Peacock* if she had heard of the peace treaty being signed. CAPT Lewis Warrington, in *Peacock,* suspected an enemy trick to escape, and demanded that the brig surrender, firing one gun when surrender was not forthcoming. *Nautilus* answered with a broadside, and the battle was on. *Peacock* returned the fire, killing six and wounding eight British crewmen, and *Nautilus* struck her colors. No one was wounded or killed in the American ship.

After the surrender, when the rumor of peace was confirmed as fact, Warrington carefully repaired damage to *Nautilus* and returned her to the British.

Attack Against Pirates at Qualla Battoo, Sumatra (6 February 1832)

On 7 Feb. 1831, Malay pirates at Qualla Battoo, Sumatra, raided and seized the American merchantman *Friendship,* killing three of her crew and wounding three others. *Friendship's* captain escaped by rowing 25 miles in one of the ship's boats to another port, where several American merchantmen were anchored.

That summer word of the affair reached Washington, and President Andrew Jackson, upon learning that such attacks had been made for over 40 years by the Sumatran pirates without the United States seeking reprisal, ordered USS *Potomac,* under CAPT John Downes, to the island.

Upon arrival off Qualla Battoo, CAPT Downes landed a party of sailors and marines which attacked four pirate forts. These were taken after severe fighting, during which two Americans were killed and 11 wounded. More than 150 Malays died in the battle, including Po Mohamoet, a local rajah who had led the attack on *Friendship,* and on the following day CAPT Downes moved closer to shore and fired a broadside into a fifth fort, which his landing party had not been able to reach. Shortly thereafter a party of emissaries, representing all the local rulers, came out to the ship, bearing gifts, and promised no more attacks would be made.

Attack on Pirates at Quallua Battoo, Sumatra (1 January 1839)

While at the Portuguese colony of Goa, in the Indian Ocean, COMO George C. Read learned that Malayan pirates had robbed and murdered the master of the American merchantman *Eclipse,* and wounded several of her crew. He sailed for Qualla Battoo in USS *Columbia,* 44 guns, in company with USS *John Adams,* 18 guns, and, after local authorities delayed producing the parties guilty of the atrocity, decided to take retaliatory action. A party of 320 seamen and marines were landed under CDR Thomas W. Wyman of *John Adams,* while both ships kept a steady fire pouring into the town, which lay on a peninsula. Dwellings of the local leaders, together with five forts, were destroyed, as well as 22 cannon. As a result of the attack the local Rajah agreed to pay $2,000 indemnity to the owners of *Eclipse,* and nearby rulers made haste to assure COMO Read their subjects would not prey on American commerce again.

Siege and Capture of Vera Cruz, Mexico (9-29 March 1847)

American strategy called for capturing the capital city of Mexico as a means for ending the war, so accordingly plans were made to land troops at Vera Cruz, on the eastern coast, for a march inland. Ships of the amphibious attack force rendezvoused at Anton Lizardo, some distance north of Vera Cruz. There troops were moved from their transports into warships which steamed to Collardo, about three miles from the city to be attacked.

USS *Spitfire* and *Vixen* (steamers) together with *Bonita, Reefer, Petrel, Falcon,* and *Tampico* (schooners) then moved out to bombard the city walls from seaward. On the 24th, some 1,200 seamen and marines were with GEN Winfield Scott's army and on the 26th overtures of surrender came from the Mexican commanders. The city surrendered on the 27th, and was occupied on the 29th.

COMO Matthew C. Perry commanded the U.S. Naval forces throughout the first part of the siege; was relieved by COMO David Conner.

Attack Against Forts of Canton, China (16-22 November 1856)

When hostilities broke out between the British and Chinese at Canton, CDR Andrew H. Foote, USN, at the request of the American consul at Canton, sent 81 seamen and marines from USS *Portsmouth* ashore to protect American lives and property. These were later reinforced by 69 men from USS *Levant*.

COMO James Armstrong, upon hearing of Foote's action, decided not to compromise America's neutrality, and ordered all forces evacuated except for one ship, which was to stand by and protect Americans in case of fighting. As USS *Portsmouth* moved to carry out these orders she was fired upon and hit five times by Chinese forts at Canton. *Portsmouth* returned the fire, then all exchanges ceased for some time. Thinking the Chinese no longer hostile, Armstrong decided to inquire of the Imperial Commissioner the reason for the firing, and while so doing learned the forts were being reinforced and strengthened. He told Foote to take what action was necessary to render the forts harmless.

Levant, San Jacinto, and *Portsmouth* moved in, took the forts under fire, and landed sailors and marines to storm them. In two days of fighting the shore party captured all four forts, together with 176 guns. American losses were seven killed and 22 wounded, while Chinese casualties were more than 400 men.

Battle of Hampton Roads (8 March 1862)

On 8 Mar. 1862, the Confederate ship *Virginia* under CAPT Franklin Buchanan, CSN, left Norfolk and proceeded to attack Union wooden ships at Hampton Roads. This ship was the former USS *Merrimac,* rebuilt by Confederate forces as an ironclad after they captured the Norfolk Navy Yard. Uninjured by heavy fire from Union ships and shore batteries, *Virginia* rammed and sunk USS *Cumberland,* anchored under the protection of batteries at Newport News Point. Then, accompanied by two gunboats, *Virginia* attacked USS *Congress,* which ran aground and was forced to surrender. Buchanan destroyed *Congress* with red hot shot, and started to attack the other Union ships, but a falling tide forced him to

return to Norfolk. Union ships had 250 men killed in this battle
while Confederate casualties were 21 killed or wounded. In *Virginia*
only two men were killed and the ship itself was uninjured. CAPT
Buchanan was wounded by a musketball.

Battle Between USS *Monitor* and CSS *Virginia* (9 March 1862)

On 25 Oct. 1861, the Union commenced building the ironclad
USS *Monitor* to match the *Virginia*. It was built in 100 days by a
private firm in Long Island; after plans by John Ericsson. It was
an iron-plated raft on which were mounted an iron conning tower
and a revolving iron turret containing two guns. The night of 8
Mar. 1862, *Monitor* arrived in Hampton Roads, after having nearly
sunk in the open sea on the way south. On 9 Mar., *Virginia*, under
LT Thomas Catesby Jones, returned to Hampton Roads to complete destruction of the Union ships. She was met by the *Monitor*,
LT James L. Worden commanding, midway between Newport
News Point and Ft. Monroe. The battle lasted four hours, neither
ship lost a man, although minor injuries were caused by splinters
and concussion. Finally an exhausted crew and a falling tide forced
Virginia to return to Norfolk. The Union ships had been saved and
the Union blockade remained unbroken. The battle was never re-
newed: each side was afraid to risk its only ironclad in another
battle. The Confederates destroyed *Virginia* when they abandoned
Norfolk later, and *Monitor* foundered at sea while being towed to
Charleston, S.C.

Capture of New Orleans (29 April 1862)

CAPT David G. Farragut in USS *Hartford*, with a fleet of 16
ships and a mortar flotilla, was sent to capture New Orleans. The
Confederates had as defenses two powerful forts 80 miles down-
stream from the city, 13 gunboats, and two ironclad rams. In addi-
tion there was an obstruction of iron chains, logs, and hulks of
vessels stretched across the river between the forts. Farragut took
two weeks to get his deep draft ships across the bars at the mouth of
the Mississippi River. Then his mortar boats bombarded the forts
for six days and nights, and two gunboats cut an opening in the
obstruction between the forts. At 2 A.M., 24 Apr., Farragut ordered
his fleet to get underway and pass the forts. Ships were trimmed
by the bow to prevent their swinging around in the current if they

grounded. Anchor chains protected their sides; coal bags and hammocks padded their boilers. A heavy bombardment by mortar boats was used to keep down fire from the forts in accordance with Farragut's principle that "the best protection against the enemy's fire is a well directed fire from our own guns." *Hartford* grounded under the guns of the forts and was set on fire by a Confederate fire raft. CAPT Thomas T. Craven, in *Brooklyn,* fouled the obstruction, but finally got clear and stood by *Hartford* until she put out her fires and got afloat again. After passing the forts, the fleet defeated the Confederate ships and sailed upstream to New Orleans, The city surrendered shortly after the fleet arrived, and the forts followed suit. This capture of the South's largest city closed the mouth of the Mississippi to Confederate shipping.

USS *Essex* vs. CSS *Arkansas* (6 August 1862)

Though U.S. forces held New Orleans, thus controlling the mouth of the Mississippi River, the Confederate river defense fleet made passage upriver to Vicksburg a hazardous prospect. CSS *Arkansas,* only Confederate ironclad on the river at that time, posed the most dangerous threat. The Confederates believed she could rid the water around Baton Rouge, La., of all Union vessels. On 5 Aug., Confederate troops attacked Union troops at Baton Rouge, but were driven off, thanks to an attack on their flank by USS *Kineo* and *Katahdin.* The next day, smoke from an approaching Confederate vessel was sighted, and *Essex,* under CDR William D. Porter, stood out with *Cayuga* and *Sumter* to meet her. *Essex* first sighted *Arkansas,* and opened fire at once, following up her first shots with incendiary shells until *Arkansas* burst into flames. The Confederate crew tried to moor their craft to the shore, but were driven off by *Essex. Arkansas* drifted out to mid-stream, blew up and sank.

USS *Hatteras* vs. CSS *Alabama* (11 January 1863)

After Galveston, Tex., was recaptured by Confederates, RADM David G. Farragut sent CAPT Henry H. Bell, in USS *Brooklyn,* with six other gunboats, to retake the city. Off the Texas coast a sail was sighted and USS *Hatteras,* CAPT Homer C. Blake, challenged the ship. The stranger was CSS *Alabama,* CAPT Raphael Semmes, CSN, though she answered the hail as "Her Majesty's steamer *Vixen!*" When Blake lowered a boat to investigate *Alabama* opened up with a broadside at 100 yards range. *Hatteras* started sinking almost at once, and *Alabama* picked up the Union crew out of the water, then steamed away before the rest of the Union squadron arrived. Though *Hatteras* was hopelessly outmatched, this sinking "of a U.S. warship" enhanced *Alabama's* reputation abroad.

USS Wachusett vs. CSS Florida (7 October 1864)

The Confederate raider had captured or destroyed 37 U.S. ships by the time she entered the harbor at Bahia, Brazil, to find USS *Wachusett*, under CDR Napoleon Collins moored there. CAPT Charles Morris, CSN, feeling *Wachusett* would not dare violate Brazilian neutrality, calmly went about provisioning and fueling his ship.

CDR Collins considered the possible violation of neutrality and the trouble it would cause, then decided that the Confederate raider had to be destroyed at any price. When darkness fell he got underway and rammed *Florida,* hoping to sink her. The collision brought down *Florida's* mainyard and mizzenmast, *Wachusett* opened up with small arms fire and three broadsides, whereupon 69 *Florida* crewmen surrendered. *Wachusett* then towed the prize to sea, though fired upon three times by Brazilians enroute.

The U.S. government apologized to Brazil, and acceded to the South American republic's demands that *Florida,* with all her crew, be returned to Bahia. Moored at Newport News, *Florida* sank at her moorings before this could be done. American sailors and citizens did not inquire too closely into reasons for the sinking, and *Florida* sat out the war in 10 fathoms of water.

Sinking of CSS Albemarle (27-28 October 1864)

The Confederate ram had helped capture the town of Plymouth, N.C., and had sunk USS *Southfield.* She was a constant threat to U.S. operations in Albermarle Sound, and the possibility of her emerging from Roanoke River and attacking blockaders kept some U.S. warships tied up in North Carolina waters. It was decided to sink her by whatever means were available, and LT William B. Cushing, USN, devised a plan and volunteered to head an expedition upriver.

On the night of the 27th, with 13 men in a small steamer, he steered into the river. He made a run for the ram, crashing over a log boom rigged about it for protection. Then he lowered a spar to which was attached a "torpedo," and by pulling a line, detonated its charge. *Albemarle,* holed, sank at her moorings. Cushing and his men, unable to stand against the rifle fire from *Albemarle's* crew, dived overboard and swam for their lives. All but two men survived the engagement. Cushing was spot-promoted for his exploit.

USS *Housatonic* vs. CSS *Hunley* (17 February 1864)

The new steam sloop *Housatonic* was moored off Charleston, N.C., when *Hunley* attacked her. *Hunley* was a 25-foot submarine, armed with a spar torpedo, which had sunk five times previously in tests, and drowned five crews. At about 9 P.M., her skipper, infantry LT G. E. Dixon, CSA, steered his craft to within 100 yards of *Housatonic* before he was discovered. *Housatonic* tried to back away from the approaching Confederate, but before her engines could respond Dixon ran into her and detonated his torpedo. Both craft went down. All of *Hunley's* crew perished. For the first time in history a submarine had sunk a warship in combat.

USS *Kearsarge* vs. CSS *Alabama* (19 June 1864)

Alabama was a British-built ship sold to the Confederacy and fitted out as a commerce raider in the Azores, in violation of Portugals' neutrality. Under CAPT Raphael Semmes, CSN, she burned 57 Union merchantmen and captured many more. While she was at Cherbourg, France, for refueling and overhaul, CAPT John A. Winslow, USN, arrived off that port in USS *Kearsarge.* Semmes had everything to lose and nothing to gain by a battle. The French, anxious to see a naval engagement, told him the presence of the *Kearsarge* off the port was a challenge no man of honor could refuse. Yielding to public opinion, Semmes agreed to take his ship to fight on a Sunday morning. The railroads ran special excursions from Paris, and on 19 June 1864, the bluffs near the city were covered with spectators. *Alabama* was accompanied from the harbor by a French man-of-war, to insure the battle took place outside the three-mile limit, and by the English yacht *Deerhound* whose owner wanted a good view of the engagement. The battle took place seven miles offshore and was rapidly being won by *Kearsarge* when Semmes ran for safety inside the three mile limit. *Kearsarge* cut between him and the shore, forcing him to surrender. *Alabama* sank before her crew could be removed to *Kearsarge*. *Deerhound* helped rescue the Confederate crew, and took Semmes and some of his men back to England. After the war, England paid 16 million dollars to the United States as damages for the part which she took in fitting out this and other Confederate commerce raiders.

Battle of Mobile Bay (5 August 1864)

The defense of Mobile consisted of three forts at the entrance to the bay, a triple line of "torpedoes" (mines) in the channel, three gunboats, and the ironclad ram *Tennessee,* commanded by ADM Franklin Buchanan, who had previously commanded the CSS *Virginia* (see Battle of Hampton Roads). On 5 Aug. 1864, ADM David G. Farragut in *Hartford,* with four ironclads and 14 wooden ships, attacked these defenses. His leading ship, *Tecumseh,* under CDR Thomas A. M. Craven, hit a torpedo and sank. The ships immediately astern of *Tecumseh* stopped and backed, while the remaining ships continued up channel. The fleet was in danger of becoming hopelessly entangled under the guns of Fort Morgan. When Farragut was informed that torpedoes were holding things up, he shouted, "Damn the torpedoes!" and ordered *Hartford* to make full speed. The other ships followed him and all passed safely into the bay. The Confederate vessels were defeated, though two escaped to the protection of the fort. Later *Tennessee* returned and engaged the entire Union fleet, but finally had to surrender after her steering gear was disabled, some of her gun ports jammed shut, and her armor began to fall off. The Confederate forts were captured later by combined land-sea attacks, and the Union blockade of Confederate Gulf ports was complete.

Battle of Manila Bay (1 May 1898)

Spanish forces in the Orient consisted of a fleet under ADM Montojo, an army in the Philippines, and fortifications in Manila Bay. COMO George Dewey in *Olympia,* with five other warships and several auxiliaries, was ordered to destroy the Spanish ships. Manila Bay was supposed to be mined and its entrance strongly fortified. On the night of 30 Apr., Dewey's squadron entered Manila Bay, with no opposition other than a few wild shots from a shore battery. Daylight of 1 May 1898, showed the Spanish fleet of nine ships (somewhat smaller than the American ships) anchored under the protection of shore batteries at Cavite, about seven miles from Manila. The Spanish ships opened fire at long range. Dewey held his fire for almost half an hour, until his ships were in the formation he desired. Then he turned to the captain of *Olympia* and said, "You may fire when you are ready, Gridley." During the battle all Spanish ships remained at anchor, but Dewey kept his ships underway. At 7:30 A.M. the American ships withdrew to replenish ammunition and to give their crews breakfast. Then Dewey returned to the battle, sinking all Spanish ships and silencing the shore batteries in short order. The American casualties numbered six; Spanish 381.

Sinking of Collier *Merrimac* in Santiago Harbor, Cuba (3 June 1898)

The Spanish fleet had entered Santiago Harbor, and RADM William T. Sampson, USN, wanted it trapped there. Naval Constructor Richard P. Hobson proposed rigging the collier *Merrimac* with explosives, then sinking her at the harbor's narrow entrance. At night, with seven volunteers, he maneuvered *Merrimac* toward the desired position, but was sighted by Spanish shore batteries, whose aim was so poor that 14 Spanish were hit by their own crossfire, while no American sailors were injured. *Merrimac* was damaged enough so Hobson could not swing her about to sink in the channel. The Americans scuttled *Merrimac,* took to a raft, and were captured by Spaniards. While the attempt was unsuccessful, it has been credited with alarming ADM Cervera so that, still fearing permanent blockade a month later, he sailed forth with his fleet to complete destruction.

Battle of Santiago (3 July 1898)

Santiago, Cuba, was held by the Spanish Army. A Spanish fleet of four cruisers and two destroyers under ADM Cervera was anchored in the harbor. The city was besieged by American troops and the harbor blockaded by ADM W. T. Sampson with four battleships, two armored cruisers, and a converted yacht. On 1 July Cervera was ordered by CAPT GEN Blanco at Havana to take the first opportunity to get out of the harbor with all his ships. Although Cervera had a very inferior force and was almost out of coal, he gallantly attempted to carry out his orders. At 9:30 A.M., 3 July 1898, he left the harbor and headed west. In a running fight along the coast, the Spanish ships were sunk one by one or forced ashore in flames. The last ship surrendered at 1:20 P.M. Seeing the Spanish ships burning, the crew of USS *Texas* cheered, but CAPT John Philip called out, "Don't cheer, boys. Those poor fellows are dying!" The Spanish lost about 350 killed and 150 wounded. The Americans had one man killed and two wounded.

World War I The Navy had no major engagements.

World War II

Pearl Harbor (7 December 1941) (See *Calendar*)

Wake Island (8-23 December 1941)

This small atoll, some 2,000 miles west of Hawaii, of no use as a harbor but a highly important location for an air base, was defended by a group of 388 Marines under MAJ James P. S. Devereux. They had 12 Grumman Wildcats and some 3-inch antiaircraft guns. Only other military men on the island were about 75 Navy and Army personnel, all unarmed, under CDR Winfield S. Cunningham, the island commander. The island also had 1,200 civilian workers. The Japanese hit Wake Island on 8 Dec.; with no radar warning, eight Marine planes were caught on the ground and six of them destroyed. Air raids continued for three days, and on 11 Dec. the first Japanese surface attack was made, with troop transports supported by nine combatant ships. The Marines sank two destroyers, damaged three destroyers and three other ships. Before the second attack, Wake was pounded by both land and carrier-based air strikes, but the Marines bravely held out for almost two more weeks. Finally, on 23 Dec., in the face of overwhelming odds, the valiant defenders of Wake Island surrendered to the Japanese.

Battle of Balikpapan (24 January 1942)

During the Japanese campaign against Borneo, the U.S. submarine *Sturgeon* sighted a convoy heading heading for the oil center of Balikpapan. When the cruisers *Boise* and *Marblehead* were prevented from entering action, due to grounding and engine trouble, respectively, four U.S. destroyers: *Ford, Pope, Paul Jones* and *Parrot,* aided by Netherlands pilots who dropped bombs to silhouette shipping targets, raced into Balikpapan Bay at 27 knots and fired torpedoes. This was followed up by gunfire from the U.S. ships. Four Japanese transports and one patrol craft were sunk before the destroyers retired at high speed.

This was a tactical victory only, as it did not slow the Japanese advance.

Battle of Badoeng Strait (19-20 February 1942)

In an attempt to smash the Japanese invasion force in Bali, an American-Dutch force of cruisers and destroyers made an attack on the enemy transport force in Badoeng Strait. RADM Karel Doorman, Netherlands Navy, commanding the Allied forces, decided upon a three-wave attack. Allied ships in the first wave were the Dutch cruisers *De Ruyter* and *Java,* Dutch destroyer *Piet Hein,* and the U.S. destroyers *Ford* and *Pope.* They attacked late at night on 19 Feb., with a bombardment-torpedo run, damaging one Japanese transport in a melee that saw two Japanese destroyers firing on one another in the confusion. The second wave, consisting of Netherlands cruiser *Tromp* and U.S. destroyers *Parrott, Pillsbury, Stewart,* and *Edwards,* did little damage, and the third wave, a group of Dutch motor torpedo boats, reported seeing nothing at all in their attack. The Allied attack, during which *Piet Hein* was lost, failed.

Battle of Java Sea (27 February 1942)

This was an Allied attempt to stop the Japanese invasion of Java, but the Allies suffered from early loss of USS *Langley* and its deckload of planes in a Japanese air attack. Under ADM Doorman, five cruisers and 11 destroyers steamed against a convoy of 40 Japanese transports escorted by cruisers and destroyers, protected by air cover. The Allied fleet was decimated, losing the Dutch cruisers *Java* and *De Ruyter,* the British destroyers *Electra* and *Jupiter,* and the Netherlands destroyer *Kortenauer.* Difficulty in communications played a large part in the defeat of the Allies, for they were not greatly outmatched by the enemy ships. The Japanese had one destroyer damaged. The invasion of Bali continued.

Battle of Sunda Strait (28 February-1 March 1942)

While steaming from Tanjong Priok, Batavia, to Tjilatjap, Java, for rendezvous with the remnants of the American-British-Dutch-Australian naval forces, USS *Houston* and HMS *Perth* were sighted shortly before midnight by the Japanese destroyer *Fubuki* near Banten Bay. The Allied ships, sighting a Japanese transport concentration in Banten Bay, made an attack on it. They knocked out four Japanese transports in a high-speed firing run, but upon turning out of the Bay were met by the Japenese cruiser *Natori* and 10 destroyers. These made repeated attacks on the Allied cruisers, and five minutes after midnight *Perth* sank. Then two more Japanese cruisers joined the fight against *Houston,* which went down 40 minutes later.

Air Attack on Tokyo, Japan (18 April 1942)

Sixteen B-25 "Mitchell" Army bombers were taken on board USS *Hornet,* which then steamed to a point about 650 miles off Japan before launching a strike led by LT COL James H. Doolittle, USAAF. Thirteen of the planes attacked Tokyo, while one each struck Nagoya, Osaka, and Kobe with incendiary bombs. Of the 80 aircrewmen, 71 survived. Three of the nine lost flyers were beheaded by the Japanese.

Battle of the Coral Sea (4-8 May 1942)

History's first great naval air action took place when the Japanese attempted to seize Port Moresby, New Guinea, key base in their plan to dominate the waters around Australia. On 4 May, U.S. carrier planes flew strikes against Japanese on Tulagi. On 5 May Japanese planes bombed Port Moresby. On 6 May Army planes from Guadalcanal discovered one of the three Japanese naval forces, but horizontal bombing proved ineffective. On 7 May, having mistaken the tanker *Neosho* and destroyer *Sims* for a carrier and cruiser, the Japanese launched a full air strike which sank both. That same day *Lexington* and *Yorktown* planes sank the carrier *Shoho.* On 8 May Japanese carriers *Shokaku* and *Zuikaku* were damaged. USS *Lexington,* damaged by the enemy and on fire, was sunk by U.S. forces. Though U.S. losses were comparatively heavy, the Japanese southern thrust had been stopped.

Battle of Midway (4-6 June 1942)

To commit the U.S. fleet to a major action, Japan decided to attack Midway Island.

The attacking Japanese ships were located, and land-based bombers and fighters attacked them, with practically no effect. Torpedo bombers from *Yorktown* and *Enterprise* also failed to stop the Japanese advance. Then U.S. carrier dive bombers turned the tide of battle, hitting the carriers *Akagi, Kaga,* and *Soryu,* all of which sank. As the Japanese fleet retreated it also lost the cruiser *Mikuma.* Later, the Japanese carrier *Hiryu* was dive-bombed and sunk. American losses were the carrier *Yorktown* and destroyer *Hammann.* Midway, the turning point of the Pacific War, was the last truly offensive thrust made by the Japanese.

Landings on Guadalcanal (7 August 1942)

The first U.S. land offensive in World War II began when Marines stormed ashore in the Solomons Islands. Bases were needed here to protect U.S. supply lines to Australia, and also as a starting point for further operations aimed eventually at the heart of the Japanese empire.

Under cover of bad weather, U.S. and Australian ships moved up from the south and landed 11,000 U.S. Marines on Guadalcanal early on 7 Aug. Within 36 hours the Japanese airfield had been taken and the battle for the Solomons was on. In the next four months six major naval engagements were fought in the area. Six months passed before the islands were secured.

Battle of Savo Island (9 August 1942)

The first naval battle off Guadalcanal resulted in a U.S. defeat. A Japanese task force of seven cruisers and one destroyer raced into "Ironbottom Bay" between Guadalcanal and Florida islands, shortly after midnight in a brilliantly executed attack, which achieved complete surprise. U.S. cruisers *Quincy, Vincennes,* and *Astoria* and the Australian cruiser *Canberra* were sunk; Japanese forces escaped practically unscathed.

Battle of the Eastern Solomons (24-25 August 1942)

After an early defeat in attempting to reinforce its garrison on Guadalcanal, the Japanese tried another, this time massing naval support in order to keep Allied forces ashore and afloat occupied long enough for Japanese troops to gain a foothold on the island. A "bait" group, sent to divert main American strength, was discovered and attacked, and the Japanese carrier *Ryujo* was sunk.

Then an air strike was made against the U.S. carriers. *Enterprise* and *North Carolina* suffered damage, and Marines on Guadalcanal were frequently shelled and bombed, but Army, Navy, and Marine pilots teamed up to destroy enough Japanese aircraft to force their retirement.

Battle of Cape Esperance (11-12 October 1942)

Knowing that a U.S. move to reinforce Marines on Guadalcanal would arouse the Japanese to oppose it, plans were made to smash any enemy opposition to such a landing. Troop transports were sent into Guadalcanal waters, then a U.S. force of four cruisers and five destroyers intercepted a charging Japanese force of three cruisers and eight destroyers off Cape Esperance, near Savo Island. In the action, which commenced about midnight of 11 Oct. and continued the following day, the Japanese heavy cruiser *Furutaka* and destroyers *Fubuki, Natsugumo,* and *Murakumo* were sunk.

Battle of Santa Cruz Islands (26 October 1942)

Another Japanese attempt to smash U.S. naval strength and to win control of the waters around Guadalcanal resulted in this battle. USS *Hornet,* aircraft carrier, and USS *Porter,* destroyer, were sunk. American planes severely damaged the Japanese task force. The battle gained more time for U.S. forces to reinforce Guadalcanal. Japanese air strength in the area was greatly reduced, a change that was to show its effect in later battles.

Invasion of North Africa (8 November 1942)

The decision to invade North Africa was based on the assumption that Germany might otherwise end up in control of Africa's western coast, an ominous threat to the Western Hemisphere. Too, a base of operations was needed for a later attack against southern Europe. The three main objectives were Casablanca, Algiers, and Oran.

The U.S. Navy saw most of its action around Casablanca, making landings at Fydala, Safi, and near Port Lyautey. French resistance was fierce but short. The transport *Leedstown* was sunk by German submarine and air attack before the French agreed to an armistice on 11 Nov. Offensive land operations forced German troops out of Africa within a few months.

Naval Battle of Guadalcanal (12-15 November 1942)

Up until this point the Guadalcanal campaign had practically become a stalemate, with neither side able to deal the other a blow serious enough to affect the outcome. In the space of four days, however, the Japanese forces were severely damaged.

The battle began with the 12 Nov. enemy air attack on American transports. In a surface engagement the next day two U.S. cruisers and four destroyers were sunk before the Japanese retreated. On 14 Nov., U.S. motor torpedo boats attacked a Japanese bombardment force, and land-based aircraft followed up later. About midnight on 14 Nov., U.S. battleships and destroyers attacked and drove off a Japanese surface force.

The Japanese lost three battleships, one cruiser, 11 transports, and five destroyers. U.S. losses were two cruisers and seven destroyers. Japan's serious losses weakened enemy ability to reinforce the Guadalcanal garrison. The U.S. had finally become strong enough to shift from the defensive to the offensive in this campaign.

Battle of Tassafaronga (30 November 1942)

This was a night action in which a U.S. force of five cruisers and four destroyers intercepted a Japanese force of eight destroyers carrying reinforcements to Guadalcanal. In a brilliantly-executed torpedo attack the Japanese crippled the U.S. cruisers *Pensacola, Northampton, New Orleans,* and *Minneapolis* but lost the destroyer *Takanami. Northampton* sank the next day. No reinforcements were landed. The Japanese had dealt out a sharp lesson in light warship tactics, from which U.S. forces profited in later battles.

Battle of Bennell Island (29-30 January 1943)

Intelligence reports showed that the Japanese were massing large groups of ships at Rabaul, Buin, and Ontong, Java. This force was designated to evacuate the garrison from Guadalcnal but U.S. leaders, assuming that the enemy intended to continue fighting for the Solomons, interpreted it as another attempt at reinforcement. U.S. transports hurrying more troops to reinforce those already on Guadalcanal, and those escorting cruiser and destroyer forces, were attacked by Japanese aircraft at night, and although the transports escaped one destroyer was damaged and the cruiser *Chicago* was sunk.

Battle of the Bismarck Sea (2-5 March 1943)

The Bismarcks were a barrier to Allied advances on the Philippines and Japanese island chains. Allied forces were progressing on New Guinea, and the Japanese wanted to land a force that would stop any drive toward Lae. A convoy of 16 transports and destroyers was dispatched to do the job. These were bombed by U.S. Army and Australian aircraft, with PT-boats sweeping in to finish off cripples. All the Japanese transports and half the destroyers were sunk, more than 3,000 Japanese soldiers lost, and 20-30 enemy planes shot down, at a cost of five Allied aircraft.

Battle of the Komandorski Islands (26 March 1943)

This was a surface engagement. Neither side had the assistance of aircraft or submarines. The U.S. force of two cruisers and four destroyers located a Japanese force of four cruisers and five destroyers, which was escorting transports filled with reinforcements for the Japanese garrison on Attu, in the Aleutians. Both sides suffered damage in the four-hour battle but no ships were sunk. The Japanese force retired without making a landing.

Battle of Kula Gulf (6 July 1943)

After the Allies had landed on New Georgia in their march up the Solomons Islands chain, the Japanese made an attempt to land reinforcements with 10 destroyers. These were met by three U.S. cruisers and four destroyers in Kula Gulf, near Kolombangara. Some of the Japanese reinforcements got ashore, but destroyers *Niizuki* and *Nagatsuki* were lost. The USS *Helena* was sunk by Japanese torpedo attack.

Invasion of Sicily (10 July 1943)

As a prelude to invasion of Italy and a thrust at "the soft underbelly of Europe," an amphibious assault was made on this island. Allied naval forces practically ringed the island on three sides, with the U.S. Navy assigned to cover the landings at Gela, Licata, and Scoglitti. Under cover of a heavy naval bombardment, Army troops landed and in 38 days secured the island.

Battle of Kolombangara (13 July 1943)

An Allied force of 13 cruisers and destroyers intercepted a Japanese reinforcement attempt near where the Battle of Kula Gulf had been fought. The Japanese force of about a dozen ships was discovered at night. In the ensuing action the U.S. destroyer *Gwin* was torpedoed and later scuttled, the Japanese cruiser *Jintsu* sunk. The Japanese ships landed their reinforcements and retired.

Kiska Bombardment and Landings (2-15 August 1943)

This Aleutian island was bombarded 10 times in 14 days by a U.S. task force of two battleships, five cruisers, and nine destroyers. On 15 Aug., U.S. Army and Canadian troops landed on Kiska, to find that the enemy had evacuated the place earlier, under cover of Arctic fog.

Battle of Vella Gulf (6 August 1943)

Another Japanese attempt to reinforce troops on New Georgia by means of high-speed troop carrying destroyers was intercepted by six U.S. destroyers which sank three and damaged one Japanese destroyer. It was the first time in WW II that U.S. ships outfought the Japanese with torpedoes.

Invasion of Italy (9 September 1943)

Six days after British units landed in Italy, 500 British and U.S. ships moved into the Gulf of Salerno and landed American and British troops in force. Little opposition was expected, since Italy had made an armistice with the Allies the previous week. Therefore it had been requested that no preliminary naval barrage be delivered, in order to obtain the advantage of surprise. Waiting German army and air units commenced pounding the 157,000 troops on the beachhead. Not until destroyers raced in and knocked out enemy gun emplacements was the beachhead secured and troops able to move inland.

Battle of Vella Lavella (6 October 1943)

A Japanese force of nine destroyers and 12 smaller craft enroute to Rabaul, after evacuating the garrison on Vella Lavella Island, were intercepted by three U.S. destroyers. One of these, *Chevalier* was sunk by a torpedo, and the others were damaged. The Japanese escaped northbound, but lost the destroyer *Yugumo* in the battle.

Battle of Empress Augusta Bay (2 November 1943)

A day after U.S. Marines had landed in Empress Augusta Bay to seize a portion of Bougainville for an airbase that would let medium bombers and fighters augment the heavy bombers already attacking Rabual, the Japanese attempted to attack 12 U.S. transports. The enemy force of 10 cruisers and destroyers was intercepted by a dozen U.S. cruisers and destroyers. The Japanese lost the cruiser *Sendai* and destroyer *Hatsukaze,* and were turned back.

Invasion of Gilbert Islands (20 November 1943)

In order to establish a path of attack paralleling that of troops under GEN Douglas MacArthur, thus forcing the Japanese to dilute their defensive strength and combat both U.S. threats, the Marshalls Island chain had to be controlled. First, however, the Gilberts had to be taken, so that preliminary reconnaissance of the Marshalls could be made.

After a night bombardment, Tarawa and Makin were assaulted on 20 Nov. Fighting was bloody and bitter, especially on Tarawa. Both islands were secured after four days.

Battle of Cape St. George (25 November 1943)

A Japanese force of five destroyers enroute from Rabual in an attempt to land reinforcements at Buka, on Bougainville was inter-cepted west of Buka by five U.S. destroyers which launched tor-pedoes and then attacked with gunfire. This night battle was a com-plete success: not one U.S. ship was hit; the Japanese lost *Onami, Makinami,* and *Yugiri.*

Landings at Anzio, Italy (22 January 1944)

When the Italian campaign became a stalemate, it was decided to make a landing behind German lines, in an attempt to cut their lines of supply and communications in nothern Italy. It was hoped that a landing behind the enemy would make him dilute his for-ward defenses enough so that Allied troops in southern Italy could crash through. This, unfortunately, did not prove to be the case.

By midnight of the first day more than 37,000 U.S. and British troops were landed against very little opposition, but it was not long before the Germans counter-attacked. The beachhead was pinned down by the enemy for three months, with U.S. naval units supplying offshore gunfire support almost continually to prevent an enemy push to the sea.

Invasion of Marshall Islands (31 January 1944)

After the Gilberts had been invaded, the Marshalls were the next step in the thrust toward the Marianas. Land-based bombers from the Gilberts pasted enemy strong points well in advance of the invasion, and fast carrier task forces raided Japanese airfields and shipping for six consecutive days, beginning on 29 Jan. How well this job was done is evidenced by the fact that no Japanese fighter planes appeared over Kwajalein after 29 Jan.

Marines and Army troops landed at Kwajalein and Majuro atolls on 31 Jan. and on Roi and Namur the next day. By 12 Feb. this island chain was sufficiently under Allied control to begin "mopping up" operations.

Invasion of Normandy (6 June 1944)

The largest aggregation of land, naval, and air forces ever assembled struck the Nazis a blow on the Cherbourg Peninsula on this date that marked the beginning of the end in Europe. Thousands of naval vessels participated, within 24 hours 66,000 U.S. troops landed on the Omaha and Utah beaches. In a week this number grew almost to 250,000, and within three months the Allies had landed more than 2,000,000 men in Europe. U.S. battleships, cruisers, and destroyers nullified the effectiveness of German shore batteries, allowing troops to crash out of the beachhead and head inland. Only U.S. loses in the first day of the landing were the destroyer *Corry* and submarine chaser *PC-1261*.

Invasion of Marianas Islands (15 June 1944)

Saipan, Guam, and Tinian had to be taken to provide U.S. bases for long-range bombers raiding the Japanese homeland. Almost 800 ships, manned by nearly 250,000 sailors, and carrying 150,000 soldiers and Marines set out to do the job. Landings were made at Saipan on 15 June, and followed by assaults against Guam and Tinian on 21 July and 23 July, respectively. All organized Japanese resistance ended by 10 Aug., after 48,000 men of the defending garrisons had been killed. U.S. casualties were about 30,000, including 5,000 killed and missing.

Battle of the Philippine Sea (19-20 June 1944)

The Japanese planned to wipe out the U.S. fleet off the Marianas by attacking it with carrier aircraft which would land in the island chain, refuel, and strike again while returning to their ships. The plan was partly defeated when U.S. submarines *Cavalla* sank *Shokaku* and *Albacore* sank *Taiho* before these two carriers could get into action. U.S. carrier aircraft shot down over 300 Japanese aircraft.

The next day American aircraft struck the Japanese fleet again, sinking the carrier *Hiyo*, and running the total of aircraft kills to 426 ship-based planes, plus 50 land-based aircraft. The Imperial Fleet withdrew to Okinawa; its naval air arm never recovered from these losses.

Invasion of Southern France (15 August 1944)

To keep up pressure on the Germans, the Allies decided to make landings on the southern coast of France, supplementing campaigns in Italy and Normandy. After four months of preliminary bombing, ending in a 1,400-plane air strike, nearly 900 Allied ships started putting troops ashore this date. A force of nine U.S. and British escort aircraft carriers provided air cover and close support for the assault, and Allied warships destroyed opposing enemy shore guns. The invasion was a speedy success.

Peleliu (15 September-14 October 1944)

Following some five months of preliminary air bombardment by Army Air Corps planes, and several days of intensive bombing by carrier-based Navy planes, and gunfire bombardment, the First Marine Division landed on Peleliu, where the defending Japanese gave them the hottest fight of the Pacific war. The enemy was skillfully hidden in caves, the beaches were mined, and pillboxes and casemates covered every bit of ground. Within two weeks, most of the island was in U.S. hands, Peleliu was declared "secure" on 14 Oct. Many enemy troops were holed up and had to be hunted out, one by one. Not until 27 Nov. was the last Japanese organized resistance overcome. By that time, Marine casualties numbered

1,124 killed, 5,024 wounded, and 117 missing. Estimates of Japanese dead reached 10,695.

Invasion of the Philippines (20 October 1944)

As GEN Douglas MacArthur left the Philippines on 11 Mar. 1942, he promised the Filipinos "I shall return." The Navy helped him keep that promise, with 738 ships steaming into position off Leyte the night of 19 Oct. Aided by earlier U.S. carrier sweeps that had destroyed more than 1,000 Japanese planes and 150 ships, the fleet landed troops in the Philippines nearly two-and-one-half years after the Japanese had taken full control. No. U.S. ships were sunk, and initial Japanese resistance was light. Four hours after the first soldier hit the beach GEN MacArthur was ashore, broadcasting his famous "I have returned" message to the Philippine people.

Battle for Leyte Gulf (23-26 October 1944)

The Japanese plan for defense of the Philippines called for smashing the Allied invasion fleet at Leyte Gulf. Loss of Leyte meant eventual loss of the entire island chain, and complete severance of Japanese supply lines to the homeland. Three Japanese naval forces were dispatched to do the job, and entered three separate actions.

The Japanese Center Force was sighted and attacked by U.S. submarines as it headed for San Bernardino Strait. The cruisers *Maya* and *Atago* were sunk, and cruiser *Takao* knocked out of action. The force was next attacked by U.S. carrier aircraft, which sank the giant battleship *Musahi;* it then retreated, but about-faced after a time and emerged from San Bernardino Strait to attack the landing area in what became The Battle Off Samar (26 Oct. 1944).

The Battle Off Samar pitted four Japanese battleships, five cruisers, and 11 destroyers against six U.S. escort carriers and seven destroyers and destroyers escorts. The Japanese sank one escort carrier and three of the destroyer types, then suddenly retreated without following up their success.

The Japanese Southern Force, two battleships, four cruisers, and eight destroyers, was ordered to steam southeast and enter Surigao Strait, where it would combine with the Center Force to crush the Allies in a giant pincers. Though attacked enroute, it lost only one destroyer, *Wakaba,* and entered the Battle of Surigao Strait (25 Oct.) otherwise intact. There an Allied fleet of battleships, cruisers, destroyers, and torpedo boats mauled it and sank two battleships, one cruiser, and three destroyers. The Southern force turned tail and ran, losing another cruiser and a destroyer to U.S. air attacks next day.

The Southern Force had been knocked out of the battle in the early darkness of 25 Oct., and the Central Force had made its bid in the daylight hours before noon. In the afternoon of the same day the Japanese Northern Force, consisting mainly of aircraft carriers acting as a decoy to draw the large U.S. carriers away from Leyte Gulf, was attacked in the Battle Off Cape Engano. U.S. naval aircraft sank four Japanese carriers, one cruiser, and two destroyers; four U.S. forces then attacked the Japanese Central Force, which was retreating through San Bernardino Strait, and sank five more cruisers and four more destroyers.

In this greatest of all naval battles, the U.S. fleet lost one light carrier, two escort carriers, two destroyers, and one destroyer escort from all causes. The Japanese fleet lost four carriers, three battleships, 10 cruisers, and 11 destroyers. Never again would it challenge U.S. control of the Pacific.

Invasion of Iwo Jima (19 February 1945)

Because Iwo-based fighters were attacking U.S. long range bombers on their way to bomb Japan, and Japanese bombers were being shuttled through the island to attack U.S. bases, this "unsinkable airfield" had to be seized. U.S. Marines landed after 72 days of advance air bombardment and three days of intensive naval gunfire. On the first day 30,000 Marines went ashore. By the time Iowa Jima was secured on 16 Mar. over 60,000 Marines had seen combat. Of these, a third were killed or wounded, in a campaign described later by Fleet ADM Nimitz as one "where uncommon valor was a common virtue."

Invasion of Okinawa (1 April 1945)

The Navy's last major amphibious assault of WW II pitted practically all of its seaborne might against one island in the bloodiest campaign of the Pacific war. Okinawa was needed as a prelude to direct invasion of the Japanese Islands. In Japanese hands it barred the way, in Allied control it opened a clear path to the doorway of the Empire. In 82 days of fighting more than 100,000 Japanese were killed; American losses totaled 12,520. Nearly 800 Allied planes were lost, while 7,830 Japanese planes were destroyed. A total of 36 U.S. warships none larger than a destroyer were sunk, and 180 enemy ships, from fishing craft to the largest battleship in the world, *Yamato*, went to the bottom. This was the last, the largest, and one of the most costly battles in the Pacific.

Korea

Invasion of Inchon, Korea (15 September 1950)

After having been almost completely driven from South Korea, the United Nations troops staged a counter-invasion in order to engage North Korean and Communist Chinese troops once more. Under cover of an air strike and offshore bombardment from Allied surface ships, United Nations troops moved ashore at Inchon. In one day they secured the Inchon peninsula, and in three more days enveloped Seoul, capital city of South Korea.

Evacuation of Hungnam (9-24 December 1950)

Having been rolled back by hordes of Communist Chinese troops, United Nations forces had to be removed from North Korea for redeployment against the enemy elsewhere. Hungnam was chosen as evacuation port. A total of 105,000 United Nations troops, 91,000 civilian refugees, 17,500 vehicles, and 350,000 tons of supplies were moved to sea while United Nations warships laid down a protective bombardment curtain around the port area.

NAVAL EXPLORATIONS

Naval Explorations

Slacum's Voyage. In November 1835, President Van Buren directed William A. Slacum, an officer of the U.S. Navy, to proceed to the west coast of the continent and "to obtain there all such information, political, physical, statistical and geographical, that might prove useful or interesting to the Government."

Slacum traveled through Mexico to Guaymas; left there on 1 June 1835, and finally reached the mouth of the Columbia River on 22 Dec. 1836. He surveyed and plotted a chart of the mouth of that river, and also compiled a chart of the coast and country south of the Columbia. The four rivers, Klamath, Coos, Rogue, and Umpqua, which had never before been charted, were shown on this map.

Wilkes Exploring Expedition. This expedition was first proposed on 22 Jan. 1828, but Congressional action on the necessary legislation was delayed for a period of about 10 years. The expedition, consisting of the sloops-of-war *Vincennes* and *Peacock*, the storeship *Relief*, the brig *Porpoise*, and tenders *Seagull* and *Flying Fish*, under command of LT Charles Wilkes, USN, finally sailed from Chesapeake Bay on 19 Aug. 1838. The expedition returned to New York in July, 1842, having sailed about 85,000 miles.

During this expedition Wilkes recorded the first sighting of the Antarctic Continent, on 19 Jan. 1840. His ships covered the Pacific from the Antarctic Continent north to the coast of Oregon, and from the Sandwich (Hawaiian) Islands west through the Philippines.

About 280 islands were surveyed, as were 800 miles of streams and coastlines in Oregon and 1,500 miles of the Antarctic coastal regions. Hundreds of new species of fish, reptiles, and insects were brought back to the United States. Published accounts of the expedition, prepared over the next 30 years, covered hydrography, geology, ethnography, meteorology, botany, zoophytes and crustacea.

Relatively unknown, these volumes contain a wealth of information on the Pacific Ocean areas. The value of this expedition, to U.S. commerce and the world at large, has probably never been fully appreciated, except by scientists.

Expedition to the Dead Sea. Sailed from the U.S. on 26 Nov. 1847, under command of LT W. F. Lynch, in the USS *Supply*. Last part of the journey, in Syria, was made on camelback and LT Lynch was later instrumental in having a group of these beasts shipped to the U.S. for use in the southwest. His report on the expedition was hailed as a classic in its field.

Exploration in the Valley of the Amazon. The first Navy expedition to this area was led by LT William L. Herndon, whose account of his journey has remained ever since a foundation for other expedition reports, and which was reprinted in 1950 under the title "Exploration of the Valley of the Amazon." The Herndon trip, made in 1850, furnished much information on that mysterious area, and had one interesting and little known sidelight: Mark Twain said that it was his reading of Herndon's account of the expedition which led him to his life as a steamboat pilot and later, writer. Another expedition, in 1878, was led by CDR T. O. Selfridge, in USS *Enterprise*. From reports of this journey the Navy prepared and published extensive navigational charts of the Amazon and Madeira Rivers. In 1899 USS *Wilmington,* under CAPT C. C. Todd, steamed up the Amazon for 2,400 miles amassing much valuable information enroute, both practical and scientific in character.

Explorations in the Rio de la Plata. During 1854 USS *Water Witch,* under CDR T. J. Page explored the Rio de la Plata. Soundings were taken and 3,600 miles of river bed charted, surrounding country was explored, and natural history collections of great value to science, art, and commerce were brought back. This voyage proved to the world that ocean going steamers could ascend the Parana and Paraguay Rivers to a point 700 miles above Ascuncion, which city is as far from the South Atlantic as St. Louis, Mo., is from the Gulf of Mexico.

Astronomical Expedition to Chile. This expedition was made in 1853, under LT James Gilliss, who founded the U.S. Naval Observatory, published the first American volume of astronomical observations, and was a large contributor to the geographical literature of the country. Gilliss collected data concerning the geography and statistics of Chile. At the same time one of his associates, LT McRae, crossed the pampas to Buenos Aires and collected information on that region. Through the combined efforts of Gilliss and McRae, the world's geographical knowledge of this area was greatly increased.

Exploration and Survey of the Panama Isthmus. In 1844 an expedition led by LT Strain searched for a canal route across Darien. The party suffered mishaps and was on the whole unlucky, but Strain proved that the Darien route was impracticable, thus pointing the way for later emphasis of the Panama route.

Tehuantepec Canal Survey. A Navy expedition consisting of USS *Kansas* and *Mayflower,* under CAPT R. W. Shufeldt, made a survey of the Isthmus of Tehuantepec and Nicaragua in a search of a possible transisthmian ship canal route. Several months were spent taking hydrographic and topographic surveys. Although the canal was eventually built in Panama, there still remain a number of vociferous advocates of the Nicaraguan canal. About the same time the Darien expedition, under CDR T. O. Selfridge, explored four possible canal routes in that area. In 1872, CAPT E. P. Lull, who had been assistant to CDR Selfridge in his expedition, led an expedition which made a survey for the Nicaraguan route.

Nicaraguan Survey. Supplementing the expedition led by CAPT Shufeldt, as well as others in 1872 and 1873, USS *Lackawanna* sailed from New York in 1884 carrying still another expedition to plan a canal across Nicaragua. This followed the conclusion of a treaty between the U.S. and Nicaragua by which the U.S. was given the right to build such a canal. Head of the expedition was Civil Engineer A. G. Menocal, USN, who was assisted by Civil Engineer R. E. Peary and ENS W. I. Chambers. (Peary later discovered the North Pole, and Chambers was an early advocate of naval aviation.) First attempt to survey a route between Atlantic and Pacific was made in 1844 by LT Strain, USN, along a suggested Darien route; that expedition was not very successful, but created such enthusiasm among other officers that the Navy never again let the matter of an

Isthmian canal drop until plans for the Panama canal were completed.

Cruise of the *Dolphin*. First hydrographic work in the Atlantic. In 1851 the brig *Dolphin,* under LT S. P. Lee, started an eight-month survey of the North Atlantic. Lee investigated 56 areas in which rocks and shoals had been reported, many of them of doubtful character and position. He also performed valuable work in connection with Matthew Maury's investigation of winds and currents of the ocean. As a result of this voyage Atlantic navigation was rendered safer, and important contributions made to physical geography, meteorology, and other sciences.

North Pacific Expedition. Under command of LT John Rodgers, USS *Vincennes, John Hancock, John P. Kennedy, Fenimore Cooper* and *Porpoise* spent about two years on this trip beginning June, 1853. They completed 15 charts of harbors and special localities, and 20 charts of island groups coasts and seas, including the Bonin Islands, ports of Japan, Kamchatka, the Aleutian Islands, the Bering Sea, and Hawaii.

Commodore Perry's Expedition to Japan. This is probably the best known of the Navy's many expeditions to foreign shores, and had the greatest effect of any expedition on both U.S. and foreign affairs. Until Perry succeeded in "opening the door" to the practically-unknown Japanese Empire, little more was known about it than had been written by Marco Polo hundreds of years before. Through his superb diplomatic abilities Perry obtained a favorable treaty between Japan and the United States. By opening Japanese eyes to the cultural, scientific and mechanical achievements of the United States, he laid the groundwork for a long and beneficial trade between the two countries. With her entry into foreign trade and relations, Japan soon moved out of her centuries-long isolation and became a world power.

COMO Perry left the United States on 24 November 1852, in his flagship *Mississippi* and returned on 12 January 1855, in the English mail steamer *Hindostan.* During his stay in Japanese waters, he was in command of a squadron consisting of the steamers *Mississippi, Princeton, Alleghany,* and *Susquehanna;* the *Vermont,* the sloops of war *Vandalla, Macedonian, Saratoga* and *Plymouth;* and the armed storeships *Supply, Lexington,* and *Southampton.* Some of these ships were already in the Orient, others followed Perry to Japan. A complete report of this expedition, titled "The Narrative of the Expedition of an American Squadron to the China Seas and Japan," in three volumes, was published in 1856. A greatly condensed, one-volume account under the title of "Commodore Perry's Naval Expedition to the China Seas and Japan" was published in 1952.

Polaris Expedition. The expedition, which sailed in 1870, led by CAPT Charles Francis Hall, USN, passed through the waters between Greenland and British America as far as latitude 82° 16′ north, a point much nearer the North Pole than had ever been reached to that time. More than 700 miles of coastline were discovered or recharted. Land was discovered extending as far north as 84°. CAPT Hall died at Polaris Bay in 1871. The expedition was shipwrecked and so delayed in returning that a relief expedition was sent to the rescue. This was composed of USS *Juniata,* CDR D. L. Braine, USS *Tigress,* CDR James A. Greer, and the steam launch *Little Juniata* under LT George Washington De Long. The latter force obtained results which added further to the fruits of the original expedition, the records of which were recovered.

Jeannette Expedition. The ship *Jeannette* was donated by James Gordon Bennett and fitted out by the Navy Department, under authority of an act of Congress, for polar exploration. LT De Long obtained command of this expedition, and believing that the chances of success were greater by the Bering Sea route, elected to go north through Bering Strait to reach the North Pole.

Jeannette sailed from San Francisco, California, on 7 August 1879, and was crushed in the ice off Siberia on June 13, 1881. The experiences of her crew, and the rescue of the survivors, are a stirring chapter in the journals of Arctic literature. Before *Jeannette* was sunk, De Long discovered Jeannette, Henrietta, and Bennet Islands. In June 1881 USS *Rodgers,* LT R. M. Berry, was sent north to search for *Jeannette,* but was destroyed by fire a few months later off the Siberian Coast. The *Rodgers'* officers did chart Wrangell Island, proving conclusively that it was not a part of the Asiatic Coast, as had been supposed by some geographers. USS

Alliance, CDR George H. Wadleigh, also searched for *Jeannette's* crew, and brought back a large amount of valuable geographical data, together with scientific specimens.

Surveys and Exploration of China and Korea under Rear Admiral Rodgers. Although unsuccessful in his first attempt to "open up" Korea, Rodgers, in 1870 through 1873, made surveys of all parts of the coast which could be reached. He also made surveys in the Yangtze River, and brought back considerable geographical data. A later expedition under COMO R. S. Shufeldt finally completed treaty negotiations with the King of Korea at Inchon, and made extensive observations on the Korean and Siberia coasts. Three officers of this group then proceeded from Japan to the U.S. via Korea and Siberia. The report of their journey was full of geographic information, which was at that time greatly welcomed.

Surveys in Japan. LT Murray S. Day, after the return to the U.S. of the Perry Expedition, spent three years in Japan (1876-1878) organizing Japanese students into surveying parties, and superintending all the field operations underlining a scientific survey, including astronomy, triangulation, topography and hydrography.

Arctic Expeditions and Exploration. In 1848 LT Edward J. De Haven, USN, in *Advance,* and Passed MID Samuel P. Griffin, in *Rescue,* sailed to the Arctic to search for Sir John Franklin's 1847 British expedition, which had been long overdue. Although they failed to find Franklin, they did add Grinnell Land to Arctic charts. Passed Assistant Surgeon E. K. Kane, USN, who had sailed on what has been called the Kane expedition, led a second search party for Franklin expedition in *Advance.* He spent over two years in the north, but was unsuccessful in the main object of the search and so overwhelmed by insurmountable difficulties that another search party had to be sent to his rescue. This was led by CAPT Henry J. Hartstene in the bark *Release* and steamer *Arctic.* They brought back 15 members of the Kane Expedition, together with its vast store of geographical and scientific data, which would otherwise have been lost.

American Eclipse Expedition. In 1905, the U.S. Navy staged the largest expedition ever fitted out by any nation, up to its time, for the purpose of observing and recording a solar eclipse. Three ships, USS *Minneapolis, Dixie* and *Caesar* (collier) were assigned to the expedition, under command of RADM Colby M. Chester. The ships left the East coast in June of this year, Observation stations were set up at Bôe, Algeria; Guelma, Algeria; and Daroca, Spain.

Arctic Expeditions. Several expeditions into the Arctic were led by Robert E. Peary, USN, over a twenty-year period ending in 1909. His first northern journey was made in 1886, when he examined the west coast of Greenland around Disco Bay as a possible base for Arctic exploration. Peary went north again in 1891-1892, leading an expedition supported by the Philadelphia Academy of Natural Science. During the next several years he continued his work in the far north; in 1900 he surveyed the north coast of Greenland and in 1902 he reached the "farthest north" point of 84° 17′ 27″. He then held the rank of commander. In 1905 he sailed north in the *Roosevelt* for a two year trip, and in 1908 he again pushed northward in the same ship, on the trip which was to finally reach the North Pole. On 6 April 1909, accompanied by Matthew Henson, a Negro, and four Eskimos, Peary planted a U.S. flag on top of the world. For his achievement, he was later given the rank of rear admiral by Congress.

Antarctic Expeditions. The Navy's first expedition to the Antarctic was led by CDR Richard E. Byrd, who had previously flown the Atlantic non-stop (30 June 1927), and made the first North Pole flight (9 May 1926). It left the U.S. in September, 1928, and set up an extensive base, called Little America, in the Bay of Whales on the Ross Sea. The expedition carried out a comprehensive program of scientific research and exploration, during which Byrd and a crew of three made the first flight over the South Pole (29 November 1929). For this feat, he was advanced, by a special act of Congress, to the rank of rear admiral in the Civil Engineering Corps' retired list. In 1933 ADM Byrd led a second expedition to Little America, and continued to research and exploration commenced earlier. This expedition returned to the United States in May, 1935. His third expedition left the United States in 1939, and returned from the Antarctic in 1941. In 1947, the Navy sent the largest expedition up to that time—over 4,000 men and a dozen ships—to the Antarctic. Termed the Antarctic Development Project, it was popularly called OPERATION HIGHJUMP. RADM Byrd was again in technical control, while the task force commander was RADM Richard N. Cruzen, who had been ADM Byrd's second-in-command during the 1939-41 expedition, as commanding officer of USS *Bear*. The expedition utilized many World War II developments, such as radar and high speed cameras, to map hundreds of miles of previously unexplored country, and acquired increased knowledge of cold weather operations as they affected men, ships, planes, and material. All types of ships, from an aircraft carrier to a submarine, operated in the Antarctic region during OPERATION HIGHJUMP.

As one aspect of U.S. participation in the International Geophysical Year (1957-58), the Navy in November, 1955, made the first of four trips to the Antarctic, with eight ships carrying men and material with which to build a base, an air operating facility, and a runway. The operation was given a permanent designation of Task Force 43. Late each fall ships leave the U.S. for Antarctica, to unload equipment and supplies there, and return in early spring of the following year. On the first trip, a SeaBee construction battalion set up a Main Base, where approximately 120 officers and men will remain during each winter. In October, 1956, this group commenced overland transportation of supplies, equipment and a construction party to Marie Byrd Land, at 80 degrees south. At the same time, a construction group flew to the South Pole to establish a third base, material for which was air-dropped over the Pole. The first plane ever to land in the South Pole was an R4D SKYTRAIN (*Que Sera Sera*). (No person had been on the ground at the South Pole since 1911-12, when Norway's Rouald Amundsen and England's Robert Scott both marched in to 90 South. Many planes have flown over the Pole since Byrd made his first flight in 1929.)

In 1956, TASK FORCE 43 ships carried south the scientists who manned the three bases during the subsequent winter, as well as supplies for two years of operation. In 1957 DEEP FREEZE III operations, ships again made a resupply mission, and aircraft flew in to the Main and South Pole Bases. A Pan American Stratocruiser landed at McMurdo Sound, the first commercial plane to reach Antarctica.

The original four-year DEEP FREEZE operation ended in 1958. The Navy now has the job of continuing logistic support during the U.S.

Antarctic Research Program for an indefinite period. Antarctica, the last global frontier, has now become the worlds largest laboratory. Each year, hundreds of men are at work there, in many scientific fields. Their findings may have vital future importance.

DISASTER RELIEF

Disaster Relief

The Navy's role as a fighting force is well known; not so much a part of common knowledge is the Navy's peaceful mission of offering assistance and aid whenever and wherever needed. "Navy to the rescue" means not only saving lives and ships at sea; it includes assistance in time of flood and earthquake, fighting forest fires, and furnishing food, water, medicine, and even electrical power and drinking water to stricken areas.

For over a century, distressed people in many lands have been given kindly care by sympathetic officers and sailors. The response of these unfortunate people is best expressed by the message painted on a rooftop in flooded Tampico, Mexico, which greeted Navy helicopters carrying aid to the stricken city in October 1955: "God Bless You, U.S. Navy."

are:

1847

USS *Jamestown* carried food supplies to Cork, Ireland, to help relieve the famine of 1847.

1882

14 July. USS *Lancaster, Nipsic* and *Quinnebaug* landed sailors and Marines at Alexandria, Egypt, which was in a state of anarchy due to bombardment by British ships. They fought fires and helped restore order.

1890

8 Feb. USS *Omaha* landed rescue force to help fight fires at Hodogaya, Japan.

1895

4 Mar. USS *New York, Cincinnati* and *Raleigh* landed men at Port of Spain, Trinidad, to help fight fires which almost destroyed the city.

1906

18 Apr. Ships and men of the Pacific Squadron and all available yard craft and men from the Mare Island Navy Yard fought fires in San Francisco resulting from earthquake, evacuated refugees, and supplied food, clothing and medicine.

1909

6 Jan. USS *Culgoa* and *Scorpion* carried supplies to Messina, Sicily, to aid earthquake victims.

1919

USS *Chicago* aided Honduran government during outbreak of yellow fever at Amapala.

1922

September-October. Navy assisted in the evacuation of hundreds of thousands of refugees from Smyrna.

December, USS *Bainbridge* rescued 482 persons from French transport *Vinh-Long* in Sea of Marmora.

1923

September. Navy performed relief work in Tokyo and Yokohama, after earthquake did severe damage in those cities.

1924

April through June. Navy carried out extensive relief and rescue work during Mississippi Valley flood.

1925

29 June. After earthquake hit Santa Barbara, Calif., Navy moved in to perform rescue work, assisted citizens of area for next month.

1926

18-19 Sept. Navy assisted in relief work at Miami, Fla., after severe hurricane.

1929

14 Mar. Planes from Pensacola made over one hundred flights carrying relief supplies to flooded areas in Alabama and Florida.

18 Dec. USS *Lexington*, aircraft carrier, reached Tacoma, Wash., and began furnishing electrical power to the city whose regular hydroelectric supply was cut short due to drought in the Puget Sound area. *Lexington* served as power supply for Tacoma until 16 Jan., 1930.

1930

3 Sept. USS *Grebe* and *Gilmer* rushed to Dominican Republic to aid people of Santo Domingo after island was battered by severe hurricane.

1931

31 Mar. Navy and Marine forces gave aid to earthquake victims at Managua, Nicaragua.

31 Aug. Yangtze Patrol, and other ships in Asiatic area performed relief work in Hankow and Nanking after heavy floods in central China.

1933

10 Mar. Navy began relief work in Long Beach, Calif., after area was severely damaged by heavy earthquake.

1947

April. Navy planes, carrying medical personnel and emergency supplies, from air stations all over the U.S. flew to aid disaster victims in Texas City, Tex., which was almost demolished by a ship exploding in the harbor, which set off further oil and chemical explosions and fire.

1948

MATS Squadrons VR-6 and VR-8 participated in the Berlin Airlift, flying food and coal into Berlin after the Russians refused to allow supply trains through the Russian Zone of Germany.

1952

January. SS *Flying Enterprise* was disabled by a hurricane 250 miles off the Irish coast. MSTS ship *Golden Eagle* and the destroyer *Willard Keith* were sent to her aid. MSTS *General A. W. Greeley* rescued 30 survivors.

1953

During early spring, Navy ships and barges moved over 1,000,000 gallons of fresh water from Puerto Rico to St. Thomas, in the Virgin Islands, to alleviate a serious water shortage there.

August. An earthquake in the Ionian Islands killed some 400 people and left almost the entire population of 118,000 homeless. The U.S. Sixth Fleet supplied nearly a half million dollars worth of food and relief equipment.

October. A dozen villages in the Reggio Calabria area of Italy were wrecked by floods. U.S. Naval Support Headquarters in Naples gave the Italian Red Cross large quantities of food and medical supplies for disaster relief.

At various times in the year, 41 ships of MSTS gave assistance at sea, in fighting fire, medical aid, or actual rescue work. A total of 232 persons were sescued from six ships and two ditched aircraft.

1954

August. At the request of the French and Vietnamese Governments, the Navy moved units of the Amphibious Force, Western Pacific, and MSTS, to Indo-China to evacuate refugees from North to South Viet Nam. From 16 Aug. 1954 through 18 May 1955, 113 Navy and MSTS ships carried 304,740 refugees, 68,727 tons of cargo, and 8,114 vehicles.

1955

January. The Nationalist Government of the Republic of China asked the United States to provide protection against Chinese Communist seizure of Ichiang Island in the northern Tachen group, to assist in redeployment of their military forces, and to evacuate civilians. Seventh Fleet units successfully evacuated some 24,000 civilian and military personnel by 12 Feb.

1-10 Oct. USS *Saipan*, with Helicopter Training Unit 1, and the transport *Basset* conducted extensive rescue operations in the flooded Tampico, Mexico, area, where hurricane JANET left over 30,000 square miles flooded. In 2,386 sorties, 4,300 persons were rescued by helicopters, which also delivered over 180,000 pounds of food to others marooned by high waters.

December. During heavy floods in California, Navy helicopters rescued over 200 people. Doctors and nurses, medical supplies and food and clothing were air-lifted in to isolated areas.

December. A heavy rain in Tripoli flooded the center of the city, leaving 150 dead and some 2,000 homeless. The Navy flew in plane loads of food and emergency supplies, even before the Lebanese government was able to act.

1956

November. After Egypt nationalized the Suez Canal, and closed airfields to commercial travel, Navy ships moved into the area and evacuated about 1,700 people from Alexandria, Egypt, and Haifa, Israel.

During the year, the Navy carried out extensive disaster relief operations during floods in New England, Pennsylvania, the Delaware River Valley, northern California, and Mexico, in which over 10,000 persons were rescued and more than 3,700 tons of food, bedding, and medical supplies were distributed.

1957

January. The Norwegian ship *Breim,* with her hold flooding, put in to the Naval Station at Midway Island, where Navy personnel repaired her.——During one week in January, a total of 655 Navy and Marine personnel fought fires which swept 30,000 acres of ground in the Santa Monica Mountains and San Fernando region of California.—— The MSTS ship *Bull Run* rescued the disabled Honduran merchant ship *Urania* and towed her in to Cristobal, Canal Zone.——Navy destroyers picked up 126 survivors of the New Zealand merchant ship *Matua,* aground north of the Fiji Islands, and the *Kyes* later towed the ship free.

February. Hungarian citizens fleeing their country after Soviet suppression of the revolt against Communist power there were moved from Bremerhaven, Germany, to New York City by the Navy's MSTS ships *Leroy Eltinge, General W. G. Haan,* and *Marine Carp.* A total of 5,156 people were carried. When the Italian ship *Viacomo H. Altieri* was sunk by heavy seas off Cape Bonifati, Italy, destroyer *William C. Lawe* rescued all hands.

March. Navy tug provided emergency service for the merchant ship SS *Andros Trident* which lost her propeller in a storm 1,000 miles off Japan.

September. MSTS ships and Navy P2V aircraft located and rescued survivors of the German four-masted bark *Pamir* which foundered and sank during hurricane CARRIE.

October. After a flood in Valencia, Spain, left many victims homeless and without food, the USS *Lake Champlain, Washtenaw County* and *Thuban* assisted in rescue work.

December. After heavy floods in Ceylon, the Ceylonese requested disaster aid, for which the Navy assembled a Ceylonese Relief Force of an aircraft carrier and two destroyers which rushed food and medical supplies to the victims. A total of 31 helicopters were used in rescue operations. Transport aircraft flew material to Ceylon from Japan, and a seaplane tender moved to the area from the Persian Gulf to assist in the operation.

1958

January. Damaged by heavy weather, the Russian grain-ships SS *General Panfilov* and SS *Odessa* were cleared to enter Midway Defensive Sea Area, where naval forces provided fuel while the ships made emergency repairs.

February. Destroyers *Barton* and *Soley* rescued all hands from SS *St. Elefterio* which foundered and sank off Puerto Rico.——Ice breaker

Burton Island, in the Lutzow-Holm area of Antarctica, went to the relief of the Japanese survey ship *Soya Maru* and escorted her free of the ice.

July. After a severe cholera epidemic developed in Thailand, that country requested U.S. assistance. A Naval Medical Research Unit was sent to Thailand to work with local health officials. During the epidemic, 8,204 cases of cholera were reported.

October. After the Norwegian cargo ship *Hoi Wong* went aground in the Paracel Islands, the heavy cruiser *Helena* was sent to her assistance. The helicopter unit aboard *Helena* made 25 trips to the ship; in all 116 persons were saved and taken to Hong Kong by *Helena.*

December. MSTS ship *Sgt. Jack J. Pendleton* picked up 24 survivors of the Japanese fishing boat *Chiyoh Maru.*——After heavy floods inundated miles of land in the vicinity of Port Lyautey, Morocco, personnel of the Naval Facility at Port Lyautey assisted in rescue work and provided food to flood victims.

December. A fire destroyed half the town of Koniya in the Ryukyus and left nearly 6,000 people homeless. The carrier *Yorktown* and seven destroyers were sent to provide food, clothing and shelter items.

1959

January. After fire broke out aboard the Italian ship SS *Maria Amada* off the coast of Spain, heavy cruiser *Macon* went to her assistance, first fighting the fires and then taking off the crew as explosions doomed the ship.——Navy P2V aircraft from Argentia, Newfoundland, joined in a futile search for the Danish vessel SS *Hans Hedtoft* which was reported sinking after hitting an iceberg off Cape Farewell.

March. Destroyer *Strong* rescued 15 survivors of fishing boats sunk in a sudden storm in the Persian Gulf.——The icebreaker *Staten Island,* in Wellington, N.Z., carried six tons of food supplies to the New Zealand island of Niue which had been hit by a violent storm.

April. Icebreaker *Edisto* was diverted to Montevideo, Uruguay, for 10 days, to furnish food and medical supplies after heavy rains had flooded the interior of Uruguay. Hundreds of people were evacuated from flooded areas by helicopters.—— Destroyer *Eversole* rescued 14 crewmen from a sinking Nationalist Chinese fishing boat in the Pescadores Islands.

July. Landing ship *Thomaston* and salvage ship *Bolster* rescued 43 men from the Japanese freighter *Bansei Maru* aground off Formosa.—— When the Italian gasoline tanker *Ombrina* caught fire in the French Mediterranean port of Sete, sailors from the USS *Fort Mandan* assisted French firemen in fighting the blaze, then used landing craft as tugs to beach the burning ship.——USS *Altair* and USS *Marias* helped fight fire on a burning Spanish coastal freighter, then towed the ship into port.——Sailors and marines from USS *Des Moines* helped local firemen fight a forest fire on the French Riveria.

1960

February. Icebreaker *Glacier* spent several days working through Antarctic ice to aid the Argentine icebreaker *General San Martin.*

March. The icebreaker *Glacier* smashed through heavy packed ice in the Antarctic to free the British ship *Kista Dan.*

March. The Navy sent relief to Agadir, Morocco, where an earthquake killed 5,000 and injured twice that many persons. During the first day of operations, R5D SKYMASTERS from Port Lyautey flew in 175,000 pounds of emergency supplies and evacuated 1,000 survivors. USS *Newport News* provided blankets, tents, and 250,000 gallons of fresh water daily. Some 33,000 pounds of food and clothing collected in the U.S. were flown to Morocco by Navy planes. A tent city was built outside Agadir, sheltering 10,000 persons.

March. USS *Tioga* rescued crew of sinking fishing boat off Taiwan.

April. After a broken dam threatened hundreds of thousands in Brazil, the Navy diverted the icebreaker *Glacier* to Brazil with rations and medical supplies.

April. USS *Kearsarge* rescued four Soviet Navy men, adrift in the Pacific in a small boat for 49 days.

June. The destroyer *Robinson* rescued crewmen from the sinking tanker SS *George MacDonald* off the U.S. east coast.

1961

During the year at least 90 ships took part in rescue and relief operations around the world. A task force of seven ships carried aid to Galveston, Texas, in the wake of hurricane CARLA. Another group of ships carried over 300 tons of emergency supplies to Belize, British Honduras, as relief from hurricane HATTIE. One ship carried 750 tons of powdered milk to relieve famine in the Congo.

NAVAL FIRSTS

Naval Firsts

Ace, Navy, WWI—David S. Ingalls, with five kills of enemy aircraft while flying with the Royal Air Force; won British Distinguished Flying Cross and U.S. Distinguished Service Medal; served as Assistant Secretary of Navy from 16 Mar. 1929 to 15 Mar. 1932.

Ace, Navy, WWII—LT Edward Henry O'Hare, 20 Feb. 1942, shot down five twin-engined Japanese bombers, damaged a sixth in a five-minute air battle.

Action, U.S. vs. German Naval units, WWII—on 10 Apr. 1941, USS *Niblack* (DD 424) depth charged a German submarine while rescuing survivors of torpedoed Netherlands freighter off Iceland. See *air raid, battle, bombardment, engagement,* and *shot.*

Admiral Confederate States Navy—Raphael Semmes, appointed 10 Feb. 1865. Earlier, while commanding CSS *Sumter* and CSS *Alabama,* Semmes captured or destroyed 83 Union ships.

Admiral, Dental Corps—George C. Paffenberger, USNR, appointed rear admiral 1 Jul. 1955.

Admirals, "five star" fleet admirals—Ernest Joseph King, William Daniel Leahy and Chester William Nimitz, whose appointments were ratified by Senate 15 Dec. 1944.

Admiral to fly—RADM Bradley A. Fiske flew over New York City on 20 May 1912, passenger in plane piloted by Joseph Collier and Walter Brookins.

Admiral, Jewish—RADM Adolph Marix; born in Saxony, admitted to Naval Academy from Iowa, graduated in Class of 1868, advanced to the rank of rear admiral by President William Howard Taft on 4 July 1908; died 11 July 1919.

Admiral, killed in action—RADM Isaac C. Kidd, Commander Battleship Division One. His flagship, the USS *Arizona,* blew up during attack on Pearl Harbor, 7 Dec. 1941. Exact manner of his death not known; last seen manning machine gun; presumably killed when magazine exploded.

Admiral of the Navy—George Dewey, rank conferred by Congress 2 Mar. 1899. He died 16 Jan. 1917.

Admiral with two admiral brothers—Augustus Joseph Wellings, Naval Academy Class of 1920, who was appointed rear admiral in 1947. His brothers, Timothy Francis Wellings and Joseph Harold Wellings, Class of 1921 and Class of 1926 respectively, were appointed rear admiral in 1952 and 1953 respectively.

Admiral, U.S. Navy—David Glasgow Farragut, appointed to that rank 25 July 1866. Farragut was first appointed rear admiral on 16 July 1862; vice admiral on 21 Dec. 1864. He was appointed midshipman 17 Dec. 1810; died 14 Aug. 1870. Until Farragut was appointed rear admiral, the Navy had never had such a title before; previously the term had been "Flag Officer."

Aerial observation, of eclipse—made 9 May 1929, when Naval Observatory expedition, under CAPT Chester H. J. Keppler (ret), used aircraft to make observations at Iloilo, P.I.

Aeronautical Detachment, overseas in WWI—arrived in France 5 June 1917, aboard USS *Neptune*. When Armistice was signed, naval aviation forces in Europe included 16,300 officers and men, 500 planes, 50 kite ballons, three dirigibles and 27 operating bases; had aggregated about 1,000,000 miles in the air.

Aircraft, launched like a ship—on 8 Nov. 1941, at Baltimore, Md., the Martin XPB2M-MARS, construction of which begun with traditional keel laying ceremonies, was launched into the water exactly as if it had been a ship.

Air evacuation of American casualties, WWII—made by Marine transport plane, which removed wounded men from Guadalcanal 7 Sept. 1942.

Air evacuation—took place in Nicaragua, when LT C. F. Schilt, USMC, used an O2U-1 to remove wounded Marines from village of Quilali while under fire from enemy forces. Commencing on 6 Jan. 1928, he made 10 flights in three days, evacuating 18 officers and men, for which he received the Medal of Honor.

Aircraft—see *seaplanes, jet, helicopter.*

Aircraft carrier—see *carrier.*

Airship—see *dirigible, lighter-than-air, balloon.*

Airplane, catapulted from dirigible—launched by USS *Los Angeles,* on 20 May 1930. LCDR Charles A. Nicholson flew two-seater Vought observation plane to landing aboard carrier *Saratoga.*

Airplane, owned by Navy—named *TRIAD-A-1*—ordered from Glenn Curtis 8 May 1911, cost $5,500, designed speed, 45 MPH.

Airplane, to reach altitude of 10,000 feet in less than a minute—F4D SKYRAY, piloted by R. W. Rahn, Douglas test pilot, 23 Feb. 1955, reached 10,000 feet, from standing start, in 56 seconds.

Air raid on Japan, WWII—made by 16 B-25's from 17th Air Group, Army Air Force, led by LTCOL James H. Doolittle, launched from the carrier *Hornet,* about 690 miles off Japan, 18 Apr. 1942.

Airship, helium-filled—used by Navy; non-rigid *C-7* which on 1 Dec. 1921, flew from Hampton Roads to Washington, D.C., and returned. The *C-7* contained 181,000 cubic feet of helium; until that time, lighter-than-air craft were inflated with hydrogen, which had greater lifting power but was dangerous because of its explosive qualities.

Airship, lost to enemy action, WWII—*K-74,* which was brought down by a German submarine in the Caribbean on 18 Jul. 1943, was also the only airship lost in WWII. *K-74* attacked a surfaced submarine, was destroyed by gun fire.

Airship, acquired by Navy—*DN-1,* which made its first flight at Pensacola April 1917. After only three flights it was damaged beyond repair. As designed, *DN-1* was a two-engine, non-rigid type, but was unable to take-off until original engines were replaced by a single engine. Built at New Haven, Conn.; cost, $45,636.25. See *dirigible.*

Air-spotting for shore batteries, in U.S.—5 Aug. 1915, LT P. N. L. Bellinger, flying a Burgess-Dunne AH-10, spotted mortar fire for Army at Fortress Monroe, Va., signalling spots with Very pistol flares.

Air strike, by U.S. forces, WWII—1 Feb. 1942, fast carriers *Enterprise* and *Yorktown,* under VADM William F. Halsey, attacked Japanese positions in Marshall and Gilbert Islands.

American flag flown in the Navy—see *flag.*

American merchant ship lost in WWI—SS *Gulflight,* torpedoed by a German submarine 1 May 1915.

American military man killed in action in Korea—LT Hugh W. McKee, attached to USS *Colorado,* wounded during attack on Kwangsong Fortress in Han River, 11 June 1871, died on board USS *Monocacy* same day; body returned to United States, buried in Lexington, Ky. In the same fight, Seth Allen, Marine attached to USS *Benecia* and Dennis Hamahan, landsman attached to USS *Colorado,* were killed, buried on Boisee Island, off the West Coast of Korea. First American military man buried in Korea was Thomas Driver, rating not known, who died aboard USS *Alaska* on 2 June 1871, of "brain fever" was buried same day, on Boisee Island.

Amphibious landing operations—3 Mar. 1776, when squadron under Esek Hopkins took New Providence, in the Bahamas. Marines under CAPT Samuel Nichols and sailors from *Cabot* under LT Weaver captured 88 cannon, 15 mortars, and a large quantity of shot and shell.

Amphibious landing from submarine—made 17 Aug. 1942, when *Nautilus* and *Argonaut* unloaded "Carlson's Raiders" on Japanese-held Makin, Marshall Islands. Marine Raider Battalion led by LTCOL Evans E. Carlson, destroyed enemy installations and wiped out the defending enemy force of about 90 men, with their own casualties 18 killed, 14 wounded, and 12 missing.

Annapolis graduate—see *graduate.*

Antarctic Circle, ship to cross—*Flying Fish,* 90-tons, under command of LT W. N. Walker. While attached to Wilkes United States Exploring Expedition, *Flying Fish* crossed the circle in March 1839, on 25 Mar. reached 70°14' South.

Arctic Circle, ships to cross—*Advance* and *Rescue* which left N.Y. 1850 on a futile rescue search for the Franklin Expedition.

Armed Guard Crew, on board merchant ship, WWII—went aboard SS *Dunboyne* 2 Dec. 1941.

Army-Navy football game—see *football.*

Army-officer, to christen a Navy ship—see *christening.*

Atlantic crossing, by steam driven ship, U.S. Navy—made by steam-frigate *Missouri,* which reached Gibraltar from Norfolk on 25 Aug. 1843. She caught fire the following day and was destroyed. Her crew was saved.

Autogyro, Navy—*XOP-1,* delivered at U.S. Naval Air Station, Anacostia, Washington, D.C., 11 June 1931.

Automatic pilot, for aircraft—demonstrated by Lawrence Sperry 12 Sept. 1916, but not considered accurate enough for use by Navy.

Aviation Unit, to leave U.S. WWI—First Marine Aeronautics Company, which reached Ponta Delgado, Azores, 21 Jan. 1918.

Aviator, Navy, ordered for training—LT T. G. Ellyson, on 23 Dec. 1910, received orders to report to Glenn Curtiss aviation camp, North Island, San Diego, for flight training.

Aviation—*see marine officers.*

Baby, born in Arctic region to white parents—Marie Ahnighito Peary, daughter of LT and Mrs. Robert E. Peary, born 12 Sept. 1893, at "Anniversary Lodge," Peary's base camp on the northwest coast of Greenland, latitude 77°40' North. Peary was on third expedition into the Arctic.

Baby, born in helicopter—brought down by LT John E. Gregory, during flood rescue operations, Tampico, Mexico, 3 Oct. 1955: he picked up 14 women and children but unloaded 15 passengers. The extra passenger was an airborne infant who had joined the group in mid-flight.

Balloon carrier, Navy—3 Aug. 1861, an armed transport, *Fanny* launched balloon which made observations of Confederate positions at Fortress Monroe, Va. The balloon was controlled by windlass on *Fanny,* reached height of 2,000 feet.

Baptism, performed south of Antarctic Circle—on Christmas Eve, 24 Dec. 1955, aboard cargo ship *Wyandot,* en route through ice pack to Ross Sea in Operation DEEPFREEZE. Charles M. Slaton, chief machinist's mate, was baptized into Catholic faith by Chaplain John C. Condit.

Bat—see *guided missles.*

Battle, between iron-clad ships—occurred 9 Mar. 1862, Hampton Roads, Va., when *Monitor* and the Confederate *Virginia,* usually called *Merrimac,* fired at each other at close range for several hours. *Virginia* withdrew, breaking off the fight; neither ship was sunk. See *action.*

Battle, in which U.S. Marines took part—attack on English fort of New Providence, in Bahamas, 3 Mar 1776. The 200 marines were led by CAPT Samuel Nichols and assisted by 50 sailors from *Cabot.*

Battle, Naval, fought without opposing ships making contact—Battle of the Coral Sea, 4-8 May 1942. Japanese carrier *Shoho* was sunk by U.S. carrier planes, *Lexington* and *Yorktown* were damaged by Japanese carrier planes. *Lexington* later was sunk to prevent possible capture.

Battle—see also *action, engagement, bombardment, enemy action, enemy plane, shot.*

Battleship—USS *Maine;* launched 18 Nov. 1890, at Brooklyn, N.Y. Last battleships on in active service were *Iowa* (decommissioned 24 Feb. 1958) and *Wisconsin* (decommissioned 5 Mar. 1958).

Battleship, only one not named for a state—*Kearsarge;* launched at Newport News in 1898. She displaced 11,000 tons, carried a crew of 657, and had a top speed of 16 knots. After WWI, was decommissioned, converted to world's largest crane ship: in 1955 was still in use at Boston Naval Shipyard. First *Kearsarge* was a sloop, launched at Portsmouth, N.H., in 1861. She served in the Civil War, achieved fame by sinking the Confederate raider *Alabama* off Cherbourg, France, was wrecked in Gulf of Mexico. Because of her outstanding naval career, Congress made a special exception to the rule naming battleships for states, in order to give her name to an early battleship. Third *Kearsarge* is aircraft carrier, commissioned 2 Mar. 1946; scenes for Republic Motion Picture's "The Eternal Sea" were filmed on this ship.

Battleship, to visit inland city—*Mississippi,* which reached Natchez, Miss., on 20 May 1909 (300 miles upstream from the mouth of Mississippi River).

Blimp—see *airship, lighter-than-air.*

Bombardment, Navy, in Korean war—made 29 June 1950 by cruiser *Juneau* and destroyer *De Haven.*

Broadcast of ship launching—7 Apr. 1925, when carrier *Saratoga* was launched at Camden, N.J., Mrs. Curtis D. Wilbur, wife of Secretary of the Navy, christened the ship.

Camera, high speed—was developed by Naval Gun Factory, in collaboration with Edison Laboratory in 1913. Three cameras were produced, able to make 6,600 exposures per minute.

Campaign medal—"Dewey Medal," authorized by act of Congress, 3 June 1898, presented to all personnel who participated in Battle of Manila Bay on 1 May 1898.

Cape of Good Hope and Cape Horn, ship to round both—Frigate *Essex*, which rounded Cape of Good Hope 28 Mar. 1800, en route from United States to Batavia, and rounded Cape Horn 14 Feb. 1813, on a cruise to the Pacific during War of 1812.

Cape of Good Hope, submarine around—*Jallao*, 24 Feb. 1956, westbound from Port Said. *Jallao* was first U.S. submarine to visit South Africa, first to sail around Africa.

Cargo, most unusual carried by a naval ship—in 1856 USS *Supply*, commanded by LT David Dixon Porter, sailed from Smyrna with 50 camels, purchased under Congressional appropriation "to be employed for military purposes." Secretary of War Jefferson Davis believed camels would speed troop movements in southwest. They were unloaded at Powder Horn, Tex., on 13 May, 1856, and used at various times and with varying degrees of success—even hauling bales of cotton for Confederates during Civil War, but soldiers and camels regarded each other with suspicion, and camels were eventually sold out of the army. Some of them were bought by a circus, some were turned loose in Arizona. A few were seen as late as 1905.

Carrier battle—see *battle, naval.*

Carrier combat kills, in Korean action—3 Jul. 1950, when two F9Fs shot down two YAK-9s over Pyongyang.

Carrier, designed and built as such from keel up—*Ranger*, commissioned at Norfolk, Va., on 4 June 1934. (First three carriers were conversions: *Langley* from collier, *Lexington* and *Saratoga* from battle cruisers.)

Carrier, helicopters—*Thetis Bay*, reclassified as Assault Helicopter Aircraft Carrier (CVHA 1) 1 Jul. 1955.

Carrier; Langley—commissioned 20 Mar. 1922, Norfolk, Va., and long known as the "Covered Wagon." Originally the collier *Jupiter*, Navy's first electrically-propelled ship; built at Mare Island, Calif., launched 24 Aug. 1912. Renamed *Langley* 21 Apr. 1920. Sunk by Japanese bombers, Tjilatjap, Java, 27 Feb. 1942.

Carrier-launched airplanes in action in WWII—planes from Scouting Squadron Six, attached to *Enterprise*. Returning from Wake Island to Pearl Harbor, "Big E" launched planes on 7 Dec. 1941, about 200 miles west of Hawaii. They reached Pearl Harbor while the Japanese attack was in progress, and engaged enemy planes.

Carrier raid on Japan—see *air raid on Japan*.

Carrier, to launch airplanes while being towed by another—*Saratoga*, on 31 Aug. 1942 when "Sara" was torpedoed by Japanese submarine off Guadalcanal, *Minneapolis* towed her for about six hours, while repairs were being made, and during this time planes were successfully launched although towed speed was far below normal speed for flight operations.

Carrier, sunk in Atlantic during WWII—escort carrier *Block Island*, torpedoed by German submarine 29 May 1944, off the Azores.

Carrier landing—see *landing*.

Carrier operations, in Korean War—on 3 July 1950 *Valley Forge*, with Air Group 5 on board, in company with HMS *Triumph*, launched strikes against airfields, supply lines, and transportation facilities around Pyongyang, northwest of Seoul. This was also first combat test of Grumman PANTHER and Douglas SKYRAIDER.

Casualties—see *officer, Korean, American*.

Casualties evacuated by air—see *air evacuation*.

Catapult launching of airplane, successful—took place at Washington Navy Yard (now the Naval Weapons Plant) 12 Nov. 1912. Plane was Curtiss hydro-plane, piloted by LT Theodore G. Ellyson.

Catapult launching, from carrier—18 Nov. 1922, plane piloted by CDR Kenneth Whiting was catapulted from *Langley*.

Catapult launching, from ship underway—5 Nov. 1915, on *North Carolina* in Pensacola Bay. Plane was AB-2 flying boat piloted by LCDR Henry C. Mustin.

Catapult steam, installed aboard Navy carrier—placed on *Hancock* at Puget Sound Naval Shipyard, Bremerton, Wash.; first tests conducted 27 Feb. 1954.

Catapult, turntable type—successfully tested at Philadelphia Navy Yard, 26 Oct. 1921, by landing N-9 seaplane.

Chapel, built on navy property—erected at Annapolis on grounds of what is now Naval Academy. Dedicated Sunday, 5 Feb. 1854. First chapel on Pacific Coast, on Navy property, and second for entire Naval establishment, was built at Mare Island, dedicated Sunday, 13 Oct. 1901. Named St. Peter's Chapel, it is still in use; chapel at Annapolis has been replaced.

Chaplain, Catholic—Charles Henry Parks, commissioned 30 Apr. 1888, with relative rank of lieutenant; resigned 25 Jan. 1900. (Chaplains did not hold actual rank until 3 March 1899.)

Chaplain, awarded Congressional Medal of Honor—LCDR Joseph Timothy O'Callahan, 23 Jan. 1946, for heroism displayed on 19 Mar. 1945, when carrier *Franklin* was bombed off Kobe, Japan.

Chaplain, Continental Navy—Rev. Benjamin Parks, Congregationalist, date of appointment, 28 Oct. 1788.

Chaplain, Jewish—only Jewish chaplain in Navy during WWI, David Goldberg, appointed lieutenant (junior grade) on 30 Oct. 1917; retired 1 Mar. 1941.

Chaplain, after Navy's reactivation in 1798—William Balch, Congregationalist, who received commission from President John Adams, 30 Oct. 1799, served until 10 May 1801.

Chaplain school—see *school, chaplain.*

Chinese to "command" a ship of U.S. Navy—Sing Hoy, a cabin steward attached to USS *Perry* in 1906. *Perry* was undergoing repairs at Mare Island Navy Yard when San Francisco was struck by the earthquake and fire. In the press of arranging rescue expeditions, to San Francisco, on 18 Apr. Commandant at Mare Island ordered some of the officers and crew of the *Perry* to man various yard craft, and others volunteered for such duty. Not until 23 Apr. when all hands returned to the *Perry,* was it discovered that in fact "all hands and the ship's cook" had been away fighting fire in San Francisco, and only man left on board was the steward, Sing Hoy, who for several days had been in sole command of warship in full commission.

Christmas party, Naval—25 Dec. 1915, on board *New York,* CAPT Hugh Rodman commanding, at Edinburgh, Scotland, 125 children were guests of the *New York* crew.

Christening of ship by Army officer—Destroyer *Colhoun,* launched 10 Apr. 1944, named for RADM Edmund Ross Colhoun and christened by his great grandniece, CAPT Kathryn Kuntz Johnson, Womans Army Corps.

Christening of ship, by enlisted woman—*LSM 167,* launched 24 July, 1944. Sponsor was WAVE Frances Davis, Pharmacist's Mate second class. First ship christened by an enlisted Woman Marine: destroyer escort *Basilone* was named for SGT John Basilone, USMC, and christened 21 Dec. 1945 by his widow, SGT Lena M. Basilone, USMCWR. First ship christened by an enlisted woman member of the Coast Guard: *LST 854,* christened 20 Nov. 1944, by Mrs. M. A. Menkol, a seaman SPAR.

Christening of ship, by Negro woman—Destroyer escort *Harmon,* which was also first ship named for a Negro. Launched on 25 July 1943, *Harmon* was named for Leonard Roy Harmon, a mess attendant, and was christened by his mother, Mrs. Naunita Harmon Carroll.

Christening of ship, by woman—USS *Germantown* 22 Oct. 1846, at Philadelphia, by "a Miss Watson of Philadelphia." Earlier, a ship launched at Portsmouth Navy Yard was chistened by "a young lady of Portsmouth," but in those days newspapers did not mention a lady's name.

Christening of ship, by a woman not a U.S. citizen—Heavy cruiser *Canberra* launched 19 Apr. 1943, named for HMAS *Canberra,* lost in Battle of Savo Island. Ship was christened by Lady Dixon, wife of Sir Owen Dixon, Australian Minister to the United States. *Natoma Bay,* escort carrier launched 20 July 1943, was christened by Lady Halifax, wife of the British Ambassador to the United States, Lord Halifax.

Christening of ship, by women in uniform—Minesweepers *Logic* and *Lance,* launched 10 Apr. 1943. *Lance* was christened by ENS Josephine D. Cunningham, a WAVE, and *Logic* by LTJG Mary Erbenz, a SPAR. Twenty-eight ships launched during WWII were christened by women in uniform.

Circumnavigation of globe, by Confederate ship—*Shenandoah,* under CAPT James T. Waddelle, sailed from England 5 Oct. 1864, and returned to England 5 Nov. 1865. During her cruise she captured 38 ships.

Circumnavigation of globe, by submerged submarine—completed 10 May, 1960, when *Triton* ended her 84 day, 36,014 mile trip, which generally followed the path of first round-the-world voyager, Magellan.

Circumnavigation of globe, west to east—Frigate *Potomac,* which sailed from Sandy Hook 28 Aug. 1831, returned to Boston 23 May 1834.

Circumnavigation of globe by Navy—completed by *Vincennes,* sloop-of-war, commanded by CDR William Compton Bolton. She left New York, N.Y., 31 Aug. 1826, rounded Cape Horn and Cape of Good Hope, returned to New York 8 June 1830.

Civil Engineering Corps officer, to head Bureau of Yards and Docks—Mordecai T. Endicott, captain, who assumed post 4 Apr. 1898. Previously, line officers had headed this bureau; eight years later Congress ruled only CEC officers could hold post.

Coaling station, Navy, in foreign territory—established April 1901, in Mexico, on the Baja (Lower) California coast.

Coast-to-coast flight, aircraft, dirigible—see *flights.*

Combat action, for AVENGER (TBF)—4 June 1942, pilots of Torpedo Squadron 8 attacked Japanese fleet in Battle of Midway.

Combat action, for CORSAIR (F4U)—on 13 Feb. 1943, planes from VMF-124 escorted bombers attacking enemy shipping in Bougainville area.

Combat damage, to an airplane—occurred 20 Apr. 1914, when *Mississippi* and *Birmingham* with aviation detachments were at Vera Cruz, Mexico. Plane piloted by LT P. N. L. Bellinger was hit and damaged by enemy fire.

Commander in Chief (Continental Navy)—Essek Hopkins, so designated from 22 Dec. 1775 to 2 Jan. 1778.

Convoy operations, ship engaged in—*Essex* sailed from Straits of Sunda, en route to New York 1 July 1800. As a protection against French, she escorted 14 American merchantmen from Batavia to U.S. east coast, reaching New York 29 Nov. 1800.

Convoy, to sail from United States during WWI—departed Hampton Roads, Va., 24 May 1917.

Convoy operations, of WWII—on 10 Nov. 1941, Division of British troops, 22,000 men, sailed from Halifax, Nova Scotia, to India and Singapore. They were carried in transports *Mount Vernon, Wakefield, West Point, Leonard Wood, Joseph T. Dickman,* and *Orizaba,* and escorted by carrier *Ranger,* cruisers *Quincy* and *Vincennes,* and destroyers *Moffett, McDougal, Winslow, Mayrant, Rhind, Rowan* and *Trippe.*

Cook book, Navy—Written and issued in 1902, by Paymaster F. T. Arms.

Cruise, Navy (with a squadron of ships)—began 17 Feb. 1776, when ships of the Continental Navy under Esek Hopkins sailed for operations in the West Indies, climaxed by capture of New Providence in the Bahamas.

Deepest dive—see *ocean bottom.*

Diesel engines, used in submarines—Vickers air injection type, four cycle, four cylinder units, installed in *E-1* and *E-2,* commissioned 14 Feb. 1912.

Dirigible, built in U.S. (and first Zeppelin type craft to use helium gas instead of hydrogen)—*Shenandoah* (zr-1), "Daughter of the Stars." She was first test flown 4 Sept. 1923, at Lakehurst, N.J.; wrecked in storm over Caldwell, Ohio, 3 Sept. 1925.

Dirigible, commissioned as a combatant ship—USS *Shenandoah,* commissioned 10 Oct. 1923.

Dirigible, to land aboard ship—the *Los Angeles* (zr-3) aboard carrier *Saratoga,* 27 Jan. 1928.

Dirigible, to moor aboard ship—USS *Shenandoah* moored to USS *Patoka* on 8 Aug. 1924, while underway.

Dirigible, all metal—*ZMC-3,* built for Navy by Detroit Aircraft Corporation and test-flown 19 Aug. 1929. *ZMC-3* was 149 feet, 5 inches in length; 52 feet, 8 inches in diameter; had a displacement of 202,200 cubic feet.

Dirigible, to catapult an airplane—*see airplane, catapulted.*

Dirigible—see *transcontinental flight.*

Distinguished Service Medal, won by a Navy Nurse—awarded to CAPT Sue Sophia Dauser, 14 Dec. 1945.

Divine Service, first ever conducted aboard a Navy ship by a commander-in-chief—held aboard *Nourmahal* (pg-72) 1 Apr. 1934. President Franklin D. Roosevelt conducted service from Episcopal Book of Common Prayer.

Doctor, Navy—Dr. Joseph Harrison. He served aboard *Alfred,* having been appointed to such duty late in 1775, in Philadelphia. (See *women doctor.*)

Drydock, constructed by the Navy—built at Boston; second was built at Norfolk, both under construction at same time. They were designed by COL Loammi Baldwin of Boston. The Boston dock was commenced in June 1827 and finished 8 Sept. 1833, at cost of $677,089.98. The Norfolk dock was commenced in Nov. 1827, and completed 15 Mar. 1834, at cost of $943,676.73. First ship docked in the Boston dock was *Constitution,* 24 June 1833, first in the Norfolk dock was *Delaware,* 17 June 1833; the docks were not yet completed at that time.

Drydock, built on Pacific coast—commenced at Mare Island Navy Yard 13 Aug. 1872; finally completed 18 Feb. 1891, estimated total cost $2,149,099.00. First ship docked after official completion, was *San Francisco;* however, the old frigate *Independence* had entered dock 30 Oct. 1886, almost five years before it was officially completed.

Drydock, floating—built in New York during 1851 and 1852, disassembled, hauled around Cape Horn in clipper ships, and put together again at Mare Island, Calif., where first official test made 10 Dec. 1855, when frigate *Independence* was docked. Dock cost $610,000.

Election, supervised by U.S. armed forces—occurred 2 Nov. 1930, when President of Nicaragua asked for and received services of more than 400 sailors, soldiers, and Marines to help keep order.

Electric-drive ship—Collier *Jupiter,* built by Mare Island Navy Yard, where she was commissioned 7 Apr. 1913. Ship was later converted to Navy's first carrier, renamed *Langley.* (see *carrier.*) First electrically propelled combatant ship in Navy was *New Mexico,* built by New York Navy Yard, commissioned 20 May 1918.

Electric light installation, shipboard—in *Trenton,* completed on 1 Oct. 1882. Earlier installation made at Mare Island Navy Yard in 1879, on board *Jeanette,* which was fitted out for the DeLong Expedition to the Arctic. That system failed as soon as ship left San Francisco.

Electric power, furnished by ship for a city—when Tacoma, Wash., faced power shortage due to 1929 drought in Puget Sound area, carrier *Lexington* took over the task of supplying power. From 18 Dec. 1929 to 16 Jan. 1930, she furnished 4,251,160 kilowatt hours.

Electric power plant, mobile—delivered to the Navy at Philadelphia, Pa., on 10 Jan. 1944. Built by General Electric, it consisted of six railway cars carrying oil-fired boilers, steam turbo-generators, transformers and necessary switches; could generate 10,000 kilowatts of electrical power.

Enlisted women, to christen ship—(see *christening.*)

Enemy action, to damage U.S. Navy ship, WWII—Japanese bombed gunboat *Tutuila,* at Chungkin, China, 30 July 1941.

Enemy action, ship sunk by, WWI—converted yacht *Alcedo*, torpedoed by German submarine 75 miles off French coast, 5 Nov. 1917, with loss of 21 lives.

Enemy action, ship sunk by, WWII—Destroyer *Reuban James*, torpedoed by German submarine off Western Iceland, 31 Oct. 1941, with loss of 100 lives. Sinking took place before U.S. officially declared war on Germany.

Enemy planes, shot down by the Navy in Korea—claimed by LTJG L. H. Plog and ENS E. W. Drown, flying F9Fs from Fighter Squadron 51, when they knocked down two YAK-9s over Pyongyang, 3 July 1950, during first strike launched by carrier *Valley Forge*. First MIG claimed by LCDR Tom Amen of VF 111, 9 Nov. 1950.

Enemy plane, shot down, WWI—19 March, 1918, ENS Stephen Potter, on a reconnaissance flight from England, became involved in a dog-fight over Heligoland Bight, and shot down one German plane near the German base of Wilhelmhaven. Potter was killed the following month, 25 Apr., in aerial engagement over the North Sea.

Enemy plane, shot down in WWII by Marine pilot—9 Dec. 1941, during Japanese air attack on Wake Island, Marine F4Fs shot down a twin-engine bomber.

Enemy ships, biggest sunk during WWII—Japanese battleships *Musashi*, 63,000 tons, sunk by carrier based airplanes 24 Oct. 1944, during Battle of Leyte Gulf, and *Yamato*, 63,000 tons, sunk by carrier based airplanes on 7 Apr. 1945, in East China Sea. Next biggest was carrier *Shinano*, 59,000 tons, which was torpedoed by submarine *Archerfish*, 29 Nov. 1944, south of Honshu.

Enemy ships, most sunk during WWII, by submarine *Tautog*—a total of 26 Japanese ships (72,606 tons of shipping) plus another 18 ships damaged. High score ship, in total tons of enemy shipping sunk, was *Flasher* whose 21 ships sunk added up to 101,231 tons.

Enemy submarine, to sink U.S. Navy ship—Confederate submarine *Hunley*, commanded by LT George Dixon, C.S.N., a small, hand-powered craft which ran on the surface and kept its hatch open because it could not store air. *Hunley* managed to explode a torpedo underneath *Housatonic*, 17 Feb. 1864, off Charleston, S.C., but the explosion swamped the submarine and she went down with all hands.

Enemy submarine, ships to sink—Destroyers *Fanning* and *Nicholson*, which jointly sank the German *U-58*, 17 Nov. 1917, near the Hebrides. The submarine was attacked with depth charges, forced to the surface and then fired on. The crew surrendered and the submarine sank soon afterward. Commanding officers of *Fanning* and *Nicholson* were LCDRs Arthur S. Carpenter and Frank D. Berrien, respectively.

Engineer officer, Navy—Charles Haynes Haswell, was commissioned Chief Engineer 12 July 1836, and Engineer in Chief 3 Oct. 1844. Haswell was the second Engineer in Chief, having been preceded by Gilbert L. Thompson on 1 Sept. 1842.

Enlisted man, buried in France during WWI—Louis Reinhardy, seaman second class, who fell overboard from *Jupiter* on 12 June 1917. His body was recovered 16 June and buried in Pauillac, 17 June 1917.

Equator, Navy ship across—Frigate *Essex*, 7 Feb. 1800, 30 days out of New York en route to Batavia.

Escort type carrier, in Navy—*Long Island*, commissioned 2 June 1941.

Ex-enlisted officer—see *sailors*.

Expedition, Navy—Authorized by Congress 18 May 1836, was Wilkes Exploring Expedition to the South Seas, led by LT John Wilkes, which sailed 18 Aug. 1838, returned to New York, after sailing around the world, in 1842. Wilkes expedition discovered the Antarctic Continent 19 Jan. 1840. See *North Pole*.

Fatal accident, naval aviation—20 June 1913, ENS W. D. Billingsly, naval aviator No. 9, was thrown from plane 1,600 feet over Annapolis. His passenger, LT J. H. Towers, rode the plane down, receiving serious injuries.

First five-star admiral—see *admiral*.

Flag, U.S., flown in Antarctic region—carried by *Flying Fish*, attached to Wilkes United States Exploring Expedition. During March, 1839, *Flying Fish* crossed the Antarctic Circle, reached latitude of 70°14' South on the 24th of that month—almost 400 miles inside Antarctic Circle.

Flag, U.S. fifty-star—flown at Fort McHenry, Baltimore, on 4 Jul. 1960.

Flag, U.S., to fly over what is now San Francisco—Raised at village of Yerba Buena, 9 July 1846, by CDR John B. Montgomery of USS *Portsmouth*. Montgomery published proclamation that the United States had formally taken possession of California. Site now marked by a plaque in Portsmouth Plaza in San Francisco. Representation of *Portsmouth* appears on all letterheads, checks and seals of Bank of America.

Flag, U.S., raised over Midway Island—28 Aug. 1867, by CAPT William Reynolds, commanding USS *Lackawanna*, who took possession of the island for the U.S.

Flag, U.S., raised over San Pedro, Calif.—7 Aug. 1846, when Marines from USS *Congress,* led by LT Jacob Zeilin, landed there and took possession for the United States.

Flag, U.S., to fly over Sea of Galilee—raised 8 Apr. 1848, by LT W. F. Lynch, in charge of the Navy Expedition to Jordan and the Dead Sea. Ceremony took place at Tiberias, when two small boats named *Fanny Skinner* and

Fanny Mason were launched there; the boats, pre-fabricated, were hauled in from the Mediterranean coast by camels. On 19 Apr., LT Lynch flew U.S. flag over the Dead Sea for the first time, on same boats.

Flag, U.S., to fly over North Pole—on 6 Apr. 1909, CDR Robert E. Peary reached the pole after nearly 20 years of effort in the Arctic. The flag was a small, silk, American flag given him by his wife 15 years earlier, and had been carried north on each of his previous expeditions. Four other flags carried by Peary, also flew above the pole that day; the Navy League flag, the Red Cross flag, the World's Ensign of Liberty and Peace, and the colors of Delta Kappa Epsilon.

Flag, U.S., to fly over Key West, Fla.—raised 25 Mar. 1822, when LT Matthew C. Perry, commanding USS *Shark,* proclaimed U.S. possession of the surrounding area.

Flag, U.S., to fly over land not a part of the United States—raised 27 Apr. 1805, over the Tripolitan fortress of Derne on north African coast, by LT Presley Neville O'Bannon of the U.S. Marines.

"Flag of America," ever displayed by an American man-of-war—raised by John Paul Jones, who had been commissioned second lieutenant that same day, on 22 Dec. 1775, aboard the *Alfred* at foot of Walnut Street in Philadelphia. Flag depicted a rattlesnake coiled around a pine tree and bore the motto "Don't Tread on Me."

Flag, saluted by a foreign power—"Continental Union flag" flown by the *Andrea Doria.* On 16 Nov. 1776, she reached St. Eustatius, Dutch West Indies, and saluted the Dutch Flag, which salute was returned by Governor Johannes de Graaff. However, the Governor was later removed from his post and the Dutch government withdrew the recognition.

Flag, officially saluted by a foreign power—flown by *Ranger,* commanded by John Paul Jones, on entering harbor of Quiberon, France, 14 Feb. 1778. *Ranger* fired a salute of 13 guns to ADM La Motte Picquet, commander of the French Naval Forces there, and in turn received nine guns, the normal salute for an admiral of any other Navy.

Flag, flown by a ship in the Navy, with the "stars and stripes" design as adopted by Congress on 14 June 1777—raised on *Ranger* in Portsmouth, New Hampshire, 4 July 1777, by CAPT John Paul Jones. Flags flown before that date were of various designs. This first "stars and stripes" supposed to have been made by a group of young ladies in Portsmouth, from their own and their mothers' gowns. The white stars came from the bridal dress of a Helen Seary.

Fleet Admirals—see *admirals.*

Fleet of warships, to circumnavigate the globe—sailed from Hampton Roads, Va., on 16 Dec. 1907, and returned on 22 Feb. 1909. Fleet commanded by RADM Robley Dunglison Evans, later relieved by RADM Charles Stillman Sperry. Ships were: *Connecticut, Georgia, Illinois, Kentucky, Louisiana, Kearsarge, Missouri, Minnesota, Ohio, Wisconsin, Nebraska, Kansas, Vermont, Rhode Island, New Jersey, Virginia,* and auxiliaries. During 46,000-mile cruise, stops made at Honolulu, Aukland, Sydney, Melbourne, Manila, Yokohama, Amoy, Colombo, Suez and Gibralter. An earlier round-the-world cruise was made by ships of the Wilkes Exploring Expedition, which left New York in August, 1838, and returned in 1842.

Flight, carrier to carrier from Pacific to Atlantic—made 6 June 1957, from *Bon Homme Richard* off California to *Saratoga* off Florida. Two F8Us made hop in three hours, 28 minutes; two A3D SKYWARRIORS made hop in four hours, one minute.

Flight, coast to coast, by a dirigible—completed 11 Oct. 1924, when USS *Shenandoah,* commanded by LCDR Zachary Lansdowne, reached San Diego, four days after departing from Lakehurst, N.J.

Flight, from ship, Navy—made 14 Nov. 1910, at Hampton Roads, Va., when Eugene Ely took off from scout cruiser *Birmingham* in 50 H.P. Curtiss Biplane, flew two miles to Norfolk. Runway was a sloping ramp, 83 feet long.

Flight, of Martin P6M SEAMASTER, swept-wing jet seaplane—14 July 1955.

Flight, round-the-world by a Navy squadron—completed 5 May 1955, when VP-1 reached NAS, Whidby Island, Wash., after a tour of duty in the Far East, by way of the Indian Ocean, Mediterranean, and the Atlantic.

Flight, Seaplane, in the U.S.—made 26 Jan. 1911, at San Diego, Calif., when Glenn Curtiss took off from and landed on the water with a hydro-aeroplane. On 17 Feb. he landed plane alongside *Pennsylvania* in the harbor, was hoisted aboard, placed afloat again by the ship's crane, took off and flew back to North Island.

Flight, longest non-stop, non-refueling—made by Lockheed P2V NEPTUNE, *Truculent Turtle,* piloted by CDR T. D. Vavies. *Turtle* took off from Perth, Australia, 29 Sept. 1946, flew almost half-way around the world, landing at Columbus, Ohio, 55 hours and 17 minutes later, establishing world's record distance of 11,235.6 miles.

Flight, by squadron of naval planes from mainland to Hawaii—made 10 and 11 Jan. 1934. Six P2Y-1 planes commanded by LCDR Knefler McGinnis, left San Francisco, Calif., 2:22 P.M. 10 Jan., and reached Pearl Harbor 24 hours and 56 minutes later, covering 2,399 miles at average speed of 100 miles an hour.

Flight, over South Pole—made 28 Nov. 1929, by LCDR Richard E. Byrd, in a tri-motored Ford; crew was composed of Bernt Balchen, Harold I. June, and Ashley C. McKinley, photographer.

Flight, over North Pole—made 9 May 1926, by LCDR Richard E. Byrd and Aviation Pilot Floyd Bennett, in tri-motored Fokker, *Josephine Ford,* from Kings Bay, Spitzbergen, to the pole and back in 15 hours.

Flight, longest, non-stop, seaplane—made by *Caroline Mars,* which flew 4,478 miles from Honolulu to Chicago, 27 Aug. 1948, carrying 42 persons and seven tons of cargo.

Flight, of Flying Platform, a one-man helicopter—made at Hiller plant in Palo Alto, Calif. 21 Jan. 1955. Flight occurred during ground tests and was therefore accidental, but successful.

Football, game between Naval Academy and Military Academy—played 29 Nov. 1890. Score Navy-24, Army-0.

Football game, in Portugal—played 9 Oct. 1955, by teams from destroyer *Zellars* and the carrier *Valley Forge.* Game was played in National Stadium, where 45,000 spectators saw *Valley Forge* win, 12-0.

Football game, played by Naval Academy—with Clifton Football Club of Baltimore, 30 Nov. 1882. Score: Clifton Club 8, Navy 0.

Foreign citizen, first to graduate with top honors from Submarine School, New London, Conn.—Cesar S. Wycoco, steward apprentice, USN, of Manila, P.I., who graduated 22 July 1955. Wycoco made highest marks in history of enlisted course at the Submarine School—3,918 out of possible 4.000.

Fueling-at-sea, operation—took place in Oct., 1893, when *Kearsarge* passed coal to *San Francisco* at the rate of two and two-thirds tons per hour. In April, 1963, oiler *Hassayampa* pumped an average of 11,426 barrels of fuel an hour to carrier *Constellation,* with both ships under way.

General, four star, Marine Corps—Thomas Holcomb, who acceded to that rank upon his retirement, 1 Jan. 1944.

German combatant ship, captured during WWII—(and only enemy ship taken by boarding since 1814) U-505, on 4 June 1944, near the Azores, hunter-killer group composed of carrier *Guadalcanal* and destroyer escorts *Jenks, Chattelain* and *Pillsbury* attacked the submarine and forced it to the surface. The German crew abandoned the submarine, leaving it in a sinking condition, but officers and men from the *Guadalcanal* and *Pillsbury* succeeded in salvaging the craft and it was brought to the United States.

German ship, captured during WWII—Blockade runner *Odenwald,* which was disguised as American ship *Willmoto. Odenwald* was captured by cruiser *Omaha* and destroyer *Somers* in mid-Atlantic, 6 Nov. 1941.

German submarine, to engage in offensive operations in U.S. territory—U-151, which damaged three small schooners off Cape Charles, Va., 25 May 1918.

German submarine, to surrender after VE day—*U-249,* which raised specified black flag to a patrol plane of Fleet Air Wing 7 near Scilly Islands, 9 May 1945.

German submarine, sunk by Navy aircraft during WWII—*U-656,* sunk 1 Mar. 1942, by planes from Patrol Squadron 82 operating out of Argentia, Newfoundland.

Gold, from California to reach the United States—carried to the East coast by LT Edward Fitzgerald Beale, who made the journey from west to east during July, August, and September of 1848. He reached Washington with a small bag of gold and word that Marshall had discovered the magic metal at Sutter's mill, near Coloma, early that year, thus setting off the rush of "Forty-Niners" to California.

Governor of Guam, Naval—COMO Seaton Schroeder, appointed 10 Feb. 1900.

Governor, Virgin Islands—RADM James H. Oliver, who took formal possession of islands on their purchase from Denmark, 25 Jan. 1917.

Graduate, Naval Academy—Richard Aulick, according to *Register of Graduates* published by U.S. Naval Academy Alumni Association. Aulick stood one in first group of graduates for years 1846-47-48, and is assigned No. 1 in *Register of Graduates.* He was commissioned passed midshipman 11 July 1846. However, since the Naval School (then called) did not open for classes until 10 Oct. 1845, and Aulick entered service as midshipman 19 Oct. 1840, only part of time as midshipman was spent at Annapolis. In 1850 school was officially named Naval Academy, and in 1851 regular instruction by classes was begun. (Prior to that time, midshipmen studied at school only when available on shore.) Of men first admitted to Academy in 1851 directly from civilian life, as opposed to their seniors who had had seagoing experience, first in that class was Thomas Oliver Selfridge, No. 299 in *Register of Graduates,* was first to complete regular Naval Academy course of study. Aulick died 8 June 1868, in Washington, D.C., a commander. Selfridge, retired since 1898, died 4 Feb. 1924, in Washington, D.C., a rear admiral.

Graduate, of Naval Academy to reach rank of rear admiral—Edward Simpson, No. 8 in the *Register of Graduates,* who was commissioned passed midshipman on 11 July 1846; he retired 3 Mar. 1886, as rear admiral and died in Washington, D.C., on 1 Dec. 1888.

Graduation exercises, held at Naval Academy—10 June 1854. Previous classes had been graduated, as early as 1846, but with no formal ceremony.

Guam, ship to visit—Sloop-of-war *Vincennes,* CDR John H. Aulick, which anchored at Apra 19 Nov. 1835.

Guided-missile cruiser, in world—*Boston,* commissioned 1 Nov. 1955.

Guided missile, high speed—KDU-1, a target drone version of REGULUS, used operationally 31 Mar. 1955.

Guided missile, launched by Navy's first guided missile experimental test ship, the *Norton Sound*—LOON, fired 26 Jan. 1949.

Guided missile, launched from a ship—LOON, fired by submarine *Cusk,* 1 May, 1947.

Guided missiles used during WWII—launched 23 Apr. 1945, when planes of Patrol Bombing Squadron 109 took off from Palawan and released two BAT automatic homing missiles against shipping in Balikpapan Harbor, Borneo.

Guns, major caliber, used by Navy in land-based offensive—14-inch guns, mounted on railway carriages, which were landed in France and first fired 6 Sept. 1918 in the Campiegne Forest, against German railroad and troop centers. These mobile batteries were built by the Navy Gun Factory, Washington, D.C.

Gyro-stabilizer installation, Navy—made by Sperry Gyroscope Company April 1913, aboard destroyer *Worden.*

Harbor, "officially opened"—on 14 Dec. 1911, armored cruiser *California* Pacific Fleet flagship steamed up Pearl Harbor channel, across which a red, white and blue ribbon had been stretched from shore to shore, broke the ribbon and proceeded to her anchorage, first large ship of the Navy to anchor in Pearl Harbor. First ship actually to enter Pearl Harbor was gunboat *Petrel,* which anchored there 11 Jan. 1905.

Helicopter Antisubmarine Squadron—*HS-1* was commissioned at Key West, Fla., 3 Oct. 1951.

Helicopter landing, aboard a hospital ship—made 21 Dec. 1951, on *Consolation.*

Helicopter Utility Squadron—commissioned 1 Apr. 1948.

Helium, used in airship—see *airship.*

Hospital, Naval, in U.S.—built at Portsmouth, Va., where cornerstone was laid 2 Apr. 1827, building was finally completed and dedicated in 1833. First naval hospital on Pacific Coast was built at Mare Island, Calif., and received first patients in 1870.

Hospital ship, used by Navy—*Red Rover,* captured Confederate ship converted for hospital use 26 Dec. 1862, in service until 12 Aug. 1865; operated on Mississippi River, carrying sick and wounded north out of war zone. First modern hospital ship: *Relief* (AH-1), first commissioned 28 Dec. 1920, served through WWII. During which time the Navy had the following hospital ships in service: *Benevolence, Bountiful, Comfort, Consolation, Haven, Hope, Mercy, Refuge, Repose, Rescue, Samaritan, Sanctuary, Solace* and *Tranquility.*

Hospital, established for use by the Navy—set up at Syracuse, Sicily, in

1802, by Surgeon Edward Cutbush, to care for sick and wounded during war with the Barbary Pirates. Hospital abandoned in April, 1805.

Hydrofoil patrol craft—USS *High Point* (PCH 1) launched on 17 Aug. 1962 at Seattle, Wash.

"Iron Man" award to a submarine—see *Submarine.*

Iron clad, in Navy—St. Louis, launched 12 Oct. 1861.

Iron ship, built for Navy—Side-wheel steamer *Michigan* launched at Erie, Pa., 5 Dec. 1843. Renamed *Wolverine* on 17 June 1905; stricken from Navy list 12 Mar. 1927. Ship operated only at Great Lakes; never on the high seas. See *pre-fabricated.*

Island, most shot-at—Kahoolawe, about 90 miles from island of Hawaii. Although never touched by enemy shells, during WWII, the nine-mile long island was used as a bombing and gunnery range by ships training in Hawaiian area, between 1943 and 1947 was shelled by over 800 ships.

Japan, U.S. Navy ship to visit—*Columbus,* CAPT Thomas W. Wyman, carrying COMO James Biddle. She anchored in Yeddo (Tokyo) Bay on 20 July 1846, and departed nine days later. Treatment of Japanese by COMO Biddle went far toward disposing them to receive Perry Expedition several years later.

Japanese midshipman, enrolled at Naval Academy—Zun Zow Matzmulla, admitted 8 Dec. 1868. Entry was authorized by Act of Congress dated 27 July 1868.

Japanese ship, sunk by a U.S. Navy ship during WWII—Midget submarine, by destroyer *Ward* off Pearl Harbor entrance, 7 Dec. 1941. First Japanese ship sunk after U.S. officially declared war on Japan was *I-170,* submarine, sunk off Hawaii by carrier aircraft, 10 Dec. 1941.

Japanese ships, last sunk during WWII—Coast defense vessels *No. 13* and *No. 47,* both sunk in Sea of Japan, 14 Aug. 1945 by submarine *Torsk.*

Japanese suicide plane, last ship sunk by—Destroyer *Callaghan,* hit off Okinawa, Saturday, 28 Aug. 1945.

Jet flights, into eye of a hurricane—made 9 Aug. 1955, when LTs Peter Mongilardi and George D. Hudson took F2H-2P BANSHEES into Hurricane "Connie," 420 miles east of Jacksonville, Fla., to obtain aerial photographs.

Jet aircraft, to operate from a carrier—a PHANTOM piloted by LCDR James Davidson, which made landings and take-offs from *Franklin D. Roosevelt,* 2 July 1946.

Jet-powered seaplane—Convair XF2Y SEA DART made first trial runs, San Diego Bay, 17 Dec. 1952.

Jet squadron, in naval aviation history—Fighter Squadron 17-A, which received its first jet aircraft, an FD PHANTOM, 23 July 1947.

Jewish officer, to become—CAPT Uriah Phillips Levy, entered Navy on

21 Oct. 1812, as sailing master, and received rank of captain, 29 Mar. 1844.

Jewish Officer—see chaplain.

Korea, casualties—see American military man.

Landing, aboard supercarrier *Forrestal*—3 Jan. 1956. Plane was FJ-3 FURY, piloted by CDR Ralph L. Werner.

Landing, aboard *Lexington*—made 5 Jan. 1928, by LT A. M. Pride.

Landing, aboard *Saratoga*—made 11 Jan. 1928, by CDR Marc A. Mitscher.

Landing, airplane, on ship of the Navy—made 18 Jan. 1911, at San Francisco, Calif. ship was armored cruiser *Pennsylvania*. Eugene Ely, flying a Curtiss pusher-type plane, landed on a specially built platform 132 feet long and 30 feet wide at 11:01 A.M. At 11:58 A.M. he took-off and flew back to Selfridge Field, in San Francisco.

Landing, carrier by jet aircraft—made 6 Nov. 1945, when ENS Jack C. West sat down on *Wake Island* in Ryan FR-1 FIREBALL. Plane was powered by both jet and piston engines; when piston engine failed, Ensign West made emergency landing with jet power only.

Landing, night carrier—made aboard *Langley* 1 Apr. 1925, by LCDR John D. Price.

Landing, carrier, night using experimental landing mirror system—made 24 Aug. 1955, when LCDR H. C. MacKnight put an F9F-8 COUGAR down on *Bennington*.

Landing "hook-on" in Naval aviation history—made 3 July 1929, when LT A. W. Gorton, flying a *UO-1* was picked up in mid-air by dirigible *Los Angeles* flying 2,500 feet over Lakehurst, N.J.

Landing carrier, while ship was underway—made by LCDR Godfrey C. Chevalier, flying an AEROMARINE, aboard *Langley,* 26 Oct. 1922.

Landing—see *Helicopter*.

Land offensive, by U.S. forces in WWII—opened 7 Aug. 1942, when U.S. Marines landed on Florida, Tulagi, Gavutu, Tanambogo and Guadalcanal in Solomon Islands.

Legislation, concerning naming of navy ships—passed 3 Mar. 1819. Congress ordered the Secretary of the Navy to name "ships of the first class for states, of the second class for rivers and the third class for cities and towns." Ships of the second and third class were then considered to be frigates and sloops.

Legislation, concerning the Navy—enacted by Congress, 13 Oct. 1775.

Liberty Ship—SS *Patrick Henry*, launched at Baltimore, Md., 27 Sept. 1941. A total of 2,710 Liberty ships were built in the U.S. during WWII. Last one was *Albert M. Boe*, delivered 30 Oct. 1945. See *Victory ship*.

Lighter-than-air aircraft tender, constructed as such—*Wright*, commissioned 16 Dec. 1921.

Loon—see *guided missile.*

"Loop the loop," in seaplane—made by CAPT Francis T. Evans, USMC, in JENNY N-9 floatplane at Pensacola, 13 Feb. 1917.

Magellan, Straits of—first submarine through—*Cutlass,* enroute from Balboa, C.Z. to Philadelphia, early 1948.

Marine aviation unit, deployed outside continental U.S.—Flight L, Fourth Squadron, which reached Guam 17 Mar. 1921.

Marine officer, to command a naval vessel—LT John M. Gamble, who sailed into the Pacific in 1812 with CAPT David Porter in *Essex.* In April 1813, Porter captured three British whalers, one of which, renamed *Greenwich,* was made a man-of-war with a crew of 14 men under LT Gamble. In July of that year, while commanding *Greenwich,* Gamble captured the British *Seringapatam,* and was commended by Porter for his masterful display of naval tactics.

Marine officer, to enter the Corps after graduation from Naval Academy—Herbert Lemuel Droper, of Class of 1887, who transferred to Marine Corps under authority contained in act of Congress approved 5 Aug. 1882.

Marine officer, to receive flight training—1stLT Alfred A. Cunningham, who reported to the Superintendent, Naval Academy, 22 May 1912, "for duty in connection with aviation," was then ordered to Burgess Company at Marblehead for training, later designated Naval Aviator No. 5.

Marine unit, to take over a Navy unit—Marine Aircraft Group at Samoa, was assigned operational control of a Navy Scouting Squadron on 22 Apr. 1942.

Mascot, to visit Antarctic—"Sydney," Newfoundland dog belonging to LT John Wilkes, who commanded the South Seas Exploring Expedition. Although the expedition did not actually reach the newly discovered continent (first seen by Wilkes on 19 Jan. 1840), officers from *Vincennes* landed on floating ice near the ice barrier, 14 Feb. 1840, to make observations. "Sydney" also landed.

Mayor, (alcalde), of San Francisco—LT Washington A. Bartlett, USN, who was also first to apply present name to what was then, 4 Jan. 1847, 70-year-old village of Yerba Buena.

McClure Strait, transit—McClure Strait is ice-locked western entrance to Northwest Passage in Canadian Arctic, transited 4 Sept. 1954, by Navy ice-breaker *Burton Island* in company with Coast Guard icebreaker *Northwind.*

Medical officer, to publish a book—Surgeon Edward Cutbush who entered Navy 24 June 1799, resigned 10 June 1829. His "Observations on the Means of Preserving the Health of Soldiers and Sailors; and on the

Duties of the Medical Department of the Army and Navy; with remarks on hospitals and their internal arrangement," was printed by Thomas Dobson, Philadelphia, 1808. See *hospital.*

Medal—see *campaign medal, Silver Star.*

Medical Officer—see *doctor, surgeon.*

Memorial Day, observed—May 30, 1868. *Merchant ship (American), to circumnavigate globe: Columbia,* which sailed from Boston 30 Sept. 1787, under CAPT Kendrick, accompanied by sloop *Washington,* under CAPT Robert Gray, who had served in the Navy during the Revolution. Enroute to the Pacific, CAPT Gray exchanged ships with CAPT Kendrick, brought *Columbia* back to Boston, 9 Aug. 1790, after 41,899 mile trip.

Merchant ship (American) lost in enemy air attack, WWII—SS *Steel Seafarer,* sunk by German planes, Gulf of Suez, Sunday, 7 Sept. 1941.

Merchant ship (American) sunk in WWII—SS *City of Bayville,* 8 Nov. 1940, by German mine in Bass Strait, Australia.

Minelayer, built as such—*Terror,* commissioned 15 July 1942. Four earlier minelayers: *Baltimore, Yosemite, Aroostock* and *Oglala,* were conversions. First ship to lay mines: *Baltimore,* Spanish-American War cruiser, recommissioned as minelayer 8 Mar. 1915, which laid mines in WWI.

Mines, laid by carrier planes—30 Mar.-1 Apr. 1944, while operating with Task Force 58, Torpedo Squadrons 2, 8, and 16 mined Palau Harbor.

Mooring mast, designed for shipboard use—Installed on USS *Patoka.* Dirigible *Shenandoah* secured to mast 8 Aug. 1924, while ship was underway in Narragansett Bay, and remained fast until she anchored off Jamestown, R.I.

Mutiny, first and only in the Navy—terminated 1 Dec. 1842, when Midshipman Philip Spencer, son of the Secretary of War, Boatswain Samuel Cromwell, and Seaman Elisha Small, were hanged aboard the brig *Somers.* CDR Alexander Slidell Mackenzie, commanding *Somers,* had previously ordered court martial, which convicted the three of conspiring to organize a mutiny. The ringleader, Midshipman Spencer, planned to murder the officers, take over the ship, and become a pirate. Mackenzie was later tried by court martial, but exonerated.

National observatory, in America—established by Navy, Washington, D.C., 6 Dec. 1830. First instrument installed was 30-inch portable transit, built by Richard Patten of New York.

NATS scheduled flight, over Atlantic—20 Dec. 1943, from Patuxent River to Port Lyautey.

NATS (Naval Air Transport Service) scheduled flight—2 Mar. 1942, by R4D from Norfolk to Squantum, Mass.

NATS flight, over the Pacific—15 May 1942, Alameda to Honolulu.

Naval Attache—LCDR French E. Chadwick, stationed in London, England, from 15 Nov. 1882, until 3 Apr. 1889.

Naval militia—established by State of Massachusetts. Four companies were formed 29 Mar. 1890, under authority contained in Executive Order dated 18 Mar. 1890.

Navy Day—observed 27 Oct. 1922.

Navy "E" Certificates—issued by Bureau of Ordnance 25 July 1941, to 14 companies as awards for meritorious service.

Navy Nurse Corps, superintendent—Esther Voorhees Hasson, who served from 18 Aug. 1908, to 16 Jan. 1911. The corps was established 13 May 1908.

Navy Post Office—see *post office.*

Navy Regulations—adopted 28 Nov. 1775.

Navy yard, west coast—Mare Island Navy Yard, now the Mare Island Naval Shipyard. First officer at Mare Island was CDR David G. Farragut, who took possession of Mare Island on 16 Sept. 1854. First Mare Island built ship was steamer *Saginaw,* launched 3 Mar. 1859.

Negro, commissioned in Naval Reserve—Bernard Whitfield Robinson, commissioned 18 June 1942.

Negro, commissioned in Regular Navy—John Lee, of Indianapolis, Ind., commissioned ensign 15 Mar. 1947, assigned to *Kearsarge.* Lee had previously been appointed ensign, Naval Reserve, 30 July, 1945.

Negro midshipman, to enter Naval Academy—James Henry Conyers, of South Carolina, 21 Sept. 1872. Conyers did not graduate.

Negro midshipman, to graduate from Naval Academy—Wesley Anthony Brown of Washington, D.C., commissioned ensign 3 June 1949.

Negro women, sworn into WAVES—13 Nov. 1944. Miss Harriet Ida Pickens and Miss Francis Eliza Wills, officer candidates, sent to Smith College, Northampton, Mass., for training.

Negro woman to christen ship—see *christening.*

Negro woman, to serve as nurse in Navy Reserve Nurse Corps—Phyllis Mae Daley of New York City, sworn in as an ensign 8 Mar. 1945.

Night carrier landing—see *landing, carrier, night.*

North Pole expedition, to reach the Pole—commanded by CDR Robert E. Peary, who planted U.S. flag at pole, 6 Apr. 1909. Peary was accompanied by Matthew Henson, an American Negro, and four Eskimos. See *flag.*

North Pole, flight—see *flight.*

Northwest Passage—see *McClure Strait.*

Nuclear Power School—established at U.S. Naval Submarine Base, New London, Conn., 10 Jan. 1956.

Nuclear-powered aircraft carrier—USS *Enterprise* (CVAN 65) commissioned 25 Nov. 1961.

Nuclear-powered cruiser—USS *Long Beach* (CGN 9) commissioned 1 Sept. 1961.

Nuclear-powered guided missile frigate—USS *Bainbridge* (DLGN 25) commissioned at Quincy, Mass., 6 Oct. 1962.

Nuclear-powered submarine—USS *Nautilus* commissioned 20 Sept. 1954.

Nuclear-powered reactor in Antarctic—At NAF McMurdo Sound, began delivering electricity 10 July 1962.

Nuclear-powered ship in the world—*Nautilus,* submarine, commissioned 30 Sept. 1954, with CDR Eugene P. Wilkinson as first commanding officer: Keel was laid 14 June 1952, by President Harry S. Truman, whose initials are welded onto the keel plate; christened 21 Jan. 1954, by Mrs. Dwight D. Eisenhower, first wife of President to sponsor a submarine. Displacement, 3,000 tons; length 300 feet; beam 28 feet. Cost: $29,000,000.

North Pole, ship to reach—see *submarine.*

Ocean bottom, reached by man—23 Jan. 1960, Navy bathyscaph *Trieste,* manned by LT Don Walsh and scientist Jacques Piccard, reached bottom of Marianas Trench off Guam, 35,800 feet below sea level.

Oceongrapher, to chart seas for ocean travel—CDR Matthew Maury, who wrote world's first authoritative work on *Sailing Directions* in 1851, was first to advocate sailing along great circle routes, the shortest possible distance between any two points on globe.

Officer, casualty, Civil War—CDR James Harmon Ward, commanding small craft flotilla on Potomac River, at Mathias' Point, 26 June 1861, Destroyer *Ward,* named in his honor, fired first shots of WWII at Pearl Harbor, 7 Dec. 1941, sinking Japanese submarine.

Officer casualty, Spanish-American War—ENS Worth Bagley, killed 11 May 1898, while serving in torpedo boat *Winslow* during attack on Cardenas, Cuba.

Officer casualty, WWI—LT C. C. Thomas, commanding armed guard crew of SS *Vacuum* when it was torpedoed by German submarine, 28 Apr. 1917. See *admiral, killed.*

Officers, regular Navy—commissioned 22 Dec. 1775.

Officer, U.S. Navy, to reach rank of admiral—John Paul Jones, who was first commissioned in Continental Navy as a 1stLT, 1775. However, John Paul Jones was never admiral in United States Navy; highest rank was captain, held when Revolutionary War ended. Jones went to Russia and was made a rear admiral in Imperial Russian Navy.

Orbital flight—see Space flight

Pacific Ocean, Navy ship to enter—Frigate *Essex,* under CAPT David Porter, which rounded Cape Horn on 14 Feb. 1813.

Panama Canal, transit by a ship of U.S. Navy—completed by collier *Jupi-*

ter, Columbus Day, 12 Oct. 1914. *Jupiter,* enroute from Pacific to Atlantic, entered canal at Balboa, 10 Oct., stopped in Gatun Lake to determine fresh water effect on barnacles. The first *westward* transit of the Panama Canal, from Atlantic to Pacific, was made by the battleships *Ohio, Missouri* and *Wisconsin,* on 16 July 1915.

Parasite-aircraft—a glider, with LT R. S. Barnaby as pilot, dropped from dirigible **Los Angeles,** 31 June 1930, at altitude of 3,000 feet.

Passengers, most ever carried by American ship—Hungnam, Korea, 22 Dec. 1950, SS *Meredith Victory,* with normal accommodations for 12 passengers, moved 14,000 South Korean refugees to Pusan. *Meredith Victory* was government-owned cargo ship operated for MSTS by Moore-McCormick Steamship Lines.

Passengers, most ever carried on one flight—301 persons and seven crew members, were flown from San Diego to Alemeda, Calif., 19 May 1949, by Martin flying boat *Marshall Mars.*

Patrol Squadron, to fly over North Pole—VP-26, composed of P2V NEPTUNES. In support of MSTS Arctic Operations in summer of 1956, all planes and members of the squadron flew around and over the pole while operating out of Greenland, Buffin Island, and Cornwallis Island.

Patrol Squadron, to complete a round the world flight—Patrol Squadron One, (12 P2V NEPTUNES) which returned to home base, Whidbey Island, Wash. 5 May 1955.

Pay bill, for naval retired personnel—enacted by Congress 2 Mar. 1799. See *pension.*

Pearl Harbor, ship to enter—see *harbor.*

Pilot ejection seat, used in emergency escape—LT J. L. Fruit, 9 Aug. 1949, in ejection from F2H-1 BANSHEE making over 500 knots.

Pension act—passed by Congress 18 Mar. 1818. Provided $20 a month to privates who had served at least nine months in Army or Navy, and could prove their need.

Pilot—see *aviation.*

Podiatrist, commissioned in Navy—Richard S. Gilbert, commissioned lieutenant, junior grade, Navy Medical Service Corps, 3 June 1953.

Polaris missile, fired from submarine—21 July 1960, ballistic missile submarine *George Washington* successfully launched two POLARIS missiles while cruising submerged, hit target 1,100 miles away.

Polaris missile, fired from submerged submarine—on 20 May 1960, USS *George Washington,* running submerged off Cape Canaveral, fired a Polaris 1000 miles down Atlantic Missile Range.

Post offices, naval—established on *Illinois, Prairie* and *Rhode Island,* 15 Aug. 1908. Navy mail service was established 27 May 1908; enlisted men designated as navy mail clerks and assistant navy mail clerks were given annual extra compensation of $500 and $300, respectively.

Pre-fabricated ship, built for Navy—*Michigan,* launched 5 Dec. 1843, built in sections at Pittsburgh, hauled to Erie, Pa., for assembly and launching. For first pre-fabricated floating dock, (See *drydock, floating*). First pre-fabricated small boats were used by Lynch Expedition to the Dead Sea, in 1847-48; hauled overland by camels, assembled and launched at Tiberias 8 Apr. 1848.

President, through Panama Canal—Franklin D. Roosevelt, 11 July 1934, aboard cruiser *Houston.*

President, to travel in submerged submarine—Harry S. Truman, who made a dive in a captured German submarine at Key West, Fla., 21 Nov. 1946.

President, to visit foreign country—Theodore Roosevelt, who visited Panama from 14 Nov. to 17 Nov. 1906; trip was made aboard battleship *Louisiana.*

President, to visit Hawaii—Franklin D. Roosevelt, aboard cruiser *Houston,* landed at Hilo, 25 July 1934.

President, to visit South America—Franklin D. Roosevelt, aboard cruiser *Houston,* 1934.

Presidential Review—4 July 1801, on White House grounds, when Thomas Jefferson reviewed U.S. Marines, led by newly formed Marine Band.

Prize money, paid by United States Navy—collected by officers and men of *Delaware,* CAPT Stephen Decatur, Sr., which captured French *Croyable,* June 1798. Earlier awards of prize money, during Revolutionary War, were paid to members of Continental Navy, state navies, and privateers.

Prize, taken by Continental sea-going forces—ship captured by *Hannah,* 7 Sept. 1775.

Prize, taken during Spanish-American war—Spanish ship *Beuna Ventura,* with cargo worth $150,000, taken by *Nashville,* 22 Apr. 1898.

Provisioning at sea—in 1804, during War with Tripoli, ketch *Intrepid* transferred fresh provisions to squadron under COMO Edward Preble.

Radar experiments—made 27 Sept. 1922, at Naval Aircraft Radio Laboratory, Anascostia, D.C., by Dr. Albert H. Taylor and Leo C. Young.

Radar installation, on battleship—placed aboard *New York* late in 1938; it was tested early in 1939, able to detect destroyers at ranges up to eight miles. Set was constructed at Naval Research Laboratory, in Washington, D.C. First contract awarded commercial firm for radar manufacture went to RCA, October 1939.

Radio station, operation by Navy—established at Navesink, N.J., 1903, Chief Radioman Jack Scanlin in charge.

Radio transmission, from airborne source—made 26 July 1912, at Annapolis, under the direction of ENS C. H. Maddox. LT John Rodgers sent letter "D" at short intervals; this was "easily received" by destroyer *Stringham* about a mile away.

Radio transmission, between submerged submarine and surface ship— 5 Oct. 1919, submarine *H-2*, submerged in Hudson River at 96th Street, New York, communicated with destroyer *Blakely.*

Radio transmission, heard around the world—flashed from Lafayette Radio Station near Bordeaux, France, on 21 Aug. 1920, one of several built overseas by Navy during and shortly after WWI.

Radio compass, on navy aircraft—used 7 July 1920, when Curtiss seaplane flew from Norfolk, Va., to battleship *Ohio*, 90 miles at sea, and returned, guided entirely by radio signals.

Radio telephone, conversation (ship to shore)—6 May 1916, CAPT Lloyd H. Chandler of battleship *New Hampshire*, at sea off Norfolk, talked with Secretary of the Navy Josephus Daniels in Washington, D.C. Two days later, *New Hampshire* completed a trans-continental phone hook-up with Mare Island Navy Yard, in California.

Recruit training center, "boot camp"—established June 1883, Newport, R.I.

Rocket attack by U.S. aircraft—made by planes from carrier *Block Island*, 11 Jan. 1944, against German submarine.

Rockets—see Viking, *V-2*, Loon.

Round-the-world flight—see *flight, round-the-world.*

Royalty, first ship visited by—*Potomac*, visited by King and Queen of Sandwich Islands (Hawaii) in Honolulu harbor, 5 Aug. 1832. A 21-gun salute was fired both on their arrival and departure. Same voyage, 25 Jan. 1833, *Potomac* was visited by "the President of Peru and lady."

Sailors, to become admiral—so far, six of the Navy's "white hats" have worked their way up to where they pinned on admiral's stars: Archie A. Antrim, Gerald A. Eubank, and Charles W. Fox, all in the Supply Corps; Henry Hartley, Alfred M. Pride, Line; and Giles C. Stedman, in the Reserve (with Coast Guard enlisted service.)

Salute to American flag by a foreign power—see *flag, officially saluted.*

School, aerological—opened at Pensacola, Fla., 1 Nov. 1919, first class consisted of four Navy and one Marine Corps officers.

School, medical—established at old Philadelphia Navy Yard, 1820, by Surgeon Thomas Harris, later second Chief of Bureau of Medicine and Surgery. School trained newly appointed medical officers for navy medical practice.

School, nautical municipal—opened 11 Jan. 1875, aboard USS *St. Marys,* New York City. School was authorized and supported by State of New York.

School, naval air training—opened at Pensacola, Fla., on 1 Dec. 1914, under command of CAPT Henry C. Mustin; with staff of three instructors and 12 mechanics.

School, Officers training—established by COMO William Bainbridge, Navy Yard, Charleston, Mass., 10 Dec. 1815.

School, Chaplains—established at Norfolk, Va., 23 Feb. 1942.

School—see *War College.*

SeaBees, sent to overseas duty—left United States 27 Jan. 1942, enroute to Bora Bora, Society Islands.

SeaBee Training Camp—Camp Allen, Va., commissioned 21 Mar. 1942.

SeaBees, killed in action—Eight men of 6th Battalion, Guadalcanal, 16 Oct. 1942.

Seaplane (CATALINA type), last in service—on 3 Jan. 1957, the last "Cat," a PBY–6A of NARTU Atlanta, was ordered retired. The first CATALINA, a PBY-1, joined the fleet in 1937.

Seaplane, with turbo-prop engines—experimental CONVAIR P5Y, a 60-ton craft first flight tested at San Diego, 18 Apr. 1950. Four Allison T-40 engines, each turned 15 foot diameter contra-rotating propellers.

Secretary of the Navy, appointed to that office—George Cabot, of Massachusetts, whose appointment was dated 3 May 1798. He declined the appointment. The first Secretary of the Navy who actually took office as such was Benjamin Stoddard, whose appointment was dated 18 May 1798.

Secretary of the Navy, to ride in an aircraft—Josephus Daniels, Annapolis, 21 May 1913. Plane was piloted by CDR John Towers.

Ship, brick—Battleship *Illinois,* an outstanding naval exhibit at the Chicago World's Fair in 1893. An exact replica of *Oregon* class battleships then building in coastal yards, hull was made of bricks coated with cement; entire structure rested on wooden pilings extending into Lake Michigan. It gave a striking impression of being afloat. Over 3,000,000 people visited this brick battleship, many went home convinced they had been aboard an actual battleship.

Ship, built as a minelayer—see *minelayer.*

Ship, built on the Pacific Coast—Sidewheel steamer *Saginaw,* launched 2 Mar. 1859, at Mare Island Navy Yard. She was 155 feet long, displaced 505 tons, cost approximately $250,000.

Ship, built for Navy by Federal Government—*Chesapeake,* authorized by Congress, 27 Mar. 1794. Work on the ship began in 1794, at Gosport, (Va.) Navy Yard, with CAPT Richard Dale superintending. Construction halted in 1796, began again in 1797, was completed in 1799, with COMO Samuel Barron then superintendent of the yard.

Ship, built solely to train Naval Academy cadets (now termed midship-

men)—*Chesapeake*, launched 20 June 1899. Her first practice cruise commenced 10 June 1900, with 110 cadets on board.

Ship, electric drive—see *electric*.

Ship of war, captured by Continental Navy—British *Edward*, taken by *Lexington* under CAPT John Barry, 7 Apr. 1776, off coast of Virginia. Another British ship, *Hawk*, a tender, was captured three days earlier, on 4 Apr. by *Columbus* under CAPT Abraham Whipple.

Ship, captured by U.S. Navy in War of 1812—British *Alert*, taken by USS *Essex*, under CAPT David Porter, in eight minute battle off Newfoundland, 13 Aug. 1812.

Ship, to cross Rocky Mountains—Destroyer escort *Brennan:* prefabricated in Denver, Colo., shipped in sections, by rail, to Mare Island Naval Shipyard in California, assembled and launched 22 Aug. 1942. Ship was launched, first commissioned, as HMS *Bentinck;* later transferred to U.S. Navy and assigned its present name.

Ship, U.S. Navy, commissioned in Canada—Patrol gunboat *Action*, built at Collingwood, Ontario, commissioned there 22 Nov. 1942.

Ship, designed and built as seaplane tender—*Curtiss*, launched 20 Apr. 1940, at Camden, N.J. Earlier seaplane tenders, *Jason* and *Langley*, were converted colliers.

Ship, last U.S. sunk in WWI—USS *Lucia*, torpedoed 17 Oct. 1918; crew rescued by steamer *Fairfax*.

Ship, Navy, steam powered to cross Atlantic—see *transatlantic crossing*.

Ship, Navy, steam powered to circumnavigate the globe—*Ticonderoga*, which left Hampton Roads, 7 Dec. 1878 and completed the two-year cruise 9 Nov. 1880.

Ship, Navy, with all-welded hull—*YG-16*, a self-propelled garbage lighter, launched 4 Aug. 1931, at the Mare Island Navy Yard.

Ship, named for enlisted man—*Osmond Ingram*, destroyer. Osmond Kelly Ingram, gunner's mate first class, was born in Pratt City, Ala., 4 Aug. 1887, killed when the destroyer *Cassin* was torpedoed by a German submarine. Ingram was trying to throw depth charge overboard before the torpedo struck, and was blown overboard; he was also the first navy casualty due to enemy action in WWI.

Ship, named for a Negro—Destroyer *Harmon*, honoring Leonard Roy Harmon, mess attendant, who was posthumously awarded the Navy Cross for action in shielding a shipmate from enemy fire during Battle of Guadalcanal, 12-13 Nov. 1942.

Ship, named for a woman—*Harriet Lane*, a Civil-war side-wheel steamer honoring the niece of President James Buchanan. On 12 Apr. 1861, *Harriet Lane* fired first shot from a naval vessel during Civil War.

Ship, combatant type, named for a woman—WWII destroyer, *Higbee*, named for Lenah S. Higbee, Superintendent of Navy Nurses during WWI. Five transports in service during WWII were also named for women: *Dorothea Dix* for Superintendent of Nurses during Civil War; *Elizabeth C. Stanton* for early American leader in women's rights; *Florence Nightingale* for famous Crimean War nurse; *Lyon* for Mary Lyon, who founded Mount Holyoke College; and *Susan B. Anthony* for "Mother of American Woman Suffrage."

Ship, with a plural name—*The Sullivans*, honoring five brothers lost when cruiser *Juneau* was sunk on 15 Nov. 1942, off Guadalcanal. Sullivan brothers enlisted in Navy at Waterloo, Iowa, 3 Jan. 1942; their names were George Thomas, Francis Henry, Joseph Eugene, Madison Abel and Albert Leo. *The Sullivans* was christened 4 Apr. 1943, by the mother, Mrs. Thomas F. Sullivan. Loss of Sullivan brothers was first time in U.S. Navy history that five members of a family died together in battle. However, there are other ships named for as many as five members of the same family who served together in battle.

Destroyer *O'Brien* was named for CAPT Gideon O'Brien and four brothers, Jeremiah, Joseph, John and William, all of Machias, Me., principal figures in first naval battle of the Revolutionary War. They took over a lumber schooner loaded with other Yankees and defeated the British sloop-of-war *Margaretta* in a battle fought mostly with pitchforks.

Destroyer *Ellet* was named for five members of Ellet family who served during Civil War: Charles Ellet, Jr., Charles Rivers Ellet, son of Charles; Alfred Washington Ellet, brother of Charles; John Ellet, nephew of Alfred; and Edward C. Ellet, son of Alfred.

Destroyer *Nicholson* was named for CAPTs Samuel Nicholson, John Nicholson and James Nicholson, all of whom served during Revolutionary War; for William C. Nicholson, son of John, who served in both War of 1812 and Civil War; and for James W. A. Nicholson, grandson of Samuel, who was with Perry during expedition to Japan, 1852-54.

Destroyer *John Rodgers* was named for three officers, all members of same family and with the same name: COMO John Rodgers, who served during the Revolutionary War; RADM John Rodgers, who served during Civil War; and CDR John Rodgers, who served during WWI, was killed in airplane crash, 1926.

Another destroyer named *Rogers* was named for three brothers killed in one battle: Jack Ellis Rogers, Jr., seaman first class; Edward Keith Rogers, seaman first class; and Charles Ethbert Rogers, seaman first class. All three men were killed in action aboard cruiser *New Orleans*, 3 Nov. 1942.

Destroyer *Hollister* was named for three brothers killed during WWII:

Lyle Eugene Hollister, radioman second class; Richard Jerome Hollister, seaman second class; and William Howard Hollister, seaman second class.

Destroyer *Gearing* was named for three members of same family: CDR Henry Chalfant Gearing, who served in Spanish-American War; CAPT Henry Chalfant Gearing, Jr., who served during both world wars; and LT Henry Chalfant Gearing, III, killed aboard cruiser *Juneau* in WWII.

High speed transport *Barber* was named for three brothers lost when battleship *Oklahoma* was bombed at Pearl Harbor on 7 Dec. 1941: Malcolm John Barber, Leroy Kenneth Barber, and Randolph Harold Barber.

Destroyer *Meade* was named for two brothers who served during the Civil War: RADM Richard W. Meade and BRIGGEN Robert L. Meade, USMC.

Ships—see *Liberty ship, Victory ship*.

Ship, most pictured in U.S. Navy—USS *Portsmouth,* sloop of war launched at Portsmouth, N.H., 1843. She served in Pacific for many years during middle nineteenth century. While commanded by CDR John B. Montgomery, *Portsmouth* landed a detachment of Marines at Yerba Buena, Calif., 9 July 1846; these Marines raised the first U.S. flag over what is now California. When Bank of America was founded in San Francisco in 1904, its first office was on Portsmouth Square, named for USS *Portsmouth,* and the bank adopted a seal which pictured the same ship. Ever since, this ship has appeared on all Bank of America checks and passbooks, all Bank of America stationery is watermarked with the same design, staff members of the Bank wear service pins bearing the seal in miniature, and it appears in enlarged form on facades of hundreds of Bank of America buildings.

Ships, steel, in Navy—cruisers *Atlanta, Boston,* and *Chicago,* and the despatch boat *Dolphin,* authorized 3 Mar. 1883.

Smoke Screen—used 5 Sept. 1923, in tests conducted off Cape Hatteras.

Shot, fired by Navy, Civil War—12 Apr. 1861, steamer USS *Harriet Lane* fired across bow of SS *Nashville* to force her to show her colors.

Shot (last) fired in Civil War—*fired* 22 June 1865 in Bering Sea, 74 days after Appomattox and nearly two months after surrender of Confederate Army. Ship was Confederate raider *Shenandoah,* which had captured 38 U.S. ships, mostly whalers, and did not know the war was over. On 2 Aug. 1865, *Shenandoah* finally heard of the Confederate surrender, sailed to England, surrendered.

Shot, in Spanish-American War—fired by USS *Nashville* 22 Apr. 1898, when she captured Spanish steamer *Buena Ventura*.

Shot, World War I—fired 7 Apr. 1917, at Apra, Guam, as armed men from USS *Supply* went to board interned German ship *Cormorant.* The shot, fired across bow of a German launch to force its surrender, was fired by CORP Chickie, USMC.

Shot, World War II—fired by old destroyer *Ward,* 7 Dec. 1941, when she opened fire on and sank Japanese midget submarine outside Pearl Harbor, before the Japanese raid commenced.

Silver Star Medal, awarded to civilian—presented to Tony Duenas, a native of Guam, during WWII.

South Pole, flight over—see *flight, south pole.*

Space flight, by American—On 5 May 1961 CDR Alan B. Shepard in "Freedom 7" made 15-minute flight, 116 miles high, 302 miles down range from Cape Canaveral, was picked up by USS *Lake Champlain.*

Space flight, American, man in orbit—On 20 Feb. 1962 LCOL John H. Glenn, USMC, in Mercury capsule made three orbits of earth in 4 hours and 55 minutes, average speed of 17,400 miles per hour, was picked up by USS *Noa* (DD 841). (First space flight was Russian.)

"Stars and Stripes," flown—see *flag.*

Steam ship, equipped with screw propeller—USS *Princeton,* named for Princeton, N.J., designed by John Ericsson, launched at Philadelphia Navy Yard 10 Dec. 1843. All earlier steam ships had paddle wheels.

Steam warship, in world—USS *Fulton,* launched at Brown's Shipyard, N.Y., 29 Oct. 1814.

Straits of Magellan, Navy ship through—the schooner *Shark,* December 1839.

Submarine, nuclear-powered—see *nuclear-powered ship.*

Submarine, biggest—*Triton,* nuclear-powered radar picket type, commissioned 10 Nov. 1959. Ship is 447 feet long, displaces 5,900 tons.

Submarine, built for offensive use—*American Turtle,* designed by David Bushnell. Propelled by hand cranked wooden screw, carried one man, moved at three knots. On 7 Sept. 1776, Ezra Lee used the boat to attack British flagship *Eagle* in New York harbor, but with no success.

Submarine, built on Great Lakes—USS *Peto,* launched at Manitowoc, Wis., 30 Apr. 1942.

Submarine, practical—known as *Holland No. 9,* built by Holland Torpedo Co., New York, made first dive of 100 minutes 17 Mar. 1898. Ship was 53 feet 11 inches long. Commissioned in Navy on 12 Oct. 1900, as *Submarine No. 1.*

Submarine disaster—25 Mar. 1915, *F-4* sank off Honolulu, Hawaii, with 21 lives lost.

Submarine, to circumnavigate world submerged—USS *Triton* (SSRN 586) submerged 16 Feb. 1960 off Montauk Point, returned to U.S. 10 May

1960, sailing around the world submerged in 84 days, a distance of 36,014 miles.

Submarine, to fly five-star admiral's flag—*Menhaden,* which flew flag of FADM C. W. Nimitz, when VADM Raymond A. Spruance relieved Nimitz as Commander in Chief, Pacific Fleet, 24 Nov. 1945. When *Menhaden* was recommissioned 6 Mar. 1953, FADM Nimitz made commissioning address and the ship flew his five-star flag a second time.

Submarine, lost due to enemy action, WWII—*Sealion,* wrecked by Japanese bombs while drydocked at Cavite Navy Yard, 10 Dec. 1941.

Submarine, with internal combustion engine—*Argonaut,* first demonstrated by Simon Lake on Patapsco River near Baltimore, 15 Dec. 1897.

Submarine, to reach North Pole—*Nautilus,* 7 Aug. 1958. In four days she cruised 1,830 miles under polar ice.

Submarine, to sink Japanese warship—*Gudgeon,* which sank submarine *I-173* off Midway 27 Jan. 1942. *Gudgeon* was also first U.S. Navy submarine ever to sink another submarine.

Submarine, to surface at North Pole—USS *Skate* (SSN 578) 17 Mar. 1959.

Submarine, to sink Japanese ship—*Swordfish,* which torpedoed *Atsutasan Maru* 15 Dec. 1941.

Submarine lung—developed by LT Charles B. Momsen, Chief Gunner Clarence L. Tibbals, and Mr. Frank M. Hobson, first tested by Momsen and Tibbals 10 May 1929, in water over 200 feet deep. In first full scale test, 30 Aug. 1929, 26 officers and men used lungs to reach surface of Thames River from submerged submarine *S-4.*

Submarine, midget—*X-1,* commissioned 7 Oct. 1955; length 55 feet, diameter seven feet, weight 25 tons.

Submarine, to sink but serve again—*Squalus,* which sank in 240 feet of water off Portsmouth, N.H., 23 May 1939; 33 of her 59 man crew were saved. Raised and refitted, the ship was renamed *Sailfish,* fought through WWII.

Submarine, to transit Straits of Magellan—*Cutlass, sailing from Balboa,* C.Z., around South America to Philadelphia, spring of 1948.

Submarine, to round Cape of Good Hope—*Jallao,* 24 Feb. 1956, west-bound from Port Said. Also first submarine to sail around Africa.

Submarine torpedo attack—see *torpedo.*

Suez Canal, transit by ship of Navy—13 Aug. 1870, *Palos* completed passage from Mediterranean to Red Sea.

Summer cruise, midshipmen—made by steamer *John Hancock,* 1851, in Chesapeake Bay.

Surgeon, Navy—George Balfour, transferred from Army 9 Mar. 1798, served until 12 Apr. 1804.

Surgeon General, Navy—William Maxwell Wood, appointed Chief of Bureau of Medicine and Surgery 28 June 1869, served until 25 Oct. 1871.

Surrender, Japanese, WWII—22 Aug. 1945, garrison at Mili Atoll, Marshall Islands, capitulated, ceremony on board destroyer escort *Levy*.

Take-off, carrier, in the Navy—made by LCDR V. C. Griffin, 17 Oct. 1922, when he flew a Vought VE-7SF from *Langley*.

Telecast, from aircraft carrier to ship in company—by WFDR-TV, USS *Franklin D. Roosevelt* (CVA 42) on 3 Apr. 1961.

Telecast, from submarine—made on board *Trumpetfish* 10 Apr. 1947, at Brooklyn Navy Yard. Three TV cameras aboard *Trumpetfish* and one on dock alongside recorded diving operations, simulated torpedo attack, and surfacing. Telecast was carried by WNBT, New York; WTTG, Washington; WPTZ, Philadelphia; WRGB, Schenectady.

Territory, ever annexed by United States, outside continental limits—Midway Island, 28 Dec. 1867.

"Texas Tower" constructed under Navy supervision—turned over to U.S. Air Force 2 Dec. 1955. Stationed 100 miles off Cape Cod, on Georges Bank.

"Torpedo" attack, by submarine—13 Aug. 1777, in New York harbor, David Bushnell, in submarine designed by himself, made unsuccessful attempt to sink British *Cerberus*. The "torpedo" (mine) was explosive device mounted on end of a spar.

Torpedo boat, forerunner of destroyers—USS *Cushing*, launched 23 Jan. 1890, Bristol, R.I.

Torpedo, fired in WWI—launched by destroyer *Ericsson*, 21 May 1917. Missed.

Torpedo, electrical—tested successfully 4 July 1842, when inventor Samuel Colt sank gunboat *Boxer* in New York harbor. In Potomac River test, 13 Apr. 1843, he demonstrated device for President John Tyler and cabinet officials by blowing up a schooner from control point five miles distant. "Torpedo," as used here, was a mine, not self-propelled automobile torpedo used in WWI and later.

Torpedo manufacturing station, in U.S.—located on Goat Island, Newport Bay. First commanding officer, CDR Edmund O. Matthews, received orders 9 June 1869, to commence construction of the station.

Transatlantic cable—laid, jointly, by USS *Niagara* and British ship *Agamemnon*, which completed task 4 Aug. 1858.

Transatlantic crossing, by steam driven ship, Navy—made by steam frigate *Missouri*, commanded by CAPT John Thomas Newton. *Missouri* left Norfolk 5 Aug. 1943, reached Gibralter 25 Aug. destroyed by fire on the following day. No casualties.

Transatlantic flight—made between 8 May and 31 May 1919; by LCDR

Albert C. Read; LTs Elmer F. Stone, Walter Hinton, James L. Breese; ENS Herbert C. Rodd; and Chief Machinist's Mate Eugene S. Rhoads in hydroplane *NC-4* from Rockaway, Long Island, to Plymouth, England, via Newfoundland, Azores, and Portugal.

Transcontinental flight, by dirigible—made by *Shenandoah,* which left Lakehurst, N.J. 7 Oct. 1924 and reached San Diego, Calif., 11 Oct. Return flight completed 25 Oct.

Transit—(see *Magellan, (Straits of,) Panama Canal, Suez Canal.*)

Treaty, commercial between United States and an oriental power—signed 20 Mar. 1833, when CAPT Geisinger, commanding *Peacock,* representing the United States, signed a treaty with Siam.

Turreted warship—ironclad steamer *Monitor,* launched at shipyard of Thomas Rowland, Greenpoint, Long Island, 30 Jan. 1862.

Twenty-millimeter guns, used by navy planes—30 Mar. 1944, SB2C HELL-DIVERS from *Bunker Hill* carried fixed 20-mm. guns into action during Task Force 58 raid in the Western Carolines.

"Type Command" status, for naval aviation—effective 1 Oct. 1937, when Patrol Wings One through Five were placed in commission as separate administrative commands under Commander Air Force, Scouting Force.

Underwater telecast, from submarine—see *telecast.*

Uniforms, for the Navy—approved by Marine Committee 5 Sept. 1776, as follows:

Captains: Blue coat, red lapels, slash cuff, stand-up collar, flat yellow buttons, blue breeches, red waistcoat with narrow lace.

Lieutenants: Blue coat, red lapels, round cuff faced, stand-up collar, yellow buttons, blue breeches, red waistcoat plain.

Masters: Blue coat and lapels, round cuff, blue breeches, red waistcoat.

Midshipmen: Blue lapeled coat, round cuff faced with red, stand-up collar with red at the button and button holes, blue breeches, red waistcoat.

Marine Officer: Green coat faced with white, round cuff, slashed sleves and pockets with buttons round the cuff, silver epaulette on the right shoulder, skirts turned back, buttons to suit the facings. White waistcoats and breeches edged with green, black gaiters and garters, green shirts for the men (if they can be procured).

United Nations Day, observance—24 Oct. 1948.

United Nations Flag, flown by ship of U.S. Navy—by destroyer *Putnam* 23 July 1948, in Haifa Harbor, Israel, while in service of Count Folke-Bernardotte, United Nations Mediator for Palestine. Flag is now in Naval Academy Museum, Annapolis.

Utility squadron—formed in San Diego 5 Oct. 1925, when VJ Squadron

1B was made up of personnel formerly attached to VS-2B. First Commanding Officer of VJ-1B was LT J. F. Moloney.

V-2 rocket, fired from ship—launched by carrier *Midway* 6 Sept. 1947. First large bombardment rocket fired from ship at sea.

Vertical take-off, in aviation history—by "free" plane in contrast to earlier hops by "tethered" model, made at Naval Air Station, Moffett Field, Calif., 1 Aug. 1954, when J. F. Coleman, Convair test pilot, took CONVAIR XPY-1 delta-wing Navy fighter up to height of 20 feet, and then backed down for landing.

Veterans' Day, celebration—11 Nov. 1954. It replaced former Armistice Day.

Victory ship—*United Victory*, delivered 29 Feb. 1944. A total of 531 "Victory" ships built during WWII. See *Liberty ship*.

Viking rocket, launched from ship—fired from *Norton Sound* 11 May 1950, near Christmas Island, reached altitude of 106.4 miles.

War College, established—at Newport, R.I., by General Order No. 325, dated 6 Oct. 1884. First Superintendent was CDR Stephen B. Luce, appointed 13 Sept. 1884. First class, eight officers, began studies Sept. 1885.

Warship builder—Joshua Humphreys, appointed constructor at annual salary of $2,000 28 June 1794. He served until 26 Oct. 1801, constructed the *Constitution, Constellation, President, Chesapeake, United States,* and numerous other ships; sometimes called "father of the American Navy."

WAVE enlisted woman in Fleet Reserve—Chief Storekeeper Barbara Metras transferred to Fleet Reserve 10 Apr. 1962.

WAVE enlisted women, ordered to sea duty—Mavia Cain, Marie A. Myers, Eileen Paluzzi, and Annette A. Tillotson, all hospitalman third class, sent to MSTS ships.

WAVE enlisted women, sworn into Regular Navy—7 July 1948, were Kay L. Langdon, Wilma J. Marchal, Frances T. Devaney, Edna F. Young, Doris R. Robertson, and Ruth Flora.

WAVE officer, accepted as member of Civil Engineer Corps—ENS Kathleen F. Lux; Sept. 1943.

WAVE officer, admitted to practice before U.S. Supreme Court—ENS Lucille Pryor, April 1943.

WAVE officer, assigned as Engineering Duty Officer, Electronics—LT Ruth Carolyn White.

WAVE officers, sworn into Regular Navy—15 Oct. 1948, CAPT Joy B. Hancock, LCDRs Winifred R. Quick, Anne King, Frances L. Willoughby; LTs Ellen Ford, Doris Cranmore; LTJGs Doris A. Defenderfer and Betty Tennent.

Wind tunnel, used by the Navy—erected at Naval Gun Factory, Washington, completed in 1914, largest in the world for many years, with eight-foot by eight-foot section. Was used for over 30 years, decommissioned, 26 May 1952.

Woman, awarded Navy and Marine Corps Medal for heroism—Marine Staff Sergeant Barbara O. Barnwell, who rescued another Marine in heavy surf at Camp Lejeune, N.C.

Woman doctor, promoted to rank of captain, Medical Corps—Gioconda R. Saraniero, 4 Nov. 1955.

Woman Marine—Opha M. Johnson, enlisted in Marine Corps 13 Aug. 1918.

Woman Naval Inspector—Mrs. Jean Hales, of Berkeley, Calif., appointed a Junior Inspector of Engineering, Twelfth Naval District, 24 Aug. 1942.

Woman naval officer—Mildred Helen McAfee, inducted 3 Aug. 1942, with rank of lieutenant, and given command of WAVES (Women Appointed for Voluntary Emergency Service).

Woman, pistol expert, Navy—ENS Rosalie Thorne, who qualified for Navy Expert Pistol Shot Medal, 4 Aug. 1943, with 211 out of possible 240 points.

Woman, published in U.S. Naval Institute Proceedings—Constance Lathrop, whose "A Vanishing Naval Tradition—the Figurehead" appeared in November 1927 issue.

Woman, to make jet landing on carrier—16 June 1960, Jacqueline Cochrane landed aboard *Independence* as passenger in A3D Skyraider.

Women, to pass submarine-escape tests—Eleanor MacDonald and Glenn Huckstep, Reserve ensigns in Navy Nurse Corps. They completed course at Submarine-Escape Training Tank, New London, 12 July 1943.

Woman, with rank of captain—Sue Sophia Dauser, Superintendent of Navy Nurse Corps, who received this rank 26 Feb. 1944. Had previously held relative rank of captain. CAPT Dauser entered naval service 15 Sept. 1917, as Naval Reserve Nurse. On 14 Dec. 1945, became first member of Navy Nurse Corps to receive Distinguished Service Medal.

MARINE CORPS ENGAGEMENTS

Marine Corps Engagements in U. S. Naval and Land Actions 1776-1958

War of the Revolution—1775-1783

Raid on New Providence, Bahamas	2-3 Mar. 1776
Alfred and *Cabot* vs. British *Glasgow*	6 Apr. 1776
Second Battle of Trenton (Assanpink Creek)	2 Jan. 1777
Battle of Princeton	3 Jan. 1777
Reprisal vs. British *Swallow*	5 Feb. 1777
Hancock vs. British *Fox*	27 June 1777
Raleigh vs. British *Druid*	4 Sept. 1777
Randolph vs. British *Yarmouth*	7 Mar. 1778
Boston vs. British *Martha*	11 Mar. 1778
Raid on Whitehaven, England	22 Apr. 1778
Ranger vs. British *Drake*	24 Apr. 1778
Penobscot Expedition—24 July to 14 Aug. 1779:	
Battle of Banks Island	26 July 1779
Battle of Majarblguyduce Peninsula	28 July-13 Aug. 1779
Bonhomme Richard vs. British *Serapis*	23 Sept. 1779
Trumbull vs. British *Watt*	2 June 1780
Alliance vs. British *Atlanta* and *Trepassy*	28-29 May 1781
Congress vs. British *Savage*	6 Sept. 1781
Hyder Ally vs. British *General Monk*	8 Apr. 1782
Alliance vs. British *Sybylle*	20 Jan. 1783

French Naval War—1798-1801

Constellation vs. French *L'Insurgente*	9 Feb. 1799
Constellation vs. French *La Vengeance*	2 Feb. 1800
Experiment vs. Haitian Picaroons	1 Jan. 1800

War with Tripoli—1801-1805

Enterprise vs. Tripolitan ship *Tripoli*	1 Aug. 1801
Raid on Tripoli	20 May 1803
Capture of *Philadelphia* by Tripolitans	31 Oct. 1803
Constitution, Siren, Argus, Scourge, Vixen, Nautilus, *Enterprise,* and gunboats vs. Tripolitan vessels	3 Aug. 1804
Capture of fortress at Derne, Tripoli	25-27 Apr. 1805

War of 1812

Essex vs. British Alert	13 Aug. 1812
Constitution vs. British Guerriere	19 Aug. 1812
Wasp vs. British Frolic	18 Oct. 1812
United States vs. British Macedonian	25 Oct. 1812
Constitution vs. British Java	29 Dec. 1812
Hornet vs. British Peacock	24 Feb. 1813
Battle of Fort George (Canada)	27 May 1813
Chesapeake vs. British Shannon	1 June 1813
Battle of Craney Island (near Norfolk, Va.)	22 June 1813
Essex and Greenwich vs. British Seringapatam	14 July 1813
Enterprise vs. British Boxer	4 Sept. 1813
Battle of Lake Erie	10 Sept. 1813
Peacock vs. British Epervier	29 Apr. 1814
Battle of Bladensburg (Maryland)	24 Aug. 1814
Battle of Lake Champlain	11 Sept. 1814
Battle of New Orleans	8 Jan. 1815
President vs. British Endymion, Majestic, Pomona, and Tenedos	15 Jan. 1815
Constitution vs. British Cyane and Levant	20 Feb. 1815
Hornet vs. British Penguin	23 Mar. 1815

1812-1832

Battle of Twelve Mile Swamp (Florida)	11 Sept. 1812
Battle of Quallah Batto (Sumatra)	6 Feb. 1832

Florida Indian War—1835-1842

Relief of Fort Brooke (Florida)	22 Jan. 1836
Battle of Wahoo Swamp (Florida)	21 Nov. 1836
Campaign in the New River Country (Florida)	22 Oct. to 15 Dec. 1836
Battle of Hatchee-Lustee (Florida)	27 Jan. 1837

Mexican War—1846-1847

Battle of San Pasqual (California)	6 Dec. 1846
Battle of Santa Clara (California)	2 Jan. 1847
Battle of San Gabriel (California)	8 Jan. 1847
Battle of La Mesa (California)	9 Jan. 1847
Battle of Vera Cruz (Mexico)	9 Mar. 1847
Battle of Tobasco (Mexico)	15 June 1847
Battle of Chapultepec (Mexico)	13 Sept. 1847
Battle of Guaymas (Mexico)	17 Nov. 1847
Battle of San Jose (California)	19 Nov. 1847

1854-1859

Battle of Shanghai (China)	4 Apr. 1854
Battle of Ty-ho Bay (China)	4 Aug. 1855
Battle with Indians near Seattle (Washington)	26 Jan. 1856
Battle of the Barrier Forts (China)	16-22 Nov. 1856
Battle of Waya (Fiji Islands)	6 Oct. 1858
Capture of John Brown (Harper's Ferry, Va.)	18 Oct. 1859

Civil War—1861-1865

First Battle of Bull Run (Manassas, Va.)	21 July 1861
Destruction of Confederate privateer *Judah* (off Pensacola, Fla.)	14 Sept. 1861
Destruction of Confederate armed schooner, *Royal Yacht* (off Galveston, Tex.)	7-8 Nov. 1861
Battle of Port Royal (South Carolina)	8 Nov. 1861
Battle of Hatteras Inlet (North Carolina)	7-8 Feb. 1862
Battle of Fort Cobb (near Elizabeth City, N.C.)	10 Feb. 1862
Battle of Winston (North Carolina)	19 Feb. 1862
Cumberland and *Congress* vs. Confederate ironclad, *Merrimac*	8 Mar. 1862
Minnesota vs. Confederate ironclad *Merrimac*	9 Mar. 1862
Battle of Slocum's Creek (North Carolina)	13 Mar. 1862
New London vs. two Confederate steamers (near Pass Christian, Va.)	25 Mar. 1862
Battle of New Orleans	24-28 Apr. 1862
Battle of Fort Macon (South Carolina)	25 Apr. 1862
Battle of Drury's Bluff (near Richmond, Va.)	15 May 1862
Expedition up Santee River (South Carolina)	24 June 1862
Admiral Farragut's fleet vs. Confederate batteries (at Vicksburg, Miss.)	28 June 1862
Admiral Farragut's fleet vs. Confederate ram *Arkansas* (near Vicksburg, Miss.)	15 July 1862
Keystone State vs. two Confederate ironclads (near Charleston, S.C.)	31 Jan. 1863
Expedition up Red River (Louisiana)	10 Mar. to 14 Apr. 1863
Battle of Port Hudson (Mississippi)	14 Mar. 1863
Attack on Fort Sumter (South Carolina)	8 Sept. 1863
Capture of Stono (South Carolina)	28 Dec. 1863
Wabash vs. Confederate torpedo-boat (off Charleston, S.C.)	18 Apr. 1864
Four U.S. vessels vs. Confederate ram *Albemarle* (near New Bern, N.C.)	5 May 1864

Kearsarge vs. Confederate *Alabama* (off Cherbourg, France)	10 June 1864
Battle of Mobile Bay	5-23 Aug. 1864
Battle of Boyd's Neck and Honey Hill, S.C.	28-30 Nov. 1864
Battle of Derang's Neck or Tullifinney Cross Road	
(South Carolina)	6-9 Dec. 1864
Battle of Fort Fisher (North Carolina)	23-25 Dec. 1864
Capture of Fort Fisher (North Carolina)	13-15 Jan. 1865

1863-1871

Wyoming vs. three Japanese ships and shore batteries	
in Straits of Shimonoseki, Japan	16 July 1863
Battle of the Salee River forts (Korea)	10-11 June 1871

War with Spain—21 April to 13 August 1898

Battle of Manila Bay	1 May 1898
Battle of Guantanamo Bay (Cuba)	11-14 June 1898
Battle of Cuzco Well (Cuba)	14 June 1898
Battle of Santiago (Cuba)	3 July 1898

Philippine Insurrection—30 June 1898 to 4 July 1902

Battle of Novaleta (Luzon)	8 Oct. 1898
Battle of Sohoton River (Samar)	5 Nov. 1901
Battle of Sohoton Cliffs (Samar)	17 Nov. 1901
March across Samar	28 Dec. 1901 to 18 Jan. 1902

1899

Battle of Tagalii (Samoa)	1 Apr. 1899

China Relief Expedition (Boxer Rebellion)—June to August 1900

Battle of Tong-ku (near Tientsin)	19 June 1900
Battle of the East Arsenal (near Tientsin)	21 June 1900
Battle of Tientsin	24 June 1900
Battle of the Imperial Arsenal (near Tientsin)	9 July 1900
Recapture of Tientsin	13-14 July 1900
Battle of Yangtsun	6 Aug. 1900
Battle of Peking	15-19 Aug. 1900

Nicaraguan Campaign of 1912

Battle of Masaya	19 Sept. 1912
Battle of Coyotepe and Barranca Hills	3-4 October 1912
Battle of Leon	5 Oct. 1912

1914

Capture of Vera Cruz (Mexico)	21-22 Apr. 1914

Occupation of Dominican Republic—5 May 1916 to 17 September 1924

Battle of Puerto Plata	1 June 1916
Battle of Las Trencheras	27 June 1916
Battle of Guavacanas	3 July 1916
Battle of Las Canitas	7 April 1917

Occupation of Haiti—28 July 1915 to 31 August 1934

Battle of Grosse Roche	24 Oct. 1915
Battle of Fort Dipite	24-25 Oct. 1915
Battle of Fort Capois	5 Nov. 1915
Battle of Forts Selon and Berthol	8 Nov. 1915
Battle of Fort Riviere	17-18 Nov. 1915
Battle of Hinche	4 Apr. 1919
Battle of Port-au-Prince	7 Oct. 1919
Capture of Charlemagne Peralte	31 Oct. 1919
Battle of Port-au-Prince	14-15 Jan. 1920

World War I—6 April 1917 to 11 November 1918

Battle of Les Mares Farm (near Belleau Wood)	3-4 June 1918
Battle of Hill 142 (near Belleau Wood)	6 June 1918
Battle of Bouresches (near Belleau Wood)	6-7 June 1918
Battle of Belleau Wood	6-26 June 1918
Battle of the Aisne-Marne (Soissons)	18-20 July 1918
Battle of St. Mihiel	12-16 September 1918
Battle of Blanc Mont	2-9 Oct. 1918
Battle of the Meuse-Argonne	1-11 Nov. 1918

Occupation of Nicaragua—6 January 1927 to 3 January 1933

Battle of La Paz Centro	16 May 1927
Battle of Ocotal	16 July 1927
Battle of Telpaneca	19 Sept. 1927
Battle of Camino Real	30 Dec. 1927
Battle of Sapotillal Ridge	1 Jan. 1928
Battle of Quilali	1-8 Jan. 1928
Battle of El Chipote	25 Jan. 1928
Battle of Bromaderos	27-28 Feb. 1928
Battle of the Cua River	13 May 1928
Battle of the Coco River (near Ililihuas)	7 Aug. 1928
Battle of Cuje	6 Dec. 1928
Battle near Ocotal-Apali	31 Dec. 1930

World War II—7 December 1941 to 15 August 1945

Pearl Harbor-Midway	7 Dec. 1941
Guam	8-10 Dec. 1941
Wake Island	8-23 Dec. 1941
Bataan and Corregidor (Philippines)	8 Dec. 1941-6 May 1942
Battle of Badoeng Strait (East Indies)	19 Feb. 1942
Battle of the Coral Sea	4-8 May 1942
Battle of Midway	3-6 June 1942
Guadalcanal-Tulagi Landings	7-9 August 1942
First Savo Battle (naval-air)	9 Aug. 1942
Capture and Defense of Guadalcanal	10 Aug. 1942-8 Feb. 1943
Makin Island Raid (Gilberts)	17-18 Aug. 1942
Battle of the Eastern Solomons	23-25 Aug. 1942
Battle of Cape Esperance (Naval)	11-12 Oct. 1942
Battle of Santa Cruz Island (Air)	26 Oct. 1942
Battle of Guadalcanal (Naval-Air)	11-15 Nov. 1942
Battle of Tassafaronga (Naval)	30 Nov.-1 Dec. 1942
Battle of Komandorski Island (Aleutians)	26 Mar. 1943
New Georgia Group	
New Georgia-Rendova-Vandunu Occupation	20 June-31 Aug. 1943
Battle of Kula Gulf (Naval)	5-6 July 1943
Battle of Kolombangara (Naval)	12-13 July 1943
Vella Lavella Occupation	15 Aug.-16 Oct. 1943
Cape Gloucester (New Britain) Operation	26 Dec. 1943-1 Mar. 1944
Green Islands Landing	15-19 Feb. 1944
Treasury-Bougainville Operation	
Treasury Island Landing	27 Oct.-6 Nov. 1943
Choiseul Island Diversion	28 Oct.-4 Nov. 1943
Occupation and Defense of Cape Torokina	1 Nov. 15 Dec. 1943
Tarawa Operation (Gilbert Islands)	20 Nov.-8 Dec. 1943
Occupation of Kwajalein and Majuro Atolls (Marshall Islands)	31 Jan.-8 Feb. 1944
Occupation of Eniwetok Atoll (Marshalls)	17 Feb.-2 Mar. 1944
Capture and Occupation of Saipan	15 June-10 Aug. 1944
Capture and Occupation of Guam	21 July-15 Aug. 1944
Capture and Occupation of Tinian	24 July-10 Aug. 1944
Capture and Occupation of Peleliu	15 Sept.-14 Oct. 1944
Leyte (Philippines) Landings	20 Oct. 1944
Battle of Leyte Gulf (Naval-Air)	24-26 Oct. 1944
Iwo Jima Operation	19 Feb.-16 Mar. 1945
Assault and Occupation of Okinawa Gunto	1 Apr.-21 June 1945

United Nations Action, Korea—27 June 1950 to 27 July 1953

North Korean Aggression	27 June-2 Nov. 1950
Communist China Aggression	3 Nov.-24 Jan. 1951
Inchon Landing	13 Sept.-17 Sept. 1950
First U.N. Counter Offensive	25 Jan.-21 Apr. 1951
Communist China Spring Offensive	22 Apr.-8 July 1951
U.N. Summer-Fall Offensive	9 July-27 Nov. 1951
Second Korean Winter	28 Nov. 1951-30 Apr. 1952
Korean Defense Summer-Fall, 1952	1 May-30 Nov. 1952
Third Korean Winter	1 Dec. 1952-30 Apr. 1953
Korea, Summer-Fall, 1953	1 May-27 July 1953

1958

Lebanon Landings—1958	15 July-30 Sept. 1958

SHIP LOSSES

Ship Losses

All World War II loss dates are taken from the official *Naval Chronology, World War II,* prepared by the Naval History Division of the Office of the Chief of Naval Operations. Not all small amphibious craft lost in World War II are listed.

World War I and earlier losses were compiled from official Navy Department records and other sources, both official and otherwise.

In order to avoid repetition, and use of confusing initials, no attempt has been made to distinguish between ships of the Continental Navy, United States Navy, United States Naval Service, Revenue Service and Coast Guard, which latter two services have at times been under Navy control.

Ship type designators and hull numbers are used only for World War II ships, and early submarines, which were numbered instead of named.

Revolutionary War

1775

December

Washington captured by British *Fowey* off Cape Ann.

1776

October

11 through 13, Battle of Lake Champlain.

Boston sunk. *Congress* beached and burned to avoid capture. *Lee* blown up to avoid capture. *Philadelphia* sunk by gunfire. *Providence* sunk. *Royal Spitfire* burned. *Savage* beached, later burned by British. *Trumbull* captured by British. *Washington* captured by British. *Warren,* schooner, captured by British *Milford. New Haven,* burned.

1777

March

26 Cabot, 12 guns, chased ashore and captured by British *Milford,* off Nova Scotia. All hands escaped overboard.

May

Surprise, cutter, seized by French in port of Dunkirk at insistence of English.

1777

June
1 *Hannah,* frigate captured off Halifax by British.
July
7 *Hancock,* 32 guns, captured off Nova Scotia by British *Rainbow.*
7 *Fox,* 28 guns, retaken by British *Flora.*
8 *Andrew Doria,* 14 guns, burned to escape capture, Delaware Bay.
8 *Repulse,* eight guns, burned to escape capture, Delaware Bay.
8 *Racehorse,* 12 guns, burned to escape capture, Delaware Bay.
8 *Hornet,* sloop, blown up in Delaware Bay.
September
19 *Lexington,* 10 guns, captured off Ushant, France, by British *Alert.*
27 *Delaware,* 24 guns, captured by shore batteries in Delaware Bay.
October
6 *Congress,* frigate, burned to escape capture, North River, N.Y.
6 *Montgomery,* 24 guns, destroyed in the Hudson River.
November
21 *Sachem,* 10 guns, burned to escape capture, Delaware Bay.
21 *Washington,* uncompleted, destroyed in Delaware Bay.

1778

Dolphin, 8 guns, seized in French port by French government.
Fly, schooner, destroyed in Delaware Bay.
Independence wrecked in Ocracoke Inlet, N.C.
March
7 *Randolph,* 32 guns, during engagement with British *Yarmouth,* instantly destroyed by magazine explosion. Of crew of 315, only four survived: loss of 311 lives in one engagement with the enemy was the greatest wartime disaster experienced by the Navy until 7 Dec. 1941.
8 *Alfred,* 24 guns, captured by British *Ariadne* and *Ceres.*
31 *Virginia,* 32 guns, ran aground in Chesapeake Bay and captured by British *Emerald* and *Conqueror.*
April
1 *Columbus,* 20 guns, driven ashore and burned, Delaware Bay.
May
7 *Effingham,* 28 guns, destroyed by British in Delaware Bay.
September
27 *Raleigh,* 32 guns, run ashore and abandoned during engagement with British *Unicorn* and *Experiment.*
November
Wasp, 8 guns, blown up to escape capture, Delaware Bay.
Reprisal foundered off Newfoundland. All hands lost but ship's cook.

1779

August

14 *Diligent,* 12 guns, burned in the Penobscot River, Me.
14 *Providence,* 10 guns, burned in the Penobscot River, Me.
17 *Warren,* 32 guns, burned in the Penobscot River, Me.
17 *Resistance* captured by British.
18 *Morris,* 24 guns, wrecked.

September

Bon Homme Richard as a result of damaged hull received in her victory of 23 September over the British *Serapis,* sank in Holland.

1780

May

12 *Providence,* 12 guns, burned at Charleston, S.C., by British. *Boston,* 24 guns, captured at Charleston, S.C., by British. *Queen of France,* 28 guns, captured at Charleston, S.C., by British. *Ranger,* 18 guns, captured at Charleston, S.C., by British.

October

9 *Saratoga,* 18 guns, headed for Delaware Capes under full sail to escape British *Intrepid,* and never seen again.

1781

June

22 *Confederacy,* 32 guns, captured by British *Orpheus* and *Roebuck.*

1782

December

19 *South Carolina* captured by British *Astrea, Diomede,* and *Quebec,* off Delaware Capes.

Note.—From 1783 to 1798 there was no Navy.

1798-1811

1798

November

20 *Retaliation,* 14 guns, captured by French in West Indies.

1800

August

8 *Insurgent,* 36 guns, sailed from Norfolk for the West Indies and never seen again; 340 lives lost.
20 *Pickering,* 14 guns, sailed from New Castle, Delaware, for Guadalupe and never seen again; 90 lives lost.

1803

October

   31 *Philadelphia,* 38 guns, ran aground and was captured in harbor of Tripoli. Crew held in captivity until peace signed in 1805.

1804

August

   7 *Gunboat No. 8* blown up in enemy action at Tripoli; nine lives lost.

September

   4 *Intrepid,* fire ship, with volunteer crew of 13, blown up while raiding shipping in Tripoli harbor; 13 lives lost.

1805

June

   20 *Gunboat No. 7* sailed from New York for the Mediterranean and never seen again.

1810

October

   Gunboat No. 159 lost in a gale off St. Mary's, with all hands.

1811

February

   2 *Revenge,* 12 guns, wrecked off Newport, R.I., by careless pilot. No casualties.

October

   Gunboat No. 2 wrecked off St. Mary's, only two survivors; about 28 lives lost.

War of 1812

1812

July

   17 *Nautilus,* 12 guns, captured off New York by British *Shannon, Africa* and *Aeolus.*

August

   12 *James Madison,* revenue cutter, captured by British off Barbadoes.

September

   16 *Gunboat No. 62, No. 161,* and *No. 164* sunk in gale off St. Mary's; 20 lives lost.

October

   9 *Adams,* 14 guns, burned.

   25 *Wasp,* 18 guns, captured by British *Poictiers.*

   29 *Gunboat No. 46* wrecked off Newport, R.I.; 10 lives lost.

November
22 *Vixen,* schooner, captured in West Indies by British *Southampton.*
Etna, 11 guns, disappeared in New Orleans area; 30 lives lost.

1813
June
1 *Chesapeake,* 38 guns, captured by British *Shannon* off Boston.
3 *Growler* captured by British land forces, Lake Champlain.
August
10 *Hamilton* lost, with all hands in gale on Lake Ontario.
10 *Scourge* lost, with all hands, in gale on Lake Ontario.
14 *Argus,* brig, captured by British *Pelican;* 12 lives lost.
December
25 *Vixen* captured by British *Belvidera.*

1814
Greenwich, 16 guns, burned in Marquesas Islands.
Ariel, schooner, wrecked in Lake Erie.
January
17 *Viper,* 10 guns, captured by British *Narcissus.*
February
22 *Ferret,* schooner, wrecked at Stone Inlet, N.C., but all hands saved.
March
28 *Essex,* 32 guns, captured at Valparaiso, Chile, by British *Phoebe* and *Cherub;* 154 killed, wounded, or missing.
April
20 *Frolic,* 20 guns, captured by British *Orpheus* off Havana, Cuba.
June
12 *Surveyor,* schooner, captured by British in York River, Va.
30 *Alligator,* schooner, sunk in gale off North Carolina coast, with loss of 23 lives. Later raised and placed in service. (See 19 Nov. 1822.)
July
11 *Rattlesnake,* 14 guns, captured by British *Leander* off Cape Sable, N.C.
12 *Syren,* 16 guns, captured by British *Medway* off African coast.
August
22 *Gunboat No. 59* burned in Patuxent to prevent capture by British.
24 *Argus,* sloop, burned at Washington, D.C., to prevent capture by British.
New York, frigate, burned at Washington, D.C., to prevent capture by British.
Columbia, 44 guns, burned at Washington, D.C., to prevent capture by British.

1814

August

General Green, 28 guns, burned at Washington, D.C., to prevent capture by British.

Boston, 28 guns, burned at Washington, D.C., to prevent capture by British.

September

3 Adams, 28 guns, burned in the Penobscot River to prevent capture by British.

11 Growler, Tigress, Somers, Scorpion and Ohio captured by British during Battle of Lake Champlain.

23 Gunboat No. 140 accidentally blown up at Ocra Coke Inlet, N.C. (nine lives lost)

October

9 Wasp vanished at sea, sometime after this date, on which she informed Swedish brig Adonis she was "standing for the Spanish Main." Ship was never seen again; 140 lives lost.

December

12 Seahorse burned.

13 Alligator, sloop (not the one noted for 30 June) captured by British at New Orleans.

27 Carolina, 14 guns, blown up by enemy shot at New Orleans.

1815-1860

1815

Helen, schooner, lost in Delaware Bay.

Estido blown up in action.

January

15 President, 44 guns, captured by British Squadron off New York.

July

14 Epervier, brig, sailed from Tripoli on 10 July, enroute to the U.S., carrying despatches from Com. Decatur and several liberated Tripolitan captives. She passed Gibraltar this date, and was never seen again.

Gunboat No. 152 was struck by lightning and blown up in the Mississippi River; only three of the crew of about 30 survived.

1816

Chippewa, 14 guns, lost off Caicos, West Indies, crew saved.

1817

Boxer, 14 guns, lost off Honduras, crew saved.

1820

January

11 Lynx, with crew of 50, sailed for Gulf of Mexico and was never seen again.

1822

November

19 *Alligator,* schooner, wrecked on Carysfort Reef in West Indies, crew served. (See 30 June 1814)

1823

July

9 *Enterprise,* 12 guns, wrecked off Little Curaçao, West Indies.

1824

October

28 *Wild Cat,* with crew of 14, sailed from Cuba for Thompson's Island in West Indies, and was never seen again.

1825

February

4 *Ferret,* schooner, capsized in squall off Cuba, all of crew but five saved.

1829

June

4 *Fulton,* first steamer built for the Navy, exploded at Brooklyn, N.Y., killing 24, including one woman.

September

10 *Hornet,* 18 guns, driven from anchorage off Tampico, Mexico, by a gale, and never seen again. She carried a crew of 140.

1831

Sylph, one gun, sailed for West Indies and never seen again.

1835

Porpoise lost off Pt. Lizardo in West Indies, crew saved.

1839

February

25 *Seagull,* converted pilot boat with crew of 16, sailed from Orange Harbor, Tierra del Fuego and never seen again.

1841

July

18 *Peacock* wrecked off Columbia River (Oregon), but crew saved. (Location now known as Peacock Spit).

1842

October

2 *Concord,* 24 guns, wrecked in Mozambique Channel on east coast of Africa; all of crew but three saved.

1843

March

14 *Grampus,* schooner, sighted off Charleston, N.C., this date and never seen again. Believed lost in a heavy gale.

August

26 *Missouri,* steam frigate, destroyed by accidental fire at Gibraltar. No lives lost.

1844

February

28 Explosion on *Princeton* in Potomac River near Washington killed Secretary of State Upshur, Secretary of the Navy Gilmer, and several others. Accident occurred when a gun burst on firing.

1846

August

15 *Truxtun* wrecked on Tuspan Bar, Mexico. Crew imprisoned by Mexicans.

September

10 *Shark,* 12 guns, wrecked off Columbia River, crew saved.

November

15 *Boston,* 18 guns, wrecked at Eleuthera, West Indies, crew saved.

December

8 *Somers* capsized off Vera Cruz, Mexico, while chasing blockade runner; 40 lives lost.

1847

March

21 *Hunter* foundered and sunk in a gale off Vera Cruz, all hands saved.

1848

June

21 *Onkahye* wrecked on Caicos Reef, West Indies; crew saved.
Petrita wrecked off Alvarado, crew saved.

1849

August

24 *Edith,* 400 ton steamer, grounded and wrecked at Pt. Conception, on California coast; crew saved.

1850

Jefferson, Coast Survey Steamer, operating in Straits of Magellan disappeared and never seen again.

September
   6 *Yorktown* wrecked in Cape Verdes Islands; crew saved.

1854

September
   21 *Porpoise*, brig of 224 tons, parted company with *Vincennes* in the Straits of Formosa on this date and was never seen again.
   29 *Albany* sailed from Aspinwall for New York and never seen again; crew of 193.

1855

Advance, of the Franklin Expedition, lost in ice.

1859

August
   23 *Fennimore Cooper*, schooner, wrecked in East Indies.
   Fulton, side wheeler, wrecked off Pensacola.

1860

September
   18 *Levant*, sloop, sailed from Hilo, Sandwich Isles (Hawaii) for Aspinwall, Nicaragua, and was never seen again.

Civil War

1861

April
   20 *Columbia, Delaware II, Dolphin III, Germantown, New York, Raritan, Pennsylvania,* and *Plymouth* burned at Norfolk Navy Yard to prevent seizure by Confederates.

1862

O. M. Pettit, armed steamer, sunk in collision.
February
   25 *R. B. Forbes*, armed steamer, wrecked in Currituck Banks, N.C.
March
   8 *Congress* and *Cumberland* destroyed by CSS *Virginia* in action at Hampton Roads, Va.
   10 *Whitehall*, sidewheel steamer, destroyed by accidental fire at Old Point, Va.
April
   15 Boiler explosion in *Chenango*, in New York Harbor; killed 25 men.
   19 *Maria J. Carlton*, mortar schooner, sunk by gunfire at New Orleans.
   20 *Varuna*, armed steamer, rammed and sunk in battle near New Orleans.

1862

June

17 *Mound City* exploded near St. Charles, White River, Ark.; killing or wounding 150 out of crew of 174.

28 *Island Belle,* armed steamer, burned in Appomattox River to prevent capture by Confederates.

July

15 *Sidney C. Jones,* mortar schooner, grounded at Vicksburg and burned to prevent capture.

August

23 *Adirondack,* screw sloop, wrecked near Little Abaco Island in West Indies

24 *Henry Andrew,* armed steamer, wrecked at Cape Henry.
Sumter, river ram, run aground, blown up and abandoned at Bayou Sara, La.

October

11 *Madge,* armed steamer, foundered at sea off Frying Pan Shoals, N.C.

November

24 *Ellis,* gunboat, run ashore near Onslow, N.C., burned to prevent capture.
Mingo, ram, sunk in collision at Cape Girardeau, Mo.

December

12 *Cairo,* river ironclad, torpedoed in Yazoo River. (Note—Civil War "torpedoes" were what are now called mines; ships so destroyed were technically "mined".)

31 *Monitor,* ironclad, foundered off Cape Hatteras, with loss of 16 lives. (Wreck of this ship claimed to have been discovered, 1955.)

1863

January

1 *Harriet Lane,* armed steamer, captured at Galveston, Tex.
Westfield, armed steamer, blown up to prevent capture at Galveston.

11 *Hatteras,* armed steamer, sunk by CSS *Alabama* near Galveston.

13 *Hastings,* steamer, captured on Cumberland River.

14 *Columbia,* armed tug, grounded, captured by batteries in St. John's River, Fla.

21 *Morning Light,* armed steamer, captured by boarding in Sabine Pass, Tex. *Velocity,* armed steamer, captured by boarding in Sabine Pass.

30 *Isaac Smith,* armed steamer, captured by batteries at Stono River.

February

2 *Underwater* captured by boarding party off Newbern, N.C.

7 *Glide,* river steamer, accidentally burned at Cairo, Ill.

14 *Queen of the West* captured by batteries on Red River.

23 *Kinsman,* sidewheel steamer, struck a snag and sunk in Berwick Bay.

24 *Indianola,* river ironclad, captured by Confederate fleet below Vicksburg.

Dan, river steamer, sunk in Mississippi River.

March

14 *Mississippi,* paddlewheeler, sunk at Port Hudson in Mississippi River, abandoned and blown up; 64 killed or missing.

25 *Lancaster,* in use by Army at time, sunk by batteries at Vicksburg.

25 *Switzerland* sunk by batteries at Vicksburg.

April

7 *Barrataria,* gunboat, grounded in Amite River, La., burned to avoid capture.

8 *Keokuk,* ironclad, sunk by batteries at Morris Island, S.C.

27 *Preble,* sloop, destroyed by accidental fire at Pensacola, Fla.

May

3 *Lily,* steam tug, sunk in Yazoo River by collision with *Choctaw.*

18 *Shepherd Knapp* wrecked on reef, Cape Haitian.

20 *Amada,* armed bark, wrecked on Florida coast.

27 *Cincinnati,* ironclad, sunk by batteries at Vickesburg.

July

Baron De Kalb, ironclad, sunk by torpedo in Yazoo River.

August

17 *Crocus* wrecked on Body's Island.

20 *Bainbridge* lost with all hands but one.

23 *Satellite,* armed tug, captured by batteries on Rappanannock River

September

8 *Clifton,* armed steamer, damaged by boiler explosion and captured by batteries at Sabine Pass.

8 *Sachem,* armed steamer, damaged by boiler explosion and captured by batteries at Sabine Pass.

December

6 *Weehawken,* monitor, foundered off Morris Island, S.C. Entire crew of 30 lost.

1864

Cossack, armed ship, wrecked on Abaco Island.

Fulton, paddle sloop, destroyed by accidental fire.

January

11 *Iron Age,* steamer, grounded and wrecked in Folly Inlet, N.C.

February

17 *Housatonic,* steamer, torpedoed at Charleston, S.C.

22 *Linden* wrecked in Arkansas River.

1864

March

6 *Peeteehoff,* steamer, sunk by gunfire off North Carolina; crew rescued by *Florida.*

28 *Kingfisher,* armed bark, wrecked on St. Helena Island.

April

19 *Southfield,* steamer, sunk by CSS *Albemarle* in Roanoke River.

22 *Petrel* sunk by batteries in Yazoo River; 10 men lost.

26 *Eastport,* river gunboat, torpedoed in Red River, Ark.

May

5 *Covington* sunk by batteries in Red River.

6 *Commodore Jones,* steamer, torpedoed in James River, Va.

6 *Wave* captured by batteries at Calcasieu Pass, La.

6 *Granite City* captured by batteries at Calcasieu Pass, La.

23 *Columbine,* armed tug, captured by batteries on St. John's River, Fla.

June

3 *Waterwitch,* gunboat, captured by batteries at Ossabaw Sound.

4 *Courier,* sailing craft, wrecked on Abaco I., Bahamas.

12 *Lavender,* steamer, lost on Lookout Shoals.

24 *Queen City* sunk by batteries off Clarendon, Ark.

August

5 *Tecumseh,* monitor, "torpedoed" (struck moored mine) in Battle of Mobile Bay; 84 lost.

5 *Philippi,* sidewheel steamer, destroyed in accidental explosion, Mobile Bay.

8 *Violet,* armed tug, wreck off Cape Fear, N.C.

September

23 *Antelope,* armed steamer, wrecked in Mississippi River.

October

8 *Aster,* armed tug, wrecked on Carolina Shoals.

30 *Undine,* river steamer, captured by batteries on Tennessee River.

November

4 *Elfin,* river steamer, sunk by batteries on Tennessee River.

4 *Key West,* sternwheeler, sunk by batteries in Tennessee River.

4 *Tawah,* sidewheeler, sunk by action in Tennessee River, burned to prevent capture.

11 *Tulip,* armed tug, wrecked by boiler explosion in Potomac River, 49 killed.

December

9 *Otsego,* steamer, torpedoed in Roanoke River.

10 *Bazely,* armed steamer, torpedoed in Roanoke River, N.C.

24 *Louisiana,* armed steamer, expended as explosion ship at Ft. Fisher.

30 *Rattler,* steamer, driven ashore by gale and abandoned.

1865

January

1 *San Jacinto,* steamer, wrecked on No Name Key in Bahama Islands; no lives lost.

16 *Patapsco,* monitor, torpedoed in Charleston River, S.C.

26 *Dai Ching,* armed steamer, wrecked in Combabee River, abandoned to Confederates.

February

15 *Merrimac,* armed steamer, foundered at sea.

24 *Indianola,* gunboat, captured and sunk by Confederate rams.

27 *Arizona,* armed steamer, destroyed by accidental fire in Mississippi River.

March

1 *Harvest Moon,* armed steamer, torpedoed near Georgetown, S.C.

28 *Milwaukee,* steamer, torpedoed in Blakely River, Fla.

29 *Osage,* monitor, torpedoed in Blakely River, Fla.

April

1 *Rudolph,* steamer, torpedoed in Blakely River, Fla.

13 *Ida,* steam tug, torpedoed in Mobile Bay.

Sciota, gunboat, torpedoed in Mobile Bay.

22 *Black Hawk,* steamer, destroyed in magazine explosion in Ohio River.

August

23 *Commodore MacDonough,* armed steamer, foundered while being towed from Port Royal, S.C., to New York.

September

Pink, screw steamer, lost off Dauphin Island, Gulf of Mexico.

October

20 *Nettle,* steam tug, ran down and sunk by an iron-clad.

November

6 *Jacob Bell,* side wheel steamer, sunk while being towed to New York.

Itasca, gunboat, torpedoed in Mobile Bay.

Anna, armed steamer, wrecked on Florida Coast.

Rose, armed tug, torpedoed in Mobile Bay.

1866-1894

1866

January

4 *Narcissus,* armed tug, driven ashore by a gale at Egmont Key, Fla. Entire crew of 32 lost.

December

16 *New Ironsides* burned while docked at League Island, N.Y.

1867

June

19 *Sacramento,* steamer, wrecked on reef in Bay of Bengal. All hands saved.

November

18 At Frederickstadt, St. Croix, a tidal wave picked up the *Monongahela* and carried it completely over dockside buildings into the city. A following wave picked the ship up again and, upon receding, deposited it on a harbor reef, from where it was eventually refloated. Five men drowned. On the same day, the *DeSota* driven ashore at St. Thomas.

1868

July

9 *Suwanee,* side wheel steamer, wrecked in Queen Charlotte Sound, enroute to Vancouver, B.C.

August

13 *Wateree* and *Fredonia* wrecked by a tidal wave at Arica, Peru.

1869

September

21 *Idaho,* caught in the eye of a hurricane, one day out of Yokohama, when the barometer dropped to a low of 27.62; the cruiser was battered into a complete wreck, although it remained afloat. Abandoned in Yokohama harbor.

1870

January

4 *Maria,* steamer, sunk off Martha's Vineyard in collision with *Miantonohah.*

24 *Oneida,* steamer, run down and sunk by British mail steamer *Bombay,* off Yokohama, with the loss of 117 lives.

October

29 *Saginaw,* paddlewheel steamer and first U.S. naval ship built in Pacific, went aground on a reef at Ocean Island in mid-Pacific. All hands got safely ashore.

December

Chattanooga, sunk while tied up to a dock at League Island Navy Yard through having sides ripped upon by moving ice.

1872

October

24 *Polaris* of the North Pole Expedition, was abandoned after being crushed in ice near Etah, Greenland.

1875

June

18 *Saranac,* side wheel steamer, wrecked in Seymour Narrows, off Vancouver Island, Alaska.

1877

November

24 *Huron* wrecked in gale at Nags Head, N.C., with loss of 100 lives.
Alert, screw steamer, wrecked.

1881

June

13 *Jeannette* carrying the DeLong Expedition to the Arctic, crushed in ice off the Siberian Coast.

November

30 *Rogers* (originally steam whaler *Mary and Helen*) destroyed by fire in St. Lawrence Bay, on the Siberian Coast, with loss of only one man.

1883

February

18 *Ashuelot* grounded on Lamock Rocks near mouth of Swatow River, China, 11 of crew drowned.

July

23 *Proteus* crushed in ice pack.

1889

March

15 *Trenton, Nipsic,* and *Vandalia* wrecked by a hurricane at Apia, Samoa. A total of 50 lives were lost in this disaster. In June 1891, 19 bodies returned to the Mare Island Navy Yard, in California, for burial. A propeller from *Nipsic* is mounted in Alden Park, Mare Island Naval Shipyard, as a memorial.

1891

Standish, screw steamer, wrecked.

February

Despatch, dispatch boat, ran aground on Assateague shoal off Maryland coast.

March

Triana, tug, stranded on Gay Head, off Martha's Vineyard.

1894

February

2 *Kearsarge* wrecked on Roncador Reef, in West Indies, while enroute

1894

February (continued)
> from Haiti to Nicaragua. All hands were rescued eight days later by the steamer *City of Para*.

Spanish-American War

1898

February
> 15 *Maine*, battleship, sunk in Havana harbor after a mysterious explosion. Of her crew of 358 officers and men, 250 were lost. Sinking of the *Maine* was immediate cause of the Spanish-American war. Fifty-nine members of the *Maine* crew are buried in Arlington National Cemetery; the mainmast of the ship is mounted in Arlington while the foremast stands at the U.S. Naval Academy, Annapolis.

1899

November
> 2 *Charleston*, cruiser, wrecked on an uncharted reef in the Philippine Islands

1900

December
> 13 *Yosemite* wrecked in gale at San Luis D'Apra, Guam; with loss of five lives.

1903-1917

1903

January
> 21 *Leyden*, steam tug, wrecked off Block Island.

1905

July
> 21 *Bennington*, gunboat, wrecked and sunk by boiler explosion at San Diego, with loss of 65 lives. She was later refloated and repaired, but never placed in service. Bennington Monument on Point Loma in San Diego erected in memory of the men killed in this accident.

1908

March
> 17 *Monongahela* destroyed by fire at Guantanamo Bay, Cuba.

1909

> *Nezinscot*, tug capsized off Cape Ann.

September
> 25 *Yankee*, auxiliary cruiser, sunk on Spindle Rock off Massachusetts Coast. Though raised, it sank again on 4 Dec. 1909.

1910

March
15 *Nina,* tug sailed from Norfolk, Va., and was never seen again.

August
9 *Marcullus,* collier, sunk in a collision off Carolinas by steamer *Roserie di Cregoria.*

1916

July
14 *Hector,* collier, wrecked.

August
29 *Memphis,* cruiser, driven ashore and wrecked by huge waves at Santo Domingo; with loss of 33 lives.

October
3 *Franklin,* old frigate, burned on beach at Eastport, Me.

1917

January
13 *Milwaukee,* cruiser, ran ashore, sold for junk.

June
13 *McCullouch,* Coast Guard, sunk in collision with steamship *Governor* near Point Conception, Calif.; no casualties.

July
7 *Saxis,* Scout patrol craft, lost through stranding at West Point, Va.; no casualties.

October
1 *Mohawk,* Coast Guard, sunk while on patrol off Ambrose Lightship; no casualties.
4 *Rehoboth,* scout patrol craft, sprung leak, sank by U.S. gunfire; no casualties.
30 Packet boat from battleship *Michigan* foundered in Hampton Roads; 12 men lost.

November
4 *Empress,* SP 569, sprung leak, broken up; no casualties.

World War I

November
5 *Alcedo,* converted yacht, sunk by enemy submarine off French coast; 21 lives lost.
19 *Chauncey,* destroyer, sunk in collision with steamship *Rose* off Gibraltar; 21 lives lost.

1917

December

6 *Jacob Jones,* destroyer, sunk by German submarine *U-53* off English coast; 64 lives lost.

9 *Washington,* SP 1224, grounded and sunk in Ambrose Channel; no casualties.

17 *F-1,* submarine, rammed and sunk by submarine *F-3* off San Pedro, Calif.; 19 lives lost.

22 *Sub-chaser No. 117,* burned off Fortress Monroe Lighthouse; no casualties.

1918

January

12 P. K. *Bauman,* patrol craft, struck rock off French coast and sunk; no casualties.

25 *Guinevere,* SP 512, struck rock off Lorient, France, and sunk; no casualties.

26 *Cherokee,* SP 458, foundered and sunk off Fenwick Lightship; 28 lives lost.

February

26 *Mariner,* SP 1136, foundered and sunk; no casualties.

March

4 *Cyclops,* 19,360 tons, sailed from Barbadoes, W.I., with a crew of 213 officers and men and 67 passengers and never seen again.

April

11 *Lakemoor,* cargo ship, sunk by German submarine *UB-73* off Cornewall Point Light; 46 lives lost.

11 *Mary B. Garner,* SP 682, grounded and wrecked, Prime Hook Beach, Del.; one life lost.

May

12 *Zaanland,* cargo ship, sunk in collision with *Hisko* off French coast; no casualties.

18 *William Rockefeller,* tank ship, sunk by enemy submarine in North Sea; three lives lost.

20 *Annie E. Gallup,* SP 694, wrecked; no casualties.

22 *Wakiva II,* converted yacht, sunk in collision with *Wabash,* Bay of Biscay; two lives lost.

31 *President Lincoln,* troop transport, sunk by submarine *U-90,* 600 miles off French coast; 26 lives lost and one man taken prisoner by *U-90.*

June

5 *Subchaser No. 132,* sunk in collision with USS *Tacoma* off Barnegat Light; no casualties.

21 *Schurz,* gunboat, ex-German *Geir,* sunk in collision with steamship *Florida* off Cape Lookout; one life lost.

22 *California,* cargo ship, sunk by mine in Bay of Biscay; no casualties.

July

1 *Covington,* troop transport, sunk by submarine *U-86* off Brest, France; six lives lost.

10 *Motor launch #3249* sunk by German shore batteries near Nieuport, Belgium; one life lost.

10 *Oosterdijk,* cargo ship, sunk in collision with steamer *San Jacinto,* mid-Atlantic; no casualties.

11 *Westover,* cargo ship, sunk by German submarine *U-92* off French coast; 11 lives lost.

19 *San Diego,* cruiser, formerly *California,* sunk by German submarine mine off Fire Island, N.Y.; six lives lost.

August

4 *Subchaser No. 187,* sunk in collision with steamship *Capto* off Virginia coast; no casualties.

21 *Montauk,* SP 392, sunk off Cumberland Island, Ga.; nine lives lost.

27 *Subchaser No. 209,* mistaken for enemy and sunk by gunfire from SS *Felix Taussig* south of Long Island; 18 lives lost.

September

16 *Buena Ventura,* cargo ship, sunk by German submarine *U-46* off Spanish coast; 19 lives lost.

26 *Tampa,* Coast Guard, disappeared, probably torpedoed by German submarine *U-53* in Bristol Channel; no survivors; 118 lives lost.

30 *Ticonderoga,* cargo ship, torpedoed, shelled and sunk by German submarine *U-152* in mid-Atlantic; 213 lives lost, including 101 Army; two men taken prisoner.

October

1 *Subchaser No. 60,* sunk in collision with tanker *Fred M. Weller* off Ambrose Channel Lightship; two lives lost.

4 *Herman Frasch,* cargo ship, sunk in collision with USS *George G. Henry* off Nova Scotia; 23 casualties.

5 *Mary Alice,* SP 397, sunk in collision with USS *O-13,* submarine, Long Island Sound; no casualties.

7 *West Gate,* cargo ship, sunk in collision with *American* off Nova Scotia; seven lives lost.

9 *Sub-chaser No. 219,* exploded and sunk between Bermuda and Azores; four lives lost.

15 *America,* troop transport, sank at the dock in Hoboken, N.J., two men missing.

1918

October

17 *Lucia,* torpedoed by submarine. Crew rescued by steamer *Fairfax;* two lives lost. Last American ship torpedoed in World War I.

1918-1941

21 *Lake Borgne,* cargo ship, struck a rock and sank near Mathieu Point, France; no casualties.

28 *Tarantula,* SP 124, sunk in collision with steamship *Frisia* off Fire Island Light Vessel; no casualties.

November

6 *Lake Damita,* cargo ship, grounded and sank Brest, France; no casualties.

15 *Elizabeth,* SP 1092, wrecked at mouth of Brazos River, Tex.; two lives lost.

26 *Bonita,* SP 540, while moored at Coast Guard station in Boston harbor, struck and sunk by schooner *Russell;* no casualties.

December

11 *Lake Bloomington,* cargo ship, grounded and sank at mouth of Gironde River, France; no casualties.

28 *Tenadores,* troop transport, grounded about 10 miles from Brest, France, total loss; no casualties.

30 *Katherine W. Cullen,* SP 3223, sank while in tow by USS *Hernon* about 15 miles from Boston Light Vessel; no casualties.

1919

January

29 *Piave,* cargo ship, grounded and sunk off English Coast in Dover Straits; no casualties.

April

28 *W. T. James,* SP 429, sunk off Armen Light, France; no casualties.

28 *Gypsum Queen,* SP 430, blew up and sunk near Armen Light, France; 18 lives lost.

May

2 *Sub-chaser No. 58,* burned by gasoline explosion, Charleston, S.C., total loss; no casualties.

5 *Sub-chaser No. 343,* sunk by fire and explosion in His Majesty's Dockyard at Ireland Island, Bermuda; one life lost.

July

12 *Richard Buckley,* trawler, sunk by mine in North Sea; seven lives lost.

17 *May,* yacht, grounded off Santa Domingo, Dominican Republic.

30 *G-2*, submarine, accidentally sunk near New London, Conn.; three lives lost.

September

10 *Katherine K.*, sp 220, wrecked near Key West, Fla.; no casualties.

10 *Mary Pope*, sp 291, wrecked; no casualties.

November

1 *Sub-chaser No. 256*, sunk by gasoline explosion, mid-Atlantic.

1920

March

9 *Sub-chaser No. 262*, sank in Pacific; no casualties.

24 *H-1*, submarine, grounded off Margarita Island, Lower California, Mexico. During salvage operations; sunk with loss of four lives.

September

1 *S-5*, submarine, sunk about 40 miles off entrance to Delaware Bay; no casualties.

1921

February

26 USS *Woolsey* sunk in collision with SS *Steel Inventor* off Panama; 16 lives lost.

March

23 USS *Conestoga*, tug, crew of 43, sailed from San Francisco enroute to Samoa and was never seen again.

September

26 *R-6*, submarine, sunk off San Pedro, Calif.; two lives lost.

December

7 *S-48*, submarine, sunk off Bridgeport, Conn., during practice dive. Crew of 43 saved, after one escaped to surface through torpedo tube.

16 *Graham*, destroyer, wrecked in collision.

1922

May

22 *Eagle 17* wrecked between Amagansett and Easthampton, in Long Island.

1923

June

5 *Cardinal*, minesweeper wrecked off Cherikof, Alaska.

July

27 USS *Granite State*, old frigate, burned and sank off Massachusetts.

August

21 *Gopher*, tender, sunk.

1923
September
   8 Point Honda (California) Disaster. Destroyers *Delphy, S. P. Lee, Fuller, Chauncey, Woodbury, Nicholas,* and *Young* piled up on the beach as a result of faulty navigation; 22 lives lost.
October
   6 *Sub-chaser 340,* destroyed by fire.

1924
January
   16 *Tacoma,* light cruiser, wrecked on reef off Tampico, Mexico; four lives lost.
September
   3 USS *Shenandoah,* dirigible, wrecked over Ava, Ohio; 15 lives lost.
   25 USS *S-51* rammed by steamer *City of Rome,* and sunk off Block Island; 37 lives lost. Ship refloated on 5 July 1925, and towed to Brooklyn Navy Yard.

1925
December
   15 *Curlew,* minesweeper, wrecked by grounding off Panama.

1927
December
   17 USS *S-4,* submarine, rammed and sunk off Provincetown, Mass., by Coast Guard destroyer *Paulding;* 39 lives lost.

1929
October
   22 *Yantic,* old gunboat, wrecked and sunk in mooring at Detroit, Mich.

1931
January
   21 *Mayflower,* yacht, burned and sank.

1933
April
   4 *Akron,* dirigible, lost in storm off Atlantic Coast; 73 lives lost, including Adm. William Moffett, Chief of Bureau of Aeronautics.

1935
February
   12 USS *Macon,* dirigible, lost while operating with Pacific Fleet off Point Sur, Calif.; all but two of crew rescued.

1937
June
26 *Sanderling*, minesweeper, sunk.

December
13 USS *Panay*, river gunboat, bombed and sunk by Japanese aircraft while at anchor near Hoshien in Yangtze River; two killed, 43 injured.

1939
May
23 USS *Squalus*, submarine, during a scheduled dive, sank in 240 feet of water off Portsmouth, N.H.; 59 men trapped in the ship were rescued. *Squalus* was successfully refloated and fought through WWII as *Sailfish*.

1941
June
16 USS *O-9*, submarine, sunk off Portsmouth, N.H., during test dive; 33 lives lost.

October
31 *Reuben James*, destroyer, torpedoed and sunk by German submarine off Western Iceland with loss of about 100 lives; first Navy ship lost by enemy action in World War II.

World War II
December
7 Sunk by Japanese sneak attack on Pearl Harbor: Battleships *Arizona, California, Oklahoma,* and *West Virginia.* Minelayer *Oglala* and the target ship *Utah.* (All ships, except *Arizona, Oklahoma,* and *Utah,* were raised and returned to service.) Damaged: Battleships *Nevada, Pennsylvania, Tennessee, Maryland;* cruisers *Raleigh, Honolulu,* and *Helena;* destroyers *Cassin, Shaw,* and *Downes;* seaplane tender *Curtiss* and repair ship *Vestal;* total of 2,117 men killed, 960 missing, 816 wounded.

8 *Wake*, gunboat, surrendered to Japanese at Shanghai, after scuttling attempt failed. Only U.S. ship to surrender in World War II.
Penguin, minesweeper, sunk by Japanese bomber, Guam.
Robert Barnes captured by Japanese at Guam.

15 *PT-33* damaged by grounding and sunk by U.S. forces, Philippine Islands.

25 *Sealion*, submarine, damaged by Japanese bomber at Cavite, P.I., on 10 Dec., sunk by U.S. forces.

1941

December

YP-16 and *YP-17* lost, Philippine Islands.

YCK-1 lost at Wake Island.

1942

In Philippine area: *YA-52, -59, -65,* *YAG-2, -3, -4,* *YC-178, -181, -537, -643, -644, -646, -647, -648, -649, -652, -653, -654, -669, -683, -714, -715, -716,* *YD-19, -47, -56, -60,* *YF-86, -177, -178, -179, -180, 181, 212, -223, -224, -230, -317, San Felipe, Santa Rita, Rosal, Camina, Dapdap, Rivera, Magdalena, Yacal,* *YM-4,* *YO-41, -42, -64,* *YPD-22,* *YPK-6, -7,* *YRC-4, YSP-41, -42, -43, -44, -45, -46, -47, -48, -49, -50.* *YSR-2, Banaag, Iona, Mercedes,* *YW-54.*

Off Guam: *YC-664, -665, -666, -667, -668, -670, -671, -672, -673, -674, -685, -717, -718,* *YM-13.* *YW-50, -55, -58...*

January

20 *PT-31* damaged by grounding, sunk by U.S. forces, Philippine Islands.

21 *S-36,* submarine, damaged by grounding and sunk by U.S. forces in Makassar Strait, Netherlands West Indies.

23 *Neches,* tanker, sunk by Japanese torpedo off Hawaiian Islands.

24 *S-26,* submarine, sunk by collision with submarine chaser *PC-460* in Gulf of Panama.

29 *Alexander Hamilton,* Coast Guard cutter, sunk by submarine torpedo off Iceland; 20 lives lost.

February

18 *Truxtun,* destroyer, and *Pollux,* stores ship, sunk by storm at Placentia Bay, Newfoundland; 204 lives lost.

19 *Peary,* destroyer, sunk by Japanese dive bomber at Darwin, Australia.

27 *Langley,* seaplane tender, sunk by Japanese bombers off Tjilatjap, Java.

28 *Jacob Jones,* destroyer, sunk by German submarine torpedo off Delaware Capes.

March

1 *Houston,* heavy cruiser, sunk by Japanese torpedoes and gunfire in Sunda Strait, Java Sea.

Pope, destroyer, sunk by dive bombers and surface gunfire, Java Sea.

Edsall, destroyer, sunk by gunfire south of Christmas Island, N.E.I.

Pillsbury, destroyer, sunk by gunfire south of Christmas Island.

Pecos, tanker, sunk by gunfire south of Christmas Island.

2 *Stewart,* destroyer, destroyed by her crew in Soerabaja, Java.

3 *Perch,* submarine, damaged by gunfire and depth charges, scuttled by crew in Java Sea.

Ashville, gunboat, sunk by gunfire south of Java.

7 *Shark,* submarine, overdue, reported lost, Pacific Ocean area.

13 *PT-32* sunk by scuttling in Philippine Islands.

15 *Acacia,* Coast Guard tender, sunk by gunfire from unidentified submarine south of Haiti, no casualties.

26 *Atik,* auxiliary craft, sunk by German submarine torpedo east of Cape Hatteras.

YP-97, patrol craft, lost in Philippines.

April

8 *Bittern,* minesweeper, damaged on 10 Dec. 1941 at Cavite by Japanese air attack, sunk by U.S. forces in Philippine Islands.

Napa, tug, scuttled by U.S. forces in Philippine Islands.

9 *PT-34,* damaged by Japanese bomber, beached and abandoned in Philippine Islands.

10 *Canopus,* submarine tender, scuttled by U.S. forces off Mariveles Bay, P.I.

10 *Finch,* minesweeper, sunk by Japanese bomber in Philippine Islands.

Dewey, floating drydock, lost at Bataan, P.I.

12 *PT-35* scuttled by U.S. forces in Philippine Islands.

15 *PT-41* scuttled by U.S. forces in Philippine Islands.

26 *Sturtevant,* destroyer, sunk by U.S. mine off Marquesas Key, Fla.

28 *YP-77,* patrol craft, lost off Atlantic Coast.

May

4 *Tanager,* minesweeper, sunk by coastal defense guns at Corregidor, P.I.

5 *Mindanao,* river gunboat, sunk by horizontal bombers, P.I. area.

Pigeon, submarine rescue ship, sunk by horizontal bombers, P.I. area.

Genessee, tug, scuttled by U.S. forces in P.I. area.

Vaga, tug, scuttled by U.S. forces in P.I. area.

Ex-*Fisheries,* Ex-*Maryann* and Ex-*Perry* lost at fall of Corregidor, P.I.

6 *Oahu,* river gunboat, *Luzon,* river gunboat, and *Quail,* minesweeper, scuttled by U.S. forces in P.I. area.

7 *Sims,* destroyer, sunk by dive bomber in Battle of the Coral Sea.

8 *Lexington,* aircraft carrier, severely damaged by torpedo bombers and sunk by torpedoes from U.S. destroyer *Phelps,* Battle of the Coral Sea; 218 lives lost.

11 *Neosho,* tanker, damaged by dive bomber in Battle of the Coral Sea on 7 May, sunk by U.S. forces.

20 *YP-387,* patrol craft, lost off Delaware Capes.

23 *YP-277,* patrol craft, lost east of Hawaii.

Cythera, auxiliary, lost off Atlantic Coast.

June

3 *Bunting,* coastal minesweeper, sunk by collision in San Francisco Bay.

6 *Hamman,* destroyer, sunk by submarine torpedo, Battle of Midway.

1942

June

7 *Yorktown*, aircraft carrier, damaged by carrier-based aircraft on 4 June during Battle of Midway, sunk by submarine torpedo while retiring toward Hawaii.

Gannett, small seaplane tender, sunk by submarine torpedo off Bermuda.

19 *S-27*, submarine, grounded and abandoned at Amchitka, Aleutian Islands.

YP-389, patrol craft, lost off Cape Hatteras.

30 *Hornbill*, coastal minesweeper, sunk by collision in San Francisco Bay.

YP-128, patrol craft, lost off Monterey, Calif.

YP-270, patrol craft, lost off Lower California, Mexico.

August

4 *Tucker*, destroyer, sunk in United States minefield at Espiritu Santo, New Hebrides.

8 *George F. Elliott*, transport, damaged by suicide bombers in Solomon Islands area and sunk by U.S. forces.

9 *Astoria*, *Quincy*, and *Vincennes*, heavy cruisers, sunk by surface gunfire during Battle of Savo Islands; 918 lives lost.

Jarvis, destroyer, sunk by air attack off Guadalcanal, in Solomon Islands.

14 *S-39*, submarine damaged by striking reef off Rossell Island, Louisiade Archipelago, abandoned two days later.

16 *Grunion*, submarine, overdue and reported lost, Pacific Ocean area.

22 *Blue*, destroyer, damaged by surface torpedo attack in Solomon Islands area and scuttled by U.S. forces.

22 *Ingraham*, destroyer, sunk in collision with tanker *Chemung* off Nova Scotia; 218 lives lost.

30 *Colhoun*, high speed transport, sunk by horizontal bomber in Solomon Islands area.

September

5 *Gregory* and *Little*, high speed transports, sunk by surface gunfire in Solomon Island area.

6 *YP-74*, patrol craft, lost in Atlantic.

9 *Muskeget*, weather ship, disappeared shortly after this date, never seen again; 120 lives lost.

9 *YP-346*, patrol craft, lost in South Pacific. Cause of loss unknown.

15 *Wasp*, aircraft carrier, damaged by submarine torpedo near Espiritu Santo, New Hebrides, sunk by U.S. forces; 180 lives lost.

29 *YC-898* and *YC-899* lost off Key West, Fla.

October

12 *Duncan*, destroyer, sunk by naval gunfire off Savo Island, Solomon Islands.

15 *Meredith,* destroyer, sunk by aircraft torpedo off San Cristobal, Solomon Islands.

19 *O'Brien,* destroyer, en route to U.S. for battle repairs after being damaged on 15 Sept., broke in two and sank off Samoa.

24 *Seminole,* tug, sunk by naval gunfire off Guadalcanal.
YP-284, patrol craft, lost off Guadalcanal.

26 *Porter,* destroyer, damaged by submarine torpedo, sunk by U.S. forces, Battle of Santa Cruz.

27 *Hornet,* aircraft carrier, sunk by dive bombers, torpedo bombers, and destroyer torpedoes in Battle of Santa Cruz Islands.

31 *YP-345* lost southeast of Midway.

November

1 *YP-205,* patrol craft, lost near Puerto Rico.

9 *Leedstown,* transport, sunk by submarine and aircraft attack near Algiers.

11 *Joseph Hewes,* transport, sunk by submarine torpedo in Fedala Roads, North Africa.

12 *Tasker H. Bliss, Hugh L. Scott* and *Edward Rutledge,* transports, sunk by submarine tropedoes off Morocco, North Africa.
Erie, gunboat, sunk by torpedo in Caribbean area.

13 Battle of Guadalcanal: *Atlanta,* light cruiser, sunk by naval gunfire. *Juneau,* light cruiser, sunk by submarine torpedo. *Cushing,* destroyer, sunk by naval gunfire. *Monssen,* destroyer, sunk by naval gunfire. *Laffey,* destroyer, sunk by naval gunfire and surface craft torpedo. *Barton,* destroyer, sunk by surface craft torpedo.

14 Battle of Guadalcanal:
Preston, destroyer, sunk by naval gunfire.
Walke, destroyer, sunk by gunfire and torpedo from surface craft.

15 Battle of Guadalcanal:
Benham, destroyer, damaged by torpedo from surface craft, sunk by U.S. forces off Savo Island, Solomon Islands.

19 *YP-26,* patrol craft, lost in Canal Zone.

20 *YP-405* lost in Caribbean Sea.

25 *Thomas Stone,* transport, damaged by grounding in North Africa, beached and abandoned.

December

1 *Northampton,* heavy cruiser, sunk as a result of torpedo damage received in Battle of Tassafaronga (30 Nov.).

5 *Grebe,* tug, sunk by grounding, south of Fiji.

12 *PT-44* sunk by naval gunfire, Guadalcanal area.

17 *Natsek,* Coast Guard converted trawler, disappeared without trace in Belle Isle Strait, Newfoundland; crew of 24 lost.

1942

December

29 *Wasmuth,* high speed minesweeper, sunk by explosion of two of her own depth charges during gale in Aleutian Islands area.

1943

January

1 *Rescuer,* salvage ship, sunk by grounding in Aleutian Islands area.

8 *YP-492* lost off east coast of Florida.

10 *Argonaut,* submarine, sunk in attack on Japanese convoy southeast of New Britain.

11 *PT-112* sunk by naval gunfire off Cape Esperance, Solomon Islands. *PT-43* damaged by naval gunfire off Cape Esperance, beached and abandoned.

12 *Worden,* destroyer, sunk by grounding, Amchitka, Aleutian Islands. *PT-28* sunk by grounding, Dora Harbor, Alaska. *YP-183,* patrol craft, lost on west coast of Hawaii.

21 *SC-709,* submarine chaser, sunk by grounding off Cape Breton, Nova Scotia.

23 *YP-577,* patrol craft, lost in Great Lakes.

30 *Chicago,* heavy cruiser, sunk by aircraft torpedo, Battle of Rennell Island, Solomon Islands.

31 *YFD-20* lost off California Coast.

February

1 *DeHaven,* destroyer, sunk by dive bombers, Solomon Islands area.

1 *PT-37, PT-111,* and *PT-123* sunk by destroyer gunfire and aircraft attack, Guadalcanal.

3 *YC-886* and *YC-887* lost at Guantanamo Bay, Cuba.

20 *YMS-133,* motor minesweeper, foundered in Coos Bay, Ore.

22 *YP-72,* patrol craft, lost in Adak, Aleutian Islands.

23 *YP-336* lost in Delaware River.

March

2 *SC-1024,* submarine chaser, sunk by collision off North Carolina.

10 *YC-1278* lost off Atlantic Coast.

17 *PT-67* and *PT-119* sunk by fire, eastern New Guinea area.

22 *Grampus* and *Amberjack,* submarines, overdue and reported lost, Pacific area.

23 *YP-483* lost at Port Everglades, Fla. *YC-869* lost off Imperial Beach, Calif.

27 *Cutter No. 85006,* Coast Guard, sunk by explosion off Long Island.

April

1 *YP-235,* patrol craft, lost in Gulf of Mexico.

7 *Aaron Ward,* destroyer, sunk by bombers near Tulagi, Solomon Islands.

Kanawha, tanker, sunk by bombers near Tulagi, Solomon Islands.

10 *Triton,* submarine, overdue and reported lost, Pacific Ocean area.

15 *YP-453* lost in Bahama Islands.

18 *YC-891* lost off Key West, Fla.

22 *Grenadier,* submarine, sunk by enemy air attack and scuttling, Straits of Malacca.

23 *YP-422* lost off New Caledonia.

25 *YP-481* lost off Charleston, S.C.

26 *YP-47,* patrol craft, lost off Staten Island, N.Y.

May

2 *Cutter 58012,* sunk by engine room explosion off Manomet Point, Mass.

6 *YF-575* lost off Atlantic City, N.J.

12 *Pickerel,* submarine, overdue and reported lost Pacific Ocean area.

23 *Niagara,* PT-boat tender, sunk by bombers, Solomon Islands area.

PT-165 and *PT-173* sunk by submarine torpedoes off New Caledonia.

June

4 *PC-496,* submarine chaser, sunk by mine off Portugal.

11 *PT-22* lost in storm at Adak, Aleutian Islands, beached and abandoned.

12 *R-12* sunk off Key West, Florida, cause unknown.

13 *Escanaba,* Coast Guard cutter, sunk by explosion of unknown origin off Ivigtut, Greenland; 101 lives lost, only 2 survivors.

17 *SC-740,* submarine chaser, sunk by grounding, northeast coast of Australia.

18 *Ronaki,* unclassified auxiliary, lost by grounding, east coast of Australia.

20 *YF-401* lost off Atlantic Coast.

22 *SC-751,* submarine chaser, sunk by grounding, west coast of Australia.

23 *Aludra* and *Deimos,* cargo ships, sunk by submarine torpedoes in Solomon Islands area.

27 *Redwing,* salvage ship, sunk by underwater explosion in North African area.

29 *Cutter 83421,* Coast Guard, sunk in collision by *Cutter 1330* off east Florida Coast; 9 lives lost.

30 *McCawley,* attack transport, damaged by submarine torpedo and sunk by U.S. PT boat, New Georgia, Solomon Islands.

July

2 *PT-153* and *PT-158* lost by grounding in Solomon Islands area, beached and abandoned.

5 *Strong,* destroyer, sunk by submarine torpedo, Solomon Islands area.

1943

July

6 *Helena*, light cruiser, sunk by destroyer torpedoes, Kula Gulf, Solomon Islands.

10 *Maddox*, destroyer, sunk by dive bomber, Sicily.

LST-313, landing ship, sunk by horizontal bomber, Sicily.

Sentinel, minesweeper, sunk by dive bombers, Sicily.

11 *LST-158*, landing ship, damaged by horizontal bomber, beached and abandoned, Sicily.

13 *Gwin*, destroyer, damaged by destroyer torpedo in Battle of Kolombangara, Solomon Islands, scuttled by U.S. forces.

18 *LST-342* sunk by submarine torpedo, Solomon Islands.

YF-487 lost in Caribbean Sea.

K-74, blimp, shot down by German submarine in Caribbean. Only airship lost in World War II.

20 *Runner*, submarine, overdue and reported lost, Pacific Ocean area.

PT-166 sunk by strafing, Solomon Island.

August

1 *PT-117* hit by dive bomber, Solomon Islands, beached and abandoned.

PT-164 sunk by horizontal bomber, Solomon Islands.

2 *PT-109* sunk in collision with enemy ship, Solomon Islands.

Plymouth, gunboat, sunk by submarine torpedo off east coast U.S.

8 *PT-113* grounded eastern New Guinea area, beached and abandoned.

10 *LST-318* damaged by dive bomber, beached and abandoned, Sicily.

YC-970 lost in Puget Sound, Wash.

13 *John Penn*, attack transport, sunk by aircraft, Guadalcanal.

18 *LST-396* sunk by accidental explosion, Solomon Islands.

23 *SC-694* and *SC-696*, submarine chasers, sunk by dive bombers, Sicily.

Crow, coastal minesweeper, sunk by erratic torpedo from U.S. aircraft Puget Sound, Wash.

September

5 *YP-279*, patrol craft, lost off Townsville, Australia.

7 *PT-118* and *PT-172* damaged by grounding in Solomon Islands, sunk by U.S. forces.

9 *Nauset*, tug, sunk by dive bomber, Italy.

11 *Rowan*, destroyer, sunk by torpedo from surface craft, Italian area.

Navajo, tug, sunk by explosion, east of New Hebrides Islands.

17 *PT-136* damaged by grounding, sunk by U.S. forces eastern New Guinea.

19 *Cisco*, submarine, sunk; departed Port Darwin, Australia for South China Sea, never heard from again.

20 *YF-579* lost at San Francisco.

22 *APc-35,* coastal transport, grounded, beached and abandoned, New Georgia.

25 *Skill,* minesweeper, sunk by submarine torpedo, Italy.

30 *Grayling,* submarine, overdue and reported lost, Pacific Ocean area.

PT-68 damaged by grounding in New Guinea area, sunk by U.S. forces.

PT-219 foundered off Attu, Aleutian Islands, sometime in September.

30 *Wilcox,* Coast Guard cutter, foundered off Cape Hatteras, one life lost.

LST-203 beached at Nanumea, Ellice Islands, unable to retract, abandoned.

October

1 *YDG-4* lost off New Caledonia.

3 *Henley,* destroyer, sunk by submarine torpedo, eastern New Guinea area.

5 *LST-488* sunk in Solomon Islands area from damage received 1 Oct. in bombing attack.

6 *Chevalier,* destroyer, damaged by destroyer torpedo and sunk by U.S. forces, off Vella Lavella, Solomon Islands.

7 *S-44,* submarine, sunk by enemy surface craft in Kurile Islands area.

9 *Buck,* destroyer, sunk by submarine torpedo in Italian area.

13 *Bristol,* destroyer, sunk by submarine torpedo in Mediterranean area.

14 *Dow,* Coast Guard cutter, grounded and abandoned off Mayaguez, Puerto Rico; no lives lost.

15 *Pompano,* submarine, overdue and reported lost, Pacific Ocean area.

16 *Moonstone,* auxiliary, lost off Delaware Capes.

24 *Dorado,* submarine, reported lost, Atlantic Ocean area.

28 *YP-88,* patrol craft, lost in Amchitka, Aleutian Islands.

November

2 *Borie,* destroyer, sunk by intentional ramming and gunfire in encounter with German submarine *U-405,* north of Azores.

5 *YCK-1* lost off Nova Scotia.

6 *Beatty,* destroyer, sunk by aircraft torpedo, off northwest Africa.

9 *Wahoo,* submarine, reported lost, Pacific Ocean area.

12 *YC-857* lost off Cape Cod, Mass.

17 *McKean,* high speed transport, sunk by aircraft torpedo off Bougainville, Solomon Islands.

Capelin, submarine, departed Darwin, Australia for Molucca and Celebes Seas and never heard from again.

18 *PT-311* sunk by mine off Corsica.

19 *Sculpin,* submarine, sunk by destroyer gunfire, Central Pacific area,

PT-147 damaged by grounding, eastern New Guinea area, sunk by U.S. forces.

1943

November

 SC-1067, submarine chaser, foundered off Attu, Aleutian Islands.

23 *PT-322* grounded, eastern New Guinea area, sunk by U.S. forces.

24 *Liscome Bay*, escort carrier, sunk by submarine torpedo, Gilbert Islands area.

29 *Perkins*, destroyer, sunk in collision with Australian troopship in eastern New Guinea area.

December

13 *YCK-8* lost off Key West, Fla.

16 *YP-426*, patrol craft, lost off east coast of Florida.

17 *APC-21*, coastal transport, sunk by dive bomber off New Britain.

21 *Bodega*, Coast Guard cutter, grounded and abandoned off Margarita Point, Canal Zone, no casualties.

23 *Corvina*, submarine, reported lost in Pacific Ocean area.

24 *Leary*, destroyer, sunk by submarine torpedo in North Atlantic.

26 *Brownson*, destroyer, sunk by dive bomber, Cape Gloucester, New Britain.

1944

January

3 *Turner*, destroyer, sunk by explosion in Ambrose Channel, New York Harbor, 100 lives lost.

4 *PT-145* damaged by grounding, sunk by U.S. forces, eastern New Guinea area.

6 *St. Augustine*, gunboat, sunk by collision off North Carolina coast.

9 *YP-281*, patrol craft, lost in New Hebrides.

10 *YMS-127*, motor minesweeper, sunk by grounding in Aleutian Islands area.

14 *YO-159*, self propelled oil barge, damaged by submarine torpedo and sunk by U.S. forces, South Pacific area.

20 *LST-228* sunk by grounding in Azores.

22 *Portent*, minesweeper, sunk by mine off Anzio, Italy.

25 *YMS-30*, motor minesweeper, sunk by mine off Anzio, Italy.

26 *PT-110* and *PT-114* sunk in collision off New Britain.

February

11 *PT-279* sunk in collision with *PT-282*, Solomon Islands.

12 *Macaw*, submarine rescue ship, sunk by grounding, entrance to Midway Channel.

18 *YT-198*, tug, sunk by mine in Italian area.

20 *LST-348* sunk by submarine torpedo in Italian waters.

22 *PT-200* sunk by collision with unknown object off Long Island, N.Y.

24 *YC-523* lost off Portsmouth, N.H.

26 *LST-349* sunk by grounding, Italian area.

26 *Ailanthus*, auxiliary, lost in Aleutian Islands.

March

5 *YT-247* lost southeast of New Hebrides

6 *Scorpion,* submarine, reported lost, Pacific Ocean area.

7 *PT-337* sunk by coastal defense guns, eastern New Guinea area.

9 *Leopold,* destroyer escort, sunk by submarine torpedo south of Iceland, 171 lives lost.

9 *YP-331,* patrol craft, lost in Straits of Florida.

17 *PT-283* sunk by coastal defense gun, Solomon Islands area.

26 *Tullibee,* submarine, sunk, (possibly by own torpedo running in circle), north of Palau Islands, Caroline Islands.

27 *PT-121* and *PT-363* accidentally sunk by friendly bombers, Bismarck Archipelago.

30 *Grayback,* submarine, reported lost, Pacific Ocean area.
YTM-467 lost in Marshall or Gilbert Islands.

April

9 *SC-984,* submarine chaser, sunk by grounding in New Hebrides.

12 *PT-135* damaged by grounding in Bismarck Archipelago area, sunk by U.S. forces.

12 *ATR-98,* rescue tug, sunk by collision in Azores area.

17 *Trout,* submarine, reported lost in Pacific Ocean area.

20 *Lansdale,* destroyer, sunk by aircraft torpedo in western Mediterranean.

28 *LST-507* and *LST-531* sunk by torpedoes from surface craft in English Channel.

29 *PT-346* and *PT-347* sunk, accidentally by friendly aircraft, Bismarck Archipelago area.

May

1 *YP-95,* patrol craft, lost at Adak, Aleutian Islands.

5 *Fechteler,* destroyer escort, sunk by submarine torpedo in western Mediterranean area.

5 *PT-247* sunk by coastal defense gun, Solomon Islands area.

9 *Shahaka,* district craft, lost in eastern Pacific.

9 *PC-558,* submarine chaser, sunk by submarine torpedo, Sicily.

11 *YF-415* lost off Cape Cod.

21 *LST-43, -69, -179, -353* and *-480* sunk by accidental explosion at Pearl Harbor, T.H.

27 *PT-339* grounded in western New Guinea area, sunk by U.S. forces.

29 *Block Island,* escort carrier, sunk by submarine torpedo northwest of Canary Islands.

June

5 *Osprey,* minesweeper, sunk by mine off Normandy, France.

6 *Corry,* destroyer, sunk by mine off Normandy, France.
PC-1261, submarine chaser, sunk by mine off Normandy.

1944

June

7 *Tide,* minesweeper, sunk by mine off Normandy.

Susan B. Anthony, transport, sunk by mine off Normandy.

Gudgeon, submarine, reported lost, Pacific Ocean area.

8 *Rich,* destroyer escort, sunk by mine, off Normandy.

LST-499 sunk by mine, off Normandy.

9 *Meredith,* destroyer, sunk by bomber off Normandy.

LST-314 sunk by torpedo from surface craft, off Normandy.

LST-376 damaged by torpedo from surface craft, sunk by U.S. forces, off Normandy.

10 *Glennon,* destroyer, sunk by coastal defense gun, Normandy.

11 *LST-496* sunk by mine off Normandy.

Partridge, ocean tug, sunk by torpedo off Normandy.

18 *PT-63* and *PT-107* sunk by fire off New Ireland.

19 *LST-523* sunk by mine off Normandy.

21 *Cutters 83415* and *83471,* Coast Guard, sunk by storm off Normandy.

24 *PT-193* damaged by grounding, sunk by U.S. forces, western New Guinea area.

29 *Valor,* coastal minesweeper, sunk by collision off Newport, R.I.

July

2 *YMS-350,* motor minesweeper, sunk by mine, Normandy area.

4 *S-28,* submarine, sunk during training exercise off Hawaii, cause unknown.

9 *Swerve,* minesweeper, sunk by mine, Italian area.

13 *Herring,* submarine, reported lost, Pacific Ocean area.

15 *PT-133* sunk by coastal defense gun, eastern New Guinea area.

26 *Golet,* submarine, reported lost, Pacific Ocean area.

Robalo, submarine, sunk off western Palawan, P.I., cause unknown.

30 *YMS-304,* motor minesweeper, sunk by mine, Normandy area.

August

2 *Fiske,* destroyer escort, sunk by submarine torpedo, North Atlantic.

9 *PT-509* sunk by naval gunfire off Isle of Jersey, English Channel.

13 *Flier,* submarine, sunk by external explosion, Balabac Strait, North Borneo.

14 *LST-921* sunk by submarine torpedo in English Channel.

15 *LST-282* damaged by radio-controlled bomb, beached and abandoned on south coast of France.

16 *PT-202* and *PT-218* sunk by mines, south coast of France.

YMS-24, motor minesweeper, sunk by mine, south coast of France.

24 *Harder,* submarine, sunk by enemy depth charges, west of Luzon, P.I.

September

1 *YMS-21,* motor minesweeper, sunk by mine, south coast of France.

12 NOA, high speed transport, sunk by collision Palau Islands area.

12 *YMS-409*, motor minesweeper, foundered off Atlantic Coast.

13 *Warrington*, destroyer, sunk by hurricane off Bahama Islands.

Perry, high speed minesweeper, sunk by mine, Palau Islands area.

14 *Bedloe* and *Jackson*, Coast Guard cutters, sunk by storm off Cape Hatteras, N.C.

Lightship No. 73, Coast Guard, sunk by storm, Vineyard Sound, Mass.

YAG-17 lost off North Carolina.

19 *PT-371* damaged by grounding, sunk by U.S. forces in Molucca Sea.

24 *YMS-19*, motor minesweeper, sunk by mine in Palau Islands area.

25 *Miantonomah*, minelayer, sunk by mine, Normandy area.

27 *YG-39* lost off Panama, Atlantic side.

October

1 *YMS-385*, motor minesweeper, sunk by mine in Western Carolina Islands area.

3 *Seawolf*, submarine, accidentally sunk by U.S. forces off Morotai Island, Netherland East Indies.

Shelton, destroyer escort, sunk by submarine torpedo, Netherlands East Indies.

6 *Asphalt*, auxiliary, lost off Saipan.

11 *PT-368* grounded in western New Guinea area, sunk by U.S. forces.

17 *YMS-70*, motor minesweeper, sunk by storm off Leyte, P.I.

24 *Princeton*, light aircraft carrier, damaged by dive bomber in Battle of Leyte Gulf, sunk by U.S. forces.

Darter, submarine, damaged by grounding in Palawan Passage, P.I., destroyed by U.S. forces.

Tang, submarine, sunk by own torpedo running in a circle, north of Formosa.

24 *Sonoma*, ocean tug, sunk by suicide plane, Battle of Leyte Gulf.

25 *St. Lo*, escort carrier, sunk by suicide plane in Battle of Leyte Gulf.

Gambier Bay, escort carrier, sunk by naval gunfire in Battle of Leyte Gulf.

Johnston, destroyer, sunk by naval gunfire, Battle of Leyte Gulf.

Hoel, destroyer, sunk by naval gunfire, Battle of Leyte Gulf.

Samuel B. Roberts, destroyer escort, sunk by gunfire, Battle of Leyte Gulf.

PT-493 sunk by coastal defense gun, Battle of Leyte Gulf.

28 *Eversole*, destroyer escort, sunk by submarine torpedo, Leyte area.

November

1 *Abner Read*, destroyer, sunk by suicide plane, Leyte Gulf.

5 *PT-320* sunk by bomber, Leyte area.

8 *Growler*, submarine, sunk west of Philippine Islands, cause unknown.

1944

November

10 *PT-321*, grounded, sunk by U.S. forces in Leyte area.

10 *Mount Hood*, ammunition ship, sunk by explosion at Manus, Admiralty Islands.

18 *LST-6* sunk by mine in Seine River, France.

PT-311 sunk by mine in Mediterranean area.

20 *Mississinewa*, tanker, sunk by submarine torpedo, Marianas Islands area.

24 *YP-383*, patrol craft, lost in Gulf of Panama.

25 *PT-363* sunk by coastal defense gun, Netherlands East Indies area.

27 *Escolar*, submarine, reported lost in Pacific Ocean area.

Shark, submarine, reported lost in Pacific Ocean area.

December

3 *Cooper*, destroyer, sunk by torpedo from unidentified source, Ormoc Bay, P.I.

7 *Mahan*, destroyer, damaged by suicide plane in Leyte area, sunk by U.S. forces.

Ward, high speed transport, damaged by suicide plane in Leyte area, sunk by U.S. forces.

10 *PT-323* damaged by suicide plane in Leyte area, beached and abandoned.

11 *Reid*, destroyer, sunk by suicide plane in Leyte area.

SC-1059, submarine chaser, sunk by grounding near Bahama Islands.

15 *LST-472* and *LST-738*, damaged by suicide planes in Mindoro area, P.I., sunk by U.S. forces.

18 *Hull, Monoghan*, and *Spence*, destroyers, sunk by typhoon east of Philippine Islands; 765 lives lost. This same storm damaged eight aircraft carriers and 16 other ships)

20 *LST-359* sunk by submarine torpedo in eastern Atlantic area.

21 *Albacore* and *Scamp*, submarines, reported lost in Pacific Ocean area.

LST-460 and *LST-479* sunk by suicide planes in Mindora area, P.I.

22 *LST-563* sunk by grounding at Clipperton Island.

28 *LST-750* damaged by aircraft torpedo off Negros, P.I., sunk by U.S. forces.

30 *Porcupine*, auxiliary craft, damaged by suicide plane, sunk by U.S. forces in Mindoro area.

YCF-42 lost off Cape Lookout.

1945

January

4 *Ommaney Bay*, escort carrier, damaged by suicide plane, sunk by U.S. forces in Luzon area, P.I.

6 *Hovey* and *Long,* high speed minesweepers, sunk by suicide planes in Luzon area, P.I.

7 *Palmer,* high speed minesweeper, sunk by bomber, Luzon area, P.I.

11 *YMS-14,* motor minesweeper, sunk by collision in Boston Harbor.

13 *YC-912* lost in North Pacific.

14 *PT-73* grounded in Philippine Islands area, beached and abandoned.

15 *YP-73,* patrol craft, lost in Kodiak Harbor, Alaska.

24 *Extractor,* salvage ship, accidentally sunk by U.S. submarine in Philippine Sea.

28 *PT-338* grounded off Luzon, P.I., sunk by U.S. forces.

29 *Serpens,* cargo ship, sunk by explosion at Guadalcanal; 196 Navy and 57 Army men lost.

30 *Pontiac,* auxiliary, lost off Halifax, Nova Scotia.

31 *PC-1129,* submarine chaser, sunk by suicide boat in Philippine Islands area.

YCF-59 lost off Delaware coast.

February

1 *PT-77* and *PT-79* accidentally sunk by U.S. naval gunfire, Philippine Islands area.

7 *YG-44* lost at Pearl Harbor.

11 *LST-577* damaged by submarine torpedo east of Philippine Islands, sunk by U.S. forces.

14 *YMS-48,* motor minesweeper, sunk by coastal defense gun in Philippine Islands area.

15 *Swordfish,* submarine, reported lost, Pacific Ocean area.

16 *Barbel,* submarine, reported lost, Pacific Ocean area.

18 *YP-94,* patrol craft, lost in Aleutian Islands.

21 *Bismarck Sea,* escort carrier, sunk by suicide plane, Iwo Jima area.

YC-693 lost, Alaskan area.

March

8 *YF-926* lost en route to Pearl Harbor.

22 *YF-724* and *YF-75* lost off Farallones Islands, Calif.

26 *Halligan,* destroyer, sunk by mine in Okinawa area.

28 *Skylark,* minesweeper, sunk by mine off Borneo.

YCF-23, -29, -36, -37 lost en route to Eniwetok Atoll.

April

3 *YMS-71,* motor minesweeper, sunk by mine off Borneo.

4 *Dickerson,* high speed transport, damaged by suicide plane and sunk by U.S. forces, Okinawa area.

6 *Bush,* destroyer, sunk by suicide plane, Okinawa area.

Colhoun, destroyer, damaged by suicide plane, sunk by U.S. forces, Okinawa area.

Emmons, high speed minesweeper, damaged by suicide plane, sunk by U.S. forces, Okinawa area.

1945

April

    LST-447 sunk by suicide plane, Okinawa area.

  7 *PGM-18,* motor gunboat, sunk by mine, Okinawa area.

 12 *Mannert L. Abele,* destroyer, sunk by piloted bomb, Okinawa area.

 16 *Pringle,* destroyer, sunk by suicide plane, Okinawa area.

    Kete, submarine, reported lost, Pacific Ocean area.

 22 *Swallow,* minesweeper, sunk by suicide plane, Okinawa area.

    SC-1019, submarine chaser, grounded and sank in Yucatan Channel.

 23 *PE-56,* gunboat, sunk by explosion off Portland, Me.

 24 *Frederick C. Davis,* destroyer escort, sunk by submarine torpedo, Atlantic Ocean area.

May

  1 *Trigger,* submarine, reported lost, Pacific Ocean area.

  2 *YMS-481,* motor minesweeper, sunk by coastal defense gun, Tarakan area, Borneo.

  3 *Luce, Little,* and *Morrison,* destroyers, sunk by suicide plane in Okinawa area.

 16 *Snook,* submarine, reported lost, Pacific Ocean area.

    Longshaw, destroyer, damaged by coastal defense gun, sunk by U.S. forces, Okinawa area.

 24 *Lagarto,* submarine, reported lost, Pacific Ocean area.

 25 *Bates,* high speed transport, sunk by suicide plane, Okinawa area.

 27 *Drexler,* destroyer, sunk by suicide plane, Okinawa area.

    YC-961 lost at Biorka Island.

    YO-156 and *157* lost at Sitka, Alaska.

June

  6 *Sheepscot,* tanker, grounded by a storm at Iwo Jima, and abandoned.

  8 *Salute,* minesweeper, sunk by mine, Borneo area.

 10 *William D. Porter,* destroyer, sunk by suicide plane, Okinawa area.

 16 *Twiggs,* destroyer, sunk by aircraft torpedo, Okinawa area.

 18 *YMS-50* damaged by mine, Balikpapan area, Borneo, sunk by U.S. forces.

 26 *YMS-39,* motor minesweeper, sunk by mine in Balikpapan area, Borneo.

    YMS-365 damaged by mine, sunk by U.S. forces in Balikpapan area, Borneo.

    YC-1272 lost near San Pedro, Calif.

July

  9 *YMS-84* sunk by mine, Balikpapan area, Borneo.

 10 *SC-521,* submarine chaser, foundered, Solomon Island area.

 24 *Underhill,* destroyer escort, damaged by piloted torpedo, sunk by U.S. forces, Luzon, P.I.

28 *Callaghan,* destroyer, sunk by suicide plane in Okinawa area.

30 *Indianapolis,* heavy cruiser, sunk by submarine torpedo in Philippine Sea, 880 lives lost.

30 *Bonefish,* submarine, reported lost in Pacific Ocean area.

August

6 *Bullhead,* submarine, sunk in Java Sea (presumed date).

24 *Magnolia,* Coast Guard, sunk in collission with SS *Marguerite Lehand* in Mobile Ship Channel; one life lost.

October

9 *PC-590* foundered and broke in two in storm at Okinawa. (20 lives lost)

1949

August

26 USS *Cochino,* submarine, sunk as the result of internal fire and explosion, while on training cruise in the Arctic.

1950

August

25 *Benevolence,* hospital ship, on trial run after being taken out of mothballs for Korean service, collided with SS *Mary Luckenbach* outside Golden Gate, and sunk with loss of 18 lives.

October

1 *Magpie* sunk by mine off Korea; 20 killed and 12 wounded.

12 *Pirate* sunk by mine off Korea; killing six and wounding 48.

12 *Pledge* sunk by mine off Korea; killing seven and wounding 39.

1951

February

2 *Partridge* sunk by mine off Korea; killing eight and wounding seven.

1952

April

26 USS *Hobson,* destroyer, collided with USS *Wasp,* aircraft carrier, during maneuvers in Atlantic. *Hobson* sank with loss of 176 lives.

August

27 *Sarsi* sunk by mine off Korea; two killed, three missing and four injured.

1963

April

10 USS *Thresher* (SSN 593) sank while conducting diving tests, 220 miles east of Cape Cod, with loss of entire crew of 112 and 17 civilians.

NAVAL TERMS AND PHRASES

Naval Terms and Phrases

Navy men pride themselves on familiarity with naval customs and expressions, and their origin and meaning. Without such knowledge, technical and professional proficiency, while adequate to the task at hand, cannot be augmented by the inspiration and zeal which is the rightful portion of men using customs, words, and tools passed down to them for over 3,000 years. Some of these were borrowed from the British Navy, but their origins go back through history to the Vikings, the Romans and Phoenicians.

Abaft—behind or farther aft; astern or toward the stern.

Abeam—at right angles to the centerline of, and outside a ship.

Aboard—on or in a ship. Close *aboard;* near a ship.

Abreast—lying, or moving side by side.

Absentee pennant—special pennant flown to indicate absence of commanding officer, admiral, chief of staff, or a division, squadron, or flotilla commander.

Acey-Ducey—Navy game; also slang: sudden fit or display of temper, as "he threw an *acey-ducey.*"

Wherever Navy men assemble, there will be found the familiar backgammon board, a handful of checkers (or washers), a pair of dice, two contestants, and a crowd of kibitzers shouting "Kick him!" "Run for it," or "Shut the door!"

Acey-Ducey is a variation of backgammon, the oldest known game: equipment for playing backgammon has been found in an Egyptian tomb of 3,000 B.C. Romans called their version of the game *Scripta Dodecim,* the French called their game *Tric Trac,* and the early English called their game *Tables.*

Acey-Ducey boards, similar to backgammon boards, are sometimes painted on canvas or oilcloth, which can be rolled up and stowed away. The 30 "men" can be checkers, poker chips, or brass and steel washers. Many sailors already have the necessary dice.

Rules for play resemble those for backgammon, with the exception that when a player rolls an *Acey-Ducey,* a 1 and a 2, he takes the moves indicated, then four moves of any number he desires from 1 to 6, and then takes another roll of the dice.

Accommodation ladder—a portable flight of steps down a ship's side.

Admiral—from the Arabic Amir-al-Bahr—commander of the seas, first used during the Crusades, England's first admiral was William de Leyburn, appointed "Admiral of the Sea of the King of England" by Edward I in 1297. First U.S. Navy admiral was David Glasgow Farragut. There have been only three admirals of the U.S. Navy—David Farragut, David Porter, and George Dewey. In W.W. II, rank of fleet admiral (five stars) was created 15 Dec., 1944, and conferred on Ernest J. King, William D.

Leahy, and Chester W. Nimitz. William H. Halsey was later appointed fleet admiral. As of 1 Jan., 1960, there were 293 active duty flag officers in the Navy.

Adrift—loose from moorings, out of place.

Advance—distance traveled by a ship on a given course before responding to change of helm.

Aeropulse (or pulsejet)—type of jet engine in which air is rammed into motor by its forward motion.

Aft—in, near, or toward the stern of a ship.

Aground—resting on or touching the ground or bottom.

Ahead—forward of the bow.

Ahoy—once Vikings war cry. Now distinct nautical hail—"Boat, *ahoy!*"

Aiguillette—loops of cord, covered with gold or gilt thread, worn by officers designated as aides to high government officials, flag officers, representatives of foreign nations, and by naval attachés. Aiguillette originated in the days of chivalry, when an aide-de-camp or henchman carried on his shoulder the rope and pegs for tethering his knight's horse. This became the mark of one near the leader. Aiguillettes worn by Presidential aides and aides to admirals or officials of higher rank, and naval attachés, consist of four loops; all to vice admirals, three loops; all others, two loops. Presidential and White House aides wear aiguillettes on right shoulder, all others on left shoulder. Naval aiguillettes are blue and gold, those of Marine Corps are red and gold. Slang term: chicken guts.

Airdale—slang: a naval aviator; "flyboy."

All hands—officers and enlisted personnel, the entire ship's company.

Allotment—assignment of part of military pay directly to person or bank.

Allowance—numbers, ranks, and ratings of officers and men assigned to ship

when impracticable to assign the full complement.

Aloft—above the ship's uppermost solid structure; overhead or high above.

Alongside—beside a pier, wharf, or ship.

Amidships (or midships)—middle portion of ship, along the line of keel.

Anchor—from *anchora*, the only nautical word adopted into the Teutonic language directly from Latin. The hook used at the end of a chain and dropped to the sea bottom to hold a ship, boat or seaplane in one particular place. Chinese used stones as anchors 2,000 B.C. The smallest Navy anchors can be lifted by one man; four anchors used by USS *Forrestal* each weigh 30 tons.

Anchorage—suitable place for ship to anchor. A designated area of port or harbor.

Anchor's aweigh—said of the anchor when just clear of the bottom.

Anchor ball—black shape hoisted by a ship to show she is anchored.

Anchor buoy—small buoy tied to an anchor, floating on the surface to show anchor's position on the bottom.

Anchor cable—chain, wire, or line, connecting anchor and ship.

Anchor detail—group of men who handle the anchor and cable when a ship is anchoring or getting underway.

Anchor light—white light displayed by a ship at anchor; two such lights are displayed by ship over 150 feet in length.

Anchor watch—originated when ships used anchor cables of hempen rope and oil-burning riding lights. Special care was taken, at anchor to see lamps were not extinguished, cables did not part, and ship did not drag her anchor. Men responsible for this duty were called the *anchor watch*. The term is still retained, although the duties have changed considerably. Today, the *anchor watch* is a detail on deck at night to guard a ship at anchor.

Anticorrosive paint—composition applied to ship's outer bottom to prevent corrosion.

Antifouling paint—composition applied over anticorrosive paint to reduce marine growths.

Armored rope—wire rope with hemp core and flat wire wound around outside of each strand; used chiefly in salvage or similar work.

Astern—toward the stern; an object or ship abaft another ship.

Athwart, athwartships—at right angles to fore and aft, or centerline of ship.

Atol—ring-shaped coral reef often topped by low sand islands, enclosing a body of water called a lagoon.

Automatic pilot—see **Gyropilot.**

Auxiliary—assisting machine or vessel, such as air-conditioning machine or fuel ship.

Avast—from Dutch *houd vast,* hold fast, and Portuguese *abasta,* enough; a command to cease or desist from whatever is being done.

Awash—said of a ship or object so low in the water that waves wash across it.

Awning—a piece of canvas spread above a deck to provide shade. Now used to describe a shade above window or terrace of building, but probably of nautical origin. CAPT John Smith's account of his voyage to Virginia, in 1624 says: "We did hang an *awning* (which is an old saile) . . . to shadow us from the sunne."

Aye, aye—term used to acknowledge receipt of command or order from senior. It means "I have heard the order; I understand it; I will carry it out."

Azimuth—the azimuth of object is its bearing from the observer measured as an angle clockwise from true north.

Azimuth circle—instrument used to take bearings of celestial objects.

Back—the wind is said to *back* when it

changes in a counter-clock-wise direction; wind veers when the change is clockwise.

Backstay—a stay of wire or rope supporting mast from aft.

Backwash—water thrown aft by ship's propeller.

Ballast—weight in the hold of a ship necessary to maintain proper stability, trim or draft; a ship "in *ballast*" carries no cargo, only ballast.

Barbette—heavily armored cylinder within which a gun turret rotates; extending from upper part of a turret down to the lowest armored deck.

Barge—craft used to haul material; as a coal barge. A power boat used by flag officers, as admiral's *barge.*

Barnacle—small marine animal that attaches itself to hulls, and pilings.

Barometer—instrument for measuring atmospheric pressure; used in forecasting weather, and for determining altitude.

Barrier reef—a reef separated from land by channels or lagoons.

Batten—long strip of steel or wood wedging the edge of a tarpaulin against a hatch.

Batten down—to cover and fasten down; to close off a hatch or watertight door.

Battle lights—dim red lights producing minimum illumination for nighttime use aboard ship.

Battle bridge—an open bridge located near the conning tower of a surface ship.

Beach—*terra firma,* as opposed to being on board ship; not necessarily a sandy shore. A sailor on recruiting duty in Nebraska is "on the *beach.*" Verb, meaning to run a ship or boat on shore.

Beachcomber—formerly, a loafer or vagrant along the seacoast who searched beaches for material washed up from wrecked ships; now an unreliable drifter or seaman found unemployed on the waterfront.

Beam—width; breadth; greatest athwartships measurement of a ship.

Bean rag—slang for the meal pennant flown during meal hours; international signal flag ECHO.

Bear—to lie in certain direction from observer: "The island *bears* due west."

Bear a hand—speed up! Lend a helping hand.

Bearing—direction of object expressed in degrees either as relative or true bearing.

Beat the Dutch—many sea yarns and expressions make varied usage of the term *Dutch*. The "Flying Dutchman" was the ship of the legendary Dutch sea captain Van der Decken, who was condemned for impiety to cruise forever off Cape of Good Hope. A *"Dutchman's* log" is a crude device used in small slow ships for measuring speed. *"Dutch* courage" has come to mean liquor-inspired bravery. *"Dutchman's* anchor" refers to something important, forgotten or left behind. *"Dutchman's* breeches" is a small patch of sky at end of a storm—a patch "big enough to make a *Dutchman* a pair of breeches." Punishment which consisted of pumping under conditions where cessation of work meant drowning, was carried out on a *"Dutch* pump." "If that don't beat the *Dutch"* comes from early-day British-Dutch sea battles where English sailors found Hollanders unexpectedly tough.

Beaufort scale—a table indicating wind velocity.

Becket—circular metal fitting on a block, a rope eye or grommet.

Beef boat—slang: a supply ship.

Belay—to cancel an order; stop; firmly secure a line.

Bells—method of marking time, in 30 minute periods by striking bells.

On the ships in Columbus's expedition to the New World, time was marked by hour glasses, or more exactly by half-hour glasses, called *am-*

polletas. A man turned the glass over promptly at the end of each half-hour, and called out the number of glasses which had been turned during the watch. Time was still measured in "glasses" during the Revolutionary War "... we then charged ... with an incessant Fire for almost three glasses." Eventually, a bell was used to mark the turning of the glasses. The bell indicates only the passage of a certain period of time, and not any definite hour, to the confusion of landlubbers who assume that "eight *bells"* always mean eight o'clock, or that ten o'clock is "ten *bells."* Eight *bells* can mean either midnight, four or eight o'clock in the morning, noon, or four or eight o'clock after noon.

At 30 minutes past midnight, a ship's bell is struck once. At one A.M. it is struck twice. This continues, adding one stroke for each additional half hour, until eight bells are struck at four A.M. The procedure is then repeated throughout the day. An odd number of bells indicates half-hours, an even number of bells indicates the hours. Bells are struck in pairs; four *bells* for two P.M. are struck as *ding-ding ding-ding*, and three *bells* for one-thirty P.M. are struck *ding-ding ding.* See **Time.**

Bell book—a book recording various speed and direction orders sent to a ship's engine-room from the bridge.

Below—below decks; below main deck.

Bend—A general class of knots used to join two lines together.

Bend on—to secure one thing to another, as *bend* a flag onto a halyard. Also slang for acquire, *bend* on a hang-over.

Berth—space assigned ship for anchoring or mooring.

Bight—middle part of a line as distinguished from ends and standing part; single complete turn of a line; a bend in a river or coastline.

Bilge—usually refers to the bottom of ship, or more correctly to curved part of ship's hull. The lower part of the hull where waste water and seepage collect. Midshipmen dropped from the Naval Academy for academic reasons are *bilged*.

Billet—an allotted sleeping space; a man's position on his ship's organization.

Binnacle—a stand housing a magnetic compass and its accounterments.

Binnacle list—formerly, a list of names of sick persons was placed on the binnacle each morning, readily available for the captain. A modern *binnacle list* contains names of men with minor ailments which preclude employment on strenuous duty. Hospitalized personnel are named on a "sick list."

Birdcage—the air control officer's station on the island of an aircraft carrier.

Bitt—strong iron post on ship's deck for working or fastening lines, usually in pairs.

Bitter end—the end of a chain cable secured in chain locker; formerly end of a cable around the bitts.

Black gang—slang for engineering crew of a ship, known also as *snipes* or *bilge rats*.

Black shoe—an officer who is not an aviator; the latter is a *brown shoe*. At one time only aviators wore brown or tan shoes; now, all officers wear tan shoes with khaki uniforms.

Blast—sound made on whistle, siren, or fog horn. Also an uncomplimentary remark.

Blinker—signal lights operated by telegraph key; used for sending flashing light messages.

Blister—an armored hollow bulge in warship's side; protection against torpedoes.

Block—grooved pulley or sheave with its frame, supporting hooks, eyes or straps; may be metal or wood.

Blockade—a war time operation by which a naval force obstructs access to the ports and shores of an enemy nation.

Bluejacket—Navy enlisted man below the grade of CPO; *white hat.*

Blue Nose—one who has crossed Arctic Circle.

Boats—small open or decked-over craft propelled by oars, sails, or some type of engine, also larger craft built to navigate rivers and inland waters.

Boat boom—a spar or pole swung out horizontally from the side of a ship at anchor, to which boats are secured.

Boat deck—deck on which ship's boats are customarily stowed.

Boat fall—rigging used to hoist or lower boats.

Boat gripe—lashing used at sea to secure a boat hanging from its davits.

Boat hook—wooden pole with metal hook and prod at one end; used to hold a boat alongside a landing, or push it away.

Boat painter—rope used for securing a boat.

Boat plug—metal or wood plug used to close drain hole in a boat.

Boat skid—heavy wood and metal frame on ship's boat deck used to support boat's keel.

Boat sling—rope or chain sling used for hoisting or lowering boats with a single davit or crane.

Boat station—allotted place of each person when boat is being lowered.

Boatswain—pronounced "bo'sn," from the Saxon *swain* or *swein;* servant or boy.

Boatswain's chair—line secured board on which a man sits when working aloft or over the side.

Boatswain's locker—compartment where deck gear is stowed.

Boatswain's pipe—a pipe with high pitched, shrill tone easily heard above the sound of wind, engines, or gunfire, first used in early Roman and Grecian galleys, to mark time for slaves at the oars. In Crusade of 1248 English crossbowmen were called on deck by a pipe. It is mentioned in Shakespeare's *Tempest*. Correct procedure for receiving prince or admiral, as laid down in 1645, required

The ship's barge to be sent to fetch the visitor having the cockson (sic) with his silver whistle in the stern. . . . Upon the near approach of the barge . . . all such as carry whistles are to whistle a welcome three several times.

Ceremony of welcoming distinguished visitor on board ship is now called "*piping* the side." Practice of having "side boys" present comes from days when officers were required to visit a flagship at sea for conferences. If weather was too rough to permit using gangway, they were hoisted aboard in a basket or chair by two or more boys, as required. Boatswain used his pipe to signal HOIST AWAY and VAST HEAVING.

Bogey—unidentified aircraft.

Bollard—wooden or iron post on pier or wharf to which mooring lines are secured.

Boom—projecting spar or pole that provides outreach for extending foot of sails, handling cargo, etc., rigged horizontally or nearly so. See **Boat boom.**

Boondocks—slang: any remote or isolated place.

Boondockers—heavy shoes worn in the *boondocks*

Boot—slang for recruit.

Boot topping—black band painted around ship hull at the waterline.

Boss plate—metal plate fitted around propeller shaft where it emerges from the hull.

Bow—forward section of ship.

Bower anchor—either of two anchors usually carried at ship's bow. Most ships anchor by using one of the bowers.

Bowline—one of the most used knots; used to make temporary eye in end of line.

Boxing the compass—naming all compass points and quarter points in proper order, from north, east, south, through west back to north.

Break—to unfurl flag with quick motion. In ship contruction, abrupt change in fore-and-aft contour of ship's main deck.

Breaker—from Spanish *barrica*. Small container for stowing drinking water carried by boats or rafts; wave that *breaks* into foam against the shore.

Break out—to unstow or prepare for use.

Breast line—mooring line running at right angles from ship's fore-and-aft line.

Bridge—platform or area from which ship is steered, navigated, and conned; usually located in forward part of ship.

Brig—originally term for fast sailing ship used by pirates in Mediterranean; contraction of brigantine or *Brigandine,* meaning robber or brigand; later a general term for two-masted, square rigged sailing ship. Credit for current use of term goes to Admiral Nelson of British Navy, who had an unusual number of prissoners confined in a small *brig* where sailors could guard them. The name *brig* became sialor's universal term for jail.

Brightwork—metal work kept polished rather than painted.

Broach—act of running torpedo when it breaks surface of water.

Broach to—turning suddenly into the wind; to be thrown broadside in surf.

Broad command pennant—personal command pennant of an officer, not a flag officer, commanding a division, flotilla, or squadron of ships or craft of any type.

Broad on the starboard (port) beam—bearing 090° (270°) relative to bow of ship.

Broad on the starboard (port) bow—bearing 135° (225°) relative to bow of ship.

Broadside—simultaneous firing of all main battery guns on one side of warship.

Broadside to—at right angles to fore-and-aft line of ship.

Brow—large gangplank leading from a ship to pier, wharf, or float; usually equipped with hand rails.

Brown bagger—slang for married man; derived from paper bag used by shore duty personnel for carrying lunch.

Bug—special type of key used by radiomen in sending code; faster than ordinary telegraph type key.

Bulkhead—one of vertical wall-like structures enclosing a ship's compartment.

Bull horn—loudspeaker used in giving commands to small boats, or in talking to nearby ships. Before electrically powered speakers came into use, speaking trumpets or megaphones were employed; Alexander the Great used similar type horn in 335 B.C.

Bull nose—closed chock in bow of ship, on forecastle deck.

Bulwark—raised plating or woodwork running along side of ship above weather deck; helps keep decks dry and prevents men and gear from being swept overboard.

Bumboat—boat employed by civilians to carry salable provisions, vegetables, and small merchandise to ships; may have been derived from *boom-boat,* indicating boats permitted to lie at booms. Buttercup, in Gilbert and Sullivan's *HMS Pinafore,* is a *bumboat* woman.

Bunk—built-in bed abroad ship.

Bunker—storage space for fuel, either coal or oil.

Bunting—woolen material from which signal flags are made; all ship's flags. Ships at anchor may sometimes have all flags hoisted at once; this is no observation of holiday, but merely "airing *bunting.*"

Buoy—floating marker, anchored in place in harbor aproaches; shape and color conveys navigational information; may be lighted, unlighted, carry bell or whistle. Pronounced "boo-ee."

Burdened vessel—vessel which by *Rules of the Road* must keep out of way of another vessel.

Burgee—swallow-tailed flag.

Burgee comand pennant—personal command pennant of officer, not flag officer, commanding any of following units: division of ships or craft other than battleships, aircraft carriers, or cruisers; major subdivision of aircraft wing.

Bust—slang—miserable failure or mistake; reduction in rate, or act of making such reduction; also a festive night ashore.

By the board—same as overboard.

By the head—ship with greater draft forward than aft.

By the stern—opposite of by the head.

Cabin—captain's living quarters; covered compartment of boat.

Cable markings—series of turns of wire or stripes of paint on certain links of each anchor chain, showing scope or amount of chain that has run out, as follows: 20 fathoms—first studded link on each side of shackle has turn of wire around its stud, and is painted white; 35 fathoms—second studded link has two turns of wire around its stud, and two links on either side of shackles are painted white; 50 fathoms—third studded link has three turns of wire around its stud, and three links on either side of shackle are painted white; Thereafter for every 15 fathoms another turn of wire is added and another shackle on each side painted white.

Caduceus—symbol of Greke God Mercury, patron of medicine and physicians, and Navy Hospital Corps; consists of staff topped by pair of wings and two serpents entwined.

Caisson—movable gate of drydock; cofferdam. Pronounced "kay-sun." Not the kind the Army sings about.

Camber—arch in ship's deck that makes

centerline sections higher than the sides.

Can—slang, short for "tin *can*," destroyer.

Can buoy—cylindrical, flat-topped metal buoy.

Can do—agreement, assent; negative is "no can do," from pidgin English.

Canoe Navy—from 1836 to 1842 the Navy maintained a Mosquito Fleet at Indian Key, Fla., consisting of small sailing ships and barges and 140 canoes used to chase Seminole Indians into the Everglades.

Capstan or capstan head—part of vertical shaft windlass around which a line or chain is passed.

Captain—from Latin *caput* meaning head. (Until 1862, captain was highest commissioned officer in U.S. Navy.)

Cardinal point—one of four principal points of compass: north, east, south and west.

Cargo cluster—cluster of lamps rigged at night for deck work.

Cargo net—heavy, square, rope net used for hoisting cargo.

Cargo whip—rope or chain used with boom and winch for handling cargo; also called cargo hoist, cargo rope.

Carrick bend—a knot used to fasten two lines or hawsers together.

Carry away—to break loose, tear loose, or wash overboard.

Carry on—order to resume work or duties.

Cast off—to throw off; let go; unfurl.

Catapult—shipboard mechanism for launching aircraft.

Catenary—dip in a length of wire, chain, or line suspended from two points.

Cat's paw—light breeze; especially little patches of ripples set in motion by such a breeze.

Catwalk—elevated walkway between bridges; commonly found on tankers; also called fore-and-aft bridge, connecting bridge, monkey bridge.

Caulk off—*caulk* or *calk* (pronounced "cork") derived from Middle English *cauken* (to tread) which in turn comes from Old North French *caukier* (to trample). To pack oakum, cotton twinst, or other filling into seams of wooden deck or side to prevent leaking. Process is completed by paying, cover by pouring or painting, seams with melted tar or pitch. To "*caulk* off" in reference to sleeping originated in days of wooden ships when naps were taken on bare decks and sleeper's back or clothing bore marks of pitch with which deck seams were payed.

Chain of command—succession of officers through which command is exercised from superior to subordinate; also called command channel.

Chain locker—compartment in which chain cable is stowed.

Chains—originally chains were used to brace platform on which leadsman stood when heaving lead while taking soundings; gradually came to designate the platform. Today any place where a man stands when heaving lead, is the *chains*.

Change of command ceremony—the ceremony by which an officer relieves another of command of a ship, station, or fleet.

Chaplain—chaplains were carried aboard warships from earliest days, both in British and U.S. Navy. Traditionally, name originated when St. Martin, one wintry day in France, divided his coat with a beggar. Miraculously preserved, the coat later became a banned for the Kings of France. Called *chape* in French, it was preserved in small room or chapel, called *chapelle*. Keeper of this room was called *chapelain*.

Chock—steel deck member, either oval or U-shaped, through which mooring lines are passed; usually paired off with bitts.

Chockablock—completely full; full to top.

Chop—in naval operations, to transfer

control of ship or unit from one command to another: "AT 0800 MISSOURI CHOP TO COMMANDER TASK FORCE NINETY." Also, signature or approval, especially on requisition or blank form. From Oriental use of chop or mark on papers.

Chop-chop—pidgin English: quickly, in a hurry.

Christmas-tree—control panel fitted with red and green indicating lights.

Chronometer—an especially accurate timepiece set to Greenwich times; used for navigation.

Clamp down—to remove water from a deck with damp swabs; lesser form of swabbing down.

Clap on—to *clap* on a rope: catch hold in order to haul on it; to *clap* on a stopper or tackler: to put on a stopper or tackle; to *clap* on canvas: to put on more sail.

Classified matter—information or material of aid to possible enemy if improperly divulged. There are currently three categories: TOP SECRET, SECRET, and CONFIDENTIAL.

Charlie Noble—believed derived from British merchant skipper, Charlie Noble. who demanded high polish on galley smokepipe. Any galley smoke pipe is now the *Charlie Noble.*

Chart—nautical term for map. From Latin *charta* and Greek *charte;* kind of papyrus on which early charts were drawn.

Chart house or chart room—compartment on or near bridge for handling and stowage of navigational equipment.

Check—to slack off slowly; to stop a ship's way gradually by line fastened to some fixed object or anchor on bottom; to ease off rope a little, especially to reduce tension; to stop or regulate motion, as of cable when running out too fast. Also: O.K., correct.

Chinese Landing—bringing boat or ship alongside another with bow toward stern, or landing plane downwind.

Chipping hammer—small hammer used for chipping and scaling metal surfaces. Also called scaling hammer or boiler pick.

Chit—receipt, voucher, or request; word came into use on Asiatic Station; picked up from pidgin English; also used by British Army and Navy and East India Company. Derived from Hindu word *chitti.*

Church Pennant—The only flag that ever flies above the Stars and Stripes. Described as a white triangular field charged with a blue Latin cross, it is flown above the U.S. flag during divine services on ships and stations of the U.S. Navy. There is no record of when this practice was adopted; it was probably borrowed from the British Royal Navy. First authentic dated mention of the church pennant is in an order signed by Farragut:

U.S. Flagship Hartford,
Off the City of New Orleans
April 26, 1862

Eleven o'clock this morning is the hour appointed for all the officers and crews of the fleet to return thanks to Almighty God for his great goodness and mercy in permitting us to pass through the events of the last two days with so little loss of life and blood. At that hour the church pennant will be hoisted on every vessel of the fleet and their crews assembled will, in humiliation and prayer, make their final acknowledgement therefore to the Great Dispencer (sic) of all human events.

D. G. Farragut,
Flag Officer Western Gulf
Blockading Squadron

A book titled *Boat Signals, USN,* published in 1861, shows a cut of the "Church Flag," bearing a Greek cross instead of the aLtin cross. A French book of flags, *Album Des Pavillons,* published in 1858, pictures the "Church Pennant, (U.S.)" and a white flag with a blue Latin cross. A table of allowances for ships of the Navy, published in 1854, lists one "church and meal pennant" for each ship but no description.

Clean Sweep—during W.W. II, submarines returning from war patrol sometimes carried a broom hoisted from periscope shears, indicating victory over the enemy, that ship had "*swept* the seas" of all opposition. Earlier ships with high gunnery scores also displayed a broom at one of their masts. Custom originated almost 300 years ago, during war between England and Holland, when the Dutch admiral Tromp ordered brooms lashed to the masts of his ships when he sailed to meet Cromwell's fleet, signifying his intention to *sweep* the British from the seas.

Clear—to leave a port with all formalities concluded; to empty; to untangle; to take such distance from any object as to have open sea room.

Clear hawse—to disentangle anchor cables when twisted around one another.

Cleat—small deck metal fitting, used for securing lines; also called belaying cleat; short piece of wood nailed to brow or gangplank to give surer footing.

Clinometer—bridge and engine-room instrument measuring amount of ship's roll or degree of list.

Close aboard—nearby.

Clothes stop—small cotton lanyard used for fastening clothes to line after washing, or securing clothes that are rolled up.

Clove hitch—not used for fastening line to spar or stanchion.

Coaming—raised framework around deck or bulkhead openings and cockpits of open boats to prevent entry of water.

Coil—laying down line in circular turns; usually one turn atop the other.

Coins at the step of a mast—frequently, when building ship, coins are placed under step (base) of the mast; a probable survival of ancient Roman custom of placing coins in mouths of the dead to enable them to pay Charon for ferrying them across River Styx.

Collision bulkhead—watertight athwartships bulkhead abaft a ship's stem; used to isolate damage due to head-on-collision.

Collison mat—mat used to temporarily close hole in ship's hull below waterline; a slang: pancake.

Colors—National ensign; distinguishing flag flown to indicate a ship's nationality. Naval ceremonies performed when national flag is hoisted at eight o'clock in the morning and hauled down at sunset.

Combination light—running light for small craft, red on port side, green on starboard.

Command—a naval unit or group of units under one officer; definite and direct form of order; authority an officer has over his men because of rank and assignment.

Commander—title introduced into British Navy by William III, when it was spelled *commandeur;* later such officer was second in command of large ships. Rank of commander introduced into U.S. Navy in 1838 replacing that of "master commandant."

Commission—to activate a ship or station; written order giving an officer his rank and authority.

Commission pennant—in 17th century, war between Holland and Britain, Admiral Tromp hoisted a broom at his masthead, indicating his intention to sweep the British from the sea. This gesture was answered by a British admiral who hoisted horsewhip, indicating intention to chastise the Dutch. The British carried out their boast and ever since, the narrow, coachwhip pennant (symbolizing original horsewhip) has been the distinctive mark of ship of war, adopted by all nations. Modern naval commission pennant, is blue at hoist, with union of seven white stars, and a red and a white at the fly, in two horizontal stripes, number of stars has no special significance, was arbitrarily selected as providing most suitable display. In lieu of commission pennant, flagships fly commodore's or admiral's personal flag.

Commissioning ceremonies—ceremonies during which a new ship is placed in service. Captain of the yard or delegated representative of commandant reads orders for delivery of ship, ATTENTION is sounded on bugle; national anthem is played, ensign, commission pennant, and jack are hoisted simultaneously. The officer ordered to command ship reads his orders from Navy Department and orders his executive officer to SET THE WATCH. Full dress uniform is usually worn by officers at commissioning ceremonies of cruisers and battleships. It is customary to invite friends of officers and others interested to attend the ceremony, and the sponsor who christened the ship.

Commodore—rank first established in U.S. Navy in 1862; used as honorary title in Revolutionary War, and still applied, as matter of courtesy to officer commanding flotilla or squadron of destroyers or smaller ships. After 1899, there were no commodores appointed for active duty; title was applied to captains with Civil War service on retired list. Commodores were again appointed in Navy in 1943; no officers of this rank now on active duty. Title, originally from Holland, first used during Dutch Wars of 1562, adopted for British Navy by William III.

Companionway—set of steps or ladders leading from one deck level to another.

Company—military unit made up of two or more platoons, or about 50 to 150 men. Ship's company; all hands.

Compartment—space enclosed by bulkheads, deck, and overhead, same as a room in a building.

Compass—latin poem written in third century A.D. describes what may have been a compass; in 1248 a Florentine described a compass then used in Norman ships. At that time north point of compass was marked by *fleur-de-lis*, and most compasses are still so marked. Compasses were later perfected by Prince Henry, the Navigator; those used by Columbus, Vasco de Gama and other early navigators were probably result of his interest and work. Magnetic compasses are still used. Gyro-compasses, unaffected by variations in earth's magnetic field, are more accurate.

Complement—numbers, ranks, and ratings of officers and men, determined by Bureau of Naval Personnel as necessary to fight the ship most effectively or perform such other duties as may be required.

Condenser—device for converting exhaust steam from engines into water for re-use in boilers.

Con or Conn—part of ship from which it is steered; also, act of directing course of ship; word used in latter sense as long ago as 1520; exact derivation not known.

Conning tower—on larger warships, a heavily armored structure just forward of and slightly below bridge for conning ship in battle.

Consul—official in diplomatic service representing U.S. Government in foreign lands; supervises all U.S. shipping at port in which residing and assists merchant marine sailors in distress.

Contraband—prohibited or dutiable goods smuggled into a country.

Convoy—group of cargo and transport ships and their escort of warships and patrol craft.

Cordage—general term for rope and line of all kinds.

Country—general area occupied by living quarters, such as "officers' *country*," "wardroom *country*," and Marine *country*."

Course—direction steered by a ship or plane.

Court-martial—military court for trial of more serious offenses; summary, special, and general *courts-martial*.

Cowl—bell or hood-shaped opening of a ventilator.

Cowling—removable covering on aircraft, over cockpit or around engine.

Cow's tail—frayed end of rope.

Coxswain—pronounced "cox-un," derived from *cock*, small boat, and *swain* servant; originally one who had charge of boat and crew during absence of boat officer; today, petty officer or seaman in charge of boat; the man who steers a boat.

CPO—abbreviation for *chief petty officer*.

Cradle—stowage rest for ship's boat.

Crossing the line—see **Shellbacks**.

Crow—slang: *eagle* on petty officer's rating badge.

Crow's nest—platform for lookout on mast or crosstrees.

Cruise—from the Dutch. To sail with no definite destination. More commonly used to describe round trip; also to sail, "the ships will *cruise* at fifteen knots."

Cumshaw—Chinese: alms for a beggar; pidgin English for gift, or something thrown in on trade; in Navy parlance, something obtained "for free," or act of obtaining it.

Cut of his jib—nationality of early sailing ships could frequently be determined by shape or cut of jib sails. As applied to a person, originally referred to shape of nose, first feature to come into view; now describes person's appearance generally.

Cutter—type of sailing vessel, square-sterned ship's boat, now seldom seen.

Cutwater—forward edge of ships stem at and below waterline.

Damage control—measures necessary to keep ship afloat, fighting, and in operating condition.

Davit—shipboard crane used for hoisting and lowering boats and weights; often found in pairs. Pronounced "dayvit."

Davy Jones' Locker—bottom of the sea.

Day's duty—tour of duty on shipboard lasting 24 hours.

D-day—unnamed day on which an operation is to begin.

Dead ahead—directly ahead of ship's bow; bearing 000° relative.

Dead horse—in early days of Navy and merchant marine, sailors were permitted to draw money in advance of a long cruise; such payment was called *dead horse*, possibly because money was spent before earned and a man felt he might as well have bought a *dead horse*. Now an advance in pay upon being transferred, to be repaid in monthly installments, is a *dead horse*.

Dead in the water—a ship making neither headway nor sternway.

Deadlight (ventilating deadlight)—arrangement of baffles to admit air while preventing passage of light; usually a circular device that fits into ports.

Dead marine—empty bottle; supposedly first used by William IV, Lord High Admiral of British Navy, who explained, "I call them *marines* because they are good fellows who have done their duty . . ."

Dead reckoning—theoretical position of ship or aircraft, plotted on chart without reference to objects on shore or astronomical observations; originally called *deduced reckoning*; shortened in log books to "*ded reckoning*," and then changed to *dead reckoning*.

Deadweight tonnage—difference between ship's light and loaded displacement.

Deck—slang: knock down: "Get your feet off my bunk or I'll *deck* you."

Deck of ship corresponds to floor of building.

Deck ape—slang: *deck* hand, one who works topside; also known as *swab jockey*.

Deck hand—seaman of deckd compartment.

Deck house—structure built on upper of weather deck; does not extend over full breadth of ship. Deck houses are typical of smaller vessels.

Deck officers—As distinguished from engineering officers; refers to all officers who assist in navigating ship at sea, and in working cargo while in port, exclusive of staff corps officers.

Deck seamanship—practical seamanship, from simplest rudiments of marlinespike seamanship to navigation; includes small-boat handling, ground tackle, steering, heaving the lead, signaling, etc.

Deck treads—thin abrasive mats held to deck by adhesive compound; provide better footing, especially on wet decks.

Decontamination—act of clearing compartment, area or clothing of poison gases, radioactive materials, or infectious agents.

Deep—an especially deep part of the ocean, usually identified on charts by name as RAMAPO DEEP.

Deeps—in a lead line, the fathoms which are not marked on the line.

Deep six—cry of leadsman when his leadline indicates 36 feet of water or six fathoms, under ship; also to indicate something or someone has fallen overboard side; to suggest disposal of worthless object; something given "the *deep* six" is not necessarily dropped into ocean, it may only be dumped into a waste basket.

Degaussing gear—electrical gear which sets up neutralizing magnetic fields to protect a ship from magnetic-action mines.

Deploy—tactical term used for dispersal of troops; also disposition of ships in battle formations.

Depth charge—explosive charge used against submarines.

Derelict—abandoned vessel at sea, still afloat.

Devil dogs—during W.W. I Marines were called *teufelhunde* by Germans. *Teufelhunde,* or *devil dogs* were fierce, fiendish dogs mentioned in Bavarian legends.

Dilbert—slang for an aviator who "goofs off," or acts stupidly.

Dinghy—small boat, 16 to 20 feet in length, propelled by oars or sail.

Dip—lowering flag part way in salute or in answer, and hoisting it again. Flag is "at the *dip*" when flown at about two-thirds the height of the halyards.

Dipping the national ensign—old-time custom by which merchant vessels were required not only to heave to when approaching warships on high seas, but also to clew up all sails to indicate honesty and willingness to be searched. Delays resulted, and in later years, *dipping* the flag was authorized as time-saving substitute. Navy ships answer merchant ships dip for dip; no Navy ship may dip her ensign except in acknowledgement of such compliment.

Director—electro-mechanical device for directing and controlling gunfire.

Displacement—of a ship, weight of water it displaces.

Distance line—light line rigged between ships engaged in underway refueling or replenishment; marked off in 20-foot lengths; helps station keeping.

Ditty bag, ditty box—small container formally used by sailors for stowage of personal effects and toilet articles.

Division—in organization of ship or plane groups, unit between sections and squadrons; in shipboard organization, number of men and officers grouped together for command purposes.

Dock—artificial basin for ships, fitted

with gates to keep in or shut out water; water area between piers.

Dock trials—test of main engines while ship is moored alongside pier.

Dog—small, metal handles used to close watertight doors, hatch, covers, scuttles, etc.

Dog face—slang: soldier.

Dog tag—metal identification disc.

Dog watch—a corruption of *dock watch*, that is, watch that has been docked or shortened; the watches between 4 and 6 P.M., and 6 and 8 P.M., are *dog watches*.

Dolphins—cluster of piles for mooring.

Dory—small, flat-bottomed pulling boat, used chiefly by fishermen.

Double-bottoms—watertight sub-divisions of ships, next to keel and between outer and inner bottoms.

Double-up—to increase number of ship-to-pier-to-ship turns of mooring line.

Doubling—rounding point of land, e.g., "*doubling* Cape Horn."

Dowse—to take in or lower sail; to put out light; to cover with water.

Draft—depth of water from surface to ship's keel; a detail of men.

Draft marks—numeral figures on either side of stem and sternpost, used to indicate amount of ship's draft.

Drag—to drag anchor; when anchor will not hold but slides along bottom. See **Drogue.**

Dressing ship—to display national ensign at all mastheads and flagstaff; full dressing further requires rainbow of signal flags from bow to stern over mastheads.

Drift lead—sounding lead and line dropped over side of anchored ship to detect dragging.

Drogue—floating anchor usually made of spars and canvas; used to keep head of ship in wind, to lessen leeway, or to check headway; also called drag sheet and sea anchor.

Drone—pilotless aircraft remotely controlled by radio; may be full-size or model-size.

Duck—from Dutch *doek,* German *tuck;* cloth. Light canvas used for sails, bags, etc.

Ducts—large sheet metal pipes that lead air from blowers to enclosed spaces.

Dungarees—working uniform of blue jean; of Hindustani orgin.

Dunnage—loose material placed in holds for cargo to rest on, or jammed between cargo to wedge it.

Dutchman's breeches—small patch of blue sky which indicates breaking up of gale or storm, and approaching fair weather.

Eagle screams—slang: pay day.

Ear-banging—art of attempting to curry favor with a superior; one who attempts this is *ear-banger.*

Ease her—command to reduce amount of rudder or helm.

East off—to ease line; slacken it when taut.

Easy—carefully, gently.

Echelon—a formation of ships or aircraft moving in a line or bearing at an angle to the direction of movement.

Eddy—small whirlpool.

Elevator—movable section of planes tail, usually hinged to stabilizer and used to head plane up or down in flight. Aircraft carriers use platform *elevators* to move planes between hangar and flight decks.

Embark—to go aboard ship preparatory to sailing.

End for end—reversing position of object or line.

End on—head-to-head or stem-to-stem.

Engine order telegraph—apparatus for transmitting speed and direction orders from bridge to engine-room.

Ensign—lowest ranking commissioned officer. From old Norman *enseigne.* First used by British Navy in 16th century. Adopted by U.S. Navy in 1862, to replace previous "passed midshipman."

Escape hatch—in general any hatch,

usually small, that permits men to escape from compartment when usual exits are blocked.

Even keel—floating level; no list.

Executive Officer—regardless of rank, the officer second in command of ship. In early days, such officer was first lieutenant.

Eyebolt—metal bolt ending in an eye.

Eyebrow—curved metal rim above a porthole, to shed water.

Eyes—foremost part of weatherdeck in bow of ship.

Eyes of the Ship—ships in early days generally had heads of mythological monsters or patrons carved in the bow. Fore part of ship was called "head." *Eyes of the ship* followed from eyes of figures placed there.

Fairlead—eye, block, or fitting furnishing clear lead for line. Pronounced "leed."

Fair tide—tidal current running with the ship.

Fairway—in inland waters, open channel or midchannel.

Fair wind—favoring wind.

Fake—single turn of line when line is coiled down.

Fake down—the art of coiling down line so each fake of rope overlaps one underneath, and leaving the line clear for running.

Fall—entire length of rope in a tackle; end secured to block is called standing part; other end, the hauling part; also, line used to lower and hoist boat.

Falling glass—lowering atmospheric pressure as registered by barometer; normally sign of approaching bad weather.

False keel—thin covering secured to lower side of main keel of ships; affords more protection.

Fancy work—intricate, symmetrical rope work used for decorative purposes.

Fantail—main deck section in after part of flush-deck ship.

Fast—snugly secured; said of line when it is fastened securely.

Fathom—in measuring depth of water, six feet. From Anglo-Saxon *faehom.* Originally, distance spanned by man's outstretched arms.

Fender—canvas, wood, rope gear or old rubber tire used over side to protect ship from chafing when alongside pier or another ship.

Fid—wooden marlinspike.

Fiddlers' Green—traditional Elysian fields of seagoing men, comparable to Viking's Valhalla and Indian's Happy Hunting Ground. Restricted to sailormen only, Fiddlers' Green is the only heaven claimed by an occupational group. According to legends, Fiddlers' Green is well supplied with joyous demoiselles, free drinks and plenty of chow, and there are no regulations. Civilians, ineligible for entrance, should read the delightful book *Fiddlers' Green,* by Albert R. Wetjen.

Fiddley, fidley—wide opening immediately above a fireroom, through which boiler uptakes, lower stack, and fireroom ventilators are led; iron framework around ladder of deck hatch leading below decks.

Fidley deck—raised platform over engine and boiler-rooms, more particularly around the stack.

Field day—day devoted to cleaning ship or station, usually Friday. The act of cleaning office, compartment or space. Field day can be held in a desk drawer.

Field strip—to disassemble without further breakdown major groups of piece of ordnance for routine or operating cleaning and oiling; as opposed to detailed stripping which may be done only by authorized technicians.

Fife rail—wood or metal rail bored with holes to take belaying pins;

seen on Navy ships at head of flag bags.

Figure-eight fake—method of coiling rope in which turns form series of overlapping figure-eights advancing about one or two diameters of rope for each turn; usually done over lifelines.

Figure-eight knot—knot forming large knob; easily tied.

Fire control—shipboard system of directing and controlling gunfire or torpedo fire.

Fire control tower—either a separate structure, or part of conning tower containing fire control equipment; typical of major warships.

First lieutenant—officer in charge of cleanliness and general upkeep of ship or shore station; descriptive of duty, not rank.

Fish—slang: torpedo.

Fix—ship's position as determined by navigational methods.

Flag at half-mast—at times of mourning in old sailing days, yards were "cockbilled" and rigging was slacked off, to indicate that grief was so great it was impossible to keep things shipshape. Today half-masting of colors is survival of days when slack appearance characterized mourning on shipboard.

Flag bag—container for stowage of signal flags and pennants.

Flag officer—rear admirals, vice admirals, admirals and fleet admirals are flag officers. "Flag officer" was actual rank in Navy, before grade of admiral was created in 1862.

Flagstaff—small vertical pole or spar at stern of ship on which ensign is hoisted.

Flag, U.S.—design credited to Samuel Chester Reid, who once served as a midshipman in USS *Baltimore*, in the early 19th century. In 1818, when alteration of flag was being considered, Representative Peter Wendover of New York mentioned matter to Reid, who suggested 13 stripes and a star for each state, with stars in rows for official use and arranged in star-shape for other uses. Congress adopted the form on April 4, 1818, without making specific rules as to arrangement of stars. Such flag, made by Mrs. Reid, was flown over Capitol building on April 12, 1818. On July 3, 1843, Reid was appointed sailing master in Navy, which in effect gave him a pension.

Flank speed—certain prescribed speed increase over standard speed; faster than full speed, but less than emergency full speed.

Flag—slang: excitement; confusion; general misunderstanding.

Flare—outward and upward curving sweep of ship's bow; outward curve of side from waterline to deck level; also, blaze to illuminate or attract attention.

Flash burn—burn received from heat of explosion.

Flash plate—protective metal plate over which anchor cable rides; part of forecastle deck.

Flat hatting—slang: flying at low altitude, usually aimed at impressing mere groundlings.

Flat top—slang: aircraft carrier.

Fleet—from Anglo-Saxon *floet*. Organization of ships and aircraft under one commander; normally includes all types of ships and aircraft necessary for major operations; also, to draw blocks of tackle apart.

Flemish—to coil line flat on deck in clockwise direction, each fake outside the other, all laid snugly side by side; begins in middle and works outward.

Flight deck—deck of aircraft carrier on which planes land, take-off.

Flight skins—slang: flight pay, extra compensation for flying personnel.

Float—any object used to keep other objects afloat.

Floating drydock—movable dock floating in water; ships of all sizes are floated into it and repaired.

Flood tide—tide rising or flowing toward land.

Floor—flat part of bottom of boat on which she rests when beached.

Flotsam—floating wreckage or goods thrown overboard. See Jetsam.

Fluke—flat end of anchor which bites into ground.

Flush deck—continuous upper deck extending from side to side and from bow to stern.

Flying boat—seaplane which can float on its own hull in the water.

Flying Dutchman—legendary phantom ship believed to haunt the seas around Cape of Good Hope. In sailing ship days seamen regarded this specter ship as bad omen, bringing with it sudden squalls, shipwrecks, illness and other disasters. Flying Dutchman legends have inspired literature, music and motion pictures. Most commonly, *Flying Dutchman* believed to be commanded by Captain Vanderdecken, who ran into terrific storm, vowed he would continue if it took until Judgment Day. Providence took him at his word; the phantom ship still sails on with canvas spread and her crew little more than shadows.

Because of unequal light refraction around Cape of Good Hope, ships actually out of sight sometimes appear to loom in distance as if they were hanging in mid-air. This phenomenon, called "mirage ship," is the *Flying Dutchman* seen by Navymen rounding Cape today.

Fore and aft—running in direction of keel.

Forecastle—pronounced "focsul." In days of Columbus, ships were fitted with castle-like structures fore and aft. The structures have disappeared, but term *forecastle,* is retained; refers to upper deck in forward part of ship. Abbreviated fo'c'sle.

Foremast—first mast abaft bow on a two-masted ship.

Forestay—stay supporting mast from forward.

Forward—toward bow; opposite of aft.

Foul—jammed; not clear for running.

Foul anchor—anchor with cable twisted around it.

Fouled up—line, or chain which has become twisted and tangled; used to describe hopelessly confused person or situation.

Founder—to sink.

Four 0—top mark, equal to 100%. Navy grades and marks run from 0.0 to 4.0. By common usage, perfect, whether said of running condition of engine or appeal of girl friend.

Foxtail—small brush with short handle, used as a counter brush.

Frame—ribs of vessel.

Frap—to bind tightly by passing lines around; to draw together parts of tackle or other combination of ropes to increase tension.

Frapping lines—lines passed around boat falls to steady them.

Freeboard—height of ship's sides from waterline to main deck.

Fresh water king—enlisted man in charge of ship's evaporators, which produce fresh water.

Frogman—slang: member of underwater demolition team.

Full speed—prescribed speed greater than standard speed but less than flank speed.

Funnel—ship's smokestack; stack.

Furl—gathering up and securing sail or awning; opposite of spread.

Gaff—small spar abaft mainmast from which national ensign is flown when ship is underway.

Gale—wind between a strong breeze and storm; wind force 28 to 55 knots.

Galley—ship's kitchen.

Gangplank—see *Brow*.

Gangway—opening in bulwarks or rail of ship to give entrance; order to stand aside and get out of the way.

Gangway ladder—see *Accommodation ladder*.

Gantline—rope and block on top of

mast, stack, etc., used to hoist up rigging, staging, boatswain's chairs, etc.

Garboard strake—strake next to keel.

Garble—unintentional mix-up of a radio message. See *Snafu*.

Gather way—to gain headway.

Gear—general term for lines, ropes, blocks, fenders, etc.; personnel effects.

Geedunk—slang: ice cream soda, malted milk, anything from soda fountain or *Geedunk* stand.

General quarters—battle stations for all hands.

Gig—one of ship's boats designated for commanding officer's use.

Gimbals—pair of rings, one within the other, with axis at right angles to each other; supports compass and keeps it horizontal despite ship's motion.

Gipsey, Gipsy—cathead; drum on horizontal shaft windlass or winch for working lines.

Gizmo—slang: any gadget or unidentifiable piece of gear; may also be applied to person whose name is unknown or unusual.

Glass—barometer or quartermaster's spyglass.

Glasses—binoculars.

Go adrift—to break loose.

Gob—slang: sailor. Mostly a civilian term, not highly regarded in the Navy.

Godown—pidgin English, from Malay *godon*, warehouse.

Gook—slang: applied to an Asiatic or a Latin.

Go-to-hell hat—slang: garrison cap.

Golden dragon—one who has crossed International Date Line. Ships crossing line westward usually hold ceremonies, in which all those crossing for first time are initiated into "Realm of the *Golden Dragon*." Appropriate certificates are given new *dragons*, wallet size identification cards for *Golden Dragons* are issued by Bureau of Naval Personnel.

Grab-rope—ropes secured above boat boom or gangplank; used to steady oneself.

Granny knot—knot similar to square knot; does not hold under pressure.

Grapnel—small anchor with several arms; used for dragging for lost objects or anchoring skiffs or dories.

Gratings—wooden or iron openwork covers for hatches, sunken decks, etc.

Greenhouse—glass enclosure around airplane cockpit.

Gripes—metal fastenings for securing boat in its cradle; canvas bands fitted with thimbles in ends and passed from davit heads over and under boat for securing for sea.

Grinder—slang: drill field or parade ground.

Grog—Admiral Edward Vernon of Royal Navy habitually wore a boatcloak of *grog*ram cloth, and came to be known as "Old *Grog*." In 1740 he introduced West Indian rum aboard ship, had mixture of rum and water served to the crews as preventive against fevers. This innovation was received with enthusiasm by sailor men on flagship *Burford,* who promptly named the beverage after its originator.

Grommet—ring of rope formed by single strand laid three times around; metal ring set in canvas, cloth or plastic.

Ground—to run a ship ashore; to strike bottom through ignorance, violence, or accident.

Green Flash—a flash of green light, sometimes seen at sunset just as sun's upper arc dips below horizon. Visible only in fair weather, with smooth sea and very clear atmosphere; it is produced by refraction of sun's rays at horizon and absorption of violet and blue wave lengths, which leave green rays visible for fraction of a second. Not all persons are able to see green light, even when it does occur. Subject of old proverb: "Glimpse you e'er the green ray, Count the morrow a fine day."

Ground swell—a heavy swell encountered in shoal water. See *Swell*.

Ground tackle—refers to all anchor gear.

Gudgeon—support for rudder; consists of metal braces bolted to sternpost, with eyes to take pintles, or pivot pins, on which rudder swings.

Guess warp—line at outer end of boat boom, used for securing boat to boom; also hauling line laid out by boat.

Guidon—small flag or streamer carried by troops to distinguish company. Pronounced "guy-dun."

Gung-ho—slang: eager and aggressive beyond normal requirements.

Gunmount—gun structure with one to four guns; may be open or shielded in steel. Enclosed mounts are not as heavily armored as turrets and carry no gun larger than 5-inch.

Gunwale—upper edge or rail of ship or boat's side. Pronounced "gunnel."

Guy—line used to steady and support spar in horizontal or inclined position.

Gyrene—slang: Marine.

Gyrocompass—compass used to determine true directions by means of gyroscopes.

Gyrocompass repeaters—compass cards electrically connected to gyrocompass and repeating same readings.

Gyropilot—an automatic steering device connected to repeater of gyrocompass; designed to hold a ship on course without steersman; also called automatic steerer, iron mike, iron quartermaster.

Hack chronometer—spare or comparison chronometer, not quite as accurate as standard chronometer.

Hail—to address nearby boat or ship; also, ship or man is said to *hail* from such and such a home port or home town.

Halfdeck—partial deck below main deck and above lowest complete deck.

Half hitch—usually seen as two half hitches; knot used much for same purposes as clove hitch.

Half-mast—position of ensign when hoisted halfway; usually done as a mark of mourning.

Halyard or halliard—line used for hoisting flags or sails.

Hammocks—used as beds for sailors in warships, in some cases up until beginning of W.W. II. All ships now equipped with bunks. Hammocks were unknown until Columbus reached New World. His sailors slept on deck, wherever they could find a soft plank. Natives in Bahamas used woven cotten nets for beds, called *hammacs*, which Columbus took back to Spain, where they were called *hamaco*. Word adopted into English language during reign of Queen Elizabeth.

Hand lead—lead weighing from seven to 14 pounds, secured to line and used for measuring depth of water or for obtaining sample of bottom. Pronounced "led."

Hand rail—steadying rail of ladder; grab rail.

Hand rope—See *Grab-rope*.

Handsomely—to ease off line gradually; to execute something deliberately and carefully, but not necessarily slowly.

Handy billy—small, portable, power-driven water pump.

Hang fire—gun charge that does not fire immediately upon pulling trigger, but some time later.

Hardtack—biscuits baked without salt and kiln-dried; either round or square in shape and often used as provisions for lengthy voyages. Other names for these biscuits were sea biscuit, ship biscuit and Liverpool pantiles.

Hash mark—slang: service stripe worn on uniforms of enlisted personnel.

Hatch—opening in ship's deck for handling stores and cargo.

Haul—to pull.

Hauling part—part of fall of tackle to which power is applied.

Hawse—old term for anchor cable.

Hawsepipes and hawseholes—steel castings in ship's bow through which anchor cables are run; openings are hawseholes.

Hawser—heavy line, five inches or more in circumference, used for towing or mooring.

Head—place in ship or on shore station which might otherwise be called rest room, wash room or toilet. Captain of the *head* is individual selected to provide janitorial service in such place; called *head* because such facilities in early days were located forward, in the *head* of the ship.

Head room—clearance between decks.

Headway—forward motion of ship.

Heave—to throw or toss; to pull on lines; rise and fall of ship at sea.

Heave away—order to start heaving on capstan or windlass, or to pull on line.

Heave in—order to haul in line or anchor cable.

Heave round—to take line or anchor cable with a winch or capstan. Also "get busy."

Heave short—order to heave in on anchor chain until ship is riding nearly over her anchor.

Heave to—to bring ship's head into wind or sea and hold her there by use of engines and rudder.

Heave the lead—use the lead line.

Heaving line—small line with weight on one end; weighted end is thrown to another ship or to pier so larger line may be passed.

Heel—to list over.

Helm—helm proper is tiller; often used to mean rudder and gear for turning it.

Helmsman—steersman; man at wheel.

H-hour—unnamed hour for attack to begin or movement to be launched.

High seas—the ocean, outside international boundaries.

High line—line stretched between ships that are replenishing or passing gear; a trolley block rides back and forth on it.

Hitch—general class of knots by which line is fastened to another object, either directly or around it; also, term of enlistment.

Hoist—display of signal flags on halyard; also, to raise piece of cargo or gear.

Hoisting pad—metal piece bolted to boat's keel; has an eye to which hoisting rod is bolted.

Hold—space below decks for storage of ballast, cargo, etc.

Holiday—blank space, or an unpainted area of bulkhead or deck.

Holiday routine—followed aboard ship on authorized holidays and Sundays.

Holy Joe—slang: chaplain.

Holystones—bricks, sand stones, or soft sand-rock used for scrubbing wooden decks; name was derived from fact that at one time fragments of broken monuments from Saint Nicholas Church, Great Yarmouth, England, were used to scrub decks of ships in British Navy. Place of holystones in life at sea is best explained by old nautical ditty:

"Six days shalt thou work, and do all thou art able, and on the seventh, *holystone* the deck and scrape the cable."

Since most ships now have steel and composition decks, holystones are little used and their passing from scene has aroused very little sentimentality on the part of old sailors.

Honey barge—slang: garbage lighter.

Horns—horizontal arms of cleat or chock; projecting timbers of stage to which rigging lines are secured.

Horses, Navy—U.S. Army was required to furnish transportation for land-based Navy, by Act of Congress approved December 15, 1814:

"the respective quartermasters of the

Army shall, upon the requisition of the commanding naval officer of any such detachment of seamen or marines, furnish the said officer, and his necessary aides, with horses, accoutrements, and forage, during the time they may be employed in co-operating with the land troops as aforesaid."

Hot rock, or shot—number-one man; outstanding in ability.

House—to stow or secure in safe place; to run anchor's shank up into hawsepipe.

Housing anchor—anchor having no stock; houses itself in hawsepipe when hove in.

Housing chain stopper—chain stopper fitted with screw turnbuckle used for securing anchor in hawsepipe.

Hove taut—pulled tight.

Hug—to keep close. A ship sailing close to land *hugs* shore.

Hulk—worn-out and stripped ship unable to move under own power.

Hull—framework of vessel, together with all decks, deckhouses, inside plating, or planking, but exclusive of masts, rigging, guns, and all superstructure items.

Hull down—said of a ship when only her mast or superstructure are visible above the horizon.

Hurricane—storm originating in West Indies. From Taino word *huracan* meaning evil spirit.

Idler—member of ship's company who does not stand night watches.

Inboard—toward ship's centerline.

Inland Rules—rules enacted by Congress to govern navigation of certain inland waters of U.S.; part of *Rules of the Road*.

Inner bottom—top of double bottom; consists of watertight plating.

Inshore—toward land.

Insignia for bow and flagstaff of boats and official automobiles—boats regularly assigned to officers for individual use carry insignia as follows:
(1) For flag or general officer, stars as arranged in his flag.

(2) For unit commander, not a flag officer, replica of his command pennant.

(3) For commanding officer, or chief of staff not flag officer, an arrow. Staffs for ensign and personal flag or pennant in boat or official automobile assigned to personal use of flag or general officer, unit commander, chief of staff, or commanding officer, or in which civil official is embarked, are typed by devices as follows:
(1) Spread eagle: For official or officer whose official salute is 19 or more guns.
(2) Halberd:
    (a) For flag or general officer whose official salute is less than 19 guns.
    (b) For civil official whose official salute is 11 or more guns but less than 19 guns.
(3) Ball:
    (a) For officer of grade, or relative grade, of captain in the Navy.
    (b) For career minister, counselor or first secretary of embassy or legation, or consul.
(4) Star: For officer of grade, or relative grade, of commander in the Navy.
(5) Flat truck:
    (a) For officer below grade, or relative grade, of commander in the Navy.
    (b) For civil official not listed above, and for whom honors are prescribed for official visit.

Iron Man—Navy athletic trophy, officially known as Navy Department General Excellence Trophy—Pacific Fleet. Iron Man was first competed for by unts of Pacific Fleet in 1919. During W.W. II it was lost for several years; after a world-wide search through Navy supply and storage facilities, was finally discovered in storeroom at Fort Washington, near Washington, D.C. about 1948. These were Iron Man winners:

1919 *Mississippi*   1921 *Mississippi*
1920 *Mississippi*   1922 *Mississippi*

1923 *Mississippi*	1932 *West Virginia*
1924 *California*	1933 *Maryland*
1925 *California*	1934 *Tennessee*
1926 *California*	1935 *West Virginia*
1927 *Pennsylvania*	1936 *Tennessee*
1928 *Tennessee*	1937 *Nevada*
1929 *Mississippi*	1938 *Tennessee*
1930 *West Virginia*	1939 *California*
1931 *West Virginia*	1940 *West Virginia*

Intercardinal points—four points midway between cardinal points of compass: northeast, southeast, southwest, northwest.

Interior communication—telephone or communication systems within ship.

International Rules—rules, established by agreement among maritime nations, to govern navigation on high seas; part of *Rules of the Road*.

Irish pennant—unseamanlike, dangling, loose end of line or piece of bunting.

Island—superstructure on aircraft carrier; contains conning tower, navigation bridge, etc.

Jack—flag similar to union of national ensign; flown at jackstaff when in port; plug for connecting electrical appliance to power or phone line.

Jack-of-the-dust—enlisted man in charge of issuing provisions from storerooms.

Jackstaff—small vertical spar at bow of ship from which jack is flown.

Jacob's ladder—ladder made of rope used over side and aloft; originally led to skysail. Probably allusion to Jacob's dream in which he climbed up to sky.

Jetsam—goods which sink when thrown overboard. See **Flotsam**.

Jettison—to throw goods overboard.

Jetty—landing; small pier.

Jew's harp—anchor shackle; ring to which anchor cable bending shackle is secured; found at upper end of anchor shank.

Jigger—light handy tackle for general work about deck.

Jimmy legs—master-at-arms; senior police petty officer.

Joint—refers to operations in which more than one Service participates; for example, *Joint* Army-Navy exercise.

Jury rig—makeshift rig of mast and sail or of other gear, as jury anchor, jury rudder; any makeshift device.

Kapok—water-resistant fibrous material packed into lifejackets to make them buoyant.

Kedge—anchor used for kedging or moving ship short distance at a time by taking anchor out in boat, letting it go, and then hauling ship up to it. If done merely to change heading of ship it is called warping. See **Warp**.

Keel—backbone of ship, running from stem to sternpost at bottom.

Keelhauling—a verbal reprimand; originally, a cruel form of punishment consisting of binding an offender hand and foot, weighting his body, then pulling him under ship's bottom from one side to the other. If bottom was covered with sharp barnacles, punishment often proved fatal. Abolished late in 19th century after international press outcry.

Keelson—timber or steel fabrications bolted on top of keel to strengthen it.

Kick—distance ship's tern is thrown away from direction of turn by action of rudder; also swirl or backwash in water caused by this action.

King post—short mast supporting a boom.

Kiyi—slang: small hand brush used for scrubbing clothes or canvas.

Knee—angular piece connecting ship's frames to beams.

Knife edge—smooth polished edge of coaming against which rubber gaskets of watertight doors and scuttles fit when closed.

Knock off—cease what is being done; stop work.

Knot—measure of speed for ships and aircraft, as "the destroyer was making 30 *knots*," or "the top speed of the plane is 400 *knots*." Expressions such as "thirty *knots* per hour," are incorrect, since knot is based on both time and distance, and "thirty *knots*" means "thirty nautical miles per hour." Originated in days of sailing ships, when a "log" fastened to long line marked at intervals by *knots* was tossed overboard to determine ship's speed. Distance between *knots* had same ratio to nautical mile as 28 seconds had to one hour. As log pulled knotted line overboard, it was timed with 28-second sand glass, and at end of 28 seconds, count was announced as "She made 10 *knots.*" Since W.W. II, both Air Force and commercial aviation have adopted Navy system of nautical miles expressed in knots. Knot consists of 6,076.103333 feet or 1,852 meters.

Labor—a ship labors when she works heavily in rough sea.

Lacing—line used to secure canvas by passing through eyelets or grommets in canvas.

Ladder—in a ship, corresponds to stairs in a building.

Lamp—electric light bulb.

Landfall—first sighting of land at end of sea voyage.

Landlubber—seaman's term for one who has never been to sea.

Landmark—any conspicuous object on shore, used for piloting.

Lanyard—line made fast to article for securing it; for example, "knife *lanyard,* bucket *lanyard.*

Lash—to tie or secure by turns of line.

Launching the ship—from earliest days of sea-borne craft, there has been religious connection with launching ceremonies, records of which go back to 2100 B.C. Ancient Chinese had elaborate ceremonies which continued unchanged for centuries. In Tahiti, launching ceremonies were marked by human sacrifice. Norsemen fastened human victims to rollers used in ship launching. Practice is referred to in the *Eddas,* as *blun-rod,* or roller-reddening. Wine was used in launching rituals long ago, but Greeks later used water in their ceremonies. In Catholic France during 18th and 19th centuries, priests performed launching ceremony which was similar to ceremony of baptism. Women did not take part in ceremonies until early in 19th century. First known woman sponsor for ship of U.S. Navy was "Miss Watson of Philadelphia" who christened USS *Germantown* on October 22, 1846, using mixture of wine and water. First ship launched on Pacific coast, USS *Saginaw,* was christened at Mare Island, California, in 1859 with California-made wine. While 18th Amendment was in force in U.S., ships were christened with water, or sometimes cider. See **Sponsor.**

Lay—go: "*lay* aloft," "*lay* below," etc.

Lea or sounding lead—weight used for sounding or measuring depth of water.

Lead line—line secured to lead used for sounding.

Leadsman—seaman detailed to heave sounding lead.

Leatherneck—term was probably applied to U.S. Marines by sailors on account of leather-lined collar once part of Marine uniform. Collar, about same height as that of present uniform collar, was designed to give more military appearance to uniform; when damp with perspiration it was highly uncomfortable and caused throat trouble. Abolished by Marine Corps about 1875. See **Devil dogs.**

Lee—direction away from wind.

Lee helmsman—assistant or relief helmsman (steersman).

Leeward—in lee direction, pronounced "lu'ard."

Leeway—drift of vessel to leeward.

Let go by the run—allowing line to run free.

Liberty—authorized absence of individual from place of duty, not chargeable as leave. No period of liberty shall exceed total of 96 hours.

Lieutenant—derived from French, meaning "holding in lieu of" or "one who replaces." The rank was first used in British Navy in 1580 to provide ship captains with an assistant or relief when necessary. For many years in both British and U.S. Navy, such assistant was called "first lieutenant." Now, he is the "executive officer."

Lieutenant commander—title of rank first used in 1862. Earlier, lieutenant in command of small warship was called "lieutenant commanding."

Lifeboat—small boat particularly adapted for use in open sea.

Lifebuoy or life ring—ring or U-shaped buoy of cork or metal to support person in water.

Life jacket or life preserver—belt or jacket of buoyant or inflatable material; worn to keep person afloat.

Lifelines—lines or metal pipes stretched fore and aft along weather decks to furnish shipboard personnel safety against falling or being washed overboard.

Life raft—float constructed either with metallic tube covered with cork and canvas, or made of balsa wood or other suitable material.

Lighter—small vessel used for working (loading and unloading cargo) ships anchored in harbor.

Lighthouses—one of earliest known lighthouses was built on Pharoes Island about 285 B.C. Light was made by burning fuel in brazier hung from pole. Many lighthouses were built by Romans; the most remarkable one, at Boulogne, was 12 stories high and was used for more than 1450 years. Modern lighthouses date back to 1756-59 when John Smeaton, "Father of modern lighthouses," constructed one at Eddystone, England, 14 miles from Plymouth,, marking reef in English channel. It was 72 feet high. Famous first light in American history was Minot's Ledge in Cohasset, Mass., built in 1849; destroyed in 1851, after which Congress appropriated money for construction of new light.

Lightship—earliest forms were called light boats; burned oil-soaked wicks lying in bath of oil aboard oversized row boats. Fish oil was used in 1820; followed by sperm oil, colza oil, lard oil and kerosene. In 1892 first U.S. lightship with electric lights was Cornfield Point Lightship No. 51, in Long Island Sound.

Line—rope or cable; the equator.

Line officer—officer who may succeed to military command as opposed to staff corps officer who normally exercises authority only in specialty, cannot succeed to command.

Line-throwing gun—small caliber gun which projects a weighted-at-one-end line a long distance; used to pass larger lines from ship to ship or ship to pier.

List—inclination or heeling over of ship to one side.

Lizard—line fitted with thimble or thimbles used as leader for running rigging. Traveling lizard is fitted to middle of lifeboat's falls for use in taking up slack when hoisting.

Lock—compartment in canal for lowering or lifting vessels to different levels.

Locker—small metal or wooden stowage space; either chest or closed.

Locker stick—fictional piece of equipment used by sailors to jam gear into overcrowded locker.

Log—instrument for measuring ship's speed through water. See **Knot**.

Logbook—official record of ship's activities and other pertinent or required data.

Longest ship in the Navy—according to midshipmen at Annapolis, the USS *Maine,* because her foremast stands on a pier at the Naval Academy, while her mainmast stands in Arlington Cemetery.

Longitudinal frames—frames of ship running fore and aft.

Longshoreman—laborer who loads and unloads cargo; stevedore, from the Spanish *Estivador*, packer.

Lookout—seaman assigned to watch and report any objects of interest; lookouts are "the eyes of the ship."

Loran—Long Range Navigation. Electronic system that fixes position of ship by measuring difference in time of reception of two synchronized radio signals.

Lubber's line—line marked on inner surface of compass bowl to indicate direction of ship's bow.

Lucky bag—originally bag in which master-at-arms of ship kept articles of clothing, bedding, etc., left about ship by crew members; now a locker or small compartment.

Mackerel skies and mare's tails—cloud formations: mackerel skies describe mottled cirrus clouds; mare's tails are spreading cirrus clouds.

Magazine—compartment for stowage of ammunition and explosives.

Maggie's drawers—red flag used on rifle range to signal miss.

Main battery—largest caliber guns carried by warship.

Main deck—highest complete deck extending from stem to stern and from side to side.

Mainmast—second mast from bow of ship with two or more masts. If ship has but one mast, that is considered the mainmast.

Make colors—to perform ceremony of colors.

Make the land—landfall.

Manhole—round or oval hole cut in deck, bulkhead, or tank top to provide access.

Man-of-war—warship. A hospital ship, oiler, "beef boat" is not a man-of-war.

Manrope—side rope to ladder used as handrail; rope used as safety line anywhere on deck; rope hanging down on side of ship to assist in ascending ship's side.

Mariner—seagoing Navy man.

Maritime—pertaining to the sea.

Martime Service—merchant marine; commercial shipping.

Mark—call used in comparing watches, compass readings, or bearings; fathoms in lead line that are marked. Also, model or type of equipment, as "*Mark* XIV torpedo."

Marlinspike—pointed iron instrument used in splicing line or wire.

Marry—placing two lines together, as in hoisting boat; to sew together temporarily ends of two lines for passing through block.

MARS—Military Amateur Radio System.

MARS—designation for Martin flying boats used by Navy for over ten years on San Francisco-Hawaii passenger-freight service. Last MARS hop made in August 1956; MARS replaced by Convair R3Y TRADEWINDS. Records established by the MARS planes include nonstop flight of 4,723 miles from Honolulu to Chicago (still record for seaplanes), 34-ton cargo lift in single flight from Patuxent River, Md., to Cleveland, and passenger lift of 301 persons, plus seven man crew, on one hop between Alameda and San Diego, Calif.

Martinet—an overly severe disciplinarian. See **Sundowner.**

Maskee—pidgin English: all right, OK.

Mast—captain's *mast*, or merely *mast*, derived from fact that in early sailing days usual setting for this type of naval justice was on weather deck near ship's main*mast*.

Masthead—top or head of a mast. On a ship without masts, spot on superstructure which approximates location of fore masthead.

Meal pennant—red speed pennant hoisted from port yardarm of Navy ship at anchor when crew is at mess. See **Bean rag.**

Medals and decorations—custom of

wearing them on the left breast comes from the practice of knights during Crusades of wearing badge of honor of their order near the heart. All decorations and awards issued in U.S. are so worn on navy uniforms. Foreign awards required to be worn in manner different from that prescribed for American awards may be worn only as courtesy to country concerned when individual is attending public function honoring that country.

Meet her—order to shift rudder to check swing of ship during change of course.

Mess—meal, a place, or group of officers and men who eat together: "crew is at *mess*," "meeting was held in CPO *mess*," or "she was guest of wardroom *mess*." Mess comes from Latin *mensa*, or table; also a Gothic word *mes*, meaning dish; hence, a mess of pottage.

Mess cook—enlisted man who performs duties in mess hall.

Messenger—light line used for hauling over heavier rope or cable; also, enlisted man who runs errands.

Midshipmen—title of *midshipmen* originally given to youngsters of British Navy who acted as messengers and carried orders from officers aft to men forward. Officer candidates at Naval Academy are called *midshipmen*.

Midships—see **Amidships.**

Mind your rudder—warning to steersman to tend to business.

Misfire—powder charge that fails to fire when trigger has been pulled. See **Hangfire.**

Monkey fist—weighted knot at end of heaving line.

Mooring—securing a ship to pier, buoy, or another ship; anchoring with two anchors.

Mooring buoy—large, well anchored buoy to which one or more ships moor.

Mooring line—one of the lines used for mooring ship to pier, wharf, or another ship.

Morning order book—book in which executive officer writes instructions for next morning's work.

Mother Carey's chickens—stormy petrels, birds that fly far from land; once held in superstitious regard by sailors; manner of low flight may account for name of petrel, believed to be diminutive of name *Peter*, so called in allusion to St. Peter's walking on sea. Mother Carey, is said to be Anglicization, of *mater cara*, the Virgin Mary who was regarded as a protector of sailors.

Motor launch—large, sturdily-built powerboat used for liberty parties and heavy workloads.

Motor whaleboat—a powerboat pointed at both ends.

Mousing—small line seized across a hook to prevent unhooking.

Muster—to assemble crew; roll call.

Nacelle—enclosed section of aircraft for engine or personnel; shorter than fuselage and without tail unit.

Nautical mile—6,080.2 feet, or about a sixth longer than land mile. See **Knot.**

Naval stores—oil, paint, turpentine, pitch, and other such items traditionally used for ships.

Neap tide—tide which twice a lunar month rises and falls least from average level; that is, tide with least amount of change from high to low, occurring every 28 days.

Neckerchiefs—black tie or scarf worn by sailors. Many years ago, sailors wore long hair, braided in pigtail fashion; pigtail was made stiff and held in position with grease or tar. To protect uniforms, they wore piece of cloth around neck which was eventually sewn to uniform. During early days of U.S. Navy, black handkerchiefs, or neckerchiefs, were apparently prescribed. As Navy developed, rules of smartness and appearance were introduced; seamen's hair was cut and pigtails disappeared but the neckerchief remains.

Nest—two or more vessels moored alongside one another; boat stowage in which one boat nests inside another.

Net—group of inter-communicating radio landline stations; barrier of steel mesh used to protect harbors and anchorage from torpedoes, submarines, or floating mines.

Netting or snaking—small stuff crisscrossed and strung around forecastles and fantails of many ships; extending up about two feet from deck, it protects exposed personnel from being washed overboard.

Nothing to the right (left)—order to steersman not to let ship go to right (left) of designated course.

Not under command—said of ship when disabled and uncontrollable.

Nun buoy—cone-shaped buoy used to mark channels; anchored on right side entering from seaward and painted red.

Oakum—calking material made of old, tarred, hemp rope fiber.

Occulting light—navigation light which goes off for short periods of time as contrasted to flashing light which goes on for short periods of time.

Officer of the deck—officer on watch in charge of ship.

Officer of the watch—see **Watch officer.**

Oiler—tanker-vessel especially designed to carry fuel oil.

Oil king—enlisted man who keeps fuel oil records in ship.

Old Man—seaman's term for captain of a ship.

Old Navy—Sentimental, nostalgic state of Paradise much talked about by old timers, in effort to impress younger people. To the old timers complaint that "Things ain't like they used to be in the *old Navy,*" the proper answer is "No, and they never were."

On the beam—same as abeam; at 90° to fore-and-aft line.

On the bow—bearing of object ahead somewhere within 45° to either side of bow.

On the quarter—bearing of object somewhere astern of ship, 45° to either side of stern.

OOD—officer of the deck.

Order—directive telling what to do, but leaving method to discretion of person ordered. See **Command.**

Origin of ships—historians agree the predecessor to the ship was probably a log, first solid, later hollowed out by fire or the stone ax; *ship* comes from Greek *skaptein* which means to scoop out. Voyage of sons of Noah is first mentioned in the Bible. The *Ark,* first vessel mentioned, was little more than covered floating raft, 450 feet in length, 75 feet in beam and 45 feet high. Phoenicians, a dozen or more centuries before Christ, brought early sea knowledge to Mediterranean; developed vessels characterized by sharp prow and high stern, up to 40 feet long and rowed by 18 to 22 men. Greeks succeeded Phoenicians as masters of Eastern Sea and brought ship development within range of recorded history. Carthaginians and Romans developed the first warships during their struggle for supremacy.

Orlop—partial deck below lower deck: also lowest deck in ship having four or more decks.

Outboard—toward side of vessel, or outside vessel entirely.

Out of trim—to carry list or be down by head or stern.

Overhang—projection of ship's bow or stern beyond stem or sternpost.

Overhaul—to separate blocks of tackle; clean or repair anything for use.

Overhead—in a ship, equivalent to ceiling of building.

Pad eye—metal eye permanently secured to deck or bulkhead.

Painter—line in bow of boat for towing or making fast.

Painting of Navy ships—from 1775 until 1888 Navy ships were painted black. In the latter year, the new despatch boat *Dolphin,* under Commander George F. Wilde, began 59,000 mile cruise around world. The interior of the hull became almost unbearable in the tropics until Commander Wilde ordered ship painted white. All ships in fleet were painted white until "battleship grey" was adopted in 1908, as being less visible and more economical. During W.W. I and II, ships were painted with "dazzle camouflage," various combinations of black, blue, green, grey and white, but with installation of radar on all ships during W.W. II, camouflage became a useless art.

Palm and needle—sailor's thimble made of leather, and large needle; used for sewing heavy canvas or leather. their military duties.

Panic button—what not to push in an emergency.

Paravanes—torpedo-shaped devices towed on either side of ship's bow to deflect and cut moored mines adrift.

Parbuckle—method for raising or lowering heavy object along inclined or vertical surface; bight of rope thrown around secure fastening at level to which object is to be raised or lowered; two ends of rope then passed under object, brought all the way over it, and led back toward bight; the object itself acting as a movable pulley.

Parceling—wrapping rope spirally with long strips of canvas, following lay of rope and overlapping like shingles on roof to shed moisture.

Part—to break, as of rope or line.

Passageway—corridor or hallway on ship.

Pass a line—to carry or send line to or around object, or to reeve through and make fast.

Pass the word—to repeat an order or information to all hands.

Patent anchor—stockless anchor, usually housing in hawsepipe.

Patent log—device for measuring ship's speed through water. See **Taffrail log.**

Patrick Henry, "Patron Saint of the Navy"—fun-loving sailors sometime claim sainthood for Patrick Henry because of his famous remark and the special meaning of *liberty* in Navy. Permission to leave ship and go ashore, called *shore-leave* for officers, is called *liberty* for enlisted men. Hence, Patrick Henry is the patron saint of the Navy, for he said "Give me *liberty* or give me death."

Pay—to fill seams of wooden vessel with pitch or other substance.

Pay off—to turn ship's bow away from wind.

Pay out—to increase scope of anchor cable; to ease off or slack line.

Peacoat—Short, heavy blue coat worn by enlisted men below grade of CPO. Exact derivation of name is not known, perhaps it came from fact that such coats were originally made of material called "pilot" cloth.

Peak—topmost end of gaff; from which ensign is flown while ship is underway.

Peak tank—tank in bow or stern of ship; usually for water ballast.

Pelican—slang: a hearty eater, a "chow hound."

Pelican hook—hinged hook held in place by ring; when ring is knocked off, hook swings open.

Pelorus—navigational instrument used in taking bearings; consists of two sight vanes mounted on hoop revolving about gyro repeater.

Pendant—length of rope with block or thimble at end.

Pennant—flag that tapers off toward one end.

Periscope—optical instrument used to observe above eye level, as in a submarine.

Phonetic alphabet—words that identify letters so they will be clearly understood; example: A is ALFA, B is BRAVO, W is WHISKEY.

Pier—harbor structure projecting out into water with sufficient depth alongside to accommodate ships.

Pig boat—slang: submarine.

Pigstick—small spar projecing above top of mainmast; commission pennants usually mounted thereon.

Pile—pointed spar projecting above surface of water; when located at corners of pier or wharf, called fender *piles*.

Pilot—expert who boards ships in harbors or dangerous waters to advise captains as to how ship should be conned; also man at controls of aircraft.

Ping jockey—slang: sonarman.

Pintles—pivot pins on which rudder turns.

Pinwheel—slang: helicopter; also called "eggbeater, whirly-bird, and hoppy-choppy.

Pipe down—to give signal for crew to begin meal; take aired bedding below decks; originally call made by boatswain on pipe; it may now consist of spoken words "*Pipe* down aired bedding"; also, slang: "Keep quiet!"

Piping the side—custom of piping side; heritage from British Navy; when captains visited one another at sea and were hoisted on board in net or basket if weather was too rough to permit use of gangways. As officers increased in rank, and, usually, weight, it took more side boys to hoist senior officers on deck. Thus the custom of having side boys became regulation courtesy based on seniority of officer concerned.

Pitch—heaving and plunging motion of vessel at sea.

Pivot point—point in ship about which she turns.

Plankowner—man who has been in ship since it was commissioned.

Plan of the day—schedule of day's routine and events ordered by Executive officer; published daily aboard ship or at shore activity.

Platform deck—partial deck below lowest complete deck; called first, second, etc.

Platoon—military unit comprising two or more squads.

Pointer—member of gun crew who controls vertical elevation of gun. See **Trainer.**

Pollywog—any person who has not crossed Equator. See **Shellback.**

Poop deck—partial deck at stern over main deck.

Port—left side of ship facing forward; harbor; opening in ship's side; usual opening in ship's side for light and air is also a *port.*

Precedence—order in which officers and petty officers are listed in chain of command; those of higher precedence being authorized to order those of lower precedence about their military duties.

Preventer—line used for additional safety and to prevent loss of gear under heavy strain or in case of accident.

Pricker—small marlinspike.

Privileged vessel—vessel with right of way. See **Burdened vessel.**

Prolonged blast—blast on whistle of from four to six seconds' duration.

Promotion—advancement from one rank to the next higher rank. Now governed by the Bureau of Naval Personnel. On board USS *Constellation,* 23 February 1799, Capt. Thomas Truxton wrote to Acting Lt. Samuel B. Brooks:

"Sir, from the first day of March next ensuing, you are to consider yourself as a Lieutenant in the Navy of the United States, and act on Board this Ship as such, for which you are to consider this as your Order, until a Commission is procured for you. You must prepare yourself with the Naval Dress as a Lieutenant; Join the Gun Room Mess, conduct yourself in all Respects as becoming a Gentleman,

and Officer, and at the Hazard of your life, aid your Superiors at all Times in Executing the Orders of the Ship, and supporting the Honor & Dignity of the Flag of the United States. If you want a little Money to give you an outfit, the Purser shall furnish it. I am with every consideration,
Your Obedt humble servt."

Protective deck—deck fitted with heaviest protective plating.

Prow—part of stem above water; old term for bow.

mining humidity of air

Psychrometer—instrument for determining humidity of air by difference in readings of wet-bulb and dry-blub thermometer.

Pulling an oar—rowing a boat.

Punt—rectangular flat-bottomed boat usually used for painting and other work around waterline of ship.

Purchase—any mechanical arrangement of tackle which increases force applied by combination of pulleys.

Pyrotechnics—chemicals, ammunition, or fireworks which produce smoke or lights of various colors and types.

Quadrant—metal fitting on rudder head to which steering ropes are attached.

Quadrantal correctors or spheres—two iron balls secured at either side of binnacle; help compensate for ship's magnetic effect on compass.

Quarter—part of ship's side near stern.

Quarterdeck—part of main (or other) deck reserved for honors and ceremonies and the station of the OOD in port. Ancient Greek and Roman ships carried a pagan alter, sometimes with fire from a certain temple, to which the crew made obeisance. Later, the same respect was paid to a shrine of the Virgin. The custom continued after the shrines were removed. Eventually, the king's colors became symbolic of church and state combined, drew the same shipboard marks of respect earlier paid to altars and shrines. The quarterdeck is the most honored part of the ship and is

saluted by officers and men as they cross it.

Quartering seas—seas hitting ship on quarter.

Quarters—living spaces assigned to personnel aboard ship; government-owned housing assigned to personnel at shore stations; assembly of personnel for drill or inspection.

Quay—wharf; landing place for receiving and discharging cargo. Pronounced "key."

Rack—slang: bunk; "to *rack* out" means to sleep.

Radar—RAdio Detection And Ranging. Principle and method whereby objects are located by radio waves; radio wave is transmitted, reflected by object, received, and illustrated by oscilloscope or cathode ray screen.

Radar picket—ship with special radar equipment, stationed so as to give early warning of enemy approach.

Rdio direction finder—apparatus for taking bearings on source of radio transmissions.

Rail loading—loading davit- or crane-supported boat while it is swung out and even with deck.

Rake—angle of vessel's masts and stacks from vertical.

Range—distance in yards from ship to target; two or more objects in line to indicate direction.

Rank—grade of official standing of commissioned and warrant officers.

Rate—grade of official standing of enlisted men; identifies pay grade or level of advancements; within rating a rate reflects levels of aptitude, training, experience, knowledge, skill, and responsibility. See **Rating.**

Rat guard—sheet metal disk constructed in conical form with hole in center and slit from center to edge; installed over mooring lines to prevent rats from boarding ship from shore.

Rating—occupation which requires basically related aptitudes, training experience, knowledge and skills; rating of yeoman comprises clerical and verbal aptitude, filing, and knowledge of correspondence and reporting forms.

Ratline—in ships rigging, lengths of small stuff running horizontally across shrouds; used for steps.

Ready room—compartment on aircraft carriers in which pilots assemble for flight briefing.

Recognition—process of determining friendly or enemy character of ship, plane, or other object or person.

Reducer—metal fitting between fire main outlet and hose coupling of smaller diameter.

Reef—chain or ridge of rocks, coral, or sand in shallow water.

Reefer—refrigerator vessel for carrying chilled or frozen foodstuffs.

Reeve—to pass end of rope through any lead, such as sheave or fairlead.

Registered publication—any official document or publication which for security purposes is given registry number; accounted for by Registered Publications Section of Naval Communication Service.

Relative bearing—bearing or direction of object in degrees in relation to bow of ship; bow of ship is taken as 000° and imaginary circle drawn clockwise around ship; objects reported as being along line of bearing through any degree division of circle.

Relieving (the watch, the duty, etc.)—to take over duty and responsibilities, as when one sentry relieves another.

Request mast—mast held by captain or executive officer to hear special requests for leave, liberty, etc.

RHIP—Rank Has Its Privileges.

Ribs—frames of ship to which sides are secured.

Ride—to lie at anchor; to safely weather storm.

Riding lights—lights carried by vessel when not underway. Same as anchor lights.

Rifle—personal weapon of a Marine; never called "gun."

Rig—general description of ship's upper works; to set up, fit out or put together.

Rigging—general term for all ropes, chains, and gear used for supporting and operating masts, yards, booms, gaffs, and sails; two kinds: standing rigging, the lines that support but ordinarily do not move; and running rigging, the lines that move to operate equipment.

Right—to return to normal position, as ship righting from heeling over.

Right-handed—twisted from left to right or clockwise; yarn and rope are usually right-handed.

Rig ship for visitors—word passed as warning to all hands to have ship and persons in neat order for expected visitors; all preparations made for receiving visitors.

Riser—vertical branch pipe; pipe going up and down between decks having branch connections or offshoots.

Roaring forties—area between 40° and 50° north or south latitude in which prevailing or stormy westerly winds are encountered.

Roll—side-to-side motion of ship at sea.

Room to swing a cat—*cat* is a whip, i.e., *cat-o'-nine-tails* Refers to size of compartment or room, and especially height of ceiling or overhead. With low overhead, there is not room to swing a *cat*.

Rope—general term for cordage over one inch in diameter; if smaller, known as cord, twine, line, or string; if finer still, as thread or double yarn. Size is designated by diameter (for wire rope) or by circumference (for fiber rope).

Rope-yarn Sunday—usually Wednesday afternoon holiday; crew ceases all but most necessary work about ship; formerly time for sailors to wash and mend clothes.

Round line—three-stranded, right-handed small stuff, used for fine seizings.

Rouse in—to haul in, especially by man power.

Rudder—from old Anglo-Saxon *rother*, that which guides; flat, vertical, moveable apparatus at stern of a ship by which its course is controlled.

Ruffles and flourishes—traditional fanfare by drums and a band, used in many ceremonies. The proper number of ruffles and flourishes to be rendered for official visits of flag officers and civil officials is prescribed by U.S. Navy Regulations.

Rules of the Road—traffic laws of the sea. On high seas, ships are governed by *International Rules of the Road*, which first went into effect July 1, 1897. *Inland Rules of the Road*, made effective in the U.S. October 7, 1897, govern traffic on waters off U.S. within boundary line. There are special rules for Great Lakes and Western Rivers, and *Pilot Rules* applicable to all three.

Running bowline—bowline made over standing part of own rope to form free-sliding nose.

Running lights—lights required by law to be shown by ships or planes when underway between sunset and sunrise.

Sack—slang: bunk or bed. *"Sack rat"* is one who spends as much time in his sack as possible.

Sailor's Friday—to old time sailors Friday was day of bad luck and not a day to undertake anything as important as a sea voyage. Some authorities claim sailor's Friday superstition was founded in religious beliefs. Early Christian clergy was supposed to have bidden sailors about to start cruise, "Out of respect for the day of universal redemption, to await the morrow's sun.'
in brine, but name was also applied to either salt beef or salt pork. See **Hardtack**.

Salutes—hand salute used in U.S. Navy came from British Navy, which in turn borowed it from British Army; salute probably originated in days of chivalry, when knights in armor raised visors when meeting. Officers in the open uncover only for divine services; enlisted men uncover when at *mast* and in officer's country when not wearing duty belt. Civilians may be saluted, when appropriate, but hats or caps are not to be lifted as form of salutation; salutes are given and returned with right hand, but may be made with the left hand when circumstances make it necessary. All salutes received when in uniform and covered shall be returned; persons not wearing hat or cap shall not salute, except when failure to do so would cause embarrassment or misunderstanding.

Salute with guns—salutes were originally act of one who first saluted, rendering himself or ship powerless for time during which honors were rendered. Thus, the gesture was one of friendship and confidence. Internation salutes grew out of custom and usage; all nations adhere to 21 guns salute. Salute over a grave: originally the three volleys fired into air, were supposed to drive away evil spirits as they escaped from the hearts of the dead. Today gun salutes are fired as a ceremonious gesture of respect.

Salvo—one or more shots fired at target by battery; called a broadside if all guns in ship's battery fire at once on same target; also name of pencil-and-paper game played in Navy.

Samson post—king post; short mast supporting auxiliary cargo booms; in small craft, single bitt amidships.

Santa Barbara—patron saint of cannoneers and ordnance men is said to have lived at close of third and beginning of fourth century of Christian era, considered as protectress against thunder, lightning, and explosive flame of all kinds; when gunpowder came into use, she became patron saint of cannoneers and ordnance men.

Scoff—slang: eat. Hearty eater is *scoffer*.

Scoop—slang: information.

Scope—length of anchor cable out.

Scow—large, open, flat-bottomed boat for transporting sand, gravel, mud, etc.

Screw—propeller; rotating, bladed device that propells vessel through water.

Scullery—compartment for washing and sterilizing eating utensils.

Scupper—opening in side of ship to carry off water from waterways.

Scuttle—small opening through hatch, deck, or bulkhead to provide access; similar hole in side or bottom of ship; cover for such opening; to sink a ship intentionally.

Scuttlebutt—a drinking fountain in Navy is called *scuttlebutt*. *Butt* is cask or hogshead. To *scuttle* means to make hole in ship's side causing it to sink. A *scuttlebutt* in old days was cask that had opening in side, fitted with spigot; also "rumor," from the fact that sailors used to congregate at the *scuttlebutt* or cask of water, to gossip.

Sea anchor—See **Drogue**.

Sea bag—large canvas bag for stowing man's gear and clothing.

SeaBees—members of Navy construction battalion.

Sea chest—sailor's trunk; intake between ship's side and sea valve or seacock.

Seacock.—valve in pipe connected to sea; vessel may be flooded by opening seacocks.

Sea dog—old, experienced sailor.

Seagull—slang: chicken; also, a girl who "follows the fleet."

Sea keeping—ability of ship to stay at sea for long periods of time.

Sea ladder—rope ladder, usually with wooden steps, for use over side.

Sea lawyer—a person who likes to argue; usually one who thinks he can twist regulations and standing orders around to favor personal inclinations.

Sea marker—dye for brightly coloring water to facilitate search and rescue.

Sea painter—long line running from well forward on ship and secured by toggle over inboard gunwale in bow of boat.

Sea room—far enough away from land for unrestricted maneuvers.

Seas—agitated surface of water; swells, waves, wavelets, etc.

Sea stores—cigarettes on which no federal tax is paid; sold only at sea.

Seaworthy—capable of putting to sea and meeting usual sea conditions.

Secondary battery—guns of lesser caliber than main battery; used against surface vessels; secondary battery refers to guns used for surface fire and should not be confused with antiaircraft battery.

Second deck—complete deck below main deck.

Section—unit of division.

Secure—to make fast; tie; order given on completion of drill or exercise, meaning to withdraw from drill stations and duties.

Seize—from Dutch *seizen*. To bind with small rope.

Seizing stuff—small cordage for seizing.

Semper Fi—marine term derived from their motto *Semper Fidelis* which means "always faithful"; Semper Fi means "I got mine. How're you doing?"

Sennet, sennit—ornamental, braided, fancy ropework, formed by interweaving number of strands.

Service force—organization of ships and other elements necessary to perform various services for fighting forces.

Service stripes—diagonal stripes on lower left sleeve of enlisted man's uniform denoting periods of enlistments; usually called "hashmarks."

Serving—additional protection over parceling, consisting of continuous round turns of small stuff.

Serving mallet—wooden mallet with groove cut lengthwise in its head; used for serving large rope.

Set—direction of leeway of ship or of tide or current.

Set taut—order to take in slack and place strain on running gear before heaving it in.

Set the course—to give steersman desired course to be steered.

Set the watch—order to station first watch when ship is commissioned.

Schackle—u-shaped piece of iron or steel with eyes in ends through which bolt passes to close.

Shaft alley—spaces within ship surrounding propeller shaft.

Shakedown cruise—cruise of newly-commissioned ship to test machinery and equipment and train crew as working unit.

Shanghai— to coerce against one's will; in old days, sell person into service in a ship.

Sheave—wheel of block over which rope reeves.

Sheer—longitudinal upward curve of deck; amount by which deck at bow is higher than deck at stern; also, sudden change of course.

Sheer off—to turn suddenly away.

Shell—casing of a block; an explosive projective fired from a gun.

Shellback—one who has crossed equator.

Shell room—compartment for stowage of projectiles.

Shift the rudder—order to swing rudder equal distance in opposite direction.

Ship—large oceangoing craft.

Shipping Articles—written agreement between government and enlisted man; covers terms of his enlistment.

Ship's company—all men and officers serving in and attached to ship; all hands.

Shipshape—neat, orderly.

Ships of the Desert—camels. During war with Tripoli joint task force composed of sailors, marines and Arabs on camelback crossed 600 miles of Libyan desert to Derne, which they captured. Sailors again served as "camel coxswains" in 1840's, when expedition to Sea of Galilee and Dead Sea used camels for transportation.

Ship with the wrong name—*USS Hamul* (AD-20), destroyer tender. Many ships in this class are named for stars, and it is assumed that this ship was named for the star Hamal, but the letter authorizing the ship's name spelled it "Hamul."

Shore patrol—naval personnel detailed to maintain discipline, aid local police in handling naval personnel on liberty or leave.

Shore up—to prop up.

Short blast—whistle, horn, or siren blast of about one second's duration.

Short stay—when anchor chain has been hauled in until amount of chain out is only slightly greater than depth of water and ship is riding almost directly over anchor.

Short timer—one whose enlistment or tour of duty is about completed.

Shot—short length of chain, usually 15 fathoms; slang for hypodermic injection.

Shove off—to leave; order to boat to leave landing or ship's side. Slang: Go away.

Show a leg—synonymous with "rise and shine."

Shroud—side stay of hemp or wire running from masthead to rail to support mast.

Sick Bay—ship's hospital or dispensary.

Side Boys—*non-rated men manning* side when visiting officers or distinguished visitors come aboard. See **Piping the side.**

Side lights—red and green running lights carried on port and starboard sides respectively.

Single up—to reduce number of mooring lines out to pier preparatory to sailing; to leave only one easily cost-off line in each place where mooring lines were doubled up for greater security.

Sister hooks—twin hooks on same swivel or ring; closed, they form eye.

Sister ships—ships built on same design; may number in the hundreds.

Skeg—continuation of keel aft to protect propeller.

Skids—beams fitted over decks for stowage of heavy boats.

Skipper—from Dutch *schipper*, meaning captain.

Skivvy—slang: undershirt.

Skoshi or skosh—slang: from Japanese *sukoshi*, meaning small, few, scarce.

Slack—part of line hanging loose; to ease off; state of tide when there is no horizontal motion. See **Stand.**

Slings—fittings for hoisting boat or other heavy lift by crane or boom; consist of metal ring with four pendents.

Slip—to let go by unshackling, as anchor cable; space between two piers; waste motion of propeller.

Small stuff—small cordage designated by number of threads (9 thread, 12 thread, etc.) or by special names, such as marline, ratline stuff, etc.

Smart—snappy, seamanlike.

Smokestacking—slang: over-acting.

Smoking lamp—In old days matches were prohibited to members of crew, and for convenience oil lamps were swung in several parts of ships were they could light pipes. Smoking was permitted only when the smoking lamp was lighted. The expression has been retained. Before drills, fuelling, receiving ammunition, etc., officer of the deck orders word passed, "The *smoking lamp* is out."

Snow job—slang: extension of truth.

Snub—to check suddenly.

Snipes—slang: members of engineering department.

Snafu—slang: Situation Normal, All Fouled Up. Supposed to have been suggested by a five letter garble in a WWII coded radio message. Led to other slang terms: TARFU—Things Are Really Fouled Up; JANFU—Joint Army-Navy Foul Up. FUBAR—Fouled Up Beyond All Repair.

So-long—originally sailor's farewell, supposed to be derived from East Indian *salaam*.

Sonar—Sound Navigation And Ranging, device for locating objects under water by emitting vibrations similar to sound and measuring time taken for vibrations to bounce back from anything in their path.

Sound—to measure depth of water by means of lead line; also, to measure depth of liquids in oil tanks, voids, blisters, and other compartment or tanks.

Sounding—sonic depth finder or fathometer measures depth of ocean; sends sound to bottom, measures time it takes to return to surface; machines then compute this against speed of sound and pin-points depth of ocean at any one spot. For many years, soundings were made by leadsman with lead line. For soundings in deeper waters, deep-sea (pronounced dipsey) lead was used.

Sound-powered phone—shipboard telephone powered by voice alone.

Span—line made fast at both ends with purchase hooded to its bright; wire rope located between davit heads and set up by turnbuckle.

Spanner—tool for coupling hoses.

Spar—steel or wood pole serving as mast, boom, gaff, pile, etc.

Spar bouy—long, thin, wooden spar used to mark channels.

Speed cone—cone-shaped, bright-yellow signal used when steaming in formation to indicate engine speeds.

Speed light—white or red light mounted high on Navy ship; indicates changes in speed at night when speed cones cannot be seen.

Spit kit—cuspidor. Also slang: small craft.

Splice—to join two lines by tucking strands of each into the other.

Splinter deck—deck fitted with lightest protective plating.

Splinter screen—protective plating around gun mount.

Sponsor—Navy ships are christened by woman selected by Navy Department. For ships named after naval heroes or famous citizens, sponsor is usually widow, mother, daughter, or direct descendant. Ships' named for states, cities, or geographical features are sponsored by wife or daughter of appropriate governor, senator, or mayor. The Society of Sponsors of the United States Navy, includes all ladies who have sponsored Navy ships, has published four volumes listing all sponsors through the year 1958. A sponsor receives no pay; provides own transportation. Principal duty is to smash bottle of champagne against bow of ship, and say "I christen thee . . ." Because women have been known to miss a ship completely with the bottle, it is now secured to bow of ship by ribbon, and man is stationed in bow to take care of breaking it if necessary.

Spring—mooring line leading at angle of about 45° off centerline of vessel; to turn vessel with line.

Spud coxswain—slang: man who prepares vegetables for use in general mess.

Squall—sudden gust of wind.

Square away—to get things settled down or in order.

Squilgee—drier for wooden decks made of flat piece of wood with rubber blade and long wooden handle. Pronounced "squeegee."

Stack—ship's smoke pipe. See **Funnel**.

Stadimeter—Instrument for measuring distance between ships in a formation.

Staff officer—officer of staff corps, as medical, dental, supply, etc. whose duties are primarily within his specialty; also, a line officer when assigned to the staff of high-ranking officer.

Stage—platform rigged over ship's side for painting or repair work.

Stanchion—wood or metal upright used as support.

Stand—condition of tide when there is no vertical motion. See **Slack**.

Stand by—preparatory order meaning "Get ready," or "Prepare to." Slang for person taking another person's duty at particular time.

Standard speed—speed set as basic speed by officer in command of unit.

Starboard—right side of ship looking forward. In Viking ships, right side of ship was called *steerboard* side because ships were steered by means of heavy board mounted on that side. Gradually, *steer board* was corrupted to *starboard*. Left side of old ships was called *load board*, (the place of loading) finally became *larboard*. Because *starboard* and *larboard* sounded so much alike, *port* was substituted in U.S. Navy for *larboard*.

Station keeping—keeping ship in proper position in formation of ships.

Stay—piece of rigging, either wire or fiber, used to support mast.

Steady—order to steersman to hold ship on course.

Steerage way—slowest speed at which ship can be steered.

Steersman—man who operates wheel or lever which controls rudder and steers ship.

St. Elmo's Fire—eerie, but natural phenomenon, frequently witnessed on old sailing ships, occasionally seen in modern ships and around airplanes in flight; a greenish-yellow glow, sometimes diffuse, sometimes collected in distinct balls of radiance. Generally seen in stormy weather. St. Elmo (or St. Ermo), bishop of central Italy, was venerated by mariners centuries ago. At sea, during a storm, he became ill; told frightened mariners as he was dying he would appear after death if they were to be saved from storm. According to legend, after he died a light appeared at masthead and was named for him. The phenomenon is caused by differences of electrical potential between atmosphere and objects on earth's surface; can be observed on mountain tops or on high projecting points of churches and other buildings.

Stem—upright post or bar at most forward part of bow of ship or boat.

Stern—after part of ship.

Sternsheets—space in boat abaft the after thwart.

Sternway—backward movement of ship.

Stopper—short length of rope or chain firmly secured at one end; used in securing or checking running line.

Stove—broken in; crushed in.

Stow—to put gear in proper place. From Dutch *stoewen,* to cram or press.

Strake—continuous line of planks or plates running length of vessel.

Strand—part of line or rope made up of yarns.

Striker—enlisted man in training for particular rating.

Strip ship—to prepare ship for battle action by disposing of any unnecessary gear.

Strongback—spar lashed to pair of boat davits; acts as spreader for davits and provides brace for more secure stowage of lifeboat at sea.

Survey—examination by authorized competent personnel to determine whether piece of gear, equipment, stores, or supplies should be discarded or retained.

Sundowner—harsh disciplinarian; martinet; formerly, a captain who ordered his men to be aboard by sundown.

Superstructure—that part of a ship above the main deck.

Superstructure deck—partial deck higher than main, forecastle, and poop

deck; not extending to ship's sides.

Swab—rope or yarn mop; also a not highly flattering term for a sailor.

Swabbo—complete miss, as in target practice.

Swamp—to sink by filling with water.

Swash bulkhead—bulkhead with numerous openings built in tank or compartment to prevent free water from sloshing back and forth when ship rolls or pitches.

Swell—heaving motion of sea.

Swing ship—moving ship through compass points to check magnetic compass on different headings and make up deviation table.

Swivel—metal link with eye at one end, fitted to revolve freely and thus keep turns out of chain.

Swords—worn by officers as badge of honor and rank, on appropriate occasions. Chaplains and WAVE officers do not wear swords.

Tachometer—mechanical device indicating revolutions, as RPM.

Tackle—arrangement of ropes and pulleys to increase available hauling force. Pronounced "take-el."

Tackline—short length of line used to separate flags in hoist.

Taffrail—rail at stern of ship.

Taffrail log—device which indicates speed of ship through water; trailed on line from taffrail and consists of rotator and recording instrument.

Take a turn—to pass a line around cleat, bitts, or bolard and hold on.

Taksan—slang: derived from Japanese *takusan,* meaning much, great, large, many, as the case may be.

Taps—bugle call; from Dutch *taptoe,* or time to close up all taps and taverns in military town; last routine call to be sounded on board ships and stations each day; by custom last call sounded over graves of military men. *Tattoo* is bugle call sounded five minutes before taps as signal to make ready for night, also, derived from same source. Taps (as now played) composed by General Daniel

Butterfield of Army of Potomac; first sounded in July 1862, at Harrison's Landing on James River in Virginia. Playing of taps is one American custom which has been adopted in Europe. In 1932 French Army announced that taps, as used by U.S. Army and Navy, would also be used in that service to end day, mark burial or dead.

Tarpaulin—heavy canvas used as protective covering.

Task force—temporary grouping of units under one comander; formed for purpose of carrying out specific operation or mission.

Taut—with no slack; also, strict as to discipline.

Telephone talker—man who handles sound-powered phone during drills.

Tender—auxiliary ship which supplies and repairs ships or aircraft.

That's high—order to cease hoisting.

Thwart—crosspiece used as seat for boat.

Thwartships—see **Athwartships.**

Tide—vertical rise and fall of the sea, caused mainly by gravitational attraction of the moon. The tide puzzled peoples of antiquity and many superstitions grew up to explain it. There is no noticeable tide in the Mediterranean, so early sailors were terrified when they first witnessed this phenomenon elsewhere. Caesar's soldiers thought they were witnessing the end of world when they first saw ebbing tide on north coast of Europe. Plato believed world was a living thing and tides were caused by its breathing.

Tidal currents—horizontal currents in more or less confined waters caused by tides.

Tideway—part of channel in which tide ebbs and flows.

Tier—to stow cable in chain locker.

Tiller—short handle fitted into head of a rudder, used to steer a boat.

Time—as used in naval correspondence and communications, is expressed by a four digit system based on a day of 24 consecutive hours. The first two digits indicate the hour and the second two the minute. Thus, 0100 is 1:00 AM, 0145 is 1:45 AM, and 1245 12:45PM. The principal difference is that in the civil system one starts "around the clock" again at 1:00 PM, whereas the Navy calls it 1300 and keeps on going to 2400, or midnight. Navy time is spoken exactly as it is written: 1300 is "thirteen hundred," not "thirteen hundred hours." 0730 (7:30 A.M.) is "zero seven thirty."

Titivate—to dress or smarten up, make neat.

Toggle—wooden or metal pin slipped into becket; furnishes rapid release.

Tompion—plug placed in muzzle of gun to keep dampness and foreign objects out. Pronounced "tompkin."

Top—platform at top of mast; to top boom is to lift up its end.

Topping lift—line used for topping boom and taking its weight.

Topside—from pidgin English, meaning upper level, or above decks; CATALINA PBY flying boats were sometimes referred to as "*topside* sampans.*"

Tow—to pull through water; the object being pulled; towing ships in Navy are tugs, not towboats.

Towing lights—special white lights displayed by towing vessel at night.

Towing spar—spar towed by ships in fog as aid to ship astern in column; following ship can see spar where it cannot distinguish ship ahead; also called position buoy.

Track—path of vessel.

Tracking—keeping gun directed at moving target.

Trades—steady winds of tropics that blow toward equator; NE in northern hemisphere; SE in southern hemisphere.

Train—group of auxiliary ships; also, to move gun horizontally onto target.

Trainer—gun crew member who controls horizontal movement of gun in aiming at target.

Transom—athwartship piece bolted to sternpost; planking across stern of square-stern boat.

Trice up—to hitch up or hook up, such as trice up shipboard bunk.

Trick—period of time steersman is at wheel, as "to take a *trick* at the wheel."

Trim—angle to horizontal at which ship rides, that is, how level the ship sits in the water; shipshape.

Trimming tanks—tanks used for water ballast, by flooding or emptying ship may be trimmed, i.e., balanced on water.

Trip—to release catch of quick-acting device, such as pelican hook.

Tripod mast—three-legged mast.

Tripoli Monument—located on grounds of Naval Academy at Annapolis; its third location in U.S. First erected in Washington Navy Yard in 1808; later moved to Capitol grounds; in 1860, moved to Annapolis. Monument was sculptured in Italy, brought to U.S. in Frigate *Constitution.*

Truck—flat, circular piece secured at top of mast or top of flagstaff and jackstaff; also, uppermost part of mast.

Trunk—vertical open shaft within a ship.

Tumble home—amount vessel's sides slope in from perpendicular.

Turbine—high-speed rotor turned by steam or other hot gases.

Turn to—order to begin work.

Turn turtle—to capsize.

Turnbuckle—metal appliance capable of being made taut or slacked, used for setting up standing rigging.

Turret—heavily armored housing containing a grouping of main battery guns; extends downward through decks and includes ammunition handling rooms and hoists. See **Gun mount.**

Two-blocked—when two blocks of tackle have been drawn as closely together as possible; said also of pennant or flag when hauled up to top of yardarm or flagstaff.

Typhoon—from Chinese *T'ai-fun,* or great wind. A circular storm, often exceedingly violent, which occurs in western Pacific, Philippine Islands, Japan, Okinawa area; same storm is called *hurricane* in West Indies. (See **Windfall**)

Unbend—to cast adrift or to untie.

Uncle Sam—the United States. Most commonly accepted version says expression originated during War of 1812. In those days, Elbert Anderson, food contractor for U.S. Army, purchased quantities of beef and pork near Troy, N.Y. Items were inspected by Ebenezer Wilson and his uncle Samuel Wilson, known as "Uncle Sam." Wilson's workmen marked "E.A.–U.S." on each case, thus identifying contents as having been procured by Elbert Anderson on behalf of U.S. Many Wilson employees were recruited as soldiers and whenever they saw the "E.A.–U.S." stamp, they would laugh and refer to it as some more of "Uncle Sam's" supplies. The joke caught on, and "Uncle Sam," soon became favorite expression to personify United States.

Uncover—to remove headgear.

Underway—ship is underway when not at anchor, made fast to shore or aground. It need not be actually moving; in which case it is under way with no way on.

Undertow—seaward current near bottom in heavy surf.

Unit—an entity in itself made up of one or more parts; unit is member part; thus, two destroyers (units) form section; two sections form division; two divisions form squadron.

Up anchor—order to weigh anchor and get underway.

Up and down—perpendicular (pertaining to anchor cable.)

Up behind—order to cease pulling and furnish slack rapidly so gear may be belayed.

Upper deck—partial deck amidships above main deck.

Uptake—enclosed trunk conecting boiler(s) to stack.

Vane—piece of bunting flown at truck to indicate direction of wind.

Vast—short for "avast"; order to cease.

Veer—to let anchor cable, line, or chain run out by its own weight; also wind is said to veer when changing direction clockwise or to right.

Very's pistol—type of pistol used to fire pyrotechnic charges.

Very well—reply of senior officer to junior officer or enlisted man to indicate information given is understood or permission is granted.

Wagon—slang: battleship, short for battle*wagon*.

Waist—part of deck between forecastle and poop on cargo-type vessels.

Wake—track left in water behind a ship.

Wale shores—stout timbers of various lengths used to prevent drydocked ship from toppling over; rigged between ship sides and sides of drydock.

Walk back—order to keep gear in hand but to walk back with it toward belaying point.

Wardroom—probably from British Navy. In 18th century, there was a compartment aboard ship near officers' staterooms used as storage room, particularly for officers' clothing. It was called *wardrobe*, term later corrupted into *wardroom*. When this compartment was empty, lieutenants met there informally and for meals. Gradually used entirely as officers' mess room, and such was custom when U.S. Navy came into being.

Warp—to move a ship by line or laid-out anchor, as "*Wrap* the ship into the slip." See **Kedge.**

Watch—period of duty, usually of four hours' duration. From time imme-

morial, the day at sea has been divided into watches, which are now called: midwatch (midnight to 4 A.M.), morning watch (4 to 8 A.M.), forenoon watch (8 A.M. to noon), afternoon watch (noon to 4 P.M.), first dog watch (4 to 6 P.M.), second dog watch (6 to 8 P.M.) and first watch (8 P.M. to midnight.)

Watch cap—knitted wool cap worn by enlisted men below CPO in cool or cold weather; canvas cover placed over stack when not in use.

Watch officer—officer regularly assigned to duty in charge of watch or of portion thereof; for example, "OOD," or "engineering officer of watch."

Watch, quarter, and station bill—large chart showing every man's location in ship's organization and his station in various shipboard drills.

Water breaker—drinking-water cask or container carried in boats.

Waterline—line painted on hull showing point to which ship sinks in water when properly trimmed.

Water-logged—filled or soaked with water but still afloat.

Watertight integrity—system of keeping ship afloat by maintaining water tightness.

Waterway—gutter at side of ship's deck to carry water to scuppers.

Weather—exposed to wind and rain; to windward, as "to face the *weather*," or "to *weather* a storm."

Weather cloth—canvas spread for protection from wind and weather.

Weather deck—portion of main, forecastle, poop, and upper deck exposed to weather.

Weather eye—to keep a *weather* eye is to be on the alert.

Weigh—from Anglo-Saxon *woeg*. To weigh anchor is to lift it from bottom on which it rests. As soon as it is off the bottom, the "anchor's *aweigh.*" Ship not fast to the bottom by her anchor is "under *weigh*" even though she may have no "way" on her, that is, not in motion; moving ship is "under way."

Well—order meaning sufficient; "That's *well*."

Well deck—low weather deck.

Whaleboat—sharp-ended lifeboat, pulled by oars and/or fitted with sails; when equipped with engine, called motor whaleboat.

Wharf—harbor structure alongside which ships moor; wharf generally is built along water's edge; pier extends well out into harbor.

What-the-hell pennant—unofficial signal flag, flown over appropriate speed and course flags, said to mean "*What-the-hell* is your speed?" or "*What-the-*hell is your course?" By itself, it expresses amazement or disbelief.

Wheel—ship's steering wheel.

Wheelhouse—pilothouse; topside compartment where on most ships OOD, steersman, quartermaster of the watch, etc., stand watches.

Where away—answering call requesting location of object reported by lookout.

Whipping—keeping ends of rope from unlaying, by wrapping with turns of twine and tucking ends.

White hat—slang: enlisted man.

Wide berth—plenty of clearance.

Wildcat—sprocket wheel on windlass for taking links of chain cable.

Winch—hoisting engine secured to deck; used to haul lines by turns around horizontally driven drum or gypsy.

Windfall—at one time in England, certain of British nobility were permitted to hold land on condition no timber would be cut except for British Navy, but trees blown down by storms were exempt; *windfalls* caused by heavy gale might mean profit for owner; thus windfalls came to mean an unexpected bit of good fortune.

Windlass—engine used for heaving in anchor.

Windward—into the wind; toward direction from which wind is blowing; opposite of leeward.

Wind scoop—metal scoop fitted into port to direct air into ship for ventilation.

Wind ship—to turn ship end for end, usually with lines at pier. Pronounced "wined."

Wire rope—rope made of wire strands, as distinguished from fiber rope.

With the sun—in clockwise direction; proper direction in which to coil line; right-handed.

Word, the—information, news, dope. Probably derived from old Navy custom of "passing the *word*."

Work a ship—to handle ship by means of engines and other means; for example, to *work* ship into a slip using engines, rudder, and lines to docks.

Working—general shipboard term meaning to operate, man, service, etc. A yard oiler goes about harbor *working* various ships by servicing them with fuel oil.

Worming—filling lays of line preparatory to parceling and serving.

Yard—spar attached at middle to mast and running athwartships; used as support for signal halyards or signal lights; also place used for shipbuilding and as repair depot.

Yardarm—either side of a yard.

Yardarm blinker—signal lights mounted above end of yardarm and flashed on and off to send messages.

Yarn—twisted fibers used for rough seizings, which may be twisted into strands; also, story, as to "spin a *yarn*," meaning to tell a story not necessarily true.

Yaw—zigzagging motion of vessel as it is carried off heading by strong overtaking seas; motion swings ship back and forth across intended course.

Yoke—piece fitting across head of boat's rudder, to end of which steering lines are attached.

Zoomie—an aviator.

TRIMMED SIZE:	5¼ × 8 inches
TYPE PAGE:	25 × 39
TYPE FACE:	Lino Baskerville
TYPE SIZE:	10 point on 12
	9 point on 11
CHAPTER TITLE:	18 point Bodoni Bold
BODY STOCK:	50 lb. White Winnebago English Finish
COVER STOCK:	Buckeye Duplex Cover, Sapphire and White